Essentials of Trauma-Informed Assessment and Intervention in School and Community Settings

Essentials of Psychological Assessment Series

Series Editors, Alan S. Kaufman and Nadeen L. Kaufman

Essentials of 16PF® Assessment by Heather E. P. Cattell and James M. Schuerger

Essentials of Adaptive Behavior Assessment of Neurodevelopmental Disorders by Celine A. Saulnier and Cheryl Klaiman

Essentials of ADHD Assessment for Children and Adolescents by Elizabeth P. Sparrow and Drew Erhardt

Essentials of Assessing, Preventing, and Overcoming Reading Difficulties by David A. Kilpatrick

Essentials of Assessment Report Writing, Second Edition by W. Joel Schneider, Elizabeth O. Lichtenberger, Nancy Mather, Nadeen L. Kaufman, and Alan S. Kaufman

Essentials of Assessment with Brief Intelligence Tests by Susan R. Homack and Cecil R. Reynolds

Essentials of Autism Spectrum Disorders Evaluation and Assessment by Celine A. Saulnier and Pamela E. Ventola

Essentials of Bayley Scales of Infant Development-II Assessment by Maureen M. Black and Kathleen Matula

Essentials of Behavioral Assessment by Michael C. Ramsay, Cecil R. Reynolds, and R. W. Kamphaus

Essentials of Career Interest Assessment by Jeffrey P. Prince and Lisa J. Heiser

Essentials of CAS2 Assessment by Jack A. Naglieri and Tulio M. Otero

Essentials of Child and Adolescent Psychopathology, Second Edition by Linda Wilmshurst

Essentials of Cognitive Assessment with KAIT and Other Kaufman Measures by Elizabeth O. Lichtenberger, Debra Y. Broadbooks, and Alan S. Kaufman

Essentials of Conners Behavior Assessments™ by Elizabeth P. Sparrow

Essentials of Creativity Assessment by James C. Kaufman, Jonathan A. Plucker, and John Baer

Essentials of Cross-Battery Assessment, Third Edition by Dawn P. Flanagan, Samuel O. Ortiz, and Vincent C. Alfonso

Essentials of DAS-II® Assessment by Ron Dumont, John O. Willis, and Colin D. Elliott

Essentials of Dyslexia Assessment and Intervention by Nancy Mather and Barbara J. Wendling

Essentials of Evidence-Based Academic Interventions by Barbara J. Wendling and Nancy Mather

Essentials of Executive Functions Assessment by George McCloskey and Lisa A. Perkins

Essentials of Forensic Psychological Assessment, Second Edition by Marc J. Ackerman

Essentials of Gifted Assessment by Steven I. Pfeiffer

Essentials of IDEA for Assessment Professionals by Guy McBride, Ron Dumont, and John O. Willis

Essentials of Individual Achievement Assessment by Douglas K. Smith

Essentials of Intellectual Disability Assessment and Identification Alan W. Brue and Linda Wilmshurst

Essentials of KABC-II Assessment by Alan S. Kaufman, Elizabeth O. Lichtenberger, Elaine Fletcher-Janzen, and Nadeen L. Kaufman

Essentials of KTEA™-3 and WIAT®-III Assessment by Kristina C. Breaux and Elizabeth O. Lichtenberger

Essentials of MCMI®-IV Assessment by Seth D. Grossman and Blaise Amendolace

Essentials of Millon™ Inventories Assessment, Third Edition by Stephen Strack

Essentials of MMPI-A™ Assessment by Robert P. Archer and Radhika Krishnamurthy

Essentials of MMPI-2® Assessment, Second Edition by David S. Nichols

Essentials of Myers-Briggs Type Indicator® Assessment, Second Edition by Naomi L. Quenk

Essentials of NEPSY®-II Assessment by Sally L. Kemp and Marit Korkman

Essentials of Neuropsychological Assessment, Second Edition by Nancy Hebben and William Milberg

Essentials of Nonverbal Assessment by Steve McCallum, Bruce Bracken, and John Wasserman

Essentials of PAI® Assessment by Leslie C. Morey

Essentials

of Trauma-Informed
Assessment and
Intervention in School and
Community Settings

Kirby L Wycoff

Bettina Franzese

WILEY

Registered Office(s)
John Wiley & Sons, Inc., 111 River Street, Hoboken, NJ 07030, USA

Editorial Office
John Wiley & Sons, Inc., 90 Eglinton Ave. E., Suite 300, Toronto, Ontario M4P 2Y3, Canada

For details of our global editorial offices, customer services, and more information about Wiley products visit us at www.wiley.com.

Wiley also publishes its books in a variety of electronic formats and by print-on-demand. Some content that appears in standard print versions of this book may not be available in other formats.

Library of Congress Cataloging-in-Publication Data is available:

9781119274612 (Paperback)
9781119276456 (ePDF)
9781119276173 (epub)

Cover Design: Wiley

Cover Image: © Greg Kuchik/Getty Images

Set in 10.5/13pt AGaramondpro by SPi Global, Chennai, India

PB Printing C10007077_122618

CONTENTS

About the Authors   xi

Series Preface   xiii

Acknowledgements   xv

Section One History: Trauma, Adversity and the
             Trauma-Informed Movement

        One Adverse Childhood Experiences   3
             Kirby L. Wycoff

        Two Impact on Children, Teens, Families,
             and Communities   17
             Kirby L. Wycoff

      Three Public Health and the Trauma-Informed
             Movement   35
             Kirby L. Wycoff

       Four Trauma–Informed Schools   59
             Kirby L. Wycoff

Section Two   Complex Trauma and the Role of Functional
               Impairment

        Five   Child Development   79
               Bettina Franzese

         Six   Complex Trauma and Its Impact
               on the Brain   93
               Bettina Franzese

       Seven   Domains of Impairment: Functional Impact
               of Complex Trauma and Stress   127
               Kirby L. Wycoff

Section Three Trauma-Informed Assessment Framework

       Eight   Considerations for Trauma Screening in School
               and Community Settings   157
               Kirby L. Wycoff

        Nine   Individual and Familial Assessment Tools   181
               Kirby L. Wycoff

Section Four   Trauma-Informed Intervention Framework

         Ten   Competencies and Components of
               Trauma-Informed Interventions   201
               Kirby L. Wycoff

      Eleven   Trauma-Informed Interventions and
               Treatments   219
               Kirby L. Wycoff

Section Five   **Ethical Considerations in Trauma-Informed Assessment and Intervention**

Twelve   Ethical Considerations   243
Kirby L. Wycoff

Thirteen   Emerging Treatments and Additional Resources   251
Kirby L. Wycoff

References   253

Index   295

ABOUT THE AUTHORS

Kirby L. Wycoff, Psy.D., NCSP, is a Nationally Certified School Psychologist and Associate Professor and Co-Director of the School Psychology Program at Eastern University. Her research and clinical interests are centered around the needs of high-risk youth and their families. Dr. Wycoff is currently pursuing her Masters of Publlic Health from The Dartmouth Institute for Health Policy and Clinical Practice to continue to build her understanding of the impact of trauma and adversity on communities. She is also serving a two-year fellowship in Leadership and Education in Adolescent Health (LEAH) through the Children's Hospital of Philadelphia and PolicyLab. The LEAH Fellowship is a national fellowship funded through the Maternal and Child Health Bureau of the Health Resources and Service Administration of the U.S. Department of Health and Human Services. LEAH Fellowship Training programs have been awarded to the leading children's hospitals across the country, where its mission is to prepare professionals from a variety of health care disciplines to be leaders in clinical care, research, public health policy, and advocacy as it relates to adolescent health.

Bettina Franzese, Psy.D., ABSNP, is a Pennsylvania Licensed Psychologist and Certified School Psychologist. She holds a Diplomate in School Neuropsychology from the American Board of School Neuropsychology. She recently retired from the Milton Hershey School, a residential school in Hershey, PA for income-eligible children.

SERIES PREFACE

In the *Essentials of Psychological Assessment* series, we have attempted to provide the reader with books that will deliver key practical information in the most efficient and accessible style. Many books in the series feature specific instruments in a variety of domains, such as cognition, personality, education, and neuropsychology. Other books, like *Essentials of Trauma-Informed Assessment and Intervention in School and Community Settings*, focus on crucial topics for professionals who are involved in any with assessment—topics such as specific reading disabilities, evidence-based interventions, or ADHD assessment. For the experienced professional, books in the series offer a concise yet thorough review of a test instrument or a specific area of expertise, including numerous tips for best practices. Students can turn to series books for a clear and concise overview of the important assessment tools, and key topics, in which they must become proficient to practice skillfully, efficiently, and ethically in their chosen fields.

Wherever feasible, visual cues highlighting key points are utilized alongside systematic, step-by-step guidelines. Chapters are focused and succinct. Topics are organized for an easy understanding of the essential material related to a particular test or topic. Theory and research are continually woven into the fabric of each book, but always to enhance the practical application of the material, rather than to sidetrack or overwhelm readers. With this series, we aim to challenge and assist readers interested in psychological assessment to aspire to the highest level of competency by arming them with the tools they need for knowledgeable, informed practice. We have long been advocates of "intelligent" testing—the notion that numbers are meaningless unless they are brought to life by the clinical acumen and expertise of examiners. Assessment must be used to make a difference in the child's or adult's life, or why bother to test? All books in the series—whether devoted to specific tests or general topics—are consistent with this credo. We want this series to help our readers, novice and veteran alike, to benefit from the intelligent assessment approaches of the authors of each book.

Essentials of Trauma-Informed Assessment and Intervention in School and Community Settings is a book about how to help young people do and be the best versions of themselves. While the superb authors talk a great deal in this book about the impact of adversity and trauma, it is critically important that they also call readers' attention to the fact that *risks* do not have to be *realities*. It is critically important to acknowledge that youth exposed to adversity hold within themselves an incredible capacity for growth and resiliency. Helping young people find their own stories of strength, and supporting their ability to grow in the face of adversity is not only possible, but necessary. As the authors emphasize, trauma-awareness must be followed by a focus on resilience if we are to truly empower and support all young people.

Alan S. Kaufman, PhD, and Nadeen L. Kaufman, EdD, Series Editors

Yale Child Study Center, Yale University School of Medicine

ACKNOWLEDGEMENTS

I would like to thank all of my friends and family for supporting me on this incredible journey of bringing this book to fruition. I could not have done it without your help and support. To my husband Patrick, thank you for your endless encouragement and faith in my ability to actually write a book. You never doubted that I could do this, even on the days that I wasn't sure I could. Thank you for being you. To my parents, thank you for your endless commitment to my education and desire to learn. Every time I tell you I want to learn more and grow, I am met with love and support. Thank you. To my grandmother, Elizabeth, who taught me that education was the key to a future and writing was the way we shared with others, I did it. I told you I would write a book one day – and here it is. I know you would be proud of me! To my former supervisor and colleague, Dr. Franzese, thank you for all that you have taught me. Your contributions to my professional and personal growth will not be soon forgotten! It has been quite the journey. To my sweet Sophia Rose, who for the last twelve years, has been my faithful companion through every single phase of my professional education. Snuggles on the couch during dissertation writing, reminders for fresh air and walks during graduate school and book writing and everything in between. For showing me, through your work as a therapy dog, how to connect deeply with young people who had been terribly victimized and hurt. I miss you deeply. Your impact will not be soon forgotten. Cricket, Shady and Bodhi – thank you for being part of my self-care plan and keeping me active with hikes, tennis ball sessions and rides through the country side! And finally, to my students and clients – thank you for all that you have taught me and continue to teach me every single day. You have my humble gratitude.

Kirby L. Wycoff

I dedicate this book to my dear mother, Vera, who was always encouraging of my endeavors. And to my loving husband, Steven, and talented son, Evan, who continue to make me a very proud partner and mother to their own achievements and many accomplishments.

Bettina Franzese

Essentials of Trauma-Informed Assessment and Intervention in School and Community Settings

Section One

HISTORY: TRAUMA, ADVERSITY AND THE TRAUMA-INFORMED MOVEMENT

One

ADVERSE CHILDHOOD EXPERIENCES

Kirby L. Wycoff

INTRODUCTION

We are a nation in crisis. Our schools, our communities, and our families are under fire. Physically, emotionally, spiritually, we are increasingly feeling the impact of adversity and trauma on a scale of massive proportions.

Take Mateo for example. Mateo is 9 years old and now resides in a therapeutic foster care home. He was removed from his home after his parents were jailed for drug possession. During the time he lived with his parents, Mateo and his siblings were left alone and unsupervised for days at a time. Sometimes there was no food in the house and the utilities were often turned off. Mateo, the middle son, was often punished severely due to his father's perceptions of him being an oppositional and willful child. All of the children witnessed domestic violence and Mateo's mother was hospitalized on several occasions. Mateo's mother, when abusing drugs, became agitated and angry and told the children they were "stupid and worthless." The siblings were split up after they were removed from the home. Mateo does poorly in school, gets into physical altercations, and spends a good deal of time in the principal's office for behavioral problems. Mateo is alternatively very clingy towards his teacher but also aggressive towards her as well. Teachers cannot understand why Mateo is so angry and can blow-up over the slightest incident. Between the ages of 6–8 years he was diagnosed with learning disabilities, attention deficit hyperactivity disorder and oppositional defiant disorder. Mateo has now been suspended from school three times and school administrators and teachers are running out of options.

Consider Rosalyn. Rosalyn is 17 years old and while she is committed to her schooling and education, she was recently suspended for sleeping overnight in the locker room on school grounds. Rosalyn was born to a drug addicted mother who had a significant history of mental illness. Rosalyn's mother has been hospitalized on multiple occasions for depressive symptoms, suicidality, and undedicated bipolar disorder. Her father was largely absent during her early childhood. Up until the fifth grade, Rosalyn lived with her mother and grandmother. Rosalyn's grandmother struggles with drug and alcohol abuse and becomes violent and aggressive when using substances. On multiple occasions Rosalyn has landed in the ER with head trauma and bruising as a result of her grandmother's violent outbursts. Roslyn lives in an area of the city that makes it unsafe for her to walk to and from school. She has to alter her route on a regular basis to avoid gang violence and gun activity. What should be a 5-minute, 3 block walk often takes her 45 minutes as she navigates her dangerous neighborhood to make it home safely. Rosalyn often eats breakfast and lunch at her school, and these might be the only meals she gets all day. Frequently, the last meal she will have before the weekend is Friday at lunch. She will not eat again until she is in school on Monday morning. Child Protective Services has been involved with the family for many years. The agency is under-resourced and despite multiple failed interventions, Rosalyn still resides in the home. Recently, Rosalyn has been sleeping in the girls' locker room because she felt safer than walking home in a dangerous neighborhood and residing with two unstable adults who are unable to meet her needs. Unfortunately, in doing this, Rosalyn was suspended for violating the schools security policy. She has now been out of school on a suspension for 23 days.

We are a nation in distress and Mateo and Rosalyn are just two of hundreds of thousands of children in this country who have experienced chronic, traumatic stressors. More than half of the school-aged children in the United States have experienced at least one Adverse Childhood Experience (ACE). Research indicates that anywhere between 3 and 10 million children per year witness violence in their homes and communities (American Psychological Association, 2008). Research shows that at the last count approximately 906,000 children were found to be victims of child abuse and neglect by Child Protective Services (American Psychological Association 2008). There has been considerable coverage and publicity about the lifelong effects of ACEs lasting well into adulthood and the negative mental and physical health outcomes. Subsequent chapters in Section 1 will discuss the ACE Study including the role of the Centers for Disease Control (CDC) and Kaiser Permanente as well as introduce a discussion on the impact of stress and adversity. The effects of trauma exposure are long lasting and often life changing. The need for trauma-informed assessments and interventions in school and community settings continues to grow exponentially in our country and beyond.

Children like Mateo and Rosalyn are in your communities, neighborhoods, classrooms, and schools, and on our caseloads. This book is designed to provide school, clinical, and related psychologists and mental health practitioners and their trainers with science-based information about the negative and toxic effects of ACEs (also referred to as chronic or developmental trauma) on children's functioning, adjustment, cognitive, social–emotional, behavioral, academic, and neuropsychological outcomes.

The Invisible Suitcase provides a meaningful metaphor for understanding the social, emotional, educational, and behavioral challenges of traumatized youth. The National Child Traumatic Stress Network uses this exercise in helping individuals understand children and youth in the foster care system as part of their Child Welfare Trauma Training Toolkit. We offer it as an opportunity to consider any traumatized child that we interact with in school and community settings. Instead of calling it the invisible suitcase, here we will refer to it as the "invisible backpack." Children who enter our school buildings and community centers may come with personal belongings and items. They may have pencils, notebooks, and pens as they gear up for their learning in the schools. They also, however, arrive with another piece of luggage. It is one that not even they are aware they have. This is their invisible backpack and it is full of the beliefs they have about themselves, the people who care for them, the people who educate them, and the world at large.

For children who have experienced trauma, particularly the abuse and neglect that leads to foster care, the invisible backpack is often filled with overwhelming negative beliefs and expectations. Beliefs not only about themselves. . .

- I am worthless.
- I am always in danger of being hurt or overwhelmed.
- I am powerless.

But also about you as a caregiver. . .

- You are unresponsive.
- You are unreliable.
- You are, or will be, threatening, dangerous, rejecting. (Child Welfare Trauma Training Toolkit: The Invisible Suitcase, March 2008, p.1)

As individuals who interact with children and youth who have been exposed to trauma, whether that is in school settings, community settings, outpatient, or inpatient settings in roles as direct care providers, foster parents, educators, and coaches or mentors, our ability to be sensitive to these negative beliefs is critical to the child's welfare. We must remember that these beliefs that these children and teens have are not about us; and if we do not understand them and where they come from, we will not be able to effectively connect and work with these children. (NCTSN 2008). This book sets the stage for community and school professionals to better understand the invisible backpack and how to help trauma-impacted children and their families.

These ACEs, which are often chronic and occur within caregiving and family systems, can throw children off a normal developmental trajectory and may have negative effects on mental and physical wellbeing that can last well into adulthood (Felitti & Anda, 2009). Current research on brain areas and cognitive processes typically associated with academic achievement has focused on the realms of language functioning, comprehension, executive functions, conceptual reasoning, learning, long-term retrieval, phonemic awareness, information processing, and related brain areas that are associated with mental health and neurodevelopmental disorders. These relationships will be discussed as they relate to early chronic stressors.

Early chronic stressors and developmental trauma can have damaging effects on children's functioning in school, home, and their communities. Youth impacted by chronic stressors are frequently referred for academic, neuropsychological, psychoeducational and/or psychological evaluations. When assessing such children, the importance of going above and beyond typical evaluations by gathering additional data from formal and informal testing, family and developmental history, and child and caregiver interviews allows for more comprehensive, trauma-focused evaluations. These evaluations can lead to targeted treatments to help understand the strengths and challenges of so many of our nation's vulnerable, at-risk children and youth.

The purpose of this book is to provide the knowledge base and tools to conduct trauma-informed assessments, develop and provide evidence-based interventions, a means in which to consult with caregivers about best practices in working with these students, and provide expertise in helping schools consider a trauma-informed perspective on children's educational and mental health services.

This book is organized and developed with the practitioner in mind. The book contains three different sections that each represent an important aspect of understanding the topic of trauma, adversity, and youth. We suspect that for the experienced clinician, you might brush up on the history of the trauma-informed movement in Section 1, and then jump right into assessment tools, services, and interventions in Section 3. This book does not need to be read chronologically and we encourage you to make this Essentials Book work for you.

Section 1: History: Trauma, Adversity, and the Trauma-Informed Movement
- Chapter 1: Adverse Childhood Experiences
- Chapter 2: Impact on Children, Teens, Families, and Communities
- Chapter 3: Public Health and the Trauma-Informed Movement
- Chapter 4: Trauma-Informed Schools

Section 2: Complex Trauma and the Role of Functional Impairment

Section 3: Trauma-Informed Assessment Framework

As we read ahead in Chapter 1, we will take a closer look at the ACEs Study and the impact that this has on our understanding of adversity and stress in the lives of children, teens, and families.

ADVERSE CHILDHOOD EXPERIENCES

The Adverse Childhood Experiences Study (1998) is one of the largest, longitudinal studies of its kind to document the harmful impact of early adversity on later physical and mental health in adults. ACEs refers to a myriad of negative experiences, including child abuse, neglect, and parental substance abuse and other traumatic stressors that occur prior to the age of 18. In the 1990s two prominent researchers, Dr. Vincent Felitti and Dr. Robert Anda, joined forces to better understand the impact of early childhood adversity on later health behaviors.

In 1985, Dr. Vincent Felitti was the chief physician at Kaiser Permanente's Department of Preventative Medicine in San Diego, CA, where he was researching obesity in an adult health clinic. He noticed over time that many of his study participants dropped out of the research protocol and never completed the program (Stevens, 2012). The Preventative Medicine Department, which housed the obesity clinic, was opened in the 1980's. Over the years, Dr. Felitti had established one of the leading preventative health clinics in the world, primarily focused on reducing health costs. Over 50,000 people were screened for disease on an annual basis, and research was being conducted to establish paths of illness and methodology for preventing illness. The dropout data at the obesity clinic puzzled Dr. Felitti. He and his team decided to dig into the medical records of all of their clients to better understand why they had dropped out. He noted that these overweight clients (most who had to lose between 100 and 600 pounds) actually left the clinic at the very moment that they were losing weight. The team wondered why someone who started at 300 pounds–and who had already lost 100 pounds–would stop just when they were feeling successful (Stevens, 2013a,b).

This phenomenon was terribly frustrating to Dr. Felitti and he wanted to know more. He noted that the situation "was ruining my attempts to build a successful program" and he wanted to know why (Stevens, 2012, Para. 7). This unexplained phenomenon would become the foundation of a career-long journey and partnership between the CDC and Kaiser Permanente to understand the impact of early childhood adversity. Based on the early research by Felitti and his team, which included approximately 17,000 subjects, we know that early exposure to adversity directly relates to multiple chronic health issues in adulthood. We know that adverse experiences in childhood are quite common, even for middle-class individuals, and that these chronic health issues cost our country billions of dollars on an annual basis.

What Dr. Felitti found in those clients' medical records was that all of clients had been born at a normal weight and most were not obese in childhood. This was shocking. He assumed that clients would gain extra weight, slowly over time. This was not the case. Instead, he found that they gained weight all at once and stayed at their heavier weight. If they lost weight, they would quickly gain it back. "I had assumed that people who were 400, 500, 600 pounds would be getting heavier and heavier year after year. In 2,000 people, I did not see it once," says Felitti (Stevens, 2012, para. 10). To dig deeper, Dr. Felitti and his team conducted in-depth interviews with a number of the clients who dropped out of his research study. He did face-to-face interviews and for many weeks, he learned nothing new that helped him solve his puzzle. Until one day he stumbled upon something accidentally. Dr. Felitti was interviewing an obesity clinic patient and working through his standard interview protocol, which included questions like these: "How much did you weigh when you were born? What was your weight in the first grade? What was your weight upon entering High School?" (Stevens, 2012, para. 11). Stumbling on one part of the interview, Dr. Felitti asked a female patient "How much did you weigh when you were first sexually active?" (Stevens, 2012, para. 11). The patient gave the physician quite a shock when she responded with "40 pounds" (Stevens, 2012, para. 12). Felitti asked again, seeking clarity. He was certain he had misunderstood. The patient went on to clarify that indeed, she was 40 pounds and 4 years old when she first became sexually active. Her father was her perpetrator.

Dr. Felitti recalled thinking that this was one of the first and only times in his 20-year career that he had worked with or even met a client with a history of incest (Stevens, 2012). As a physician, Felitti was trained on the medical side of the physical human body, but not necessarily on the mental health side. He recalled not knowing how to handle the information that this client had shared (Stevens, 2012). Felitti also recalled feeling distraught when he had another client just a few days later report the exact same experience. He wondered how he had missed this critically important piece of information in his medical training. More concerning, he wondered if perhaps this was just not something that professionals or patients were talking about. Felitti wondered if he had unintentionally biased his participants in the way he worded his interview questions. Perhaps it was his flawed research methodology and design that created the shocking outcomes. Perhaps there was something about the way he was doing the interviews that was misleading or biased. He revisited his design protocol and asked colleagues to interview the remaining participants (Stevens, 2012). Unfortunately, it was not bias that was revealing these startling trends. In fact, of the 286 people interviewed by the team, most had reported being sexually abused as children. One particular respondent revealed another piece of the puzzle. This patient reported that she had not been born overweight, but was raped at 23 years of age. In the year following her attack, she gained over 100 pounds. Stevens (2012) noted in her now widespread article on this topic that Felitti reported the following in reference to the 23 year old client: "As she was thanking me for asking the question, she looked down at the carpet and muttered 'Overweight is overlooked and that's what I needed to be'" (Stevens, 2013a,b, para. 18).

Felitti was struck by a fact that had eluded so many others who were attempting to address the obesity epidemic. As Felitti reflected, for many of these people the weight was not the problem, it was the solution (Stevens, 2013a,b). For many of these participants, food had become a way to manage an intense emotional experience. Instead of processing the deep and complex feelings that occur as a result of trauma, mindlessly eating created a numbing experience. In many ways, the weight became a protective factor. Instead of becoming incredibly vulnerable and addressing the shame and guilt of the traumatic experience, eating became a distraction. Similar to the use of drugs, it was both a solution and distractor; a self-medication of sorts in which food provided a mechanism for coping. For some, being overweight in-and-of-itself works as an invisibility cloak in a society that is seemingly obsessed with being thin and attractive. Being overweight lets individuals fade into the margins of a society if they choose to do so. To the 23-year-old woman discussed above, becoming overweight after her rape was a safeguard against being sexually assaulted again. Another participant, who was also a sexual abuse survivor, recalls that every time she lost weight and men would comment on how attractive she was, she became paralyzed with fear; not surprisingly, she would again gain weight (Stevens, 2012). Obesity served as a protective factor to something more painful and scary. Losing weight caused significant anxiety and discomfort and with this line of thinking in mind, it was no wonder that so many of Felitti's participants dropped out of the study, right at the time that they were "successfully" losing weight. Multiple subsequent researchers have documented the impact of early adversity on physical health and obesity. In a sample of 471, the prevalence of obesity (BMI>/= 85%) was greater (45.2%) among participants who had experienced four or more childhood adversities, compared to those that had no childhood adversity (Burke, et al., 2011). This critical aspect of obesity had largely been ignored by mental health professionals, physicians, and public health policymakers. Felitti's discovery led him down an entirely new path of inquiry—understanding the impact of adversity on later mental and physical health outcomes (Stevens, 2012).

In many ways this new information turned the public health and medical fields entirely upside down. For a long time researchers had been looking at the behavior as the problem, with rates of addiction and obesity skyrocketing across the country. Felitti's work suggested a different line of inquiry might be worth pursuing. With Felitti's discovery, the field began to turn their attention to the underlying causes of these behaviors. It would appear that the addictive behaviors of overeating (or doing drugs, or drinking alcohol, or smoking cigarettes) were coping mechanisms for unresolved early traumatic experiences (Stevens, 2012).

Felitti was invigorated by this new finding and took his data to a conference in Georgia in 1990 to spread the word. At the North American Association for the Study of Obesity, a conference largely attended by psychologists, psychiatrists, and obesity researchers, Felitti was sure his data would have an impact (Stevens, 2013a,b). It did not. Many in the audience criticized the work and noted that his findings were not generalizable. They criticized his sample size for being too small and generally discounted his findings. However, one attendee at the conference took note. Dr. David Williamson, who also happened to be an epidemiologist for the United States Centers for Disease Control and Prevention, approached Felitti with an idea. He told Felitti that with a larger sample size from the general population (instead of just those from an obesity clinic), folks might be more inclined to hear what he had to say. Williamson introduced Dr. Felitti to Dr. Robert Anda, a medical epidemiologist. Dr. Anda was a physician, who had become interested in public health and epidemiology. Broadly speaking, epidemiology is the study of disease from a population perspective. "Epidemiology is the study of the distribution and determinants of health-related states or events in specified populations, and the application of this study to the control of health problems" (Last, 2001, p.1). It is the study of the health in an overall population and it involves connecting research-driven data and outcomes to community-based practice (Cates, 1982; Greenwood, 1935).

At the time that Felitti and Anda met, Anda was researching the relationship between depression and coronary heart disease at the CDC. He had found in his work that these things were connected and wondered if there was something about the underlying feelings of hopelessness in his sample population that was influencing the prevalence of heart disease. The two decided to join tasks and tap their collective expertise and resources. Together, they agreed that if they were to collaborate and bring the resources of both the CDC and Kaiser-Permanente together, they might be able to uncover some important information about health and wellness in our country.

The team decided that Kaiser-Permanente in San Diego would make an ideal setting for this large-scale data collection. As in any research endeavor, the population that researchers have access to can completely change the significance of the findings. When considering sample size, typically, the bigger the better. At the time that they were planning their research there were approximately 50,000 individuals who would be seen by the Department of Preventive Medicine in any given year, and all of them would have completed an extensive biopsychosocial history form prior to physical examination and laboratory testing. The two researchers decided to use this opportunity as an initial source for recruiting participants for their own study. Through that screening process, the team asked 26,000 people "if they would be interested in helping us understand how childhood events might affect adult health" said Felitti (Stephens, 2012, para. 1). A total of 17,421 or 68% of that 26,000 agreed to participate in the study with the understanding that the information that they provided about their childhood experiencers would not be kept in their permanent medical files (Burke, 2011; Felitti, 2002; Hillis, 2004; Stevens, 2012; Williamson, 2002). Approximately two weeks after their annual health and wellness evaluation, the participants that agreed to participate in the study, received (via email) an ACE questionnaire. The questionnaire surveyed self-reports of 10 different categories of childhood abuse and household dysfunction (Burke, 2011; Felitti, 2002; Hillis, 2004; Stevens, 2013; Williamson, 2002). The questionnaire yielded an "ACE score" for each individual. This was a count of the number of categories (not the number of incidents) that had occurred to any given individual prior to the age of 18. It is important to note that this retrospective aspect of the study may have resulted in recall bias, and it is possible that not all of the individuals accurately remembered their earlier trauma exposure. Each positive endorsement (an answer of yes) received one point towards the total point tally. The questions on the ACEs inventory asked "While you were growing up, during your first 18 years of life" and included the following:

1. Did a parent or other adult in the household often. . .
   - Swear at you, insult you, put you down, or humiliate you? (Or)

- Act in a way that made you afraid that you might be physically hurt?
2. Did a parent or other adult in the household often. . .
   - Push, grab, slap, or throw something at you? (Or)
   - Ever hit you so hard that you had marks or were injured?
3. Did an adult or person at least five years older than you ever. . .
   - Touch or fondle you or have you touch their body in a sexual way? (Or)
   - Try to or actually have oral, anal, or vaginal sex with you?
4. Did you often feel that. . .
   - No one in your family loved you or thought you were important or special? (Or)
   - Your family didn't look out for each other, feel close to each other, or support each other?
5. Did you often feel that. . .
   - You didn't have enough to eat, had to wear dirty clothes, and had no one to protect you? (Or)
   - Your parents were too drunk or high to take care of you or take you to the doctor if you needed it?
6. Were your parents ever separated or divorced?
7. Was your mother or stepmother:
   - Often pushed, grabbed, slapped, or had something thrown at her? (Or)
   - Sometimes or often kicked, bitten, hit with a fist, or hit with something hard? (Or)
   - Ever repeatedly hit over at least a few minutes or threaten with a gun or knife?
8. Did you live with anyone who was a problem drinking or alcoholic or who used street drugs?
9. Was a household member depressed or mentally ill or did a household member attempt suicide?
10. Did a household member go to prison? (Felitti & Anda, 1998, p. 4)

The full measure for scores can be found by visiting the following address:
   https://www.ncjfcj.org/sites/default/files/Finding%20Your%20ACE%20Score.pdf

One of the critiques of the original data was that it was not robust or representative enough of the population. The new sample would address those concerns. The Kaiser Health Plan patients were solidly middle-class Americans who had access to high-quality health insurance. In any four-year period, a total of 81% of San Diego plan members came in for comprehensive medical evaluations. This was a resourced, knowledgeable population who had access to services and support. Approximately 80% of the population was White (which included Hispanics), 10% were Black, and 10% were Asian. Furthermore, 74% had attended college and the average age of the participants was 57 years. Almost exactly half of the population was men and half was women. This solidly middle-class group hailed from the seventh largest city in the United States and the results surely could not be dismissed as being atypical, the result of poverty, or some other confounding variable. Felitti wanted to be certain that sample size and population would not be a limitation of the study moving forward (Felitti & Anda, 2009).

In preparation for the joint work ahead—what would become the largest scale, longitudinal study in the world examining childhood adversity—Dr. Anda brought himself up to date on the childhood trauma literature and immersed himself in the data that Dr. Felitti had already collected (Stephens, 2012). Dr. Anda noted that prior to that, he never even considered childhood adversity as being related to his work (Anda, et al., 2012) For the next 6 months, Anda did a large-scale literature review and read every single abstract for every single article in MedLine that had the words "child abuse and neglect" in it, going back 15 years. Most of the studies he reviewed looked at one single form of abuse and most of them looked at sexual abuse and physical abuse (Anda, et al., 2012). Some looked at exposure to domestic violence, but all looked at these issues singularly. The outcomes were limited and none of the studies considered the cumulative effects of multiple traumas or adversities. He noted that most outcomes were related to later depressive symptoms, and not a single one considered adult physical health as being related to early adversity. Dr. Anda recalled feeling that there was a lot of fragmented information across different fields related to childhood adversity, but nothing that tied it all together.

Based on the research Anda did and the work that Felitti had already done, the team established eight primary types of childhood trauma that were the focus of the original research. They included three different types of abuse: sexual, physical, and verbal, and five other types of family-related problems: a mentally ill parent, an alcoholic parent, a mother who had been the victim of domestic violence, an incarcerated family member, and parental loss via divorce or abandonment (Felitti & Anda, 1998; 2010; Hillis, 2004; 2010; Stevens, 2013a,b). Dr. Anda added emotional abuse and physical neglect to the list, which brought the inventory to a total of 10 types of childhood adversity.

The joint research endeavor officially began in 1995 and was carried through until 1997. The participants in the initial dataset were followed for over 15 years, using a retrospective and prospective cohort study (IRB approval through Kaiser-Permanente and Emory University and the Office of Human Research Protection). In the end, the study was both retrospective (looking backwards) and prospective (looking forward). The big picture, endgame goal of the ACEs study was to match (retrospectively) an individual's current health status and wellness to an ACE score based on experiences in the past (adversity before age 18). The second aspect was then to follow that cohort forward into the future (prospectively) and match those individuals' records against future doctor visits, ER visits, hospitalizations, pharmacy costs, and finally, death. At the time of the printing of this book (2018) we have just passed the 20 year mark from the original data collection and have gathered a longitudinal body of information (Nakazawa 2015).

The data was collected in two periods to allow for a mid-point correction and adjustment to the collection protocol if needed. The first phase was from August to November of 1995 and January to March of 1996. The second phase was from June to October in 1997. The response rate averaged 68% across both phases, 70% for phase 1 and 65% for phase 2 (Felitti & Anda, 2009; Felitti et al., 1998a,b,c). Dr. Anda noted: "Everything we've published comes from that baseline survey of 17,241 people" (Stevens, 2012, para. 1). He recalled that when the dataset first came in, he was at his home in Atlanta. He logged into the database and was shocked. "I wept. I saw how much people had suffered and I wept" (Stevens, 2012, para. 1). This was the first time that anyone had looked at these individual trauma incidents or experiences in a cumulative way. The data set showed a number of striking patterns. The bottom line was that the higher the number of categories of childhood adversity someone was exposed to, the higher their likelihood of experiencing adult health risk behaviors, disease, and possibly even death (Felitti et al., 1998a,b,c; Stephens, 2012). There was a strong, proportionate link between exposure to childhood trauma and not only mental illness, incarceration, and addiction, but also chronic physical illness and disease. Experiencing early adversity and trauma could actually make you sicker as an adult? Maybe even cause you to die younger? This was a ground-breaking discovery in the mid 1990s.

Speaking at the University of Alaska, Anchorage, Dr. Anda recalled his early professional career and path that lead him to the ACEs work. Dr. Anda noted that he was working as a resident in internal medicine at the Veterans Hospital in Madison Wisconsin from 1979 to 1982, where he first remembered seeing the impact that experiences could have on health. Working primarily with World War II veterans, he saw men who were dying of things like smoking related illness, chronic lung disease, substance abuse, and mental illness, all at a time before Post Traumatic Stress Disorder was part of the common language for clinicians.

Citing a quote from a videotaped speech, he noted that "I saw things that didn't need to be there" (Anda et al., 2012), and wondered why these men behaved the way they did. He recalls one specific client named Ed, who was dying of smoking related illness and was gasping for breath just to get from his bed to the bathroom. It would take Ed many minutes to catch his breath after this short walk. After this, Ed would meander his way down to the community room where he would smoke for hours on end while interacting with his peers. Dr. Anda wondered why Ed, and the many others like him, did what they did. In this University Hospital setting, Dr. Anda was seeing end-stage cancer and heart disease patients. If preventative options had been available, things would not have gotten this bad for so many of them (Anda et al., 2012).

Dr. Anda also recalled his time working in the Wisconsin prison systems where he saw many rural young men struggling with substance abuse issues. He wondered how they got there and what they were doing in the prison system. His work in the Emergency room also got him thinking about the intersection between substance abuse and violence. All of these experiences converged and Dr. Anda decided to pursue a career in preventative medicine. He felt strongly that something (ANYTHING) had to be done to help these people before they found themselves in difficult health and social situations. This led him to his work at the CDC where he focused largely on chronic disease (Anda et al., 2012).

After many years of working at the CDC, Dr. Anda found himself increasingly disillusioned by what he was seeing relative to chronic illness. He was frustrated because over time he realized how challenging and difficult it was to change risk-taking behaviors. He noted that these were entrenched, habitual behaviors that contributed to things like smoking, hypertension, obesity, and diabetes. He found that they were not only difficult to treat, but quite expensive. This got Dr. Anda to thinking about the emotional origins of these problematic, risk-taking behaviors. He increasingly realized that there was some emotional distress that was underlying many of these behaviors, and until he addressed this distress, he was fighting an uphill battle (Anda et al., 2012).

To explore this further, Dr. Anda looked at smoking and depression and found that the more depressed someone was, the more likely they were to smoke (Anda et al., 1990). Dr. Anda and his team did a national study and followed these individuals over the course of years. The team noted that depressed people were less likely to quit over a period of multiple years. From this study came substantial contributions to the origins of the "self-medication" hypothesis (Anda, et al., 2012; Markou, et al., 1998). Individuals with mental illness are twice as likely to smoke as those without mental illness (Lasser, et al., 2000). Addiction to drugs is intimately connected to human suffering (Khantzian, 1987). It is possible that individuals use a substance of some sort (alcohol, drugs, prescription medications, food, and/or other compulsive behaviors) to engage in emotional numbing around their own mental health distress and disease.

Dr. Anda was heavily involved in this research and getting some traction on understanding the emotional underpinnings of chronic disease before he met Felitti in 1991, when a colleague introduced them after that brown bag lunch seminar at the CDC. The two researchers (who had never encountered each other's work prior to this) agreed that there were mutual interests and mechanisms that deserved their serious research attention; and the now infamous, ACEs study was born. The team noted that this topic was too important to ignore: "In the context of everyday medical practice, we came to recognize that the earliest years of infancy and childhood are not lost but, like a child's footprints in wet cement, are often life-long" (Felitti & Anda, 2010).

Two

IMPACT ON CHILDREN, TEENS, FAMILIES, AND COMMUNITIES

Kirby L. Wycoff

INTRODUCTION

What does the Adverse Childhood Experiences (ACEs) study tell us about children, teens, families, and communities? The information provided by the ACEs study offered more insight to the complex physical, mental, and behavioral health needs of our society. The partnership between these two eminent researchers, Dr. Felitti and Dr. Anda, provided the foundation for one of the most important public health research studies in our country's history. The data analysis was robust and compelling. The findings were that the more exposure one has to adversity under the age of 18, the higher the risk for a whole host of other problems later in life. Yet it is still undetermined how specifically early adversity can impact various aspects of functioning. This next section will dig deeper into the impact that adversity has on individuals and what this means for community and school-based practitioners who are working with children and families at risk.

As noted earlier, major and toxic stressors take many forms: sexual, physical, psychological abuse and neglect (child maltreatment), as well as chronic bullying, out of home placement, foster care, children and youth services involvement, parental substance abuse, parental criminality, loss of loved ones, parental mental health problems, severe financial hardship, living with racism and bigotry, witnessing interpersonal and community violence, exposure to discrete trauma, and undergoing painful childhood medical procedures (Carrion & Wong, 2012; DeBellis et al. 2003; Teicher, 2000). Brown et al., (2009) in their study of ACE's exposure and mortality found a shocking 19 years of potential life lost for those individuals who had multiple ACE exposures (Brown et al., 2009).

This exposure to stressors in childhood causes a whole host of problems for children, adolescents, families, and communities. Per Felitti and Anda, "there is a long-lasting, strongly proportionate, and often profound relationship between adverse childhood experiences and important categories of emotional state, health risks, disease burden, sexual behavior, disability and healthcare costs – decades later" (Felitti & Anda, 2009, p. 4). As noted in the previous section, the ACE study helped us look broadly at childhood adversity and included three forms of abuse: emotional, physical, and sexual (Anda et al., 2006a,b,c; Felitti et al., 1998a,b,c). The outcomes were striking. The data showed that 1 in 6 people had an ACE score of 4 or more and 1 in 9 had an ACE score of 5 or more. If one category was endorsed there was an 87% likelihood that there was at least one other category present. Women were reportedly 50% more likely than men to have 5 or more categories of ACEs (Anda et al., 2006a,b,c; Bloom, 2017; Felitti et al., 1998a,b,c). There was a staircase effect in the data. As the ACE score goes up, so do the potential risks for problems. At the high end, the risks become almost exponential; more is worse (Nakazawa, 2015). The research team reported that:

> More than half of respondents reported at least one, and one-fourth reported two categories of childhood exposures. We found a graded relationship between the number of categories of childhood exposure and each of the adult health risk behaviors and diseases that were studied (P < .001). Persons who had experienced four or more categories of childhood exposure, compared to those who had experienced none, had 4- to 12-fold increased health risks for alcoholism, drug abuse, depression, and suicide attempt; a 2- to 4-fold increase in smoking, poor self-rated health, ≥ 50 sexual intercourse partners, and sexually transmitted disease; and a 1.4- to 1.6-fold increase in physical inactivity and severe obesity. The number of categories of adverse childhood exposures showed a graded relationship to the presence of adult diseases including ischemic heart disease, cancer, chronic lung disease, skeletal fractures, and liver disease. The seven categories of adverse childhood experiences were strongly interrelated and persons with multiple categories of childhood exposure were likely to have multiple health risk factors later in life.

(Felitti et al., 1998a,b,c, p. 1)

The following list is of the prevalence of childhood exposure to abuse and household dysfunction. *Prevalence* refers to the extent to which a condition is prevalent or common:

Abuse by Category
1. Psychology–recurrent threats, humiliation (11.1%)
2. Physical–beating, not spanking (10.8%)
3. Contact sexual abuse (28% women, 16% men, 22% overall)

Household Dysfunction
1. Mother treated violently (12.5%)
2. Substance use (household member alcoholic or drug user) (25.6%)
3. Criminal behavior in household (3.4%)
4. Household member chronically depressed, suicidal, mentally ill, or in psychiatric hospital (18.8%)
5. Not raised by both biological parents (23%)

Neglect
1. Physical (10%)
2. Emotional (15%) (Anda et al., 2006a,b,c, p. 5).

Some exposure to stress is necessary and beneficial as it allows children to develop self-regulation, resiliency, and coping skills. However, prolonged or toxic stress, especially in the absence of warm, nurturing, protective relationships (positive attachment figures), activates the biological stress response system, keeping it on high alert. This initiates a cascade of neurochemical and hormonal changes in the body that can lead to neural cellular death, altered synaptic chemical production, disrupted pruning of nerve cells, weaker and fewer neural connections, abnormal electroencephalograms (EEGs), and altered brain architecture, structure, and functioning (DeBellis & Keshavan, 1999; Gunnar & Quevedo, 2007; Harvard Center on the Developing Child).

Considering the impact of healthy stress and stress overload that leads to unfolding of disease pathways, the concept of *allostatic* load is relevant. The body has a number of stress response systems in place to respond to an increased burden of wear and tear. *Allostasis* refers to the concept by which the body seeks to find and maintain homeostasis, even in the face of stressors. The burden of allostatic load is one way that we can conceptualize the impact of chronic traumatic stressors on the physical body at a cellular level.

With regards to our physical health, allostasis allows us to maintain physiological balance through changing circumstances and stressors. When a healthy organism is confronted with physiological arousal or stress, the body calls forth a protective response. The body works hard to return to a state of balance, equilibrium, and homeostasis. However, if the body's natural coping response is ineffective, damage (or allostatic load) will remain present, which can result in current or future illness (Felitti & Anda, 2010).

In the physical domain a healthy organism is capable of "allostasis"--the maintenance of physiological homoeostasis through changing circumstances. When confronted with physiological stress, a healthy organism is able to mount a protective response, to reduce the potential for harm, and restore an (adapted) equilibrium. If this physiological coping strategy is not successful, damage (or "allostatic load") remains, which may finally result in illness.

(Huber et al., 2011, p. 236)

As presented by Dr. Melissa Merrick of the CDC's National Center for Injury Prevention and Control, ACEs are related to some of the leading causes of death in the United States. Citing the National Vital Statistics in a webinar on "Preventing Early Adversity through Policies, Norms and Programs" for the organization MARC (Mobilizing Action for Resilient Communities, http://marc.healthfederation.org/BrownBag#ARCHIVES). Dr. Merrick noted that the top 10 leading causes of death in the United States and ACE's have been empirically connected to at least seven of them. The leading causes that underlie death in the United States in 2014 are listed below; causes impacted by ACE's exposure will appear in italics: (The National Vital Statistics Report (NVSR) "Deaths: Final Data for 2014").

1. *Heart Disease*
2. *Cancer*
3. *Chronic lower respiratory diseases*
4. Unintentional injuries
5. *Stroke*
6. Alzheimer's disease
7. *Diabetes*
8. Influenza and Pneumonia
9. *Nephritis, Nephrotic Syndrome, and Nephrosis (Kidney Disease)*
10. *Intentional self-harm (suicide)* (NVSR, "Deaths: Final Data for 2014").

Exposure to chronic stress and adversity in childhood has negative impacts on individuals' mental and physical health later in life. A meta-analysis in *The Lancet* (2017) analyzed the impact that early adversity has on health. The research team did a systematic review of five electronic databases for any cross-sectional, case–control, or cohort studies that had been published up until May 6, 2016. The team focused on looking for studies that discussed health outcomes (e.g. substance abuse, sexual health, mental health, weight and physical exercise, violence, physical health status and conditions) associated with ACEs (Hughes, et al., 2017). The team was interested in studies that considered risk estimates for individuals with at least four ACE exposures compared to those with zero ACE exposures. The population of interest was adults over 18 years of age and the sample sizes for the studies needed to be over 100 participants. The team was able to compare apples to apples by using an odds ratio based on a random-effects model (Hughes et al., 2017). An *odds ratio* is the likelihood that a given individual will be impacted by a specific outcome. An odds ratio of 1: 1 indicates that there is no greater risk of experiencing a specific outcome based on a specific exposure; that is the same level of risk. An odds ratio of higher than 1 indicates an increased risk, and a ratio of less than 1 indicates a decreased risk (Merrick, 2017). The initial search yielded an astounding 11,621 possible studies for inclusion with a total of 253,719 pooled participants in the meta-analysis.

In the meta-analysis, Hughes et al. found that individuals who had 4 or more ACEs compared to 0 ACEs were more likely to experience the following:

- 7.51 – 37.48 times more likely to make a suicide attempt
- 3.70 – 4.73 times more likely to experience anxiety or depression
- 2.24 – 4.36 times more likely to have poor self-rated health and low life satisfaction
- 5.92 times more likely to have a Sexually Transmitted Infection (STI)
- 1.38 – 3.05 times more likely to experience chronic diseases (diabetes, cancer, liver and digestive issues, lung disease)
- 1.25 – 6.86 times more likely to engage in risky behaviors like smoking, unsafe sex, and drug and alcohol abuse. (Hughes, et al., 2017, p. 361)

Hughes et al. summarized their findings as follows:

To have multiple ACEs is a major risk factor for many health conditions. The outcomes most strongly associated with multiple ACEs represent ACE risks for the next generation (e.g. violence, mental illness, and substance use). To sustain improvements in public health requires a shift in focus to include prevention of ACEs, resilience building, and ACE-informed service provision.

(Hughes et al., 2017, p. 1)

Among so many other negative behavioral, physical, and psychological health outcomes, individuals with ACE scores of 4 or more are 2 times more likely to smoke, 7 times more likely to be alcoholics, and 6 times more likely to have sex before the age of 18 (Bloom, 2017). More is worse. The jump from zero ACEs to even just one ACE suggests a potential increase of problems by up to 30–40%. For the purposes of this book, we will now further explore the specific impacts of ACEs exposure on children, teens, families, and communities.

MENTAL HEALTH RISK AND IMPACT

Childhood exposure to adversity has a well-documented negative impact on later psychiatric health (Boney-McCoy, 1995; Chapman et al., 2004; Dube et al., 2001; Horowitz, 2001; Karatekin 2017; Kendall-Tacket et al., 1993; Kessler et al., 1997; Runyon et al., 2014; Singer, 1995; Turner et al., 2006). Children who experience multiple adversities and chronic, traumatic stress prior to the age of 18 are at a higher risk for a whole host of mental health challenges, including increased rates of depression, antisocial behavior, psychosis, anxiety, suicidality, and posttraumatic stress disorder (PTSD) symptoms, among others. Felitti and Anda (2009) noted a strong and clear connection between ACE scores and self-reported chronic depression; this is true for other psychiatric conditions as well. The higher the number of ACEs you experienced, the higher the odds that an individual will self-report depressive symptoms later in life. They further noted a similar (but stronger) step-wise relationship between ACE exposure and future suicide attempts. Interestingly enough (and certainly relevant from a public health and economic lens), there has also been a demonstrated relationship between ACE scores and higher anti-depressant prescription medication use over the lifetime of the individual (Felitti & Anda, 2009). An individuals' exposure to childhood adversity and trauma is likely to contribute to later psychiatric illness.

Whitfield et al. (2005a,b) identified a consistent incline of relationship between ACE scores and later hallucinations. Using the original dataset and an adjusted odds ratio from logistical regression models, the relationship between ACE exposure and self-reported hallucinations was assessed. There was a clear, graded, statistically significant connection between childhood trauma exposure and hallucinations, while statistically correcting for a history of substance abuse (Whitfield et al. 2005a,b; Whitfield, 2005). The researchers specifically sought to disentangle the relationship between substance abuse, which could also be related to hallucinations, and hallucinations alone. The researchers wanted to isolate ACEs as the core aspect of the relationship between early trauma and later hallucinations, without the mediating effect of alcohol. This study included a total of 17,337 participants from the original Felitti and Anda dataset, 54% (9,367) of whom were women and 46% (7,970) of whom were men. The mean age was 57 years and the majority of the respondents were white, middle class, and educated. The authors noted that the risk for hallucinations increased 1.2–2.5 times by exposure to any ACE, irrespective of the type of ACE exposure (Whitfield, et al., 2005a,b). This relationship was further explored for individuals who both had and did not have substance abuse histories. After statistically adjusting for age, sex, education level, and race, there was a persistent graded increase in the prevalence of hallucinations (p < 0.001) (Whitfield, et al., 2005a,b) Compared to individuals who had no ACE exposure in childhood, individuals with exposure to seven or more ACEs categories had a fivefold increase in the risk of reporting hallucinations (Whitfield, et al., 2005a,b). These findings are both significant and relevant, and strongly suggest the need for assessing childhood trauma histories among individuals who have experienced hallucinations.

Mersky et al. (2013) found that ACE exposure contributed to a robust and significant relationship to more frequent depressive and anxiety symptoms and poorer self-rated life satisfaction. Using data from the Chicago Longitudinal Study (CLS), the dose–response relationship was assessed in an ethnically diverse, economically disadvantaged population. The CLS tracked a cohort of low socio-economic status (SES), minority youth in an urban setting who were born in 1979 and 1980. The sample population included 1,539 children in a full-day kindergarten program within a public school district from 1985 to 1986 (Mersky, 2013). The majority (2/3, n = 989) of the children attended pre-school through Chicago's Child–Parent Center (CPC) program, and the rest of the sample attended local pre-schools in similarly disadvantaged neighborhood (Mersky, 2013). The CPC program was established in 1967 and is a center-based early intervention program that provides comprehensive family support and educational services to low-income children and their parents in Chicago (Chicago Longitudinal Study, 2013, para. 3: http://www.cehd.umn.edu/icd/research/CLS/ch2.html). The CLS had multiple data points obtained from public record dating back to the child's birth and later survey data was collected from parents, teachers, and participants over the next twenty years (Mersky, 2013).

The present study assessed the adults (n = 1142, 74.2% of full sample) between the ages of 22–24 years old (2002–2004) (Mersky, 2013). The research team used mail, telephone, and in-person surveys to assess the sample population. For both men and women, those with higher ACE scores from the 1985–1986 data collection reported more frequent depressive symptoms and more frequent anxiety symptoms (Mersky, 2013). To assess depressive symptoms, participants endorsed how they felt in the past month: (i) very sad, (ii) hopeless, (iii) lonely, (iv) depressed, or (v) life isn't worth living. Any symptom endorsed was rated for frequency: (1) once a month to (5) almost every day. A similar scale was built to assess anxiety symptoms as well (Mersky, 2013). The outcomes of the research indicated that four out of five (79.5%) participants in the CLS had experienced at least one ACE and approximately half of the CLS sample (48.9%) had multiple ACE exposures (Mersky, 2013). There was a significant dose–response relationship between ACE exposure and later depression symptoms (OR = 2.01–8.09 comparing 0 ACEs or multiple ACEs), anxiety symptoms (OR = 1.77–4.19 comparing 0 ACEs or multiple ACEs), and decreased life-satisfaction (OR = 0.52–0.22 comparing 0 ACEs or multiple ACEs) (Mersky, 2013). Using "No/Zero ACE Exposure" as the referent group, those with an ACE score of 2 (OR = 0.50), a score of 3–4 (OR = 0.57), and scores of five or more (OR = 0.45) indicated significantly poorer health outcomes (Mersky, 2013). The results of this study confirmed other outcomes that indicated increased exposure to ACEs are related to poorer mental health in early adulthood.

Karatekin (2017) sought to explore the role of ACEs in college students using a short-term longitudinal study. This researcher was interested in the extent to which a history of ACEs could potentially be used in early identification of college students who are at risk for mental health challenges as well as exploring the role that current stress played in that interaction (Karatekin, 2017). Acknowledging the fact that early stressors have long-lasting impacts on the stress-response systems in the brain, Karatekin considered the role that current stress played in making individuals more vulnerable to stress later in life in a sample of college students. At the beginning of an academic semester, the team collected information on ACE's history and current depression, anxiety, and suicidality for n = 239 college students at a public university in the Midwest (Karatekin, 2017). The same metrics were collected at the end of the semester. Given that the college transition can be a stressful time and that many mental health issues emerge in early adulthood, this population offered the opportunity to explore ACEs, mental health outcomes, and current stressors. The hypothesis was that ACEs assessed at the outset of the semester would predict a worsening in mental health (e.g. depression, anxiety, and suicidality) at the end of the semester, which could indicate that an ACE history leads to greater vulnerabilities of future stressors. This hypothesis was tested using the Early Adverse Experiences Questionnaire (Felitti et al., 1998a,b,c), the Life Events Scale for Students (Clements & Turpin, 1996), and the Patient Health Questionnaire (PHQ) (Karatekin, 2017). The outcomes of this study indicated that approximately 19% of the population met criteria for clinically significant depression or anxiety.

In addition, more than twice as many (21%) high-ACEs students met screening criteria for at least one anxiety or depressive disorder at Time 2 (when they had not met criteria for any of these disorders at Time 1) compared to low-ACEs students (9%). A logistic regression showed that ACEs made a significant contribution to the prediction of who would develop a depressive or anxiety disorder. A relative risk calculation indicated that a student in the high-ACEs group was more than twice (2.32) as likely to show this deterioration as a student in the low-ACEs group.

(Karatekin, 2017, para. 17)

This suggested the significant role that early adversity exposure plays on later stressors and mental health in a college-aged population. Karatekin also found a significant relationship between a history of ACEs and suicidality, which is also a great concern.

Over a tenth of the students indicated at least some suicidal ideation in the past month at both Time 1 (11%) and Time 2 (12%). Rates were higher in the high-ACEs compared to the low-ACEs group. In the low-ACEs group, 6% of the students expressed no suicidal ideation at Time 1 but did so at Time 2. The corresponding percentage was 11% in the high-ACEs group. A relative risk calculation indicated that a student in the high-ACEs group was almost twice (1.85) as likely to develop suicidal ideation at Time 2 than a student in the low-ACEs group. Adverse childhood experiences made a significant contribution to the prediction of suicidal ideation at Time 2 even after controlling for suicidal ideation at Time 1.

(Karatekin, 2017, para. 19)

Having at least one ACE has been estimated to account for two-thirds of suicide attempts in adults (Dube et al., 2001).These results support the ongoing need to both assess and intervene with ACE-exposed young adults who may be experiencing current anxiety, depression, or suicidality.

In addition to the outcomes noted above, Felitti and Anda considered the role that early adversity and trauma may have in later somatization disorders. Somatization disorders are those that are believed to be physical in nature, but often present as mental health distress. That is, emotional distress will present in the form of a physical symptom. This is notable because somatization disorders and other physical disorders with no clear medical basis are often challenging for clinicians to diagnose and treat. The Felitti and Anda research indicated that the higher the likelihood of childhood sexual abuse, the higher the likelihood of unexplained physical symptoms in adulthood. The authors noted that this is consistent with all of the rest of the original ACE study outcomes and also part of what makes the study so groundbreaking. "What one sees, the presenting problem, is often only the marker for the real problem, which is buried in time, concealed by patient shame, secrecy and sometimes amnesia–and frequently, clinician discomfort" (Felitti & Anda, 2009, p. 6). It is increasingly clear that the mental health and psychiatric risks and impact related to ACEs are significant and warrant our serious attention and concern. Anda and Felitti noted in their work that it is abundantly clear that ACEs have a "profound, proportionate and long-lasting effect on emotional state, whether measured by depression or suicide attempts, by protective unconscious devices like somatization and dissociation, or by self-help attempts that are misguidedly addressed solely as long-term health risks" (Felitti & Anda, 2009, p. 6).

PHYSICAL HEALTH RISK AND IMPACT

The ACEs study clearly demonstrated that there is a significant relationship between childhood exposure to adversity and biomedical disease and disease pathways in adulthood. The fact that emotional distress and adversity can not only relate to later mental health issues, but actually impact the body in acute, physical ways, is a profound finding (Felitti & Anda, 2009). That is, life experience can transmit into organic disease over time (Felitti & Anda, 2009). This is largely a departure from the common medical model beliefs wherein disease was considered genetic (Felitti & Anda, 2009).

There are four specific examples of medical illness and disease that were connected to ACEs in the original study. These are: "liver disease /Hepatitis/Jaundice (Dong et al., 2003), Chronic Obstructive Pulmonary Disease/COPD (Anda et al., 2009), Coronary Artery Disease (Dong et al. 2004a,b) and autoimmune disease (Dube, 2009)" (Felitti & Anda, 2009, p. 9). All of these indicated that a higher ACE score in childhood would lead to increased risk in adulthood for these diseases. This proportionate relationship is also corrected for other related risk factors. For example in Coronary Artery Disease (CAD), the dataset was statistically corrected to account for other risk factors for coronary disease like smoking and hyperlipidemia (Felitti & Anda, 2009). Felitti and Anda addressed the biomedical disease process in their research where they acknowledged how the pathway might seem straightforward at first glance. They addressed this assumption by noting that while we might assume that COPD and CAD are results of cigarette smoking behavior alone, and that stressful early life experience lead to these negative coping behaviors, this is not the full story (Felitti & Anda, 2009). The authors noted a strong relationship between ACEs and coronary disease, even after statistically adjusting for typical risk factors like smoking and cholesterol (Felitti & Anda, 2009). This is ground breaking information. Felitti and

Anda hypothesized that early adversity in childhood was related to adult illness and through two mechanisms or pathways:

1. Conventional risky behaviors (like smoking) are actually self-help attempts. i.e. Nicotine with multiple psychoactive benefits.
2. Chronic stress mediated through chronic inflammatory stress responses on the developing brain/body and regulatory systems, causes disregulation of stress response and subsequent disease pathways turned on (Felitti & Anda, 2009, p. 10).

What is the Medical Impact?

(Quick Glance Figure Box)

When considering the role of disease pathways and the impact of ACEs on physical health, we can consider how ACEs increases the likelihood of heart disease exponentially. For each ACE category, an odds ratio has been calculated to assess how much more likely an individual is to experience heart disease if they had one of these ACE exposure categories:

- Emotional Abuse (1.7 times more likely to have heart disease)
- Physical Abuse (1.5 times more likely to have heart disease)
- Sexual Abuse (1.4 times more likely to have heart disease)
- Domestic Violence (1.4 times more likely to have heart disease)
- Mental Illness (1.4 times more likely to have heart disease)
- Substance Abuse (1.3 times more likely to have heart disease)
- Household Criminal (1.7 times more likely to have heart disease)
- Emotional Neglect (1.3 times more likely to have heart disease)
- Physical Neglect (1.4 times more likely to have heart disease)
  (Bloom, 2017, p. 2)

It had been well established in the literature that emotional distress at an early age could contribute to emotional distress in adulthood. But Felitti and Anda found something that no one else had. The fact that early adversity could actually increase the likelihood of physical disease in adulthood completely turned the field of medicine on its head and was incredibly relevant to our work in school and communities.

ADDICTION RISK AND IMPACT

Understanding addiction through a trauma-informed lens is an important aspect of considering the role that trauma plays in behavioral and mental health outcomes. *Addiction* refers to when an individual is addicted to (or has a dependence on) a particular substance or activity. Smoking, drug use, alcoholism, and compulsive overeating are all examples of addictive behaviors that are both challenging and costly to treat but may be rooted in early traumatic stress. One aspect of why these are so difficult to treat is that they have, at least in the short term, some beneficial or distress-alleviating characteristics. Nicotine, for example, can reduce anxiety. Overeating is one of the behaviors that leads to obesity, and is known as an emotional management strategy for emotional distress, anxiety, and/or feelings of depression. These health risk behaviors are often viewed as solely problematic, which fails to recognize that at some point they served as a purpose for the user.

The original ACEs study found a strong, directly proportionate relationship between ACE scores and the use of psychoactive substances and behaviors. Felitti and Anda noted that there are many common categories of addictions that are particularly relevant to the ACEs study. They noted that an addiction is an "unconscious, compulsive use of a psychoactive agent" (Felitti & Anda, 2010; p. 7). Felitti and Anda, among other researchers, noted the three most common addictions are:

1. Smoking, (Anda et al., 1999; Edwards, 2007)
2. Alcoholism (Felitti et al., 1998a,b,c; Anda, 2002; Dube et al., 2006)
3. Injection drug use (Dube et al., 2003a,b).

These three categories are proportionately related to several categories of adversity in childhood. (Anda et al., 2002, 2006a,b,c; Dube et al., 2003a,b; Edwards et al., 2003; Felitti et al., 1998a,b,c).

The costs of addiction to our communities are significant. "The health, economic, and human burden of substance misuse and addiction is staggering. More than 20 million Americans, nearly 8% of the population, meet diagnostic criteria for substance use disorder" (Office of the Surgeon General, 2016, para. 1). When we consider that an individual's need for self-medication may in part drive the addiction cycle, reducing this through primary prevention is one important avenue to consider. This can be further articulated through things like reducing the stigma of substance misuse and addiction, increasing protective factors, improving interdisciplinary treatment collaborations, and improving prevention efforts (Dube et al., 2006, 2009).

For male children with an ACE score of 6 or more, there is a 4,600% increased likelihood of them later becoming an injection drug user (Anda & Felitti, 2009), when compared to a male child who has an ACE score of zero. This indicates that exposure to cumulative early adversities places an individual at an exponential risk for later drug and addiction behaviors. When considering the dramatic impact that ACE exposure may have on later injection drug use, this warrants our serious consideration for the importance of trauma-informed assessments in school and community settings. This also suggests that the basic causes of addiction are "predominately experience-dependent during childhood and not substance dependent." (Anda Felitti, 2010, p.7).

Using a retrospective cohort study design to assess illicit drug use, the Healthy People 2010 Initiative (Dube et al., 2003a,b) articulated the need to understand the impact of ACEs on the initiation and maintenance of drug abuse. With a sample size of 8,613 adults in a primary care clinic in California, ACEs were assessed, as were self-reports of illicit drug use and other health-related topics. The study specifically measured the initiation of drug use during three age groups: under 14 years old, 15–18 years old and 19 or older. The findings were significant. Like we have seen in other outcomes, there was a strong, graded relationship between each ACE and every variable of interest. For every cumulative ACE category, the likelihood for early initiation of drug use went up two to fourfold. (Dube et al., 2003a,b). Furthermore, for all age groups, ACE scores had the same step-wise relationship to overall lifetime drug use.

> Compared with people with 0 ACEs, people with ≥5 ACEs were 7- to 10-fold more likely to report illicit drug use problems, addiction to illicit drugs, and parenteral drug use. The attributable risk fractions as a result of ACEs for each of these illicit drug use problems were 56%, 64%, and 67%, respectively.
>
> *(Dube et al., 2003a,b, p. 1)*

These authors conclude that ACEs appear to account for one-half to one-third of the drug related problems in our country (Dube et al., 2003a,b). They further noted the significant need for programmatic approaches to reduction of childhood adversity exposure (Dube et al. 2003a,b).

What is clear from the initial ACEs study and many subsequent ones is that the impact of early adversity on later addictive behavior is noteworthy. When considering the economic cost that treating and managing addiction has on our country's resources, not to mention the lost economic and work force contributions for those individuals who are struggling with addiction, this deserves our serious attention.

SEXUAL BEHAVIORAL RISK AND IMPACT

Having an early history of adversity does more than just impact mental health wellness, physical wellness, and addiction risk. Sexualized behaviors are an additional area often impacted by early adversity exposure. Felitti and Anda used teen pregnancy and promiscuity as measures of sexualized behavior and found that ACE scores had a direct proportionate relationship to sexualized behaviors. The higher your ACE score, the more likely you would be to have sexual intercourse by age 15, have a teenage pregnancy if female, and experience teen paternity if are male (Felitti & Anda, 2010). Additionally, miscarriage of pregnancy was also higher for those with higher ACE scores, which again speaks to the complexity of early adversity and things that are typically considered purely biomedical outcomes (Hillis et al., 2004). An adjusted odds ratio demonstrated that the higher your ACE score, the higher the likelihood that you would have more than 50 sexual partners in your lifetime.

Exposure to family dysfunction and childhood abuse are risk factors related to teen pregnancy. Hillis et al. determined that teenage pregnancy increased as ACE score also increased. The study also examined whether it was ACEs or the teenage pregnancy that was the principal risk factor for long-term psychosocial consequences and possible fetal death. These authors used a retrospective cohort study that included 9,159 women with a mean age of 56 years. These were women who were seen through the primary care clinic at Kaiser Permanent between the years of 1995–1997. The study demonstrated that 66% (6,015) of women reported at least one or more ACE and that teenage pregnancy risk increased as ACE scores increased:

- 0 ACEs = 16% increased risk of teen pregnancy
- 1 ACE = 21% increased risk of teen pregnancy
- 2 ACEs = 26% increased risk of teen pregnancy
- 3 ACEs = 29% increased risk of teen pregnancy
- 4 ACEs = 32% increased risk of teen pregnancy
- 5 ACEs = 40% increased risk of teen pregnancy
- 6 ACEs = 43% increased risk of teen pregnancy
- 7–8 ACEs = 53% increased risk of teen pregnancy (Hillis et al., 2004, p. 1)

Additionally, the ACE score was associated with increased fetal death after a first pregnancy. The authors concluded that the connection between ACEs and teenage pregnancy was statistically significant; proportionately graded such that when one score goes up the risk of teen pregnancy rises as well (Hillis et al., 2004). They further concluded that the negative impacts of fetal death that are often attributed to teenage pregnancy appear to be related to the underlying ACE score rather than the actual pregnancy (Hillis et al., 2004). It is also important to note that unwanted teenage pregnancy is a potential risk for perpetration of child abuse (on the un-wanted child), and that this could be one potential mechanism wherein the intergenerational transmission of trauma continues.

Despite the fact that teenage pregnancy rates have decreased in recent decades (Kaufman et al., 1998), the United States continues to present with higher rates than most other developing countries. There are a number of common risk factors often attributed to teenage mothers. These include lower socio-economic status (SES), lower educational attainment, and greater risk of being a single parent (Anda et al., 2002; Dong, et al., 2004a,b). In addition, there are a number of impacts on the fetus, as the result of being born to a teenaged mother. The risk of fetal death is reportedly higher, and these infants may also have lower birth weight, be premature, exhibit poorer cognitive development, and face lower educational attainment, more frequent criminal activity, and higher risk of neglect, abandonment, and behavioral challenges in childhood (Anda et al., 2007; Dong et al., 2004a,b; Dube et al., 2001; Seeman et al., 2001a,b). The debate here lies in understanding whether teenage pregnancy leads to those negative outcomes or if they are the cause; that is, the same environment of adversity that led to the teen getting pregnant in the first place. It is a complex problem and a number of risk factors for teenage pregnancy have been identified. These include: higher unemployment rates, higher violent crime rates, higher teenage suicide rates, higher high school dropout rates, lower parental education, inadequate health care insurance coverage, having an older sister or friend who was an adolescent parent, minority race/ethnicity, lower family connectedness, physical or sexual abuse, general maltreatment by family members, a greater number of sex partners, alcohol use, substance use, and attempted suicide (Anda et al., 2009; Dong et al., 2003, 2004a,b; Dube et al., 2003a,b; Hillis et al., 2004). Despite understanding these factors as those related to teenage pregnancy, there has been less research specifically on ACEs and the role they play in teenage pregnancy. These authors used the original ACE dataset to explore the extent to which ACE exposure increased the risk for teen pregnancy. The research team hypothesized that each ACE category would independently increase the risk, and as overall ACE scores increased, so would the risk for pregnancy. This team also wanted to explore if it was the ACE exposure or if the teenage pregnancy was the primary mechanism for long-term, negative outcomes, serious family problems, job problems, financial problems, high stress, uncontrollable anger, and so forth.

Teenage pregnancy was defined as being pregnant between ages 11–19, which was also collected through the original data collection. During Wave 1 of data collection, the first occurrence of pregnancy was estimated from a question regarding when the first pregnancy ended. Specifically it asked: "During what month and year did your first pregnancy end?" (Felitti & Anda, 2010). The age of when the first pregnancy ended was calculated by using the participant's date of birth and subtracting the age at which the first pregnancy ended. This information, along with the outcome of that first pregnancy (live birth, stillbirth/ miscarriage, tubal pregnancy, or elective abortion) was used to uncover the age when the participant first became pregnant. For live births, they assumed the individual became pregnant eight months before pregnancy ended. In computing age for those where a fetal death occurred, (stillbirth, miscarriage) age at first pregnancy was estimated at four months before the pregnancy ended (Felitti & Anda, 2010). For elective abortion or ectopic pregnancies, researchers assumed the age at first pregnancy was two months prior. As noted earlier, the original ACEs data was collected in two waves, to allow for a mid-point correction (Felitti & Anda, 2010). The team came to realize that they could ask this question very directly and very bluntly in order to get the information they needed. In Wave two, they changed the question to, "How old were you the first time you became pregnant." This research team integrated their analysis from the Wave 1 and Wave 2 data so that they could have more direct estimates of the age at which the participants first became pregnant, although the frequency of teen pregnancy was almost identical in Wave 1 and Wave 2. Wave 1 came out to 23.2% using the estimated variable, and Wave 2 was 23.8% using the actual variable. The researchers took those numbers and lined them up against other psychosocial outcomes questions from the Kaiser Health Appraisal Questionnaire. These included family, work, and financial stressors. Questions asked included: "Are you now having serious or disturbing problems with your family (yes/no), job (yes/no), finances (yes/no)?" (Felitti & Anda, 2010). There was also a question used to assess high stress. This question asked "Please fill in the circle that best describes your stress level (high/medium/low)." The final relevant question they used was in regards to uncontrollable anger (which could speak to emotional dysregulation). The question asked was "Have you ever had reason to fear your anger getting out of control?" (Felitti & Anda, 2010).

A Mantel–Haenszel statistical analysis was used to assess for linear trends in proportions, to assess if the risk for teenage pregnancy increased as the number of ACE categories increased. Separate logistic regression models were used to obtain an adjusted odds ratio (as estimates of relative risks) for the association between ACE score, teenage pregnancy, fetal death, and long-term psychosocial consequences. That is, researchers wanted to uncover if it was the teenage pregnancy that was leading to the negative long-term psychosocial outcomes noted above (Felitti & Anda, 2010). They found highly significant differences based on whether participants had been exposed to ACEs or not. This suggested that connection between teen pregnancy and those negative outcomes are different for those with and without ACEs (Felitti & Anda, 2010).

The bottom line was that exposure to each of the 10 types of ACE categories placed women at a higher risk of experiencing teen pregnancy. As ACE scores increased, serious family problems, job problems, financial problems, high stress, and uncontrollable anger steadily increased. In stark contrast, however, teen pregnancy *without* exposure to ACEs was not associated with a single one of the negative outcomes noted above (Felitti & Anda, 2010). For those women who had been pregnant, there was also a strong relationship between ACE scores and fetal death as an outcome to the first pregnancy (Felitti & Anda, 2010). There was also a clear dose-gradient effect of ACEs on teenage pregnancy (Dube et al., 2003a,b; Hillis et al., 2004; Felitti et al., 2010). These outcomes were unchanged between Wave 1 and Wave 2 data. Wave 2 included additional behavior data and this allowed the team to control for possible confounding factors like multiple sexual partners, drinking during adolescence, drug use during adolescence, being the daughter of an adolescent mother, and suicide attempt during adolescence (Felitti & Anda, 2010). One might assume that exposure to ACEs caused adolescent pregnancy, which based on the computations of this team indicated that the population attributable risk is 33%; and that one-third of teenage pregnancies could be prevented by eliminating exposure to ACEs (Dube et al., 2003a,b; Hillis et al., 2004; Felitti et al., 2010). From a public health perspective, this suggested that putting resources into reducing family dysfunction and violence would be one way to combat the problems associated with teen pregnancy.

The public health implications in these outcomes are jaw-dropping. Essentially, a large number of the female participants who experienced teenage pregnancy as well as ACEs during childhood described significantly impairing problems years later with families, jobs, and finances. While those things are commonly thought to be attributed to the teenage pregnancy, this study shows that they may actually be a result of being raised in a family with exposure to ACEs (Dube et al., 2003a,b; Felitti et al., 2010; Hillis et al., 2004). When the family environment did not have ACEs, teenage pregnancies did not have nearly the same long-term, negative, psychosocial sequelae (Dube et al., 2003a,b; Felitti et al., 2010; Hillis et al., 2004).

LIFE EXPECTANCY RISK AND IMPACT

As established throughout this chapter, exposure to early adversity clearly results in a number of negative mental and physical health outcomes. What is perhaps the most concerning outcome of the original ACE study is the fact that actual life expectancy is reduced for those who have experienced multiple ACEs. Yes, that is correct. The more ACEs you have, the more likely you are to die at a younger age. Felitti and Anda's work found that older people are more likely to have lower ACE scores (score of 0) and are less likely to have higher ACE scores (scores of 2 or 4). One reasonable explanation that the researchers note is that those with higher ACE scores die at younger ages, which would account for why older individuals (the only ones still alive) would have lower scores. The others in that original birth cohort in the study are less likely to have survived, and less likely to be included in the study as a result (Felitti & Anda, 2010).

Another possibility is that patients were so impaired by their physical health status, or perhaps so embarrassed by it as it relates to their early exposure to adversity, that they simply avoided all medical care (Felitti & Anda, 2010). As such, they would not have come in to the Kaiser Permanente clinic and would not have had the opportunity to be included in the study.

While this may be a possibility, Felitti and Anda directly addressed this by noting this rationale is not supported by their research. They explained that at one point during the study, they brought a psychoanalytically trained psychiatrist into the study who (for a period of six months) saw high ACE score clients immediately after their comprehensive medical evaluation. This was different from the typical protocol which included a referral to psychiatry for follow-up, instead of an immediate, same-day visit with a psychiatrist. Anda and Felitti noted that they administered an anonymous questionnaire to those clients (with a response rate of 81%) who reported that the hour-long session with a trained mental health professional was viewed as highly desirable and positive (Felitti & Anda, 2010). Anda and Felitti interpreted this as evidence that when clients feel heard and understood, and have a chance to disclose painful and upsetting secrets from their past, patients viewed this as being highly beneficial. They further extrapolate that this negates the assumption that someone who had a high ACE score would simply choose not to participate in medical care. The prospective phase of the study indicates that early death may in fact be related to higher ACE scores. The data showed that individuals with an ACE score of 6 or more had a lifespan almost two decades shorter than an individual with a zero ACE score (Brown et al., 2009) The analysis to date does support the hypothesis that ACEs and premature mortality are related.

Three

PUBLIC HEALTH AND THE TRAUMA-INFORMED MOVEMENT

Kirby L. Wycoff

INTRODUCTION

"We have this incredible proof about the expense that trauma is causing our society and how all of these physical ailments are related. And yet, what do you do to change it?"

–Patricia Wilcox, head of the Traumatic Stress
Institute at Klingberg Family Centers.

The trauma-informed care movement has its roots in public health policy and mental health services. The public health and policy arena will help us answer the "Now what" question that Wilcox posed above. The focus of this chapter will be about how the public health sector intersects with the trauma-informed care movement. Public health has historically been involved with the health and welfare of large communities of people and management of communicable disease, but this has shifted. In more recent decades the public health sector has turned its attention to understanding social determinants of health. There is also particular interest in prevention and it is natural that the trauma- informed care movement and the public health sector intersect in meaningful ways. A major point in this conversation is that there has been increasing awareness in the United States that our overspending on healthcare costs is undermined by our underspending and low investments on social services and supports for entire communities. The trauma-informed care movement includes issues of equity, public health, and policy (Health Affairs, 2014).

Social determinants of health include things like income, wealth, family and household structure, social support and isolation, occupation, discrimination, neighborhood conditions, social institutions, and education. The Centers for

Disease Control defines social determinants as things that are not directly controllable by the individual but affect the individual's environment (Centers for Disease Control and Prevention [CDC], 2010). The World Health Organization defines social determinants as "the conditions in which people are born, grow, live, work, and age and which are shaped by the distribution of power, money and resources at global, national and local levels" and . . . "mostly responsible for health inequity" (World Health Organization, 2002, para. 1). Social determinants of health are often used to refer broadly to any non-medical factors that influence overall health and wellness (Braveman, et al., 2011). We can use this understanding of social determinants of health to consider how adverse chronic traumatic adversity may impact the health and wellness of communities. This also helps us consider why some populations are healthier than others, and how policy, research, and resource allocation can contribute to this (Kindig & Stoddart, 2003).

The understanding of social determinants of health also frames for us the conversation around social inequity, early exposure to adversity, and understanding how stress impacts later functioning. Peggy Thoits stated that, "the bulk of the literature indicates that differential exposure to stressful experiences is one of the central ways that gender, racial-ethnic, marital status, and social class inequalities in health are produced" (Thoits, 2010, p. 51). As noted elsewhere, the physiological mechanisms related to stress cause cumulative damage and lead to chronic, negative health outcomes. There are a number of harmful and permanent health effects that are the result of early adversity and stress. Thoits noted that this is a significant consideration when evaluating the impact of stress on health and related policy (Thoits, 2010).

This is precisely why the topic of early exposure to adversity and trauma must include aspects of social inequity and wealth distribution. It is also why health policy has often been presented as actually being economic policy, and even more recently it has been noted in the literature that health policy is in all policy. Pearlin has noted,

> People's standing in the stratified orders of social and economic class, gender, race, and ethnicity have the potential to pervade the structure of their daily existence . . . shaping the contexts of people's lives, the stressors to which they are exposed, and the moderating resources they possess.
>
> *(Pearlin 1999, p. 398)*

Our country needs to investigate how we invest in our health care as it impacts the overall health of our country, and our understanding of how to alleviate the impact of early, chronic, traumatic stress on children and families. The better we recognize issues of inequity and how this connects to the experience of chronic stress in community members, the better able we are to address and intervene in meaningful ways. For example, early childhood investments offer a promising cross-cutting solution to many social determinant pathways. Early life exposures affect health over the life course, including the propensity for risky health behaviors. Research shows that early life exposures affect cognitive and non-cognitive development (for example, executive function and prefrontal cortex development), which, in turn, affects time preferences and self-control skills (delayed gratification), which are major determinants of risky health behaviors (Health Policy Brief, 2014, p. 7). If we are truly to understand the role that public health plays in trauma-informed assessments, interventions, and organizations, we must take a brief look at the history of the public health movement.

HISTORICAL CONTEXT OF PUBLIC HEALTH

Understanding the historical context of public health will help us understand how we can move towards a trauma- informed culture. This research will give us the historical context for the public health sector, and how it intersects with trauma-informed care practices.

How do we define public health and why is this relevant to a conversation on trauma-informed practices in school and community settings? Understanding the trauma-informed movement in our country relies on an understanding of the public health system and how community-based prevention works. Understanding the public health system also gives us a background for understanding and using cost–benefit analysis in considering the impact that adverse childhood experiences (ACE) and chronic, traumatic stress has on our communities and taxpayers' pocketbooks. The World Health Organization (WHO) defined health in a broader sense in its 1948 constitution as "a state of complete physical, mental, and social well-being and not merely the absence of disease or infirmity." (World Health Organization, 2002, para. 2).

A brief history of the public health system in our country will provide a useful background for moving forward (Turnock, 2012). A conceptual framework that allows us to approach public health issues from a systems lens will be critical. We continue to note that childhood adversity and chronic traumatic stress is a public health crisis in our country. In order to understand what to do about it, we need to understand how the system works.

Early efforts at public health in the United States and worldwide were largely focused on epidemic and disease management. With only a cursory understanding of how and why disease spread, public health efforts were focused on mitigating risk. These public health efforts also looked to assist people with a better understanding of illnesses and their transmission processes to help their chances to stay alive. For many centuries, disease was analogous to epidemics and things like the plague, smallpox, tuberculosis, and cholera were the focus of attention for public health practitioners (Turnock, 2012, p. 3). As cities became more crowded and industrialism grew in our country, so did poor living and working conditions. Between crowded living situations and unsanitary conditions, disease spread rapidly with little understanding of how or why it was happening. Interestingly, the national capital was moved from Philadelphia in 1793 due to a disastrous epidemic of yellow fever, which led the city to develop a Board of Health (the first in the United States) in that same year (Turnock, 2012). The primary mechanism for addressing epidemics like these at that time was to evacuate a specific location. But with the growth of science came increased understanding of how disease was actually spread from one person to another, and an understanding of germs and bacteria unfolded. In 1976, Edward Jenner developed and used a vaccination protocol to address a devastating disease which is now nonexistent: small pox (Turnock, 2012). With increasing awareness of sanitation and social conditions came a movement to understand the role of poverty and disease. Edwin Chadwick published "An Inquiry into the Sanitary Conditions of the Laboring Population of Great Britain" in 1837 where he developed a framework for improving sanitation. Chadwick believed disease caused poverty and poverty was "responsible for the great social ills of the time, including societal disorder and high taxation to provide for the general welfare" (Turnock, 2012, p. 4). This conceptualization connected poverty to poor health, but in an opposite way as we see it now. Early clinicians believed that disease caused poverty, but today we have a more nuanced understanding of the fact that poverty, in many ways, causes disease.

As noted in this chapter's introduction, this concept of how wealth and resource disparity contributes to overall health is a critical underpinning to the topic of trauma-informed assessments and interventions in schools and communities. It essentially speaks to a philosophy of social justice and can be considered through the lens of the social determinants of health. Essentially, it is this concept that public health policy is actually economic policy, which is actually social justice policy.

> The poor health of the poor, the social gradient in health within countries, and the market health inequities between countries are caused by the unequal distribution of power, income, goods, and services, globally and nationally, and the consequent unfairness in the immediate, visible

circumstances of peoples' lives. Their access to healthcare, schools, and education, their conditions of work and leisure, their homes, communities, towns, or cities– and their chances of meeting a flourishing life. This unequal distribution of health damaging experiences is not in any sense a natural phenomenon but is the result of a top combination of poor social policies and programs unfair economic arrangements and bad politics. Together, the structural determinants and conditions of daily life constitute the social determinants of health and are responsible for a major part of health inequities between and within countries.

(WHO Commission, 2008, p.1)

Public health emerges from a conceptual, systems perspective and framework that allows us to identify the multiple dimensions of health and wellness. It is in subsequent chapters here, that we will explore the systems level perspective, the impact of early chronic adversity on functioning, and what school and community professionals can do to alleviate their impact. We encourage readers to investigate Turnock's book on public health for a more robust discussion on what public health is and how it is relevant to this topic.

HEALTH POLICY AND INITIATIVES

Public health policy and initiatives are relevant to the increasing movement in our country towards trauma-informed care and trauma-competent interventions. This section will briefly outline a few such federal program and policy initiatives.

The Substance Abuse and Mental Health Services Administration

The Substance Abuse and Mental Health Services Administration (SAMHSA) is an agency within the United States Department of Health and Human Services. SAMHSA is the government agency that provides leadership and resources to developing policies, programs, and initiatives to help address behavioral and mental health. This group focuses on prevention and effective treatment in the recovery of mental health and substance abuse issues. The agency is responsible for initiating, developing, and implementing health efforts that contribute to the overall behavioral and mental health and wellness of the entire country. One of the core aspects of SAMHSA's mission is to reduce the negative impact of mental illness and substance abuse in our country, and we strongly encourage readers to visit their website (https://www.samhsa.gov/about-us).

In 1992, Congress developed the SAMHSA as a public health initiative to make substance abuse and mental illness issues more visible and accessible in our country. The SAMHSA has an entire initiative developed around addressing trauma and violence in our communities. The initiative seeks to address the impact that trauma can have not just on individuals but also families and community members. There is also a clear focus on the healing and recovery for those who been exposed to trauma. SAMHSA has developed a working definition of trauma that is broad in scope and useful to consider:

> An event, series of events, or set of circumstances that is experienced by an individual is physically or emotionally harmful or life-threatening and that has lasting adverse effects on the individual's functioning and mental, physical, social, emotional or spiritual well-being

> *(SAMHSA, 2017, para. 3)*

SAMHSA is leading federal efforts in addressing trauma in our country. Focusing on trauma is one of their six strategic initiatives for the organization. The development of trauma-informed interventions and trauma-informed approaches are being investigated by SAMHSA. The organization is engaged in grant funding of technical assistance centers, publications, trainings, and partnerships with government and nongovernment agencies to meet this goal. The specific initiatives that are related to trauma include the following:

- Developing and promoting trauma-specific interventions
- Expanding trauma-informed care services and training among the workforce and capacity of organizations
- Publishing a conceptual framework for trauma and implementing trauma-informed approaches to guide SAMHSA's work and to support the efforts of other agencies, systems, and organizations
- Recognizing trauma and its behavioral health effects across health and social service delivery systems (SAMHSA, 2017, para. 9).

The organization disseminates multiple free resources and publications to help agencies across the country become more trauma-informed. One such resource that is freely available to the public and highly recommended, is the "TIP 57: Trauma- informed care and behavioral health services" manual (SAMHSA 2014). This manual is intended to help behavioral health professionals understand how trauma affects individuals and communities and includes information on assessment, treatment planning, interventions, and ways to support recovery.

SAMHSA has multiple other partnership initiatives that support individuals seeking help for mental, physical, and behavioral health issues.

The organization meets their goal of increasing knowledge and awareness of the impact of trauma throughout our country by developing a trauma-informed approach model. We believe that this model has utility across sectors in organizations, including schools. The trauma-informed approach for SAMHSA includes the following four R's:

1. *Realizes* the widespread impact of trauma and understands potential paths for recovery;
2. *Recognizes* the signs and symptoms of trauma in clients, families, staff, and others involved with the system;
3. *Responds* by fully integrating knowledge about trauma into policies, procedures, and practices; and
4. Seeks to actively resist *Re-traumatization*. (SAMHSA, 2016, para. 2)

A trauma-informed approach can be implemented in any type of service setting or organization and is distinct from trauma-specific interventions or treatments that are designed specifically to address the consequences of trauma and to facilitate healing. The overarching goal of this organization is to both develop and promote trauma-specific interventions, while also expanding the conceptual understanding and implementation of trauma-informed care. Increased awareness is at the foundation of this, by helping organizations understand the impact of trauma on behavioral mental health. Borrowing from multiple other sources, the trauma-informed approach to mental and behavioral healthcare asks "what happened to this person?" instead of "what's wrong with this person?" (Bloom, 2007). This is a fundamental shift in mindset that allows the conversation to be about trust and safety in relationships between providers and clients, while employing a holistic view of an individual's current presentation and life history. This is where recovery and healing can begin, allowing those impacted by trauma to seek services that are supportive, and not punitive.

In addition to the four R's there are six key principles that SAMHSA promotes. A trauma-informed approach that reflects these six principles does so in the spirit of building relationships and guiding organizational climate and culture. They include:

1. *Safety.* Throughout the organization, staff and clients should feel physically and psychologically safe.
2. *Trustworthiness and transparency.* Organizational operations and decisions are conducted with transparency and the goal of building and maintaining trust among staff, clients, and family members.

3. *Peer support and mutual self-help.* Both are seen as integral to the organizational and service delivery approach, and are understood as key vehicles for building trust, establishing safety, and empowerment.
4. *Collaboration and mutuality.* There is true partnering between staff and clients and among organizational staff from direct care staff to administrators.
5. *Empowerment, voice, and choice.* Throughout the organization, and among the clients served, individuals' strengths are recognized, built on, and validated, and new skills developed as necessary.
6. *Cultural, historical, and gender issues.* The organization actively moves past cultural stereotypes and biases, considers language and cultural considerations in providing support, offers gender-responsive services, leverages the healing value of traditional cultural and peer connections, and recognizes and addresses historical trauma (SAMHSA, 2016, para.4).

From SAMHSA's perspective, promoting the connection between resilience and growth is critical and their framework aims to assist trauma-affected families and individuals in this way.

The National Child Traumatic Stress Network (NCTSN)

An additional resource that originates with SAMHSA is the National Child Traumatic Stress Network (NCTSN) and we strong encourage readers to visit this website: http://www.nctsnet.org/about-us/who-we-are. This organization is also rooted in public health initiatives originating within the U.S. government. In 2000, the U.S. Congress, as part of the children's health act, created the NCTSN. The NCTSN is funded by the Center for Mental Health Services, SAMHSA, and the U.S. Department of Health and Human Services, and is jointly led by UCLA and Duke University. The National Center for Child Traumatic Stress provides the organizational structure and leadership as well as grant funding to a number of organizations across the country for support in implementing trauma-sensitive practices and evidence-based, trauma-informed interventions. The organization also provides technical assistance to the group grantees (NCTSN 2017).

The network of grantees, which is where the name National Child Traumatic Stress Network originates from, has grown over time from a collaborative network of 17 to over 150 funded affiliate centers that deliver trauma-informed care to children and families. The NCTSN, is funded through the SAMHSA. One of the primary purposes of the network is to provide training resources and support to professionals across the country who work with children and families exposed to trauma and adversity. As noted earlier, this exposure to adversity can include domestic abuse, community violence, physical, sexual, or emotional abuse, natural disasters, or other life-threatening complications (NCTSN, 2017). In addition to providing the support to direct service providers, the organization is involved in research, program development, policy development, systems level change, and advocacy work. The NCTSN articulated its mission of serving traumatized children and their families in the country through the following initiatives:

- Raising public awareness of the scope and serious impact of child traumatic stress on the safety and healthy development of America's children and youth.
- Advancing a broad range of effective services and interventions by creating trauma-informed, developmentally and culturally appropriate programs that improve the standard of care.
- Working with established systems of care including the health, mental health, education, law enforcement, child welfare, juvenile justice, and military family service systems to ensure that there is a comprehensive trauma-informed continuum of accessible care.
- Fostering a community dedicated to collaboration within and beyond the NCTSN to ensure that widely shared knowledge and skills become a sustainable national resource (NCTSN, 2017, para. 2).

The Centers for Disease Control and Prevention: Essentials for Childhood

Another initiative that is guided by the government is the CDC's National Center for Injury Prevention and Control initiative "Essentials for Childhood" (Merrick, 2017). The mission of the Essentials for Childhood initiative is in "assuring safe, stable, nurturing relationships and environments for all children" (Merrick, 2017). We strongly encourage readers to visit this website directly, as it is an excellent resource for helping support children and families exposed to adversity: https://www.cdc.gov/violenceprevention/childmaltreatment/essentials .html. The CDC offers the following framework for how they strive to articulate the goals noted above:

1. Raise awareness and commitment to support safe, stable, nurturing relationships, and environments
2. Use data to inform action

3. Create the context for healthy children and families through norms changes and programs
4. Create the context for health children and families through policies (Centers for Disease Control and Prevention, Division of Violence Prevention, 2014, p. 8)

The entire framework document can be accessed for free, here: https://www.cdc.gov/violenceprevention/pdf/essentials_for_childhood_framework.pdf

The CDC is currently funding five states in their action plans to meet the goals noted above. Those states are California, Colorado, Massachusetts, North Carolina, and Washington (Merrick, 2017). In addition to these, there are 31 other states in the US who are self-supported and participating in the program in some capacity. All the involved states are eligible for training and technical assistance in putting the "Essentials for Childhood" framework into action (Merrick, 2017). The National Center for Injury Prevention and Control provides a number of free technical documents to help communities and organizations guide their efforts in creating safe, stable, and nurturing relationships for all children and we strongly encourage readers to access those materials here: https://www.cdc.gov/violenceprevention/childmaltreatment/essentials.html

Also of importance from the public health lens is that a total of 39 states in the United States have included the ACE module in their Behavioral Risk Factor Surveillance System (BRFSS). Administered by the CDC, the BRFSS is the nation's largest health-related telephone survey that collects information on health-related risk behaviors of more than 400, 00 adults a year. It is the most comprehensive, continuously conducted health survey system in the world (CDC, BRFSS, 2017). This is relevant to our later conversation on how we might use publically available public health data to better understand the needs of local communities relative to trauma-informed practices and interventions.

All of these resources and initiatives speak to the growing interest and focus on not only the treatment of trauma outcomes, but also the prevention of the conditions that create the adversity in the first place. We encourage readers to explore these resources and others on their journey to becoming trauma-competent professionals.

TRAUMA-INFORMED CARE MODELS

The Sanctuary Model

The Sanctuary Model is a systems-level framework that focuses on trauma-informed organizational change. It was developed by Dr. Sandra Bloom and her colleagues in the 1980's in Philadelphia. The framework is not intended to offer a one-hit wonder intervention, but rather reflects on a cultural and organizational shifts. This whole culture approach is theory-based, trauma-informed, and evidence-supported (Bloom, 2015, 2011; Bloom et al., 2005). For anyone truly committed to understanding more about the impact that trauma has on individuals and how to help them, we encourage you to read Bloom's three books on this topic. They are titled: (i) Creating Sanctuary: Toward the Evolution of Sane Societies, (ii) Destroying Sanctuary: The Crisis in Human Service Delivery Systems, and (iii) Restoring Sanctuary: A New Operating System for Trauma-Informed Systems of Care.

Essentially, the model seeks to shift the mindset regarding the behavior of traumatized individuals. As Dr. Bloom notes often, that there is a shift in perspective about those who have experienced trauma. Instead of asking "What's wrong with you?" we instead ask "What happened to you?" (Foderaro 1991). We move from a less pejorative and marginalizing position of viewing traumatized individuals as sick, unwell, and unstable, and instead focus on the fact that these individuals have experienced both psychological and physical injury (Bloom, 2007). The model, which has its roots in inpatient psychiatric hospitals in Philadelphia provides a comprehensive blueprint for both clinical and organizational change (Esaki et al., 2014).

History of the Sanctuary Model

In the early 1980s Dr. Sandra Bloom (a psychiatrist), Joseph Foderaro (a social worker), and Ruth Ann Ryan (a nurse manager) were all working in an inpatient psychiatric unit in Philadelphia. By the mid 1980s the team began to realize that a large portion of the patients that they were treating in the inpatient setting had significant histories of trauma in their past. They further noted that these were often seriously stressful experiences for the individuals and the traumatic experiences typically originated in childhood (The Origins of the Sanctuary Model, Community Works, 2017).

Bloom and colleagues noted that for their most vulnerable, acute, and high-needs clients, instead of finding healing and recovery in the units, they found more trauma (Esaki et al., 2014). The team of three joined with other mental health providers to create an acute care model on a psychiatry unit in a general hospital of north Philadelphia. The team worked in the late 1980's into the early 1990s and developed an inpatient, trauma-informed approach for treating adults with significant mental illness. Based around the concepts of therapeutic communities, the team worked to facilitate an organizational culture that "counteracts the wounds suffered by the victims of traumatic experience and extended exposure to adversity" (Esaki, 2014, p. 1). Their intent was to create communities within inpatient units that promoted safety and recovery and allowed staff and clients to work together to build a trauma-informed culture. These therapeutic communities had the goal of encouraging both staff and clients to collaboratively participate in building a system and culture of healing (Jones 1953, 1968; Lees et al., 2004; Main, 1946; Silver, 1985, 1986). These units became a "Sanctuary" and the model of healing and hope was born (Bloom, 2007).

The Sanctuary Model was implemented in a number of inpatient hospital programs in the greater Philadelphia area including the following:

- 1980–1991: Quakertown Community Hospital, Quakertown, PA
- 1991–1996: Northwestern Institute of Psychiatry, Fort Washington, PA
- 1996–1999: Friends Hospital, Philadelphia, PA
- 1999–2001: Horsham Clinic, Ambler, PA
- 1999–2001: Hampton Hospital, Rancocas, NJ (Sanctuary Model, 2017) http://sanctuaryweb.com/TheSanctuaryModel/ORIGINSOFTHESANCTUARYMODEL.aspx

In the early 1990s several adult-focused mental health organizations sought consultation from Dr. Bloom and her team and the model has since been implemented in multiple organizations. In the 1990s the Jewish Board of Family and Children's Services of New York partnered with Dr. Bloom in establishing the Sanctuary model in multiple residential treatment programs for children and teens in Westchester County, New York. As part of a large-scale National Institute of Mental Health (NIMH) research study, the model's effectiveness was implemented at the following three organizations: Hawthorne-Cedar Knolls, The Goldsmith Center, and the Linden Hall School. The outcomes of this research were positive and the programming has since been expanded to other organizations serving children and teens.

Dr. Bloom sought to impress upon staff, administrators, and the larger community that "a traumatic experience impacts the entire person–the way we think, the way we learn, the way we remember things, the way we feel about ourselves, the way we feel about other people, and the way we make sense of the world" (The Sanctuary Institute, Bloom, 2017, para. 1). Dr. Bloom and her team worked to develop a cohesive context for healing and recovery and did so with a focus on democratic processes, positive relationships, and a restorative culture. At its core, the model was "designed to facilitate the development of structures, processes, and behaviors on the part of staff, clients, and the community as a whole that can counteract the biological, affective, cognitive, social, and existential wounds suffered by the victims of traumatic experience and extended exposure to adversity" (Esaki, 2014, p. 2).

As more and more organizations began to appreciate the trauma-informed approach, the Andrus Children's Center (Yonkers, NY) sought partnership with Bloom and her team to implement a trauma-informed culture in multiple treatment programs. The Andrus Children's Center, which provides services to over 3,000 children and families, instituted the Sanctuary Model in their residential programs, day treatment programming, as well as school and community based programming. The Sanctuary model remains a core feature of the Andrus program. In 2005, Bloom and Andrus worked together to build "The Sanctuary Institute" which provides support, training and technical guidance for programs seeking to institute the Sanctuary model. At the most recent count, over 300 national and international programs are a part of the professional Sanctuary Network.

A partial list of the programs that utilize the Sanctuary Model can be found below:

- Astor Services for Children and Families, Rhinebeck, NY
- Arizona's Children Association, Phoenix, AZ
- The Andrus Children's Center, Yonkers, NY
- Brooklyn State Island, Office of Child and Family Services, NY
- Bronx, Office of Child and Family Services, NY
- Brentwood, Office of Child and Family Services, NY
- The Bradley Center, Pittsburgh, PA
- Bethany Children's Home, Womelsdorf, PA
- Bethanna, Philadelphia, Southeastern, and Central PA
- Baker Victory Services, Lackawanna, NY
- Children's Home of York (CHOY), York, PA
- Children's Home of Poughkeepsie, NY
- Carson Valley Children's Aid, Philadelphia, PA
- Care Visions, UK
- Children's Recovery Center, Oklahoma Department of Mental Health
- Holy Family Institute, Western, PA
- Manhattan Office of Children and Family Services, NY
- Mid-Hudson Office of Children and Family Services, NY
- Mercy First, NY
- Mercy Home for Boys and Girls, Chicago, IL
- Lutheran Settlement House, Philadelphia, PA
- Lansing Office of Children and Family Services, NY
- Lancaster General Hospital, Lancaster, PA
- KidsPeace, PA

- Juconi Foundation, Mexico
- Jewish Child Care Association, NY
- The Jewish Board, NY
- House of Good Shepherd, Watertown, NY
- Hawthorn Children's Psychiatric Hospital, Missouri Department of Mental Health
- Harbor Creek Youth Services, Harborcreek, PA
- Green Chimneys, Brewster, NY
- Good Shepherd Services, New York City
- Glade Run Lutheran Services, Zelienople, PA
- Friendship House, Scranton, PA
- Eagle Ridge Family Treatment Institute, Oklahoma
- Drexel University School of Public Health: Center for Nonviolence and Social Justice, Philadelphia, PA
- Devereux Foundation, Villanova, PA
- Department of Human Health and Services, Philadelphia, PA
- Crossnore School and Children's Home, Crossnore, NC (The Sanctuary Institute, 2017)

The Sanctuary Theoretical Framework

The theoretical model that drives the Sanctuary framework is both dynamic and diverse. As an organizational framework and intervention, the Sanctuary framework seeks to create change in organizational culture. Through the education of staff on the effects of trauma and stress, shifts in mindset can be achieved. The framework itself has psychodynamic origins, including aspects of self-psychology, social learning, and cognitive development (Esaki, 2014). It pulls from the fields of social psychiatry, systems theory (Bertalanffy, 1974), burn-out theory (Maslach & Jackson, 1981; Maslach et al., 2001), constructivist self-development theory (McCann & Perlman, 1990; Perlman & Saakvitne, 1995a,b), attachment theory (Bowlby, 1988), therapeutic communities, and organizational change theory (Hermans, 1991; Weatherize et al., 2009).

Constructivist self-development theory is an integrative personality theory. It provides a framework or a way of understanding how childhood abuse affects the development of the sense of self and internal resources (McCann & Perlman, 1990; Pearlman & Saakvitine, 1995a,b; Saakvitine et al., 1998). As a constructivist theory of personality, it seeks to explore how traumatic events affect the individual's development (Brock et al., 2006). As it relates to the Sanctuary model, this theory talks about three different capacities related to an individual's sense of self. The first is the extent to which an individual is able to maintain connections with others. The second is the individual's ability to experience and tolerate strong emotions. The third is the individual's ability to view themselves as positive and worthy. (Esaki, 2014). This model allows us to understand disruptions to social and behavioral functioning and the connection between those disruptions and both attachment and affect regulation. (Esaki, 2014).

Drawing on the work of Bowlby's attachment theory (1988), this model suggests that an individual develops their sense of self and internal resources through the creation and maintenance of early relationships with caregivers. These healthy, early attachment experiences allow the individual to regulate emotions, manage stress, and navigate the environment. (Brock et al., 2006; Tishelman et al., 2010; Cook et al., 2005). Critically important in the treatment of trauma is that the Sanctuary model seeks to create a safe community environment that allows individuals to restore their connection with others, develop multiple healthy relationships, and in turn regulate their own internal emotional experience (Esaki, 2014).

Drawing on Bertalanffy's (1974) systems theory, Sanctuary acknowledges that complex organizations are systems that are defined by multiple components that interact in multiple ways. Bertalanffy drew on the physical sciences and understanding of how an organism is impacted by both inputs and outputs. That is, different parts of the organization are all interacting in complex ways. A system which can either be opened or closed, is an entity with both interrelated and interdependent parts. It is important to note that boundaries are relevant in systems and the entity as a whole is the sum of its parts, or subsystems. When one aspect of the system is changed or modified, it affects the entire rest of the system. When a system is open it is perceived as being accessible, allowing input from the greater environment, and is able to be influenced by the external environment. We see the influence of systems thinking in multiple family therapy models. In these systems there are healthy boundaries, related and connected subsystems, and overall balance and equilibrium. Those systems that are healthy are adaptable and flexible. Closed systems are often disconnected from external influence (Bertalanffy, 1974, 1968, 1950; Bertalanffy & Rapport, 1956). Essential to the Sanctuary model is that when one part of the system is adjusted or changed, it exerts influence on other aspects of the system.

Organizations, schools, residential treatment facilities and other care-providing organizations are all systems, essentially a confluence of interacting and interconnecting parts. These authors believe that the Sanctuary model can be useful in understanding organizational change in school and community settings as it relates to trauma-informed care. As the primary vehicle for delivering change, these organizations are well-positioned to address the impacts of trauma.

Trauma Survivors and the Sanctuary Model

The Sanctuary model is predicated on the idea that trauma survivors have the ability to be resilient if they are connected to positive care service individuals (Harney, 2007; Larkin et al., 2012). There is clear evidence between the impact of childhood adversity and trauma and later psychiatric disturbances. The therapeutic milieu–which focuses on containment, support, structure, involvement, and validation–seeks to repair damage done through trauma exposure (Gunderson, 1978).

Bloom advocated for a combination approach that includes the therapeutic milieu as well as daily individualized treatment, group therapies, community meetings, family therapy, psychopharmacology, art therapy, and psychodrama (Bloom 1994). We would also suggest that the use of Animal Assisted Interventions in addressing the needs of trauma-impacted individuals would be valuable (Wycoff & Murphy, 2017).

Individuals with trauma exposure typically enter psychiatric units for both positive and negative PTSD symptoms. The positive PTSD symptoms include things like hyperarousal, irritability, inability to control rage, flashbacks, behavioral reenactments, and pseudo-hallucinations. The negative PTSD symptoms could include denial, numbness, depression, withdrawal, and anhedonia (Bloom, 1994). Irrespective of the specific symptoms they are exhibiting, most of these individuals have a significant deficit in their ability to trust, form stable relationships, and engage interpersonally (Bloom, 1994). Essentially they often have disturbance in comprehending normal interpersonal boundaries (Bloom, 1994). These survivors struggle to establish and maintain healthy relationships and understand healthy, protective boundaries around self; and often misunderstand or misinterpret the boundary operations of others (Bloom, 1994). Bloom noted that the quality of relating in these individuals is often intense and even unrealistic (Bloom, 1994).

> Victims of overwhelming life experiences have difficulty staying safe, find emotions difficult to manage, have suffered many losses, and have difficulty envisioning a future. As a result, they are frequently in danger, lose emotional control, or are so numb that they cannot access their emotions, have many signs of unresolved loss, and are stuck in time, haunted by the past, and unable to move into a better future.
>
> *(Bloom, 2007, p. 2)*

Bloom further noted that these individuals may be sensitive to boundary violations of any sort and may try to compulsively reenact those violations.

(Bloom, 1994). She further indicated that these individuals struggle to regulate and monitor their own feelings of rage, fear, and grief and demonstrate extreme ranges of the emotional expression continuum. These individuals often have little understanding of how those past traumas affect their present emotional experience (Bloom, 1994).

There are a number of aspects of the Sanctuary model that help address the impact of trauma. Bloom (1994) built off the "Stages of Treatment" the work of Horowitz (1986) to conceptualize the Sanctuary approach to trauma work. While they are articulated in phases, they are interactive and iterative. Herman (1991) noted that trauma treatment can be articulated in three stages:

1. Safety
2. Reconstruction
3. Reconnection

Safety. Safety refers to the fact that an individual exposed to trauma has lost their sense of safety in the world. In order to heal, this sense of safety must be restored. Further, it must include not only physical safety (i.e. the client no longer lives with the partner who perpetrated domestic violence) but also that the individual experiences emotional and social safety as well (Bloom, 1994). When we consider how this might play out in child-serving organizations like schools, we may consider the need for policies and practices that make both staff and students feel safe and maintain safety. There must be clear expectations and unacceptability of violence across the entire system. School with high levels of violence, aggression, behavioral infractions, and suspensions, for example, are unlikely to provide trauma survivors the sense of safety that they need to function and in many ways, may in fact be re-traumatizing.

Reconstruction. Reconstruction, the second stage of recovery, references the reconstruction of lost memories which may include multiple aspects of the trauma experience. Those memories may include physical, somatic, affective, and cognitive aspects of the trauma (Bloom, 1994). It is also important to note that in this stage, there may be an emergence or reemergence of positive posttraumatic stress disorder (PTSD) symptoms like hyperarousal, flashbacks, nightmares, disassociation, sleep disturbance, and concentration problems and psychosomatic symptoms (Bloom, 1994). In almost all trauma treatments, there is a memory retrieval or trauma narrative aspect of treatment. It is critical to note that this aspect should be planned, organized, and controlled, and ONLY occur AFTER safety has been established. There may be intense feelings of shame and guilt around recalling the traumatic event and a strong therapeutic alliance that features safety and trust must be established before proceeding. "Ultimately the survivor must integrate the traumatic experience into a new definition of and attitude towards life that transcends that experience" (Bloom, 1994, p. 9). At its core, this model moves away from pathologizing the trauma response.

Many individual approaches follow the medical model, which assumes that "sick" youth have an internal, mental disease and should be passive recipients of expert treatment. In contrast, the group, milieu, and therapeutic community approaches adhere to a model which assumes that the resident's problems stem from the interaction between the individual and the environment and that the youth themselves are capable of active, responsible participation.

(Abramovitz & Bloom, 2003, p. 127)

Reconnection. The final stage of the model that drives our understanding of trauma treatment is reconnection. Here is where we help clients move from the past into a new and different future. The client begins to reconnect in realistic and meaningful ways and ultimately reconstruct their reality and identity without trauma as the core feature (Bloom, 1994). This sends the implicit and explicit message around the belief that the survivor is capable of transcending their pain (Bloom, 1994). "Memories begin to become actual memories and no longer carry the same power to control thought, action, and feelings" (Bloom, 1994, p. 9).

The Sanctuary model understands and recognizes the concept of parallel processes. The model notes that just as individuals may experience trauma and adversity, so too can organizations. There is an inherent understanding in the dramatic symptoms that client might experience and those that an organization might experience.

Just as we see individuals who have experienced trauma responding with isolative behavior and withdrawal from the community, we also see organizations facing financial or political stressors respond with isolationism, rigidity and hierarchical decision-making. Intervening in this parallel process requires shifting behaviors and thinking to align with a specific set of values

(The Sanctuary Institute, 2017, para. 7)

This speaks to the overall significance and importance of addressing not only trauma treatment for individuals but also building trauma competency in organizations and communities (Maslach, 1982).

It is important to note that the model is intended to be culturally sensitive in and of itself; trauma is universal, and this model acknowledges that.

The overrepresentation of increasingly poor, minority, and immigrant youngsters with trauma backgrounds combined with staff responses to their behavior have severely tested the standard treatment models used by most residential centers around the nation and suggests the need for new types of intervention.

(Abramovitz & Bloom, 2003, p. 121)

The model further integrates an important public health concept: *shared decision-making*. Shared decision-making acknowledges the role that the client has in making decisions about their own health and wellness. It de-centralizes the role of the expert to the clinician and instead acknowledges that both the client and the clinician have information to offer in the decision-making process. This is an important concept in public health, and it is critically important in working with individuals who have been traumatized. By acknowledging the role of the individual client in telling their story and being an agent of change for themselves, we give them the opportunity for growth and healing. We also return control back to the client, which is often the very thing that has been lost through the traumatic experience.

Healing requires a vision of restored health. What is the shared goal of treatment? What is the vision the client holds of "emancipation"- of freedom from being haunted by the past? All treatment debates and decisions must be informed by this vision of where everyone is headed. In service of this vision, debates about whose job is more important– therapist, educator, childcare worker–fall away in service of the larger goal of bringing about a healthy empowerment and enhanced social function of each individual child.

(Abramovitz & Bloom, 2003, p. 131)

Sanctuary Components
There are a number of aspects of the Sanctuary model that help address the impact of trauma. It is an organic process that unfolds over time, as an organization moves towards becoming more trauma-informed. Essentially, it is intended to reduce the

negative effects of adversity and stress. The Sanctuary model appreciates and recognizes that all individuals are vulnerable to the impact of stress and trauma and seeks to create organizations that can help mitigate those stressors. There are four central pillars to the Sanctuary model and these drive key theories (Abramovitz & Bloom, 2003; Sanctuary Institute, 2012). They can be found below. Note, that the first pillar is an understanding of trauma theory which is the foundation to all of the other aspects of the program. That is our understanding of traumatic stress and adversity, and drives the evidence base for the entire model. The components of the framework are organized around the pillars noted below.

Four Pillars of the Sanctuary Model

Trauma Theory. Overview of information about how traumatic experiences affect the brain and therefore influence thoughts, feelings, and behaviors

Seven Sanctuary Commitments. Philosophical underpinnings of the Sanctuary model that describe how community members agree to behave with each other and the values to which the organization subscribes

S.E.L.F. Acronym for organizational categories of safety, emotional management, loss, and future, used to formulate plans for client services or treatment as well as for interpersonal and organizational problem-solving

Sanctuary Toolkit. Set of 10 practical applications of trauma theory, seven commitments, and S.E.L.F. which are used by all members of the community at all levels of the hierarchy and reinforce the concepts of the model (The Sanctuary Model 2014, para. 1)

Trauma theory has been covered extensively elsewhere in this book and we will now turn our attention to the "Seven Sanctuary Commitments" which reflects the second pillar in the model. The entire Sanctuary model is built on these seven primary sanctuary commitments. These commitments guide the overall philosophical and theoretical system that the model is built on. They represent the commitments of the model, and in turn the clinicians, staff members, clients, and organizations that prescribe to them. These values, outlined in the Sanctuary model, give individuals and organizations a roadmap in moving towards trauma competency. We suggest here that any organization–including school-based and community organizations that are serve children–can use the Seven Sanctuary Commitments as guiding principles to their organizational culture and ethos.

The Seven Sanctuary Commitments

1. Commitment to Nonviolence: Building and modeling safety skills
2. Commitment to Emotional Intelligence: Teaching and modeling affect management skills

3. Commitment to Inquiry and Social Learning: Building and modeling cognitive skills
4. Commitment to Democracy: Creating and modeling civic skills of self-control, self-discipline, and administration of healthy authority
5. Commitment to Open Communication: Overcoming barriers to healthy communication, reduce acting out, enhance self-protective and self-correcting skills, and teach healthy boundaries
6. Commitment to Social Responsibility: Rebuilding social connection skills, and establishing healthy attachment relationships.
7. Commitment to Growth and Change: Restoring hope, meaning, and purpose (The Sanctuary Institute 2017, para 3).

S.E.L.F is the acronym that is used to present a shared language for professionals from a variety of backgrounds. This shared language allows multidisciplinary teams to work together and move towards competent caregiving. They provide an organizing framework for activities including treatment planning, community conversations, and collaborative decision-making. With regards to safety, this focuses on helping individuals maintain safety in themselves and their relationships. Emotional management refers to the identification and management of emotions and emotional responses. Loss focuses on dealing with feelings of grief. Future refers to helping individuals explore new ways of moving forward (Rivard et al., 2005, p 3).

The Sanctuary toolkit is a series of practical, supplied tools that can be used day in and day out to bring the trauma-informed perspective to life. These include things like community meetings, safety plans, self treatment planning conferences, team meetings, self-care planning, and psychoeducation. For example, in a community meeting, there are three questions that are asked twice-daily: "How are you feeling?", "What is your goal for today?", and "Who can you ask for help?" (The Sanctuary Model, 2012).

Evidence Base for Trauma-Informed Care Models

There is an extensive evidence base for moving towards trauma-informed care models. An increasing recognition in the literature notes that working with traumatized individuals is about more than just isolated interventions and techniques, but about a systems-wide approach that has an appreciation for the overall impact of stress and adversity. The ethos of this trauma-informed culture is about the fact that:

We need to stop viewing people as either "sick" or "bad"–philosophical positions that inevitably lead to the problems associated with the mental health system or the criminal justice system–and instead begin viewing all of these problems as the result of injuries–some to the body, some to the mind, some to the ability to relate, some to the sense of right and wrong, and some to the soul.

(Bloom, 2007, p 1)

There are over 300 organizations in the Sanctuary Institute professional network. A look at the outcomes of the NIMH grant data may prove helpful in considering how other schools and organizations might integrate the Sanctuary model approach. The Jewish Board of Family and Children's Services began implementing the Sanctuary model in three of the residential treatment centers in Westchester County, New York. Approximately 70% of the residents had suffered abuse and neglect. As has been noted elsewhere, these traumatized youth were more volatile, had an unpredictable aggression, and were exceedingly reactive (Rivard et al., 2005). The Sanctuary model helped the team recognize that trauma was a central organizing life experience for these individuals.

The Sanctuary Model shifts the debate about the nature of the problem by changing the definition of institutionalized children from "bad" kids or "sick" kids (or both) to children who have sustained physical, psychological, social, and moral insults that lead to developmental injuries. These injuries to the body, mind, and soul often exacerbate each other, so that the optimal treatment environment must be directed at healing all of them simultaneously.

(Abramovitz, & Bloom, 2003, p. 131)

The project was funded by the NIMH as an exploratory developmental study (MH62896). The team that was involved in the implementation and assessment of the grant noted:

That within the context of safe, supportive, stable, and socially responsible therapeutic communities, a trauma recovery treatment framework could be used teach youths effective adaptation and coping skills to replace nonadaptive cognitive, social, and behavioral strategies acquired as means of coping with traumatic life experiences.

(Rivard et al., 2005, p. 1)

The outcomes of the data collection related to this grant were impressive.

Residential units implementing the model are significantly stronger on dimensions of the treatment environment that assess support, autonomy, spontaneity, personal problem orientation, and safety in comparison to residential units not implementing the model. Youth made gains over time in one measured domain of coping skills and on another scale assessing the extent to which they had a sense of control over their lives.

(Rivard et al., 2005, p 7)

The Sanctuary model is an evidence-driven, organizational intervention that helps build community capacities to respond to the needs of individuals who have been exposed to trauma. It reflects both a blueprint and framework for reconceptualizing service provision through the lens of trauma competency. While the model was initially established for inpatient and residential settings, these authors would strongly suggest that the tenets here can be useful for non-residential organizations serving children and adolescents across the community.

Four

TRAUMA–INFORMED SCHOOLS

Kirby L. Wycoff

INTRODUCTION

There is an increased need for trauma-informed practices and frameworks in school systems. With as many children exposed to adversity as we know there are, trauma-informed, school-based practices support not just adversity exposed children, but *all* children. It is the belief of these authors that uploading these four pillars of trauma-informed care are central to supporting the needs of all students. All organizations that serves individuals who have been exposed to traumatic stressors, which includes schools, can incorporate these four tenets into practice and provide trauma-informed care (Ridgard et al. 2015). In fact, Ridgard et al. noted that this is a social justice imperative; we would add a public health crisis of epic proportions. How can schools be a part of the solution of addressing the significant number of children in the country who have been exposed to adversity?

TRAUMA-INFORMED SCHOOLS

Trauma-informed schools are organizations that integrate a trauma and adversity informed perspective to their entire organizational system. This often includes the development of Tier 1 (school-wide) interventions that are good for *all* kids, not just kids exposed to adversity. As we have noted throughout this book, there is a significant prevalence of trauma among youth. The National Survey of Children's Exposure to Violence (2011) indicated that 41.2% of children had been victims of physical assault within the past year, with 10.1% of those incidents causing physical injury and 6.2% which included use of a weapon (Finkelhor et al., 2013). During the same time, 5.6% of children and teens had been sexually victimized, with rates as high as 22.8% among teenage girls. In addition, 13.8% of youths were subjected to neglect, physical, sexual, or emotional abuse by their respective caregiver (Crouch et al., 2000). The survey also noted that 22.4% of them had witnessed violence at home, school, or experienced community violence. On the whole, considering 50 different victimization categories, 57.7% of youths had some exposure to violence and 15.1% were exposed to six or more categories, while 4.9% were exposed to 10 or more categories (Crouch et al., 2000). Rossen and Cowan (2013) noted that instead of focusing on learning, traumatized students are instead focused on basic survival. Trauma-exposed youths had challenges in their ability to engage in learning, socializing, and engaging with school in meaningful ways (Rossen & Cowan, 2013).

As noted earlier, there is significant disproportionality in rates of exposure to community violence and it is especially high for children in urban, low-income, ethnic/racial minority communities. Teens from families with annual incomes of less than $20,000 are more likely than those from families with an annual income of $50,000 or more to have witnessed violence (49.8% for low-income teens vs. 34.8% for higher-income teens), and have been the victim of physical assault (24.2% for low income teens vs. 15% for higher-income teens) (Crouch et al., 2000).

In addition to this, the lifetime prevalence of witnessing violence is higher among teens from minority groups. Specifically, the lifetime prevalence of witnessing violence for different racial groups is as follows: 57.2% for African Americans, 50% for Hispanics, and 34.3% for Caucasians. The lifetime prevalence of being the victim of physical assault also differs along racial lines: 24.2% for African Americans, 20.7% for Hispanics, and 15.5% for Caucasians (Crouch et al., 2000).

Also of note and great concern is that the protective factor of increased income was found only to be relevant for Caucasian adolescents. Children from high-income African American and Hispanic households were exposed to more violence than teenagers from low-income white households (Crouch et al., 2000). This suggests that even more than income, race plays a significant role in who is exposed to adversity and trauma. In fact, even after accounting for overall levels of traumatic exposure and other demographic variables, African Americans, Hispanics, and Native Americans all demonstrate higher rates of posttraumatic stress syndrome (PTSD) as a result of traumatic violence (APA, 2013). This disparity also extends to children who are new to the United States. Children who are recent immigrants are at an especially high risk of victimization or violence exposure. Approximately 32% of this group reported symptoms of PTSD and 16% reported clinically significant symptoms of depression (Jaycox et al., 2002).

In addition to issues of disparity, trauma-informed school frameworks can also reduce and address discipline and behavior problems in schools. We know that increased exposure to violence increases likelihood of truancy and school suspension (Kataoka et al., 2007). Research suggests that providing effective interventions for students exposed to violence may help reduce disproportionality in discipline (Ramirez et al., 2012).

Focusing our attention on helping students cope with trauma around community violence can help address issues of school engagement and success, and is a reasonable avenue to pursue in improving overall school climate. As noted earlier, trauma may disproportionally impact students and families from ethnic and racial minorities, and trauma-informed approaches and care in schools may potentially minimize disparity in academic, behavior, and psychosocial outcomes related to trauma. School-based mental health services are one possible avenue for decreasing this disproportionality (Kataoka et al., 2007). These authors firmly believe that "treating behavior that may be related to trauma as a disciplinary concern, rather than a mental health concern is neither effective nor socially just" (Ridgard et al., 2015, p.1).

UNDERSTANDING THE WHY: COMPTON, CALIFORNIA

The trauma-informed schooling movement has risen to a fever pitch in our country and it is due in part to a landmark class action law suit in the state of California. Peter P., et al. v. Compton Unified School District (CUSD) is a first of its kind class action lawsuit filed in 2015 in the state of California which has brought the impact of trauma on learning into the public spotlight (Peter P., et al. v. Compton Unified School District, 2015).

The Los Angeles public counsel and the law firm of Irell & Manella LLP filed the suit on behalf of five students and three teachers. The suit indicated that for students who had been exposed to trauma, CUSD had failed to provide services and accommodations that the students needed to access the free and appropriate public education that is entitled to them under federal law. The suit contended that the school should be required to adapt and provide services to help these students learn, in the same way they adapt and provide services for students who have other physical, emotional, or neurological barriers to learning under the Americans with Disabilities Act (ADA).

In September 2015, Federal Judge Michael Fitzgerald denied the district's motion to dismiss the case. Judge Fitzgerald essentially agreed with arguments filed on behalf of students and teachers that the students who had experienced ongoing, traumatic stress and been exposed to significant trauma could be considered "disabled" under the Americans with Disabilities Act. This would in turn require that the school provide services to these students, in the same way they would to students disabled by a learning disability, autism, attention deficit hyperactivity disorder (ADHD), visual impairments, or any other documented disability. This is the first case of its kind that seeks to use federal disability law to require schools to provide services to children who have been exposed to adverse childhood experiences. The original suit that was filed contended that untreated experiences of chronic traumatic stress and exposure to adversity, are a significant indicator of later academic failure (Blodgett, 2015).

Based on the inordinate wealth of data to support their position, in their initial complaint (Peter P., et al. v. Compton Unified School District, 2015) the suit noted:

> Schools are obliged under the Rehabilitation Act and Americans with Disabilities Act to accommodate students who are being denied benefits of educational programs solely by reason of experiencing complex trauma. Schools must intervene early and consistently according to professional standards in order to ensure that trauma does not determine a young person's educational attainment and life chances. Experiences in California and across the country have repeatedly shown that appropriate interventions, which teach skills proven to bolster the resilience of young people, can effectively accommodate the disabling effects of trauma. This gives students affected by trauma meaningful access to the public education they deserve. Experts agree that to effectively provide reasonable accommodations to students whose learning is impaired by complex trauma, particularly in schools that serve high concentrations of trauma-impacted students, access to an individualized plan is insufficient. Rather, implementation of school-wide trauma-sensitive practices that create an environment in which students are able to learn is required
>
> *(Peter P., et al. v. Compton Unified School District,*
> *Initial Complaint, 2015, p. 2, line 3)*

The suit contends that CUSD did not appropriately train staff on trauma-informed practices nor do they have mechanisms in place to identify and support students who have had exposure to traumatic stress. The suit goes on to contend that the district does not use restorative justice practices to help students work through behavioral challenges. The suit notes that CUSD did not address conflict and violence in a trauma-sensitive way and did not help students exposed to trauma work towards increased self-regulation. Perhaps most concerning, the lawsuit claimed that rather than providing all of these trauma-sensitive practices, which the research indicates works well for trauma-exposed students (and *all* students), the district subjected the "trauma-impacted students to punitive and counter-productive suspensions, expulsions, involuntary transfers and referrals to law enforcement that push them out of school, off the path to graduate, and into the criminal justice system" (Peter P., et al. v. Compton Unified School District, Initial Complaint, 2015, p. 5, line 3).

The lawsuit cited the infamous Brown v. Board of Education ruling, 347U.S. 483 (1954) where the Supreme Court recognized the need for a free and appropriate public education for all students and that this was a foundational right on which good citizenship is founded. The suit contests that 60 years later, trauma-impacted students in Compton were not able to access that right (Peter P., et al. v. Compton Unified School District, Initial Complaint, 2015). The suit reminds readers and the court that children exposed to chronic, toxic, traumatic stress have altered neuro-regulatory systems that affect their experiences in school on multiple levels: learning, memory, emotional regulation, relationship building, conflict management, and more (Perry et al., 1998, 1995).

A neurotypical student might respond to an everyday stressor with a capacity for self-management and conflict resolution, but a trauma-impacted student will respond quite differently; their ability to cope is greatly altered (Lenore, 1991). The suit is careful to note that some of these students will quality for a Diagnostic and Statistical Manual of Mental Disorders.

(DSM) diagnosis of PTSD, but others may not (Stein et al., 2003). In addition, a number of other mental health diagnosis may be associated with traumatic experiences in childhood.

In response to the original law suit not being dismissed, public counsel Mark Rosenbaum noted that "this historic and life-changing decision recognizes that children who suffer the disabling effects of complex trauma resulting from exposure to violence, racism, extreme poverty, and other adverse childhood experiences are entitled to equal access to education and the provision of appropriate services" (Palta, 2015, para. 5).

Alternatively, Compton's attorney reflected on the case by noting "just because a child lives in Compton doesn't mean they are disabled by trauma" (Palta, 2015, para. 7) These differing perspectives are at the crux of this conversation: Does a district have a responsibility to provide interventions and accommodations to students exposed to trauma, and does every child who has been exposed to trauma potentially have a disability? These are complex questions and the authors of this book contend that it is indeed the school's responsibility to provide services to all children who have disabling conditions that interfere with their access to a free and appropriate public education, and that trauma may be one of those conditions. We call for a trauma-informed approach to assessment that will allow schools to better identify which children exposed to trauma are experiencing significant impairments.

In considering the profile of a trauma-impacted child who may be in your school or your community, one only has to look to the history of Peter P. to see how his story is echoed across this country, day in and day out. There is a Peter P. in your school, and in your community right now. At an interdisciplinary action research conference at the Rutgers University Law School's "Center on Law, Inequality, and Metropolitan Equity" (May, 2017) public counsel Jeff Rosenbaum noted that he asked the plaintiff what pseudonym he wanted to go by for the case. The young man chose Peter Pan, hence, Peter. P—a deeply symbolic reflection on how he viewed himself and what he was going through (Rosenbaum, 2017). If we unpack Peter's story more fully, we can appreciate further how he slipped through the cracks and what we might learn from him. Learning more about Peter P. sheds some light on his profile and helps us consider children in our own communities who may have similar backgrounds. We strongly suggest readers visit the Trauma and Learning website that provides additional information on Peter, his peers, and the current state of affairs in Compton: http://www .traumaandlearning.org/home.

Plaintiff Peter P. was a 17-year-old male student at Dominguez High School in Compton, California. According to the formal suit filed, the following can be said to be true about Peter's early life experiences:

- Biological mother was a drug user
- Was the victim of sexual and physical abuse (mother's multiple boy-friends perpetrated)
- Witnessed physical abuse of siblings and mother (mother's multiple boyfriends perpetrated)
- At age 5, Peter and siblings were removed from care of biological mother and placed in foster system
- Peter was separated from his siblings when they entered into foster care system
- Peter moved frequently and was in a number of foster homes; during this time, Peter was occasionally sent back to the home of biological mother for weeks at a time before being placed again in foster care
- At age 10 or 11 years, his biological mother's rights were terminated; at that time he and some (but not all) of his siblings were adopted
- Peter witnessed and was the victim of violence

- In 2014, while in Middle School, Peter witnessed his best friend getting shot and killed
- In 2014, Peter received stab wounds that required stitches when he stepped in front of a friend who was being attacked with a knife
- Peter has reportedly witnessed over 20 gun shootings
- Peter's older brothers are incarcerated
- The man who lived with his mother (and cared for Peter and siblings) at the time they entered the foster care system is currently incarcerated for murder
- During March and April 2015, Peter was homeless; during this time he slept on the roof of the High School cafeteria (Peter P., et al. v. Compton Unified School District, Initial Complaint, 2015).

At the time of the suit, his clinical presentation also included:

- Peter has flashbacks (of mother and siblings being victimized and experiencing sexual abuse at hands of male perpetrators) and he often reports feeling aggressive when males approach

The critical question of the lawsuit is around the impact of childhood adversity and trauma on later functioning. Does a child exposed to early, chronic, traumatic stress have a condition that disables learning and access to education? The answer may well be "it depends." This book becomes of critical important now. It is incumbent on school and community based practitioners who are working with children like Peter to do two things: (i) Create schools that are trauma informed for ALL children (i.e. Tier 1) and (ii) build response processes that allow us to provide trauma-informed, evidence-based treatments for children who are most functionally and clinically impacted by their trauma history (i.e. Tier 2 and 3). This occurs through Tier 1 interventions that integrate trauma-informed practices and Tier 2 and Tier 3 practices that assess children who did not respond to intervention at Tier 1 and/or Tier 2, or are so symptomatic that more individualized clinical support is warranted.

Across the country, the response to intervention (RTI) model is in various stages of implementation and with a wide range of fidelity. An in-depth discussion on RTI is well beyond the scope of this book, but it is important to note that at EVERY stage, trauma-informed practices can be integrated. Furthermore, when a student gets to the level of requiring an intensive psycho-educational and clinical assessment for consideration of special education inclusion, a trauma-informed assessment is essential. We contend that all clinicians in school and community settings should be screening for and considering trauma for any child referred for a full evaluation. There may in fact be circumstances when Tier 1 screenings are either clinically relevant, appropriate, or warranted, pending outcomes of basic screening measures that are either done in the context of the actual evaluation or performed at Tier 1 or 2 screenings. This data is critical in understanding the underlying needs of any child and considering the possibility that exposure to adverse childhood experiences is a part of their clinical picture. This is precisely what was missing in Compton.

TRAUMA AND POLICY LEARNING INITIATIVE

Building entire school-wide, trauma-informed practices is a large undertaking. Discussing this topic in its entirety is beyond the scope of this book, however we believe that trauma-informed assessments need to be embedded within trauma-informed schools and organizations. We direct readers to the extensive volume entitled *Helping Traumatized Children Learn: Creating, and Advocating for Trauma-Sensitive Schools*, which can be found here: https://traumasensitiveschools.org. This is the second of two volumes released by the Trauma and Learning Policy Initiative (TLPI) which is a partnership with the Massachusetts Advocates for Children (MAC) and Harvard Law School (Cole et al., 2005a,b, 2013).

The mission of the TLPI is to ensure that all children who have been exposed to childhood adversity and trauma are able to succeed in their schools. TLPI works as an advocacy group, supporting schools to develop trauma-informed practices and become trauma-informed organizations. This also includes a great deal of logistic legislative work as well as policy development. MAC started in the mid-1990s as a way to address the needs of children in Massachusetts who were being expelled and suspended from school. MAC developed a task force for children affected by domestic violence, produced a number of working papers and documents, and were directly related with policy and law development. In 2000, MAC partnered with Lesley University's Center for Special Education to host a professional training and conference on trauma and learning (Cole et al., 2005a,b, 2013). These two organizations came together to provide a multidisciplinary workgroup that included mental health professionals, educators, attorneys, and advocates. Together they published the "Helping Traumatized Children Learn" volume (Cole et al., 2005a,b, 2013). The publication developed and disseminated to something more; they created something called a *flexible framework*. The flexible framework is a tool for integrating and creating trauma-sensitive schools (Cole et al., 2005a,b). In 2004, MAC developed a partnership with Harvard Law School, and the Trauma and Learning Policy Initiative was born. The TLPI group has since disseminated hundreds of thousands of free copies of their publications to educators and mental health providers all over the country and world (Cole et al., 2005a,b, 2013). The TLPI is directed by attorney Susan Cole, who also has a background in special education (Cole et al., 2005a,b, 2013). Susan and her team have since expanded TLPI into advocacy work, and she now also leads the Safe and Supportive Schools Commission for the State of Massachusetts (of which this author is a participant), which is directly connected to building trauma-sensitive and safe schools for all children in the entire state. The Trauma Sensitive Schools and TLPI provide an exhaustive list of resources for community and school-based professionals invested in understanding and building trauma-sensitive schools, and we encourage readers to visit this website to learn more: https://traumasensitiveschools.org/about-tlpi.

Bill H. 4376: An Act Relative to the Reduction of Gun Violence

On August 13, 2014, House Bill 4376–an act relative to the reduction of gun violence–was signed into law by Governor Deval Patrick (D). While the primary thrust of this bill was around universal background checks and the reduction of gun violence in the state, it also focused on a safe and supportive framework for schools. The bill went through multiple rounds of revision and compromise from both sides of the aisle. This bill was related to the sale and possession of firearms in the commonwealth, and it was declared an emergency law, necessary for the immediate preservation of the public convenience. The controversial bill, now law, reflected a long and challenging legislative process that began largely in response to the 2012 school shootings in Newtown, Connecticut. After the mass shooting, law makers in the state of Massachusetts filed over 60 bills relative to gun violence (Schoenberg 2014). The process of getting House Bill 4376 into law was largely a partisan process with a great deal of controversy around gun ownership and Second Amendment rights (Schoenberg 2014). A state-wide task force was established and ultimately House Speaker Robert DeLeo (D) proposed this gun violence bill. The revised bill also required the courts in Massachusetts to share all relevant mental health and substance abuse commitments, domestic violence convictions, restraining orders, and guardianship appointments with the criminal justice system (Eger, 2014). This information was then added to the FBI's National Instant Criminal Background Check system (Eger, 2014). Essentially, the law focused on expanding broad background checks for all gun sales in the state. A summary of all of the details of the bill related to fire arm licensing and acquisition can be found here: http://www.mass.gov/eopss/agencies/dcjis/key-changes-to-the-massachusetts-gun-laws-august-2014.html

In addition to focusing on gun control, Bill H. 4376 also improved a number of other parameters that were related to safety in schools and communities. The bill mandated that all schools in the Commonwealth create comprehensive school safety plans and addressed students' mental health needs (Schoenberg, 2014). Bill H. 4376 ultimately led to the creation of the Safe and Supportive Schools Commission for the State of Massachusetts, which is essentially a task force of education, mental health, public health, policy, and legal professionals who meet throughout the year to enact and make recommendations. While it is a less publicized aspect of the bill, the Safe and Supportive Schools Commission was created as part of the Safe and Supportive Schools Framework Law (Massachusetts General Laws, chapter 69, section 1P), through An Act Relative to the Reduction of Gun Violence (Safe and Supportive Schools Commission, 2014), and works in partnership with the Department for Elementary and Secondary Education. Section 1P. The Safe and Supportive Schools Framework noted that the work of the commission is to create schools that are safe for all students; promote positive, healthy, and inclusive school environments; and support students in reaching academic and non-academic success in school with a focus on maintaining physical and psychological health and well-being (Cole et al., 2005a,b, 2013). The framework seeks to create an integrated and aligned service provision model and school-wide culture that supports social–emotional learning, mental health, positive approaches to behavior management, and trauma sensitivity. The goals of this task force were built off of the earlier work of The Behavioral Health and Public Schools Task force of the Department of Elementary and Secondary Education that was created under section 19 of Chapter 321 of the acts of 2008 and both of these can be found in full here. We strongly encourage readers to visit the following two websites: https://malegislature.gov/Laws/GeneralLaws/PartI/TitleXII/Chapter69/Section1P and https://malegislature.gov/Laws/SessionLaws/Acts/2014/Chapter284.

THE ROLE OF SCHOOLS

As noted elsewhere, the impact of trauma and chronic, toxic stress on learning and school functioning is significant. This will be further expanded in subsequent chapters, but needless to say, trauma has a critical impact on a child's day-to-day functioning in the school setting. Despite the significant and widespread impact of trauma exposure and the subsequent mental health distress that impact our youth, relatively few have access to high-quality treatment. Those who receive treatment often get low-quality care (Weist & Evans, 2005).

This is where the role of schools comes into play. All children, by law, have to be enrolled in some type of educational program, with the majority of those being in the public sector. Due to these compulsory education requirements, schools offer the opportunity to provide public health services through the public education system. Essentially, providing community-based mental health services can happen in the context of the school system (Farmer et al., 2003). By integrating mental health services into the school system, we are provided an opportunity to access high-risk populations that might not otherwise be accessible. By using the opportunity that we already have with large groups of children and teens in schools every day, and moving mental health services into this setting, we may also decrease the racial disparities relative to who is even able to access services (Kataoka et al., 2007).

Pushing mental health services into schools allows us to access all kids for screening, identification, prevention, and intervention. This also lends itself to the partnership between schools, families, and community agencies to provide high-quality, evidence-based, data-driven prevention and intervention programs in schools (Weist & Evans, 2005). This is the very foundation of the intersection between public education and public health. Schools that integrate a public health perspective on mental health services are better equipped to serve all children. Jaycox et al. (2007) showed that schools with comprehensive mental health programs in place already respond better to traumatic events and crisis (Jaycox et al., 2007).

It is increasingly clear that the more effective mental health systems in place within the school system, the better equipped these schools are to handle single incidence traumatic events. (Brock & Cowan, 2004; Cowan et al., 2013). Our focus here is to consider how schools can become more prepared and effective at managing chronic, community based, traumatic stressors that lead to complex trauma that occur over time.

Trauma-informed approaches are not specific interventions, but rather a way of providing services to children and families that facilitates improved functioning of those negatively impacted by trauma (Kessler 2014; SAMSHA, 2014). Single-event, catastrophic traumas like Hurricane Katrina, the Sandy Hook school shootings, and the terrorist attacks of 9/11 have created a sense of community urgency around response to traumatic events. Well-prepared schools have crisis intervention plans and teams in place to respond to everything from a natural disaster to a suicide in the student body. Increased public awareness has led to increased efforts in training staff and building district-level capacity to respond to these events swiftly, thoughtfully, and often with evidence-based response approaches (Brock & Cowan, 2004; Cowan et al., 2013).

However, what about schools with a significant portion of their student population who are living in adversity and toxic stress on a regular basis? Things like community violence, poverty, housing, and food insecurity have significant impact on a student's ability to learn and function in the school setting, yet much less is known regarding how to ensure that these children get the services they need and go to schools that are prepared to meet their unique needs.

One way schools can respond to the needs of these children, and in turn all of the other students in the building, is by adopting school-wide trauma-informed models. Schools can address the negative impacts of trauma on the academic, behavioral, and psychological health of students by adopting trauma-informed approaches to schooling. As noted earlier, the use of trauma-informed approaches are more than just about robust mental health service delivery, but a social justice and equity imperative. Ms. Nicole Boykins, Principal of the Crocker College Prep School in New Orleans School whose school has garnered national attention for their school-wide approach to trauma sensitivity notes that this is about a shift in mindset (Boykins, 2017). Trauma-informed schools are not just an intervention, but rather a way of providing services and changing the mindset (Kessler 2014; Substance Abuse and Mental Health Services Administration, 2014).

In the monograph action research study, titled "Advancing Education Effectiveness: Interconnecting School Mental Health and School-Wide Positive Behavior Support," editors and authors compiled a comprehensive resources on how to connect school mental health (SMH) to school-wide positive behavior supports, which we believe is essential to this conversation on trauma-informed schools. This manuscript and related activities were developed through funding from the United States Office of Special Education Programs (OSEPs) of the Department of Education and the Maternal and Child Health Bureau (MCHB) of the Health Resources and Service Administration of the US Department of Health and Human Services. We direct you to their full document (https:// www.pbis.org/school/school-mental-health/interconnected-systems) but will summarize key points here. The Interconnected Systems Framework (ISF) is the proposed mechanisms for connecting Positive Behavioral Interventions and Supports (PBIS) and SMH and we also believe that it is the mechanism that will best support the development of trauma-sensitive schools (Barrett et al., 2013).

As noted earlier, the public health perspective is one that addresses the continuum of services and interventions from prevention through to highly specified interventions, and this framework is central to the ISF model. Schools become the most ideal place to realize this continuum and range of services. As a reminder, for all children who received mental health services, approximately

70% of them access those serves through their school (Barrett et al., 2013). Barrett et al., further noted that the marriage of the PBIS and SMH models is appropriate because PBIS has the capacity to carry the delivery of the SMH. At present, approximately one out of every five youths have a mental health "condition," and school becomes a natural vehicle for SMH services. Citing implementation science (Fixsen et al., 2009), and Communities of Practice (Wagner et al., 2005), these editors of the monograph note that the final conceptualization of ISF is informed by multiple sectors.

What is the Interconnected Systems Framework? The ISF is the platform by which PBIS and SMH come together. We believe that Trauma-Sensitive Schools can be articulated here as well. Barrett, Eber, and Weist note that ISF closes the gaps that PBIS has when it is a standalone model, focusing specifically on insufficient development of Tier 2 and Tier 3 aspects, which result in unaddressed behavioral and mental health needs for high-risk children. Furthermore, the authors note that at Tier 1, progress has been seen related to social climate and even discipline, but this has not yet been connected to broader mental health prevention. In turn, the authors note that the weaknesses of the SMH model, including lack of implementation science, lack of structure, and disconnection of services, can be leveraged by the PBIS model. Together, these two models leverage one another's weakness and drive the Interconnected Systems Framework. Core features of the ISF model include:

1. Effective teams that include community mental health providers,
2. Data-based decision making,
3. Formal processes for the selection and implementation of evidence based practices,
4. Early access through use of comprehensive screening,
5. Rigorous progress-monitoring for both fidelity and effectiveness, and
6. Ongoing coaching at both the systems and practice level (Barrett et al., 2013, p. 3)

This is of significance when considering the goals of integrating trauma-sensitive practices into schools. For example, psycho-educational models that treat anxiety and the effects of trauma have strong evidence for being effective (Stein et al., 2003). However, assistance in implementation (training, coaching, fidelity, monitoring) is needed to be truly useful to schools (Graczyk et al., 2003; Weist et al., 2007). This is where ISF can be quite useful when considering the development of trauma-sensitive schools. As Barrett, Eber, and Weist noted, "ISF builds on the foundations of PBIS and SMH to ensure greater depth and quality of prevention and intervention by building multiple tiers of support" (Barrett et al., 2013, p. 6). Citing the Systems of Care (Pires, 2002), Barrett, Eber, and Weist also noted that the ISF will achieve a number of economic and social benefits, such as:

1. Children and youth will have earlier access to a wider range of evidenced-based practices with enhanced preventative services,
2. Children and youth will be more likely to receive higher quality of care when practices a are implemented within a tiered framework,
3. Staff will have clearly defined roles and relationships among school-employed mental health staff and community-employed providers
4. Cross-system leadership and training will promote common language, and common approaches to addressing community and school system needs,
5. Interventions will have an increased likelihood of generalization with impact across settings,
6. Accessing services within the school setting will become less stigmatizing, and
7. Effective cross-teaming structures will promote communication, coordination of services, and enhanced family engagement with systematic ways to progress monitor and measure impact or fidelity (Barrett et al., 2013, p. 6)

We believe that the tenets of ISF will serve us well for considering the development and implementation of trauma-sensitive school frameworks and will use this framework as a guiding principle.

With the ISF as the framework and backdrop to trauma-sensitive schools, we can revisit the four R's of the Substance Abuse and Mental Health Services Administration (SAMSHA). According to SAMSHA, a trauma-informed organization or system is one that does the following:

1. Realizes the widespread impact of trauma and understands potential paths for recovery;
2. Recognizes the signs and symptoms of trauma in clients, families, staff, and others involved with the system;
3. Responds by fully integrating knowledge about trauma into policies, procedures, and practices; and
4. Seeks to actively resist re-traumatization (SAMSHA, 2017, para. 2)

Revisiting the four R's of the SAMSHA model—realizes, recognizes, responds, and resists re-traumatization—we see that these can be integrated across entire school-wide efforts (SAMSHA, 2014). By integrating these principles into existing school-wide efforts, we can move schools towards being more trauma-informed organizations. Trauma informed models can be integrated in schools through a multi-tier service delivery system (Kessler 2014; Walkey & Cox, 2013) This often means exploring the need for systems level changes. If we consider that a tiered model approach originally stems from the RTI world, and before that, the public health world, and instead use it to conceptualize the tenets of trauma informed frameworks, then we can integrate these concepts into all levels of the organization. For example, Tier 1 changes may include school policy, practices, procedures, and universal interventions that help realize the impact of trauma, recognize the signs and symptoms of trauma, and respond in kind. For a school to become trauma-informed, the culture and climate need to be addressed. This may include procedures that govern and manage the entire school community (Kessler 2014; Walkley & Cox 2013). Schools work towards this by integrating the four SAMSHA aspects of trauma-informed care noted above into the fabric of the school, across all levels of intervention.

Realizing and recognizing are SAMSHA's first two principles. This is what underlies all trauma-based assessments and interventions. These principles have to be in place, in order for trauma-informed interventions and assessments to exist in a school. Individual practitioners can address and provide trauma-informed assessment and intervention individually on a Tier 3 level (i.e. in their own assessments), but the best outcomes will occur when Tier 1 and Tier 2 support for a trauma-informed approach.

Realizing, and recognizing the far-reaching impact of trauma and its related symptoms can be part of professional development and staff training. This helps us lay the foundation for building a trauma-informed school (Ko et al., 2008; Walkley & Cox, 2013). Additionally, universal screenings for trauma can be put in place at the Tier 1 level. Schools utilizing a trauma-informed approach will need to implement universal screenings to consider not only if children have experienced a potential single traumatic event, but also multiple chronic ACEs. In addition, screenings should consider those who are actively demonstrating trauma-based symptoms and those who are not responding to universal interventions (Conradi & Wilson, 2010; Walkley & Cox, 2013).

Professional development for staff can be focused first on helping staff understand and realize the impact that trauma and adverse childhood experiences can have on individuals, both children and families. Schools want to impress upon staff the pervasiveness of the impact of trauma and adversity. To that end, Chapter 1 of this book can be useful reading for staff members and can be used to develop school-wide training for *all* staff—not just teachers and administrators, but also bus drivers, janitors, lunch staff, and all other support staff. By building in this foundational knowledge for all personnel in the building, we are actually addressing and shifting perceptions. Remember, trauma-informed schools represent a complete mindset shift, not just a series of interventions and programs.

Research indicates that implementing trauma-informed perspectives in organizational ethos can be quite impactful. When considering other child-service organizations (child welfare) research demonstrates that staff professional development can do the following: Increase knowledge about trauma informed care, improve attitudes towards the use of trauma-informed care, and increase use of trauma-informed approaches and practices (Brown et al., 2013; Conners-Burrow et al., 2013).

Prevention of re-traumatization can be articulated in a number of different ways. One way that this can be done is through modifications or adjustments in discipline practices. School-wide efforts to address the impact of trauma and adversity are not just good for kids who have been exposed to chronic, traumatic stress, but for all kids. This is consistent with other school-wide intervention programs that address all students at the Tier 1 level of service provision. School psychologists and other mental and behavioral health professionals who work or consult with school systems can serve a meaningful role in this endeavor.

The SAMSHA model further outlines six principles of a trauma-informed approach. We believe that these can also be integrated into school-wide trauma-informed frameworks. These six principles are noted below.

Six Principles of Trauma-Informed Approach

1. Safety
2. Trustworthiness and transparency
3. Peer support
4. Collaboration and mutuality
5. Empowerment (voice and choice)
6. Cultural, historical, and gender (SAMSHA, 2014, para. 3)

As Ridgard et al. (2015) noted, if school policies and procedures are aligned with these nine principles they will be integrated into daily practice across building trauma-informed schools and districts. This would reflect a consistent, trauma informed approach. One example would be the integration of trustworthiness and transparency into all aspects of school development. This could be defined as open and honest communication, consistent and reliable interactions, and clear expectations between staff and students (Kessler, 2014). While many schools have clear behavioral expectations for students that are visible throughout the school, they could also develop this for staff and teachers. This would improve transparency between students and staff and contribute positively to the relational aspect of student-teacher interactions. This would not only enhance transparency, but would build trust between these two groups, which is a foundational element of a trauma-informed school (Walkley & Cox, 2013).

Trauma-informed schools represent the future of building trauma-informed communities and supporting children exposed to trauma and adversity. When considering the "How" of building these communities, we can look towards the world of advocacy for assistance.

Section Two

COMPLEX TRAUMA AND THE ROLE OF FUNCTIONAL IMPAIRMENT

Five

CHILD DEVELOPMENT

Bettina Franzese

THE STUDY OF CHILD DEVELOPMENT: CHILD WELFARE AND SCIENTIFIC STUDY

It is only fairly recently that we have thought about the care and welfare of children. With the advent of the growth of urban areas and the Industrial Revolution in America near the end of the eighteenth century, children worked long hours in poorly ventilated, dimly lit factories across the country under adverse conditions with little or no pay, and little recourse. Working 12-hour days under such harsh and dangerous conditions led to illness, accidents, and death for our youngest American citizens. Social concern for their health and wellbeing led to greater social and scientific research, reforms, and child labor laws (Stearns, 2006). Children's developmental changes over time from infancy through young adulthood became established scientific inquiry as the interest in the cognitive, social, emotional, and behavioral lives of children broadened. Psychologists will note that by the end of the nineteenth century, Alfred Binet and Theodore Simon had devised a 30-item standardized test to better understand individual differences in children's mental abilities that led to the first widely used, psychometrically based intelligence measure, the 1905 Binet–Simon Scale (Sattler, 2008; Lightfoot et al., 2013).

Today, the field of child development is multifaceted and influenced by numerous disciplines including neurobiology, neuroimaging, molecular biology, genetics, the social and behavioral sciences, and public policy. While one tenet of child development continues to focus on the safety and wellbeing of children, more and more multidisciplinary efforts are focused on optimizing and advancing positive health and adaptive developmental outcomes for all children and youth. Just as research illuminates and guides our individual practice in assessment, consultation, and interventions in psychology, developmental science is illuminating policy initiatives and programs on a macro level that can reach families and children within their communities. Today's children are tomorrow's parents, thinkers, and leaders. It is our best interest to provide population-level support to ensure raising productive, responsible citizens of tomorrow. This concept of population health models and public health has been discussed elsewhere in this book and is also relevant here.

While discovering policies and practices that help maximize the odds for children to grow from healthy children to healthy, well-adjusted adults has been a focus for considerable periods of time, exactly how to accomplish this was filled with debate and competing theories. For example, it was once thought that spanking and using physical force to reduce children's aggressive behaviors was an effective means of controlling misbehavior, or that picking up crying infants or toddlers would "spoil" them and reinforce fussiness and irritability.

Historically, little recognition has been given to the fact that corporal punishment poses the risk of serious psychological harm and violates basic human rights (Lenta, 2012). In many states, countries, and geographic regions as well as within the practices of a wide range of cultural and religious practices, corporal punishment is still seen as a reasonable measure to induce behavioral change. At the time of the writing of this book (2017–2018), the country-wide commitment to ending this human rights violation has increased. A total of 53 states have prohibited all corporal punishment of children, including within the family home and 54 states have expressed commitment to a full prohibition of this practice (www.endcorporalpunishment.org). Despite this, the state laws governing a number of settings within much of the United States including daycares, schools, penal institutions, and alternative care settings still confirm a parental right to inflict physical punishment on their children. Corporal punishment is prohibited in all alternative settings in 40 states and Washington, D.C.; it is also prohibited in all early childhood care and daycare for older children in 36 states (www.endcorporalpunishment.org). This parental right further protects parents from legal provisions around violence and abuse – that is, parents are able to make decisions about using corporal punishment on their children. At present, corporal punishment legally allowed in private homes in all states and state laws confirms a parent's right to use physical punishment as a practice. State laws for violence and abuse are routinely interpreted as excluding corporal punishment (http://www.endcorporalpunishment.org/progress/country-reports/usa.html).

Corporal punishment in schools is a topic of particular interest when we consider the role of the trauma-informed, safe-and-supportive school context in helping all children learn successfully. There exists no federal law in the United States disallowing corporal punishment in public and private schools. The Eighth Amendment of the U.S. Constitution prohibits cruel and unusual punishment. However, the U.S. Supreme Court found in 1977 that this is provision did not apply to schools (see http://www.endcorporalpunishment.org/progress/country-reports/usa.html). Multiple states in recent years (August 2017 in Utah, and June 2015 in Massachusetts) have overturned cases at the state supreme judicial court level that had ruled in favor of protecting the child from undue physical punishment at the hands of a parent. The case in Massachusetts overturned the original conviction of assault and battery and noted that "the ruling set out the following "framework": ". . . we hold that a parent or guardian may not be subjected to criminal liability for the use of force against a minor child under the care and supervision of the parent or guardian, provided that (1) the force used against the minor child is reasonable; (2) the force is reasonably related to the purpose of safeguarding or promoting the welfare of the minor, including the prevention or punishment of the minor's misconduct; and (3) the force used neither causes, nor creates a substantial risk of causing, physical harm (beyond fleeting pain or minor, transient marks), gross degradation, or severe mental distress" (End Corporal Punishment, 2017, para. 3). By virtue of the specificity in the ruling, this ruling is believed to have done a better job than some others in balancing the state's responsibility to protect children while also respecting a parent's right to parent as they see fit. That is, the clarification of "unreasonable" is seen as progress and movement forward in the extent to which states can protect the rights of children. In other states, the ruling has been perhaps more concerning, wherein the burden to indicate that physical abuse actually caused harm to the child is not met.

In August 2017, the Supreme Court of Utah[2] reversed the decision of a juvenile court which had found that parents that had spanked their children using a belt were guilty of abuse under the Utah Code. The Supreme Court highlighted that the juvenile court had failed to prove that the spanking had caused "harm" to the children as defined in the Utah Code ("physical, emotional, or developmental injury or damage"), instead stipulating harm as a natural consequence to the spanking. The Supreme Court also objected to the juvenile court's adoption of the *per se* rule that "hitting a child with a belt or strap or another object is abuse" as too broad and potentially applying to inoffensive situations such as "throwing a pillow or a rolled-up pair of socks at a child" or "hitting a child with a Nerf sword playfully as part of a game"

(http://www.endcorporalpunishment.org/progress/
country-reports/usa.html, 2017, para. 4).

This information is relevant to this book and chapter for a number of reasons. First, this entire volume is intended to improve our understanding and knowledge of how to support children who have experienced chronic, traumatic stressors that are often (but not always) experienced in the context of the caregiving relationship. That it is still legally possible in our country (and many others) to use physical coercion, force, and contact to parent children makes this all the more alarming. The literature has consistently born out that there is no place for physical contact in teaching children, yet our legal systems have yet to fully embrace this. Implementing a safe and supportive trauma-informed school culture in a building that allows the use of physical contact and punishment to manage student behavior may prove to be an uphill battle. As recently as the summer of 2017, a school district in south Texas (Three Rivers Independent School) gave parents the opportunity to opt in or out of the policy that allows the school to use paddling on students. The Texas Classroom Teachers Association (TCTA) defines corporal punishment as "deliberate infliction of physical pain by hitting, paddling, spanking, slapping or any other physical force used as a means of discipline" (Texas Classroom Teachers Association 2017, para. 2). Furthermore, the TCTA noted: "Educators may use corporal punishment only if the board of trustees has adopted a policy allowing the use of corporal punishment, unless the student's parent, guardian, or other person having lawful control over the student has previously provided a written, signed statement prohibiting the use of corporal punishment for the student" (Texas Classroom Teachers Association 2017, para. 2). According to the National Center on Safe and Supportive Learning Environments (U.S. Department of Education; https://safesupportivelearning.ed.gov) Texas is one of 15 states that specifically support the use of corporal punishment in schools, while another eight states do not have a specific statute or law regulating against the use of corporal punishment (https://safesupportivelearning.ed.gov).

In November of 2016 Secretary of Education John B. Kingmade a national call for ending corporal punishment in schools. He sent a letter to all states strongly urging leaders to end all use of corporal punishment in schools, citing both the negative short and long-term outcomes of its use.

"Our schools are bound by a sacred trust to safeguard the well-being, safety, and extraordinary potential of the children and youth within the communities they serve," King said. "While some may argue that corporal punishment is a tradition in some school communities, society has evolved and past practice alone is no justification. No school can be considered safe or supportive if its students are fearful of being physically punished. We strongly urge states to eliminate the use of corporal punishment in schools—a practice that educators, civil rights advocates, medical professionals, and researchers agree is harmful to students, and which data shows us unequivocally and disproportionally impacts students of color and students with disabilities"

(U.S. Department of Education, U.S. Education Secretary John B, King, https://www.ed.gov/news/press-releases/king-sends-letter-states-calling-end-corporal-punishment-schools, para. 2).

Gershoff (2013) in their article entitled "Spanking and Child Development: We Know Enough Now to Stop Hitting Our Children" noted a number of significant concerning outcomes that are the result of hitting children. Given that physical punishment has been a part of childrearing practices likely since the beginning of time, it is not entirely surprising that ending its practice is often met with resistance (Scott, 1996). This is a practice that is still largely endorsed by a number of cultural and religious groups, but Gershoff argues that we now have enough mounting literature to support the concept that physical punishment is an outdated and ineffective practice. Spanking increases short-term noncompliance, long-term non-compliance, and aggression (Gershoff, 2013; Holden et al., 1995; Gershoff, 2002; Roberts & Powers, 1990).

While corporal punishment still remains a fairly common childrearing practice (UNICEF, 2014), research generally indicates that using it as a discipline method can actually increase children's problem behaviors, bullying, and physical and verbal aggression (Gershoff & Grogan-Taylor, 2016). The American Academy of Child and Adolescent Psychiatry does not support the use of corporal punishment as a method of behavior modification (policy statement, 2012). Additionally, it is now well established that responding to infant distress with physical comfort and warm, consistent caregiving enables babies to better handle stressors, establishes a foundation of safety and security, and is essential for children's mental health and development (National Scientific Council on the Developing Child Working Paper #1, 2004).

Today, we know that children's development is influenced by numerous factors that interact in dynamic ways including the roles of genetics, molecular biology, the environment, and social experiences. Progression through the developmental stages is the result of a unique mix of physical and mental predispositions and attributes, as well as environmental conditions such as living in poverty, a mother's prenatal drug exposure, or having a responsive, empathic parent or caregiver. The science of development is also heavily influenced by the many ways that cultural, group, and ethnic variables affect developmental processes. We are a diverse nation with different cultural and family practices, and different expectations for children's socialization and childhood behaviors embedded within our larger society. As such, children grow and mature within cultural contexts that are as integral to their histories as their biology or genetic makeup (Lightfoot et al., 2013).

BASICS OF CHILD DEVELOPMENT

Development unfolds over time in a consistent sequence for all individuals, although people develop and mature in unique and varied ways. There are certain developmental tasks and milestones that children are expected to master and attain within developmental periods. These foundational building blocks are required to acquire more advanced and complex capacities as they grow.

Sensitive periods or optimum periods (Werker & Tees, 2005) are those times in childhood when children are open and ready to profit from environmental experiences that can either facilitate or impede adaptive behaviors or skill development. We now know that certain developmental processes are open to change and modification even if they are acquired during non-optimal periods, although it may be more difficult to attain the expected skills and outcomes than if conditions occurred in more typical developmental timeframes. This is what is known as *brain plasticity*, or the brain's ability to be changed or modified to accommodate a range of positive or negative influences on development. Adverse Childhood Experiences, trauma, abuse, or neglect can alter children's stress response systems, but due to brain plasticity, evidence-based interventions can allow children to cope with and overcome negative outcomes associated with early adversity. As the developing brain matures and becomes more specialized in function, it is less able to adapt or reorganize to a changing experiential environment.

DEVELOPMENTAL PERIODS, DOMAINS OF FUNCTIONING, AND ATTAINMENTS

Generally, periods of development can be broken down in the following ways (although it is important to note that some organizations have different definitions of these time periods). Furthermore, cultural and economic shifts in society may also modify these periods. For example, emerging and young adulthood may be conceptualized to include individuals from ages 18 through to the late 20's. These individuals may be dependent on their parents well into adulthood and this will change the way we understand their needs:

- Prenatal: Conception to birth
- Infancy: Birth to 12 months
- Toddlerhood: 12–36 months
- Early childhood: 3–6 years
- Middle Childhood: 6–11 years
- Early Adolescence: 11–15 years
- Adolescence: 15–19 years (Arnett 2007)

Child healthcare providers and clinicians inquire about and observe children's developmental milestones–specific skill attainments and capacities which occur sequentially over time, building upon more basic foundational skills as children mature. Developmental milestones are the result of the dynamic interaction of developing neurobiological systems and children's unique experiences within their environment. Skill attainment is often grouped in domains of development, which include things like physical development, motor development, cognitive development, language development, social/emotional development, and moral development.

Major changes take place during these periods and the attributes described here are general and are only meant to review basic skills and abilities. While this section provides a brief summary of child development, we encourage readers to expand on this understanding with additional resources as needed. The following lists have been generated from multiple resources and we encourage readers to review these resources in full:

- Lightfoot, C., Cole, M. & Cole, S. R. (2013). *The Development of Children* (7th ed.) New York: Worth Publishers.
- Berk, L., & Meyers, A. (2016) Infants, Children, and Adolescents (8th ed.) New York: Pearson.
- Feldman, S. (2016). Child Development. (7th ed) New York: Pearson.
- The PA Child Welfare Training Program – Child and Adolescent Development Resource Book; University of Pittsburgh Office of Child Development (http://www.pacwrc.pitt.edu/Curriculum/CTC/MOD9-OLD/RsrcBk/RsrcBk.pdf).
- Centers for Disease Control and Prevention (https://www.cdc.gov/ncbddd/childdevelopment/index.html)

Most children during these time frames can do, are acquiring, and/or have attained the following:

Early Childhood: 3–6 Years
- Children may have been in preschool
- May be starting Kindergarten at age 5 or 6

Cognitive Development:
- Their thinking is rigid and concrete (ages 4–5)
- They know and can identify basic shapes
- They can sort objects by color, size, or shape
- They can understand concepts such as size including largest and smallest
- They know some colors
- They understand causality in familiar situations
- They enjoy stories
- They understand that letters and sounds are linked in systematic ways
- They have an emerging sense of time
- They can do very simple addition and subtraction

Language Development:
- They have a vocabulary of about 1,500 words (by age 4)
- By age 5, vocabulary can reach 10,000 words (girls earlier than boys)
- They use pronouns correctly
- They follow two or three-step directions
- They can answer simple questions
- They understand opposites
- They understand and begin to use prepositions
- Their conversational skills improve
- They start to use verbs properly

Social/Emotional Development:
- Their social interactions are based on learned, modeled interactions at home
- They may be bossy and aggressive
- They want to do things independently
- They understand the idea of taking turns but may not always do it
- They begin to distinguish intentional acts from unintentional acts
- They may fear noises, imaginary creatures, and storms
- They form first friendships
- Their interactive play increases
- They are proud of their achievements (age 5)

- Their emotion regulation improves
- They can use internal speech to guide emotions
- Socially competent children are popular; disruptive children tend to be socially rejected

Moral Development:
- They continue to tie their behavior to gain reinforcement and avoid punishment, but also begin to evidence a sense of justice and altruism.
- They understand social expectations such as sharing as a social obligation (by age 5)

Middle Childhood: 6–11 Years
Typically developing children during these years have been enrolled in elementary and are transitioning to middle school. Attainments are categorized from age 6 to age 11 and then broken down again in some areas from ages 9 to 11.

Cognitive Development:
There is a rapid development of mental skills with markers of logical thought
They can use memory strategies for learning
There is a decline in letter reversals
There are opportunities to become increasingly proficient in basic skills on which to build by adding new information to their academic skill repertoire.

9–11 Years:
- Executive function skills such as planning, self-monitoring, self-regulation, and working toward goals improve
- Long-term knowledge base continues to grow in size and organization
- They use memory strategies to master new material

Language Development:
- Interested in new words
- They use complete sentences
- They are beginning to read (age 6)
- They are transitioning from learning to read to reading to learn
- They converse freely and often
- Their vocabulary increases rapidly throughout middle childhood
- They enjoy riddles and jokes
- *9–11 Years* They now understand double meanings, metaphor, humor
- They use complex grammatical structures
- They adapt their conversation based on situation

Social/Emotional Development:
- They may have a special friend
- They engage in cooperative play
- They compare themselves with others
- They attend to social and emotional cues from others.
- They become more responsible and independent
- They have a theory of mind and understand that others may have differing viewpoints
- *9–11 Years* They can empathize with others
- They are better able to regulate emotions
- Their friendships are based on sharing interests and activities
- They seek peers with similar interests and ideas.

Moral Development:
- They still obey authority to avoid trouble
- They begin to understand the need for rules
- They have an increased awareness about what is fair and equal
- They connect rewards with merit

9–11 Years
- They grasp the link between moral and social conventions
- They evidence an expanded concept of right and wrong

Early Adolescence: 11–15 and Adolescence: 15–19
These youths are in middle school and high school.

Cognitive Development:
- Their thinking is less concrete and more abstract, idealistic, and logical
- They have a greater attention span and ability to focus
- They have an interest in achievement and their future
- They continue to use and apply formal abstract thought with inductive and deductive reasoning

Language Development:
- They often enjoy debate and arguing
- May be reluctant to communicate with adults
- They enjoy communicating with friends
- They may think that others do not understand them
- They may use written language skills to convey their thoughts and feelings such as journaling

Social/Emotional/Moral Development

Early Adolescence

- They are forming their identity and separation from others
- They may have increased conflict with parents
- They have increased interest in peers and more pressure to conform to attain status
- They are often egocentric and sensitive to personal appearance
- They may be moody
- Youth with different cultural backgrounds have multiple disadvantages such as dealing with prejudice and racism
- They strive to live up to expectations
- They continue to learn culture-based moral values

Adolescence:

- There is a belief of an imaginary audience watching them and their behaviors; they have a sense of personal uniqueness
- They show an active interest in personal appearance
- They continue to form their own identity in preparation for adulthood
- Minority youth learn to navigate their culture and the majority culture
- Gender-based scripts may guide dating interactions
- They are concerned about own thoughts and opinions
- They are interested in forming romantic relationships
- They may question adult authority and see themselves as nonconformists.

CORE TENETS OF CHILD DEVELOPMENT

There are four core tenets to child development that are critical to consider, particularly in the context of understanding the role that adversity and chronic, traumatic toxicity, and stress can play in children's lives.

1. **The Influence of Nature Plus Nurture and The Role of Epigenetics**
   A child's development is a complex, sequential unfolding of processes that are dynamic interactions of genetic makeup within child psychological attributes such as cognitive, temperament, and personality factors. External variables such as the child-rearing environment; and cultural contexts and circumstances or experiences within that environment. From a biological-social perspective, these five factors contribute to brain development, mental and physical health, adaptive functioning, and vulnerability to stress-related disorders. These factors

continually intertwine with reciprocal and mutual influences starting from before birth and continuing into adulthood. While genes provide basic plans for nerve cells and neuronal connections in the developing brain, the environment has a profound influence on its architecture, structure, and functioning. The brain is hardwired to be sculpted and influenced by critical age-appropriate "expected experiences" which allows for genetic predispositions to be manifested. Children's genes and their developing brains are profoundly affected by both the positive and negative experiences they encounter, especially in early childhood. The approximately 23,000 genes that children inherit from their parents comprise the genome – the complete assembly and set of DNA (deoxyribonucleic acid) instructions that make each person biologically unique. An individual's epigenome are chemical compounds that are built over time and can leave chemical signatures on genes and can affect gene expression, turning them on or off. The role of experiences helps explain why identical twins, although genetically the same, can differ in terms of health status, behaviors, personality, and their responses to the environment. Many factors can shape the epigenome including nutrition, exposure to toxins, contaminants, and the nature and timing of adaptive or maladaptive life experiences. This interplay of gene expression and environment interaction is generally referred to as *epigenetics* (Meany, 2010; Murgatroyd & Spengler, 2011; National Human Genome Research Institute Fact Sheet: Epigenomics, 2016). While childhood exposure to repeated stressors such as maltreatment, abuse, and neglect can result in disruptions in brain structure and function, there is also developmental brain plasticity which can adapt and accommodate a wide range of experiential interactions with the environment. However, as the child matures and the brain becomes more specialized for functions, it loses this capacity for reorganization and adaptation. This is how exposure to high-quality, enriching experiences builds strong foundational bases for optimal brain development, allowing children to progress on a healthy developmental track and benefit from continued positive experiences (National Council on the Developing Child, Working Paper #5, 2007).

2. **The First Five Years are Especially Important**
   During the first five years of life, children are rapidly developing critical dimensions for brain growth, cognitive development, language functioning, social/emotional learning, adjustments to stressors, moral capacities, and self regulation of thought, emotions, and behavior.

The growth of self regulation and ability to cope with stress are considered cornerstones of early childhood development and need to be implemented across a variety of social, learning, and academic settings. While there is a certain amount of plasticity during this time, positive experiences that include responsive caregiving, access to high-quality early childhood programs, exposure to enriched environments, and adequate safety, nutrition, and medical care are crucial. This is not necessarily because these factors or their absence can have immutable positive or deleterious effects, but because these experiences can set either a resilient, sturdy foundation or a maladaptive, vulnerable foundation from which other developmental capacities are built (Shonkoff & Phillips, 2000). Understanding normal child and atypical child development allows us to understand the risk and protective resiliency factors over the course of development (Cicchetti & Toth, 2009).

3. **Children Need Healthy, Supportive Environments to Reach Their Full Potential**

From adequate prenatal care for mothers to high-quality nutrition for both mother and child, raising healthy children requires commitments of time and resources from both a personal and public policy perspective. Parents may have difficulty balancing home and work responsibilities, which can make spending more time interacting with their children challenging. Parents struggling with financial hardships may not be able to afford high-quality child care or access community resources for adequate medical care for themselves or their children. Living in such circumstances makes children vulnerable to a host of adverse conditions such as residing in socially stressed and/or unsafe neighborhoods and being exposed to environmental substances with potentially brain-damaging neurotoxic effects. Exposure to neurotoxins can disrupt brain development both before and after birth, and result in detrimental lifelong consequences. The immature brain is more vulnerable to toxic exposure than the adult brain. Heavy metals such as lead (found in old plumbing and paint), mercury (found in food), and manganese (in unleaded gasoline) can disrupt normal neurobiological processes, interfere with the architecture of the developing brain, disrupt brain cell migration from one part of the brain to another, and negatively affect the formation of neuronal connections and circuits. Children living in economically disadvantaged environments are more likely to be exposed than their more advantaged counterparts. Other sources of chemical exposure occur when children are exposed in utero to nicotine, cocaine, and other drugs including alcohol. Alcohol produces pervasive and devastating effects on neurological functioning and can interfere with other biological organ systems such as the cardiovascular, digestive, and musculoskeletal systems (National Scientific Council on the Developing Child, Working Paper # 4, 2006).

4. **Relationships are Central for Healthy Development**
Most American children are raised in a family or family-like environment. As noted, the need for age appropriate, expected experiences is biologically programmed in the brain. These experiences can either assist children in attaining developmental capacities or make them more vulnerable to risk factors that can throw them off a healthy developmental trajectory. No more is this apparent than in the quality of children's early social relationships. Infants and children not only depend on adult caregivers (usually parents or parental figures) to provide food, clothing, and shelter, but also require these caregivers to provide a warm, nurturing social environment. When parents respond to their young child's distress with comfort, the child's elevated stress response is quieted and returns to a normal baseline. This parent-child interaction sets up a mutual and reciprocal relationship that builds a foundation of trust, safety, and security and is the basis for future social interactions. Forming these stable relationships, along with other factors, maximizes the odds of optimal brain growth and mental and physical health over time. Psychologists typically refer to this as *attachment*—the child's capacity to form and maintain healthy social and emotional bonds with others, deal with life stressors, and develop buffering self regulatory skills to build the protective factor of resiliency. Researchers John Bowlby, Mary Ainsworth and others have documented factors that promote secure attachments. Problems with early attachment including maltreatment and other adverse childhood experiences can facilitate numerous types of psychopathology, mental health issues, and adjustment problems across the lifespan (Bretherton, 1992; National Council on the Developing Child, Working Paper #12, 2012). It is beyond the scope of this work to provide a complete discussion of the attachment literature, but reviews of the literature can be found in Davies (2011)and Sroufe et al. (1999).

While intended to be a brief review of child development, it is clear that any discussion on the impact of adversity on child development must rest firmly on an understanding of what healthy and typical child development looks like.

Six

COMPLEX TRAUMA AND ITS IMPACT ON THE BRAIN

Bettina Franzese

HISTORY

In the history of the study of trauma and traumatic experiences, Lenore Terr was a pioneer in researching and outlining the types of trauma which can affect children. She differentiated two types of trauma, Type I and Type II. Type I traumas were discrete, single events resulting in symptoms associated with Post-traumatic stress syndrome (PTSD) such as experiencing a life-threatening event. Type II traumas were adverse, chronic experiences which tended to be repeated over time, such as being the victim of abuse or maltreatment (Terr, 1991). Many children experience single event experiences which are stressful and potentially traumatic, such as a serious accident. It is more common that children come to the clinician's awareness because of problems associated with chronic life stressors within their family constellations as most childhood trauma originates from home. The latter is referred to as complex trauma.

COMPLEX TRAUMA

The National Traumatic Stress Network (2016) defines *complex trauma* as "children's exposure to multiple traumatic events, often of an invasive, interpersonal nature, and the wide-ranging, long-term impact of this exposure. These events are severe and pervasive, such as abuse or profound neglect. They usually begin early in life and can disrupt many aspects of the child's development and self-formation. Since they often occur in the context of the child's relationship with a caregiver, they interfere with the child's ability to form a secure attachment bond. Many aspects of a child's healthy physical and mental development rely on this primary source of safety and stability" (National Traumatic Stress Network, 2016, para. 1).

One complication in trying to synthesize the literature on stressors and trauma in the lives of children is the different research outcomes of interest by discipline. Clinical child psychology and psychiatry studies might be interested in the attachment role, affect regulation, sense of self, negative emotional states, dissociative experiences, interpersonal relationships, and clinical diagnoses based on the Diagnostic Statistical Manual of Mental Disorders (American Psychiatric Association, 2013) related to trauma-exposed individuals. Neuropsychologists and school psychologists focus on understanding trauma associations with brain behavior relationships such as how early childhood trauma influenced academic achievement, cognitive processes, learning and memory, sensory-motor skills, language development, visual-spatial capacities, executive functioning, and problem-solving abilities. Medical researchers will want to understand how adverse experiences relate to the function, structure, neurochemical, and biologic aspects of the stress systems and their influences on the developing brain, organs, the immune system, and health and disease states. The truth is many of these areas realistically are questions of interest for most child and adolescent clinicians; there is much overlap in professional training and interest. What is important is to try to gain a better understanding of how exposure to trauma in childhood can negatively influence children's cognitive processes, learning, social-emotional functioning, adaptive living skills, adjustment abilities, mental health, and physical wellness. Without efforts to prevent maltreatment and other social stressors for at-risk families or evidenced interventions, these problems can last a lifetime (Anda et al., 2006a,b,c).

DEVELOPMENTAL TRAUMA DISORDER

According to the DSM, children with traumatic histories often present complex clinical pictures and their symptomology tends to be pervasive and multifaceted. They may be aggressive, disruptive, oppositional, and explosive or withdrawn, overly compliant, or socially awkward and disengaged. They may have significant internalizing symptoms such as anxiety or depression with feelings of hopelessness, helplessness, or a sense of a foreshortened future. There may be behavioral and affective dysregulation present, and many have eating and sleeping problems and somatic complaints. Encopresis and enuresis are common in young children from chaotic family environments. Children and adolescents may report suicidal ideation and may engage in non-suicidal self-injurious behaviors such as cutting and body mutilation. Interpersonal relationships are often disrupted, unsatisfying, and unhealthy. Maltreated children tend to underperform in the classroom and lag behind peers in mastery of academic skills. These children and youth often meet behavioral criteria for mental health diagnoses such as learning disorders, attention deficit hyperactivity disorder (ADHD), oppositional defiant disorder, impulse control disorders, borderline personality disorder, depressive and anxiety disorders, elimination disorders, eating disorders, and posttraumatic stress disorder. Since many children unfortunately affected by trauma present with a host of problems, they often meet criteria for several disorders collectively (Van der Kolk, 2005).

The complex trauma taskforce of the National Childhood Traumatic Stress Network suggested the clinical complexity and myriad symptom presentation of children exposed to multiple adverse experiences was not captured adequately with a posttraumatic stress diagnosis according to DSM-IV criteria. These children's problems were better understood when viewed from a trauma perspective. A proposal was initiated with the next DSM version (the DSM 5) for a provisional diagnosis called developmental trauma disorder, which has been viewed as more precise for children with complex histories. Bessel van der Kolk (2005) noted the PTSD diagnosis was adequate for acute trauma in adults, but does not translate well to children who may continue to be traumatized throughout their early years. This leaves the potential for existing problems to worsen and new ones to develop.

Proposed criteria for Developmental Trauma Disorder included the following:

Exposure. The child has experienced or witnessed adverse experiences over time.

Physiological and affective dysregulation. There is impairment in typical developmental competencies related to arousal regulation including an inability to tolerate, cope with, or recover from extreme affective states. Problems with bodily function disturbances occur in areas such as eating, sleeping, and elimination. Problems with disorganization and over or under-reactivity to social stressors in the environment may also be present, along with diminished capacity to describe or experience affective states.

Attention and behavioral dysregulation. Includes atypical competencies related to attention, learning, or dealing in adaptive ways to stressors. This may include hypervigilance to threats and misreading safety and danger cues, risk-taking behaviors which threaten the child's safety maladaptive coping skills, self-harm behaviors, and problems with goal-related behaviors.

Self and relational dysregulation. Impaired awareness of a sense of personal identity and relationships. This may involve a preoccupation on the safety of a parental figure, negative self-perceptions, distrust of others, reactive responses toward peers or adults, initiating inappropriate behaviors for intimacy, problems with empathy and regard for others' feeling states, or an excessive response to the distress of others, beyond the typical age.

Those who work with at-risk, traumatized children and adolescents in schools, inpatient and outpatient trauma clinics, within the juvenile justice system, and in residential treatment centers will recognize these symptoms and impairments as they tend to capture the myriad of presenting problems with trauma-exposed youth. Rather than identifying and treating each diagnosis or problem individually—such as a child with a learning disorder who cannot remain on task and also has significant aggression and acting out behaviors—conceptualizing and providing interventions through a trauma-focused, trauma-sensitive framework allows for a more helpful understanding of the whole child.

The Developmental Trauma Diagnosis was not included in the DSM-5. It was revised with two changes. Rather than being categorized as an anxiety disorder, DSM-PTSD is listed under "trauma-and stressor-related-disorders" with a modified criteria for diagnosing PTSD in preschool children.

For this text, the terms childhood trauma, adverse childhood experiences (ACES), early adverse life experiences, and significant stressors will be used when discussing chronic, persistent negative experiences over time. These events have the potential to undermine development, throw children off a normal developmental trajectory, and result in significant distress and impairment across various venues and functional domains.

TYPES OF CHILDHOOD TRAUMA

Children are exposed to many different adverse life experiences which can result in negative outcomes. One significant source of complex trauma is child maltreatment. Child maltreatment is generally includes physical abuse, sexual abuse, neglect, and psychological abuse.

Physical abuse means causing or attempting to cause physical pain or injury to a child or adolescent. Injuries might include leaving red marks, bruises, cuts, welts, or broken bones. It can result from punching, beating, kicking, or harming a child in other ways. An injury sometimes occurs when a punishment is not appropriate for a child's age or condition. Even if the harm was caused unintentionally, it can still be regarded as physical abuse. Physical abuse can include a single act or several acts. In extreme cases, physical abuse can result in death.

Sexual abuse is any interaction between a child and an adult (or another child) in which the child is used for the sexual stimulation of the perpetrator or an observer. Sexual abuse can include touching and non-touching behaviors. Touching behaviors may involve touching of the genitals, breasts or buttocks, oral-genital contact, or sexual intercourse. Non-touching behaviors can include voyeurism (trying to look at a child's naked body), exhibitionism, or exposure to pornography. Abusers often do not use physical force, but may use play, deception, threats, or other forms of coercion to engage children and maintain their silence. Abusers frequently use persuasive and manipulative tactics – referred to as "grooming" – such as buying gifts or arranging special activities, which can further confuse the victim.

Child neglect is when a parent or caregiver does not give a child age-appropriate attention according to his or her needs even though that adult can afford to provide the care or is offered help to provide care. Neglect can mean not giving food, clothing, and shelter. It can mean that a parent or caregiver is not providing a child with medical or mental health treatment, or not giving prescribed medicines the child needs. Neglect can also mean neglecting the child's education; keeping a child from school can be a form of neglect. Neglect also includes exposing a child to dangerous environments. It can mean poor supervision for a child, including putting the child in the care of someone incapable of caring for children. It can also mean abandoning a child or expelling them from the home. Neglect is the most common form of abuse reported to child welfare authorities.

Emotional child abuse is maltreatment which results in impaired psychological growth and development. It may involve words, actions, and indifference toward the child or adolescent. The abuser constantly criticizes, rejects, ignores, or belittles the victim. This form of abuse may occur with or without physical abuse, but there is often an overlap. Examples of emotional child abuse are verbal abuse; excessive demands on a child's performance; penalizing a child for positive, normal behavior; discouraging caregiver and infant attachment; penalizing a child for demonstrating signs of positive self-esteem; and penalizing a child for using interpersonal skills needed for adequate performance in school and peer groups. Frequently exposing children to family violence and an unwillingness or inability to provide affection or stimulation for the child in daily care may also result in emotional abuse (National Child Traumatic Stress Network-Types of Abuse; Child Welfare Information Gateway-Child Abuse and Neglect).

When working with adversity-exposed youth, psychologists, and other mandated reporters need to be aware of child protection guidelines as it is their responsibility to report suspected child abuse.

Many Childhood Adverse Experiences Can Result in Complex Trauma

Severe financial hardship

Residing in a violent neighborhood

Experiencing Racism/Sexism

Experiencing or witnessing intimate partner violence or interpersonal violence

Parental substance abuse, incarceration, mental health and physical health problems of caregiver

Numerous contacts with Children and Youth Services

Out of home placement

Residing in foster care

Homelessness

Experiencing chronic bullying

Being a victim of a crime, calamity, natural disaster, accident

Chronic and serious physical illness

Painful medical procedures

At-risk, underserved children are typically exposed to many life stressors simultaneously. It would not be not be uncommon for a vulnerable child to witness interpersonal violence at home, have a caregiver who has a serious mental health problem, live in a chaotic environment, and have ongoing contact with children and youth services all at the same time.

Complex trauma is not a DSM-5. But it is clinically useful in case formulation and conceptualization, and is consistent with the proposed provisional diagnosis of Developmental Trauma Disorder for the DSM-5.

COMPLEX TRAUMAS AND ASSOCIATED AREAS OF IMPAIRMENT

Attachment. Early responsive parental care provides a stable relational context from which children can develop internal working models of themselves and others. Responsive caregiving allows children to master developmental capacities such as self-regulation, safety to explore their environment, create a sense of instrumentality in their world, and acquire the emotional and communication skills needed to take part in healthy relationships with others. When primary caregivers alternate between acceptance and rejection of children, an ambivalent pattern of attachment may result. These children become used to anticipating unpredictability from others and may socially disconnect if they feel adults are intrusive, overly engaging, or rejecting. Attachment problems associated with neglect and early aversive consequences can result in children feeling overwhelmed and unable to organize and process their experiences in meaningful and adaptive ways. This can disrupt and alter biopsychosocial competencies and is typically referred to as disorganized attachment (Cicchetti & Toth, 1995). Disorganized attachment can result in personal boundary violations, empathy deficits in attuning to the thoughts and feelings of others, and using language to solve problems in social situations. Schore (2001) notes disorganized attachment may be the result of disrupted connecting pathways of the prefrontal cortex. Disrupted attachments put children at risk for physical disease and psychosocial problems.

Dissociation. Dissociation is generally regarded as a key symptom in complex trauma. It is described as the disconnection of experiences which are typically connected in meaningful ways. Dissociated experiences are not integrated into a person's sense of self which results in alterations of conscious awareness. The disconnection often occurs in the typically integrated functions of memory, attention, self identity, or perception to the environment. It can range from getting lost in thought while driving and realizing that you have arrived at your destination, to the absence of affect while thinking about previous upsetting traumas (emotional numbing) and feeling that one is detached from one's body, to peritraumatic dissociation during trauma triggers and exposures. When trauma is chronic, children will rely on dissociation as a coping method to manage the overwhelming feelings of distress associated with the traumatic experiences. This can lead to disrupted self-regulation of behavior, affect, and self perception (Putnam, 1997).

Behavioral regulation. Adversity-exposed children often come to the clinician's awareness because of behavioral problems. The children may evidence internalizing or externalizing behaviors or both. Impulsivity, aggression, oppositional and defiant behaviors, problems with following rules, accepting limits, or being overly compliant with adults is common.

Cognition. Children reared in abusive homes show cognitive deficits by late infancy (Egeland et al., 1983). Neglectful parents may not provide the emotional support, sensory stimulation, or opportunities to engage in enriched language and problem-solving experiences needed for development. Over time, these children show delays in language functioning and overall intelligence, which contributes to their academic achievement difficulties.

Complex trauma, toxic stress, and effects on brain development. Many factors are important for normal brain development including adequate prenatal care, nutritious diet, access to quality medical care, positive interactions with others, exposure to enriched experiences, warm, responsive caregiving, and the security of a safe living environment.

TYPICAL BRAIN DEVELOPMENT

To understand how stress and adverse experiences can negatively influence the brain, the following is a brief discussion of normal brain development and neuronal structure. This discussion is intended to provide a context to identify disruptive influences which might occur to children living in adverse environments.

Stiles (2010) stated human brain development is a protracted process which begins in the third gestational week and extends throughout adolescence (and arguably throughout the lifespan). This process depends on the dynamic and complex interaction of inherited factors (genes and the cellular mechanisms that express the information coded in the genes) and the environmental context. Acting together and in concert, these factors direct the processes which gives rise to neural architecture, structure, and function.

At all phases of growth and change, neurobiological processes and the child's unique environmental experiences help guide and direct the developing brain. After a child is born, the role of experience in defining patterns of brain organization and connectivity becomes more pronounced. The postnatal period has been defined as the time of experience-expectant learning whereby brain systems are programmed to expect certain types of experiential input from the environment in order to develop normally.

Based on information from neuroscience, this is why early childhood experiences can have such a profound effect on child development especially during the first five years of life. The following is only a basic review of important aspects of nervous system structures and functions and was retrieved from the following sources: Cognitive Neuroscience: The Biology of the Mind (Gazzaniga et al., 2014); Neuroscience, Fourth Edition (Eds. Purves et al.. 2008) and Fundamentals of Human Neuropsychology, Seventh Edition, (Kolb & Whishaw, 2015).

The brain develops sequentially from the bottom (caudal), and then upwards (rostral). Primitive areas which control autonomic functions such as heart rate, breathing, and blood pressure mature first, with higher-order cognitive functions such as reasoning and abstract thought developing as the child matures postnatally. Growth occurs from the posterior part of the brain forward to the anterior regions with the prefrontal cortex continuing to mature into the third decade of life (ZERO TO THREE, 2012). The human nervous system is comprised of two classes of cells: neurons and glial cells (often called neuroglia). *Neurons* are specialized signaling cells in the brain which function to transmit information to other nerve cells, muscles, and glands. *Glial cells* are nonneural cells, meaning that they lack the property to actually transmit rapid electrical signals to other cells, though some glial cells play a role in modulating neuronal activity and supporting neurotransmission. There are several types of glial cells whose additional functions include providing structural mechanical support, and maintaining ionic balance in the extracellular space. Some glial cells create the fatty myelin sheaths coating neuronal axons, allowing for rapid, efficient electrical communication within the brain by speeding up conduction of electrical impulses. Neurons consist of a cell body (soma) with nucleus, branching dendrites, *axons* (the neuron extensions which conduct signals away from the cell body to other cells), and nerve endings (also known as *axon terminals*).

Cell bodies contain the cell's DNA and structure which provides energy to the neuron. *Dendrites* are tree-like branching projections from the cell body that receive inputs from other neurons. The more dendrites exist, the greater potential for brain connectivity and networks. Axons are the main conducting unit for relaying nerve impulses and extend from the cell body. Many axons split into several branches carrying information to different target cells. Cells which wrap around axons within the central nervous system (oligodendrocytes) create the fatty myelin sheath which speeds nerve cell electrical transmission. Axons terminate in endfeet or terminal buttons which house synaptic vesicles. Chemical synaptic vesicles contain chemical messengers or neurotransmitters which are released into a small gap known as the synaptic cleft when a nerve cell fires. Neurotransmitters bind to the cell membrane of the postsynaptic neuron, which are called receptor sites. Depending on the type of neuron, location, and neurotransmitter released, the postsynaptic neuron can be activated to fire or be inhibited from firing.

Common Neurotransmitters

Acetylcholine is a widely distributed neurotransmitter which is involved in attentiveness, wakefulness, attention, and memory, among other things. Decreases in acetylcholine in certain parts of the brain are considered to be related to Alzheimer's disease.

Dopamine is involved in controlling motor movement. It is also involved in the brain's reward and pleasure centers. It is associated with addictive drugs and addiction. Increases in dopamine activity may be linked to schizophrenia, while decreases in dopamine are considered to be related to ADHD.

Norepinephrine is important for sleep, emotions, and learning, among other things. Decreased norepinephrine is implicated in both depression and ADHD.

Serotonin plays roles in wakefulness, sleep, appetite, regulating body temperature, and mood. It is tied to several mental health diagnoses including depression, anxiety, and obsessive-compulsive disorder.

Hormones, drugs, and other substances can mimic neurotransmitters or disrupt their function and activity.

Circuits in the brain with similar functions are grouped into neural systems and can be broken down into three general system classifications:

1. Sensory systems such as vision and hearing which acquire and process information from the environment.
2. Motor systems allow the organism to respond to such information to generate movement and actions.
3. Associational systems link the sensory and motor systems to provide the basis for higher-order brain functioning including perception, attention, cognition, memory, language, thinking and learning and emotions (Purves et al., 2008).

ATYPICAL BRAIN DEVELOPMENT ASSOCIATED WITH CHILDHOOD TRAUMA TOXIC

The following discussion is from the National Scientific Council on the Developing Child (2005/2014) *Excessive Stress Disrupts the Architecture of the Developing Brain: Working Paper 3*. Updated Edition.

There is a significant body of research outlining the mechanisms involved in how postnatal exposure to stress can have disruptive and detrimental consequences for the brain and other organ systems, especially in infancy and early childhood. Not all stressful adverse experiences are harmful. Some stress exposure is normative, expected, and necessary for infants and children to facilitate a normal biological stress response system, learn to self-regulate, and develop the coping skills needed to deal with future stressors and adversity. Several important points including categories of positive, tolerable, and toxic stress are simplified here for discussion as a way to conceptualize the potentially damaging way that ACES can affect the biologic stress responses and developing organ systems including the brain. Other biological, genetic, temperamental, and social factors can affect children's vulnerability to negative, stress-related outcomes. Studies suggest that it is the presence or absence of high-quality nurturance provided by caregivers that mediates whether children become resilient in handling stress and adversity in adaptive ways, or whether aversive experiences result in impairment and compromised development.

Positive stress is the presence of an upsetting experience or challenge accompanied by cognitive and biological processes that activates the stress system. These stressors are generally mild, and not prolonged and expected in the course of normal childhood experiences such as when a young child receives a vaccination.

The stress response is activated when this occurs, causing biological changes such as a mild elevation in stress hormones such as cortisol, and an increase in heart rate and blood pressure. When a caregiver reacts to the child's distress in warm, responsive, and positive ways, this allows children to calm down, manage, and adapt to mildly aversive experiences. This is essential for healthy child development. Other positive stressors include dealing with typical frustrations or facing new environmental and experiential challenges.

Tolerable stress is typically associated with more negative experiences and a higher activation of the body's stress response systems. Although distressing, the stressor generally tends to be time-limited. The presence of a responsive, nurturing caregiver at these times allows the child's stress system to recover and return to homeostatic balance or baseline, and the child's distress is alleviated. Examples of tolerable stressors include a childhood illness or injury, or exposure to a stressful adverse experience of a serious nature. Facing tolerable stress with responsive caregiving allows children to learn that there are others who will provide safety and comfort in a reliable and consistent manner. Adverse experiences become tolerable within the context of the caregiver-child relationship. Children with this support can learn and develop coping skills to manage difficult experiences, negative affect, and strong emotions.

The term *toxic* refers to serious and significantly distressing adverse experiences which tend to be chronic and occur without the buffering of supportive caregiving. Parents may be absent or unable to adequately attend to the needs of their offspring, leaving children to deal with distressing experiences without comfort or solace. Toxic stress also occurs when the adults children rely on for help and protection are the same people who are the source of the child's fear and aversive experiences. This causes significant distress for the child, and results in prolonged activation and hyperarousal of stress systems. Without the protection of adult support, this frequent or ongoing stress system activation can disrupt and compromise brain development, the immune system, and other organ systems, and potentially lead to vulnerability to future stress-related problems and mental and physical illnesses well into adulthood.

THE STRESS SYSTEMS

The immune system, stress systems, and the brain are interconnected, shaped, and influenced by one's experiences in the environment. Johnson et al. (2013) states "it is virtually impossible to parse the impact of experience on the developing brain from its simultaneous impact on the stress response and immune system" (p. 320).

Immediate Response to Threat

There are two interrelated stress response systems which work together and regulate the body's adaptation to stress and traumatic experiences. One is the sympathetic-adrenomedullary (SAM) system, a part of the autonomic nervous system. SAM activates the physiological responses needed for quick, immediate action to respond to danger. When a real or perceived threat is detected, the hypothalamus (a brain structure sitting above the brainstem) triggers the sympathetic nervous system by the adrenal glands to activate a fight or flight response. Epinephrine and norepinephrine are released into the circulatory system, where they activate multiple target organs. This immediately results in significant physiological changes. Heart rate, pulmonary function, and blood pressure all increase; our pupils dilate, and blood is pumped to skeletal muscles. Activation of these systems mobilizes our body's resources, maximizes vigilance, attention, and alertness, and allows us to act offensively, defensively, or flee the danger. This high-alert readiness for action in response to a threat increases the chances that the organism will survive.

A Slower Response to Stress: The HPA Axis

The second component in mounting a stress response to threat is the Hypothalamic-Pituitary-Adrenocortical Axis (HPA Axis). Sometimes the HPA axis is referred to as the Limbic-Hypothalamic-Pituitary-Adrenocortical (LHPA) axis to note limbic system involvement.

The HPA axis is not fully mature at birth and develops with age. Experience is important in shaping the reactivity of the HPA (Gunnar & Donzella, 2001).

Norepinephrine in the central nervous system is involved in activating the HPA axis (Gunnar & Quevedo, 2007). In addition to the quickly acting SAM, the slower-reacting HPA axis functions are also initiated as the result of internal or external threats, regardless of whether that danger is real or perceived.

At the moment of stress perception and with other limbic system input, the hypothalamus releases a corticotropin-releasing hormone (CRH). CRH acts on the pituitary gland (a small, peanut shaped structure located at the base of the skull), causing it to release the hormone adrenocorticotropin (ACTH). ACTH travels through the bloodstream to the adrenal glands which are situated on top of the kidneys. In the outer part of the adrenal glands (the adrenal cortex), steroid hormones called glucocorticoids are produced and secreted, one of which in humans is cortisol. Cortisol serves many purposes including involvement with memory and emotional expression. The principle function of cortisol is to restore homeostasis following stress exposure. Unlike the immediate effects on the body with the release of epinephrine and norepinephrine, the cortisol production and effects are slower. The result of glucocorticoids acting on their target tissues can alter gene transcription, which helps explain why there can be lasting physiological effects on the individual from stress response activation (Sapolsky et al., 2000a,b). Even without threat or danger, varying levels of cortisol wax and wane throughout the circadian cycle. The highest levels are in the morning and the lowest concentrations are at night. This pattern of rising and falling levels throughout the day allows our bodies to have energy for the morning and rest at night. These fluctuations are typical and healthy. When experiencing stress, the body produces additional cortisol to deal with perceived danger. Cortisol elevates glucose or blood sugar production for increased energy to fuel the physiological processes to prepare our bodies to deal with danger.

Cortisol functions to keep the body charged and on high alert. When we perceive that the threat to safety has subsided, cortisol levels decrease by signaling back to the hypothalamus and the stress response is dampened by this negative feedback mechanism. The prefrontal cortex of the brain and limbic forebrain structures are also involved in this feedback loop. Other important structures in modulating this process are the amygdala and hippocampus (Bernard et al., 2015; Gunnar & Quevedo, 2007; Harvard Medical School, 2016; Jacoby et al., 2016; Sapolsky et al., 2000a,b; Tarullo & Gunnar, 2006).

The Role of Stress Glucocorticoids and the Developing Brain

Normal brain development occurs with an overabundance of neurons, increases in neuronal growth, and increases in neural connections in utero, throughout childhood and adolescence, and on into young adulthood. An over production of synapses, dendrites, and axons is typical in the perinatal period followed by programmed cell death or apoptosis. This allows for selective pruning, in which some neural connections are reduced, while others are strengthened.

The myelination of neurons allows for greater connectivity of developing brain regions as myelinated axons transmit signals more rapidly than unmyelinated nerve cells. Both suppressed and elevated levels of glucocorticoids can happen with continued activation of the stress response, or occur with dysregulated stress response systems which are thought to adversely affect programmed apoptosis resulting in delays in myelination, disruptions in pruning, and the suppression of new cell growth (Discussed in De Bellis & Zisk, 2014 and Bick & Nelson, 2016). Glucocorticoids can damage neurons in several brain structures of the HPA axis such as the prefrontal cortex, the amygdala, hippocampus, and the corpus callosum and cerebellum. These areas are particularly vulnerable because of their high number of glucocorticoid receptors and their protracted development period, which makes them more vulnerable to the toxic effects of glucocorticoid exposure.

Children with chronic trauma and maltreatment backgrounds are known to have cortisol-regulating abnormalities suggesting stress response impairment. Ongoing activation of these systems and the increased neuronal connectivity results in sensitizing these stress networks. Children may then process other sensory input from this fear template; this is why we often see them respond to even minor stress with overblown responses. Often teachers and parents will comment that "the smallest thing sets him off" or that "she was fine this morning until something of little consequence happened and she had a meltdown" (Perry et al. 1995). Hyperarousal, dissociation, behavioral and emotional dysregulation, irritability, and fight-flight or freeze responses are frequently evident and related to physiological alterations in developing stress systems because of chronic trauma.

NEUROIMAGING

For many years, autopsy was the only way to document structural differences in people with known disorders or diseases years.

Advances in imaging science and computer assisted technology now allow us to monitor electrical and chemical activity in the brain, providing researchers with real-time functional, structural, molecular, and electrical information to better understand the clinical associations of brain-behavior-pathology relationships. Brain imaging is particularly relevant in the study of the impacts of early life adversity and stress on the developing nervous system by comparing the brain imaging of children who experienced significant traumatic stress with control groups of children who have not. Electroencephalograph techniques and neuroimaging yields important information about the timing, sequence, and processes of brain alterations often seen with adversity-exposed children. This can help with designing preventative programs and treatment planning, and help to understand what typical and normal brain development looks like in children.

While there are many studies focusing on maltreated children and adults who report histories of maltreatment, there are several limitations. Hart and Rubia (2012) explained how many maltreated individuals also carry co-morbid psychiatric diagnoses such as depression, anxiety, eating disorders, and conduct problems. It is difficult to determine if neuroimaging differences in structure and function exist because of abuse or neglect or psychiatric conditions. Some subjects may be treated for their psychiatric conditions by taking prescribed psychotropic medications which are designed to influence brain functioning. While many studies control for these factors by including or excluding individuals on medication, this also can pose problems interpreting results. Even with these concerns, neuroimaging research efforts on the effects of significant early life stressors on the brain are increasingly valuable to better understand the relationship between environmental experiences, brain plasticity, sensitive and critical periods of development, and child developmental outcomes.

Commonly Used Neuroimaging Methods

Computed Tomography (CT) scanning provides images of the gross structure of the brain by passing X-rays through the head. CT scans combine a series of X-ray images taken from different angles using computer processing to create cross sectional images, or slices of the brain. With CT, the X-ray beam moves in a circle around the body allowing for many different views of brain structure. CT scans are useful for patients with stroke symptoms, skull fractures, and acute head trauma. Concerns with CT scans on children are related to exposing them to radiation and possible deleterious health effects.

Magnetic Resonance Imaging (MRI) of the brain uses a magnetic field and radio waves to produce detailed images of the brain and the brainstem. Water molecules in the body contain hydrogen protons which react with magnetic fields. Magnetized hydrogen protons align in relation to the field. A radio frequency is applied to the magnetic field. As the hydrogen protons realign back into their normal position, they send out radio signals which are analyzed and converted by a computer into images. MRIs offer a higher resolution view of neuroanatomical structures than CT scans and do not use X-rays. Sometimes a contrast medium is used to improve visualization in brain regions of interest (ROI).

Diffusion Tensor Imaging (DTI) is an MRI method which allows the study of the micromolecular environment of the brain's white matter, the nerve fiber pathways, and the brain's connectivity.

Functional Magnetic Resonance Imaging (fMRI) provides functional data of cerebral activity during given tasks such as motor or cognitive tasks. fMRI is based on blood oxygenation (tissue perfusion). Increased blood flow is correlated with increased neuronal activity.

Electroencephalogram(EEG). While it does not produce neurological visual images of structure and functioning of the brain, an EEG provides data on the brain's electrical activity. An EEG scans, tracks, and records brainwave patterns. EEG is typically used to evaluate and diagnosis seizure disorders and sleep disturbances.

(See Noggle et al., 2011 for a full review of neuroimaging technology and brain diagnostic procedures).

Neurobiological Alterations Associated with Early Childhood Trauma: Functions and Implications for Clinicians

Because of the brain's plasticity, multifunctionality of structures and systems, and connectivity throughout brain regions, trying to associate behaviors to particular structures in a one-to-one manner belies the complexity of the human brain. And that is with typical development. With trauma-exposed children who may not be following a normally-expected developmental trajectory, it becomes even more difficult to understand how neurobiological alterations associated with trauma may affect their functioning.

There are several types of maltreatment (including sexual abuse, physical abuse, neglect, psychological or emotional abuse, and witnessing intimate partner violence). Some studies have looked at the effects of maltreatment in general or studied a particular type of abuse, like sexual abuse, on outcome measures. Some studies have focused on youth who already carry a DSM-5 diagnosis, such as children with PTSD. Many children experiencing early adverse life experiences do not experience one type of trauma. It is common for vulnerable children to have many psychosocial stressors impinging on them: poverty, living in dangerous neighborhoods, being raised by parents who may have experienced abuse themselves as children. These factors can confound research results, making it hard to tease out individual contributions for particular ACES. Brain regions and structures are highly interconnected, highly interdependent, and may have many functions on different biological systems. The hippocampus is a heterogeneous, multi-function structure with various sub-regions involved with the stress responses, anxiety, learning and memory and emotional processing. Even when there are differences in brain structure area, volume, or connectivity associated with trauma, clinicians need to be cautious about interpreting areas of possible deficits for any particular child. If studies show maltreated children have a smaller corpus callosum, one cannot assume that all children with adversity backgrounds will have a smaller corpus callosum and then make inferences about associated lower IQ. Even though the corpus callosum plays a role in higher-order cognitive functioning, this finding of smaller brain structure should be interpreted as only a risk factor and not a one-to-one mapping of brain structure to a particular area of functioning. Even with these caveats, there is ample evidence that childhood traumatic experiences can disrupt development, throw children off an adaptive developmental trajectory, alter brain architecture and function, and negatively influence children's cognitive, academic, social-emotional, adaptive, and behavioral outcomes.

Children are not miniature adults and a key feature when working with children includes understanding expected capacities at typical development stages. We assume that two-year-olds may be oppositional, defiant, and impulsive with underdeveloped regulation of affect and behavior. The brain processes involved in controlling those functions are immature in toddlerhood. We do not expect to see those behaviors in a 12-year-old. Child development norms must be taken into account for assessing and treating childhood problems for all children and adolescents. Children with trauma exposure are particularly vulnerable for not meeting developmental milestones or mastering developmental tasks, so knowledge of typical and atypical development is even more important with this population.

The Cerebrum and Cerebral Cortex

The central nervous system is made up two types of nerve cells. Gray matter (neuronal cell bodies and unmyelinated axons) processes information in the brain. White matter is myelinated nerve cells, because their fatty coating speeds up nerve cell transmission of information from cell to cell in other brain areas. Hale and Fiorello use a metaphor to exemplify the difference between gray and white matter. They suggest that you can think of the gray matter as houses and neighborhoods (where information processing occurs depending on the brain regions involved) and white matter as streets and highways of connectivity among brain regions and structures. A consistent finding in studies of institutionalized children with early deprivation shows a reduction in cortical gray and white matter. De Bellis et al. (1999) found trauma-exposed children with early onset and longer duration of abuse with a PTSD diagnosis had smaller intracranial and cerebral volumes than control children. Poverty is also associated with attenuated cortical gray and white matter (Teicher & Samson, 2016).

Functions. The cerebral cortex is comprised of a left and right hemisphere and is divided into four major lobes: the occipital, temporal, parietal, and frontal. The occipital lobe is involved the visual system and visual processing; the temporal lobe controls sound processing, language functioning and memory. The parietal lobe processes sensory information and is involved with spatial relations, and the frontal lobe handles motor operations and executive functioning skills such as planning and organizational skills. Certain areas of the cortex, such as primary cortices, receive sensory input such as visual and auditory information, or are involved with body movement. Cortical association areas include higher-order cognitive functions such as problem-solving, learning, memory, attention, language, emotional responses, judgment, and goal-directed behaviors.

Risk factors. Overall reductions in gray and white matter associated with neglect and trauma can make children vulnerable to various sensory, motor, and cognitive problems including milestone delays, developmental delays, lower IQ, language, attention, learning, and memory deficits, slower processing speed, and problems with activities of daily living (ADL). Children exposed to alcohol in utero, which is not unusual with traumatized children, can have various brain abnormalities. The most common are reduced brain volume and malformations of the corpus callosum, which is the largest white matter tract connecting the two brain hemispheres (Lebel et al., 2011). When there are concerns a child may have a fetal alcohol spectrum disorder, suitable referrals need to be made as it is a complex medical diagnosis. Updated clinical guidelines recommend a multidisciplinary clinical team approach. Team members need to include physicians such as pediatricians and may include psychiatrists, clinical geneticists, psychologists, occupational and physical therapists, and special educators (Hoyme et al., 2016).

Limbic System

Hippocampus

Many studies show a relationship with adults who report a history of early adverse life experiences and smaller hippocampal volumes as compared to adults who report no history of early adverse experiences (Teicher et al., 2012; reviewed in Teicher & Samson, 2016). There are mixed results on hippocampal volumes in traumatized children. De Bellis and colleagues found no hippocampus volume reductions in maltreated children (De Bellis et al,. 2001). In contrast to studies with adults, one study reported larger hippocampi in children and adolescents with PTSD following childhood abuse (Tupler & De Bellis, 2006). One hypothesis is that adversity-related effects on hippocampal volume of the hippocampus may not manifest until after childhood (Tottenham & Sheridan, 2009).

Functions. The hippocampus is a part of the limbic system and is located deep within the temporal lobe. It has extensive connections to other areas such as the amygdala, hypothalamus, and cortical association areas. It is involved with several systems and processes. It plays a regulatory role in the negative feedback loop with the HPA stress system as cortisol effects on the hippocampus shuts down the stress response.

It also plays major roles in learning and memory, especially episodic and spatial memory (Kolb & Whishaw, 2015). The hippocampus is crucial for most memory processing including encoding, consolidation, and memory retrieval. Carrion and Wong (2012) studied youth between age 10–17 with PTSD and history of interpersonal trauma. During a verbal memory task, the youth with PTSD evidenced reduced activity of the hippocampus with reduced retrieval accuracy on the task. In addition to learning and memory, the hippocampus is involved in social behavior, attention, and motivation (Farmer-Dougan et al., 2011).

Risk factors. Intact memory processing is related to other cognitive processes and is crucial for learning and all academic achievement in reading, written language, and mathematics. When assessing children with adversity histories, clinicians may find it useful to have added measures of learning and memory functioning including tests of short-term memory, working memory, and long-term memory in the visual and verbal domains, as well as long-term memory retrieval and recognition, narrative and episodic memory, and memory consolidation. Information from spatial memory tasks may be useful as children with trauma backgrounds may have problems remembering object locations and navigating their whereabouts in school and other settings, may forget where their classroom is located, and may wander in the halls unsure of where they need to be at a given time. Spatial memory facilitates the acquisition of early mathematical skills and may be especially important for younger children who rely more on visual spatial memory when initially learning math (Discussed in Van de Weijer-Bergsma et al., 2015). Other memory problems may include forgetting conversations and activities in daily living (Vargha-Khadem et al., 1997). When treating and providing psychosocial interventions for trauma-exposed youth, especially those who meet criteria for psychopathological disorders, clinicians should be aware they may forget appointments, clinical homework assignments, and information processed in a previous therapy session. With episodic and autobiographical memory deficits there may be difficulties remembering their trauma and relevant family histories. Trauma-focused cognitive behavior therapy in which a trauma narrative is created for therapeutic purposes can also be affected, hindering positive outcomes.

Amygdala

Although some studies have not found differences in amygdala structure in maltreated children, some newer investigations showed smaller amygdala volumes in children exposed to abuse and neglect. Infants with depressed mothers, a risk factor for unresponsive caregiving and neglect, were observed over time. MRI scans when these children grew up and were in their late childhood revealed a positive association between mother's depression and amygdala size (reviewed in Bick & Nelson, 2016).

Functions. The amygdala is a complex collection of nuclei located in the medial temporal lobe of the brain. It is extensively connected with many brain regions including the hypothalamus, hippocampus, and prefrontal cortex. It is part of the limbic and stress systems and plays a critical role in fear conditioning, emotional learning, reactivity to emotional stimuli, and social information processing. The amygdala is also implicated in the psychopathology of anxiety disorders. In primate studies, stimulation of the amygdala and associated neuroendocrine centers activated fear centers with anxiety symptoms such as hypervigilance and hyperarousal (Kolb & Whishaw, 2015). The amygdala plays a role in social judgment and cognition and is activated when perceiving relevant social signals such as eye gaze, emotional cues, and facial expression (discussed in Baron-Cohen et al., 2000). Social conventions such as abiding by personal boundaries and recognizing the importance of personal space has also been associated with the amygdala (Kennedy et al., 2009). Standing too close to others can be intrusive and make them feel uncomfortable, alienating peers and adults, compounding interpersonal communication skill difficulties which may already be present. Young people who were identified as having callous-unemotional traits showed a reduced amygdala response when viewing fearful expressions (Marsh et al., 2008). This suggests perhaps a difficulty or inability to accurately interpret the expressions (particularly fear) of others, and is implicated in autism with the hippocampal formation, frontal cortex, and limbic-frontal connections (discussed in Baron-Cohen et al., 2000). The amygdala, like the hippocampus, is particularly vulnerable to the effects of chronic trauma because of its high number of glucocorticoid receptors and increasing neural connections which continue to develop until adolescence.

Risk factors. High reactivity and emotional alertness are common among mistreated youth. Trauma-exposed children are hypervigilant to environmental cues likely because of disrupted early attachments and fear associated with abuse. While this has acted as a survival mechanism because of legitimate fears in their experiences, it is detrimental to their social interactions. These children may not have been exposed to learning and modeling pro-social behaviors from the adults who care for them. If there is conflict within the home, especially for children who have been exposed to intimate partner violence, more peaceful ways to solve social problems have not been demonstrated to act as exemplars. What is learned is that aggression is a legitimate way to get your needs met and to solve social problems. High emotional reactivity may exacerbate these problems. Amygdala dysfunction can cause children to perceive threat and fear in benign situations. This can hinder them from picking up and processing other important social cues and learn more adaptive responses to positive interactions with others (Rodriguez et al., 2016).

Children with aggression problems often misperceive social situations and make hostile attributions to environmental stimuli (Crick & Dodge, 1996). Trauma-exposed children often evidence problems with personal boundaries and indiscriminate friendliness with strangers. These children are often described as "loving" or "clingy" as they may hug strangers and be affectionate to adults they do not know putting them at further risk for abuse. Typically developing children know that those they do know provide comfort and safety and do not seek this type attention from strangers. They may be overly suspicious, avoidant, and distrustful when engaging with others due to their histories of maltreatment as noted above. They may have problems with emotional identification and emotional regulation which can make it difficult for them to understand and follow social conventions, make and keep friends, and engage in meaningful and reciprocal peer and adult relationships. Children with social competency deficits are particularly at risk for poor outcomes as they mature into adulthood. Understanding the association between trauma and children's social-emotional functioning allows clinicians to be proactive in early identification of children needing further assessment and interventions for social competency and social-emotional learning. Getting a detailed history on social skills from caregivers, teachers, direct observations, or inventories allows for targeted treatment planning. Since anxiety, depression, and trauma symptoms may be co-morbid, these symptoms can be assessed and treated as well. Screening for anxiety even in young children can be particularly helpful and monitoring over time for changes in symptom severity and impairment is a proactive way to intervene before anxiety becomes more debilitating or pervasive. Anxiety is the most common disorder in children and there are evidence-based interventions to alleviate symptoms and improve functioning. Social-emotional capacities are directly tied to early child-parent interactions. Examining those relationships with interviews or attachment-related assessment instruments can help with gaining a more thorough clinical picture of the child. Since anxiety, emotional regulation, and social skill competency deficits are more common with this population, more proactive interventions such as teaching emotional regulation, empathy, coping skills, mindfulness, relaxation methods, and social skills may help prevent more serious problems as children grow and develop.

Structural Connectivity: The Corpus Callosum
An early and consistent finding in the study of maltreatment and brain alterations in children is smaller structure and reduced integrity of the corpus callosum (De Bellis et al., 1999; Teicher et al., 2004). Several studies suggest boys may be more adversely affected than girls (De Bellis et al., 2002a,b,c; Teicher

et al., 2004). Gender and maltreatment type-specific results indicate neglect was most associated with corpus callosum abnormalities for boys and sexual abuse for girls (Teicher et al., 2004).

Functions and risk factors. The corpus callosum is the largest white matter structure in the brain connecting the homologous areas of the cortex and facilitates communication between the left and right cortical hemispheres. With more than 190 million axons, which allows for integrating neural processes, it is vulnerable to the early impacts of trauma as high levels of stress hormones interfere with glial cell division, crucial for myelination. Like other brain architecture, the development of the corpus callosum is also dependent on experience. Because of its many and elaborate connections to other brain regions, most brain functions and systems are affected by altered corpus callosum development.

Sleep problems, impaired social functioning, somatic complaints, and unusual thoughts are also reported (see Badaruddin et al., 2007 for discussion).

In the cognitive domain, the corpus callosum positively correlates with general intelligence and higher IQ, problem-solving, visual and spatial capacities, short-term visual and spatial memory, long-term verbal memory, abstract reasoning, processing speed, executive functioning, and social cognition (Hinkley et al., 2012; Kolb & Whishaw, 2015; Penke et al., 2010). Growth patterns of the corpus callosum continue as children mature. This strengthens the connectivity and efficiency of information transmission of brain regions over time and affects development of higher-order cognitive processes (Pechtel & Pizzagalli, 2011). The basic skills needed for reading such as manipulating basic sound structures of language, phonological processing, and phonological awareness are associated with corpus callosum development. Research indicates more proficient readers have larger corpus callosum area and white matter integrity than less skilled readers. The arcuate fasciculus, another fiber tract connecting Wernicke's area (located in the temporal lobe) to Broca's area (positioned in the frontal lobe) is also implicated in reading and crucial for oral language and language comprehension (Wandall & Yeatman, 2012). Those with adverse histories may evidence dissociative symptoms, disruptions in the usually integrated functions of self and consciousness. There was an association between the Child Dissociative Checklist scores neuroimaging study hypothesizing those dissociative symptoms may be due to less connectivity in the corpus callosum for maltreated children and adolescents (De Bellis et al., 1999). Other problems associated with altered corpus callosum functioning in children and adolescents include sensory-motor deficits, sleep disturbances, impaired social functioning, somatic complaints, and odd and unusual thoughts (see Badaruddin et al., 2007 for discussion). Reduced size of the corpus callosum is associated with diminished communication between the cortical hemispheres. In adult studies, diminished functioning of the corpus callosum contributes to a decline in cognitive functioning in the aged (Zahr et al., 2009).

Agenesis (the absence) or hypogenesis (partial absence) of the corpus callosum is among the most common brain malformations in humans. For children with developmental disabilities its prevalence is 2–3 affected per 100 (Bedeschi et al., 2006; Jeret et al., 1986). A commissurectomy (surgical severing) of the cerebral commissures has been a treatment for intractable epilepsy when medication is not effective in controlling seizures, preventing electrical activity from crossing over to the other side of the brain. Altered connectivity of the corpus callosum is seen in ADHD, autism, bipolar disorder, and schizophrenia. Genetic influences are associated with these disorders as well (Hinkley et al., 2012). Understanding the many capacities and skill acquisitions affected by the corpus callosum allows clinicians to monitor for a wide range of potential problems with at-risk children.

Cerebellum

The cerebellum, located under the occipital and temporal lobes in the posterior of the brain is best known for its role in motor learning, motor coordination, balance, and postural control (Evarts & Thach, 1969). There is considerable evidence that many non-motor related functions are integral parts of cerebellar activities including emotional processing, fear conditioning, language, cognitive capacities, understanding of social intentions, and executive functions (Discussed in De Bellis & Zisk, 2014; McCrory et al., 2010). The cerebellum is implicated in many psychiatric disorders including ADHD, schizophrenia, and Autistic Spectrum Disorders (ASDs), bipolar disorder, major depressive disorder, and anxiety disorders (Phillips et al., 2015; Shevelkin et al., 2014). Consistent findings in the maltreatment literature point to altered cerebellar development, smaller cerebellar volumes, and reduced gray matter in children with histories of adversity, early institutionalization, and PTSD diagnoses (Bauer et al., 2009; Carrion et al., 2009; De Bellis et al., 2014; De Bellis et al., 2015; Teicher & Samson, 2016).

Functions. The cerebellum is responsible for a wide and varied range of brain functions and processes because of its vast array of networks with other brain regions. Studies indicate its contributory role in emotional processing including evaluating emotional cues, emotional learning, regulation, modulation, perception, and emotional recognition (Adamaszek et al., 2016). It also plays a role in language processing and is involved in phonological working memory, semantic verbal fluency, verbal working memory, syntax processing, language production, rhyming tasks, verbal prosody, and reading and written language (see consensus paper on language and the cerebellum, 2014 and Booth et al., 2007). Cognitive processes and executive functions associated with the cerebellum include working memory, decision-making, and planning abilities, and are associated with its neural pathways with the prefrontal cortex (Bauer et al., 2009).

Risk factors. Understanding the neural connectivity of brain regions helps to appreciate how different brain regions work together to determine functional outcomes and areas of possible vulnerability for the child. With regard to the cerebellum, its associations with mediating cognitive, emotional, and executive functions as well as academic skills allows clinicians to also take into consideration how more primary association areas for such capacities might also be involved for children's presenting problems. Knowing that the cerebellum has an associative role in reading and written language and that the temporal and frontal lobes are primarily involved with those functions, and also may be negatively affected by early traumatic experiences provides additional information to clinicians about potential risk factors in those domains.

Temporal Lobe

The lobes of the brain have intra-lobe connections from the outer cortex to deeper structures within the lobe and inter-lobe connections among various brain regions. The amygdale is located in the temporal lobe and connects to many other brain regions including the hippocampus, hypothalamus, and frontal cortex, all involved in the stress response systems. The arcuate fasciculus runs from the temporal lobe to the frontal lobe and is a language processing pathway. The prefrontal cortex coordinates processing across wide regions of the brain with networks which link the motor, perceptual, and limbic regions (Gazzaniga et al., 2014). This massive network architecture allows structured communication among various regions, structures, and systems.

Temporal-Parietal Regions

Studies on diversity-related brain alterations of the temporal lobe have been mixed. De Bellis et al. (2002a,b) discovered that children and adolescents with PTSD when compared to control groups had larger right-sided gray matter volumes of the superior temporal gyrus (STG). Comorbidities included major depressive disorder, oppositional defiant disorder, and ADHD. They hypothesized that auditory traumatic reminders may lead to enhanced hypervigilance and behavioral dysregulation. Tomoda et al., (2011) found young adults with histories of parental verbal abuse had larger gray matter volumes of the left STG. Lesions in the posterior region of the STG typically result in language comprehension deficits associated with Wernicke's area, and temporal lobe structures may be particularly susceptible to early verbal abuse. Exposure to high levels of verbal abuse could potentially stimulate this area and alter its normal development. In a study of maltreated children from London, England, De Brito et al. (2013) found children with maltreatment histories had reduced gray matter in the left lateral temporal gyrus. Hanson et al. (2010) also found smaller brain volumes in the left inferior temporal pole and right middle temporal lobe in children who were physically abused. Electroencephalographic brain wave differences are similar to what is found in temporal lobe epilepsy and diminished development of the left hemispheres to those exposed to childhood trauma (Teicher, 2000).

In addition to significantly reduced gray matter in the left and right medial temporal lobes, Kelly et al. (2015) discovered children with verified maltreatment experiences had significantly reduced bilateral gray matter volumes in the supramarginal gyri of the inferior parietal lobe as well as the orbitofrontal cortex (OFC). They noted the maltreated group had more peer problems and emotional reactivity.

Functions. The temporal lobes are important for organizing sensory input, auditory processing, memory formation and categorization, emotional processing, visual object and facial recognition, and synthesizing past and present emotional and sensory experiences to create a continuous sense of self. The primary auditory cortex, responsible for processing sounds, acoustic information, phonological aspects of speech, perception, and production are housed in the STG (Buchsbaum et al., 2001; Warrier et al., 2009) as is Wernicke's Area, responsible for language comprehension. The STG is networked with the amygdala and prefrontal cortex, and involved in social cognition (discussed in Hale & Fiorello, 2004).

The medial temporal lobe consists of structures which are vital for semantic processing and the conscious memory for facts and events (declarative memory) because of networks with hippocampal and related regions buried deep with the temporal lobe. Declarative memory is the capacity to recollect events, situations, and facts not associated with non-declarative memory such as motor memory, which is based on performance rather than recollection. (Learning to ride a bicycle is an example of motor memory as once it is mastered, you do not consciously need to remember individual steps such as first placing your foot on the pedal, pushing off with other leg, etc. . . . .). Damage to the medial temporal lobe is hallmarked by profound forgetfulness, although immediate memory for simple material is intact (such as skills required for a digit-span task). Often perceptual abilities, vocabulary, and overall intellectual functions are intact. Psychologists are aware of the case study with H.M. who had damage to the hippocampal formation. Dysfunction of the medial temporal lobe has enormous implications for learning and school performance. Squire et al. (2004) reported that if the medial temporal lobe is not operating at the time of learning, memory is not consolidated in a usable way and is not available later for retrieval. Hale and Fiorello (2004) stated that the medial temporal lobe, because of neuronal network connections, is also involved with attention and emotion. Autobiographical memory and retrieval is associated with the medial temporal gyrus.

Because of projections from the occipital lobe to the temporal lobe, the inferior temporal gyrus, located below the medial temporal lobe, is part of the ventral stream of visual processing associated with the representation of object features such as shape and object quality. Ventral pathway representations capture a stable configuration of physical objects such as visual features, contours, and attributes (Kravitz et al., 2013). The fusiform gyrus is involved with color processing, facial recognition, and the visual processing of words. Word-finding problems such as anomia and the visual ability to recognize words are fundamental language skills and highly associated with learning to read. For those with dyslexia, the fusiform gyrus is underactivated and has reduced gray matter density (Bonner & Grossman, 2012; Rohrer et al., 2008). The supramarginal gyrus, in the inferior parietal lobe, is involved in visual word recognition, as is a distributed area of left hemisphere regions (Stoeckle et al., 2009). Shaywitz et al., (2002) suggested inferior parietal lobe involvement is also related to spelling to sound processes.

Risk factors. Trauma-exposed children have many academic and social problems in the school setting. They have more learning and information processing problems, score lower on standardized reading tests, earn lower grades, are more likely to be retained, and more likely to be referred for special education services (Crozier et al., 2013). The temporal-parietal areas which may be compromised by trauma are learning, memory, language, and reading related, as well as possible social skill problems likely to manifest in children's interactions with peers and adults. Language deficits can be particularly problematic and are associated with behavior problems, social isolation, anxiety, aggression, and rule-breaking behavior (Maggio et al., 2014).

While speech and language functions may be assessed and remediated by speech and language pathologists, school and child psychologists are tasked with assessing language, reading, and written language skills as they are crucial for academic achievement. Understanding which areas associated with reading and written language may be affected by early adversity allows them to conceptualize deficits in these areas within a trauma-informed rubric. They may want to incorporate additional assessments in language, phonological and orthographical processing (letter-sound integration), phonological storage and retrieval, reading comprehension (both inferential and abstract), word substitutions in written language, spelling mistakes (orthographic or phonetic), word attack and decoding, rapid naming, reading automaticity, reading fluency, and spoken language such as mispronunciations and word-finding difficulties. Important information from caregivers would include parental history of reading problems as they are highly heritable, the acquisition of speech and language skills, exposure to print at home, and family attitudes about reading. Attention and memory play crucial roles in reading. Children need to attend to the words on the page, remain focused, and attend to important contextual cues in text. Working memory and other types of memory deficits impair reading comprehension. Adding measures of these constructs is especially useful especially with referred children with trauma backgrounds (Ashkenazi et al., 2013; Berninger et al., 2008; Feifer 2010; Fletcher-Janzen, 2017; Gabel et al., 2010; Shaywitz & Shaywitz, 2004, 2008). See Feifer and Della Toffalo (2007) for a discussion of assessing and treating reading problems in children. Also see the earlier section in this chapter on limbic system functions for risk factors associated with memory problems in adversity exposed youth.

Frontal Regions

Many researchers have been interested in the frontal lobes and prefrontal areas of the brain as ROI with children and adolescents exposed to early trauma. Di Brito et al. (2013) reported a maltreated group of children, in comparison to matched controls, evidenced decreased gray matter in the medial OFC. In a series of studies, De Bellis et al. found that compared to control subjects, children and adolescents carrying a PTSD diagnosis had smaller prefrontal cortex gray and white matter and biologic markers for neuronal loss in the medial prefrontal cortex. Sex differences were also found, with males having larger lateral ventricles suggesting smaller brain volumes for boys who may be more vulnerable to neurotoxic effects of trauma (De Bellis et al., 1999, 2000, 2002a,b). Kelly et al. discovered cortical thickness, surface area, and gyrification abnormalities in children exposed to maltreatment. Observed areas included the anterior cingulate, superior frontal gyrus, and the OFC.

Carrion and his research group found that decreased left ventral and left inferior prefrontal gray matter volumes in maltreated children with PTSD symptoms negatively correlated with bedtime salivary cortisol levels (2010). In another of their studies, a similar clinical group had attenuation of frontal lobe asymmetry (2001) in comparison with control subjects. The right frontal lobe typically is larger than the left. The authors note that attenuated frontal lobe asymmetry has been found in adults with late onset depression and schizophrenia and that those adults with PTSD have differential hemispheric activation in frontal regions involved in cognitive functions when exposed to traumatic stimuli.

Several studies found consistent findings of attenuated development including diminished volume, thickness, and biological markers of dysfunction of the anterior cingulate cortex (ACC), located in the medial surface of the frontal lobes (Reviewed in De Bellis & Zisk, 2014; Teicher & Samson, 2016).

Functions. The frontal lobes are located in the most anterior region of the brain. They mediate several functional units such as basic neurological functions (pyramidal motor functions, continence, and olfaction), purposeful eye movements, speech and language abilities, motivational and social behaviors, and executive capabilities. There is bilateral differentiation as well, with the left frontal lobe more specialized for speech and language (Broca's area is located in the left frontal lobe for most individuals) and the right frontal area more dominant for social cognition and emotion. Imaging studies suggest self-reflection, understanding emotional cues, and other social-related behaviors activate the right frontal region compared to the left. Researchers have organized the frontal cortex both by function and by the connectivity between subcortical and frontal structures. Longitudinal imaging studies suggest that the prefrontal cortex is one of the last regions to mature in humans. New cell growth, synapses, myelination, and pruning continue into the third decade of life Depression, schizophrenia, obsessive compulsive disorder, autism spectrum disorders, ADHD, and bipolar disorder are associated with the frontal regions (Miller, 2007).

The frontal lobes are organized into three basic areas: precentral, pre motor, and prefrontal. The prefrontal cortex is of great interest to school and child clinical psychologists because of its involvement in higher-order functions such as planning, reasoning, problem-solving, judgment, memory, motivation, and attention. These are referred to as executive cognitive functions. Stuss (2007) noted executive cognitive functions are high-level capacities (e.g. monitoring, energizing, switching, inhibiting) that are involved in the control and direction of more automatic, lower-level functions. The prefrontal cortex is divided into the orbitofrontal, medial frontal/anterior cingulate, and dorsolateral prefrontal cortex (DLPFC).

Cummings and Miller (2007) reported the right OFC mediates the rules of social convention such as understanding and behaving in socially appropriate ways. Individuals with known OFC lesions have problems with interpersonal relationships. They often have poor social judgment, and lack empathy and the ability to understand how their actions affect others. Theory of mind, the ability to infer the mental states of others, is a function of the right orbitofrontal region (Stuss et al., 2001). Other behaviors related to problems with OFC functioning can include lack of motivation, indifference, and euphoria; being overly dependent on stimuli in the environment; emotional processing; and reinforcement/punishment contingencies (Sarazin et al., 1998; Ogar & Gorno-Tempini, 2007).

The supplementary motor cortex (SMC) and ACC make up the medial frontal cortex. The ACC is involved with both cognitive and emotional information processing. Motivation is a key construct associated with this region. Problems are related to apathetic behaviors, including reduced motor movements, decreased curiosity, lack of distress, and diminished social interests and engagement (Cummings & Miller, 2007). Additional functions of the ACC include modulation of attention, response inhibition, and working memory. The ACC is involved in error detection and correction and is activated by Stroop-like competing stimuli/interference tasks. Affect-related functions include the appraisal and expression of negative emotions and generating emotional responses (Discussed in Etkin et al., 2011). The ACC has widespread connections to the DLPFC (Kaufer, 2007). The ability to choose, plan, organize, and carry out purposeful goals and to monitor and evaluate their effectiveness as well as modify responses based on feedback are functions associated with the DLPFC and commonly referred to as executive skills.

Executive functions. Adversity-related experiences such as abuse and neglect, orphanage rearing, exposure to alcohol in utero, and prematurity are some of the factors that are associated with executive functioning deficits. Neural circuits and connectivity associated with the prefrontal cortex, the anterior cingulate, the striatal region, hippocampus, and the stress systems are linked to the behaviors and processes associated with executive functioning (Center on the Developing Child at Harvard University, 2011). De Prince et al. (2009) noted poorer performance on an ethnically diverse community sample exposed to familial trauma on measures of working memory, inhibition, auditory attention, and processing speed tasks.

Baron (2004) defined executive functions as "the metacognitive capacities that allow an individual to perceive stimuli from his or her environment, respond adaptively, flexibly change direction, anticipate future goals, consider consequences, and respond in and integrated or common sense way, utilizing all these capacities to serve a common purposive goal" (p. 135). Strategy selection, concept formation, reasoning, fluency, response inhibition, the ability to delay gratification, working memory, and using internal speech to guide and control behavior are also considered executive skills (Barkley, 2012; Baron, 2004; Cummings & Miller 2007; Dawson & Guare, 2010; Miller, 2013). McCloskey and Wasserman (2012) outline 32 executive function capabilities by categories including clusters for attention, engagement, optimization, evaluation/solution, efficiency, and memory.

Risk factors. Considering the development of the frontal lobes continuing past adolescence, trauma can potentially alter the structure, connectivity, and functions of the frontal region and circuitry to other brain regions. Children with poor executive functioning associated with the prefrontal cortex can manifest problems in the cognitive, academic, social-emotional, and behavioral domains and with activities related to their daily living skills. Dawson and Guare (2010) noted that the application of executive skills is needed to master developmental tasks throughout childhood and adolescence. During kindergarten and early elementary school, children are required to remember and carry out two to three-step directions and inhibit inappropriate behaviors such as not hitting classmates. By middle school, expectations for planning and organizing school work and following rules and social conventions increase. By high school, higher demands on adolescents' time, work output, organizational abilities, self-monitoring and regulation, socially appropriate behaviors and planning of future goals are needed for post-secondary success and preparation for independent adulthood. Higher-level learning draws upon a host of executive functioning skills in the frontal regions to direct and orchestrate the mastery of academic material in deliberate and meaningful ways.

ACADEMIC DIFFICULTIES

Reading

Automaticity is a hallmark of fluent reading. Skilled readers activate posterior regions of the brain whereas poor readers sound out words (frontal lobe involvement), making reading a deliberate and laborious endeavor. Reading comprehension suffers as it takes time and effort to decode individual words. During that delay, and especially if the child has working memory problems, meaningful links are lost and unavailable to extract meaning from text (Shaywitz, 2004; discussed in Feifer & Della Tofallo 2007). Feifer and Della Tofallo (2007, p. 124) outline the executive skills drawn upon as they relate to reading.

Planning skills – skilled readers approach reading with a purpose when seeking information
Organizational skills – linking text in a cohesive manner
Working memory – temporarily suspending previously read material in mind while linking it to new information being read
Cognitive flexibility – not perseverating on material

Response inhibition – remaining focused on text without jumping ahead
Concept formation – drawing meaning from text

Mathematics

Feifer and De Fina (2005 p. 78) linked math skills and the executive skills required for mastery as follows:

Sustained attention – vigilance to operational signs; procedural knowledge
Planning – needed for understanding important information in word problems; needed to estimate
Organizational skills – important for setting up problems
Self monitoring – is the answer a plausible one; double checking work
Retrieval fluency – ability to retrieve previously learned math facts.

Written language

Feifer (2013) noted that written language skills place the greatest demand on executive function skills.

Sustained attention – needed to keep track of thoughts and ideas
Inhibition – important for organizing thoughts
Planning – needed to cohesively link text

The frontal lobes are also implicated in ADHD. Children with ADHD often have motor problems and co-morbid learning disorders, with writing and written language problems being the most common (Mayes et al., 2000).

SOCIAL COMPETENCY, EMOTIONAL REGULATION, AND ACTIVITIES OF DAILY LIVING

Children with executive functioning deficits such as impaired working memory, poor rule-governed behaviors, behavioral disinhibition, impulsivity, difficulty understanding cause-and-effect relationships, and problems connecting past behaviors to the present situation are at greater risk for social isolation, rejection, and interpersonal problems with peers and adults. Emotional dysregulation and empathy deficits add to these children's problems navigating and gaining acceptance from their social environments. Parents of children with executive functioning problems know very well the challenges these children have with performing ADL independently. Commonly known as *performance deficits* rather than skill deficits, they have the knowledge and skills to perform tasks but their output or performance falls short. They frequently lose track of time so that an expected 15-minute shower turns into a 45-minute soak and at the end of that time, they have not completed required "shower tasks" such as soaping up, rinsing, and washing hair. They may start out with a goal of going to the laundry room to fold clean clothes. When caregivers check in on progress, they are often found in another part of the house doing something completely different and engaged in more preferred activity such as watching television or playing a video game. Working memory and retrieval problems may manifest as forgetting steps in a routine they should know for their developmental age. Dull, more routine tasks can be especially problematic such as chores, sitting quietly in a car, homework, classwork, and paper and pencil tasks. Another common problem is inconsistency and variability of performance. One day they can meet expectations and the next day they cannot, even though the task and the steps for completion are known and performed successfully in the past. This can be especially frustrating for teachers who may reprimand the child by saying he or she is not putting forth effort or just does not want to comply by rules. Effort allocation and regulation can be problematic with executive function deficits. Teachers may want to blame the child by saying, "you just did this yesterday, I don't understand why you can't do it today, you just don't want to put in the effort." These authors suggest that they reframe this by noting, "you did such a terrific job with this yesterday, and did everything perfectly, so let's see how we can make it happen today." Another effort allocation problem on variability in performance might be addressed with a gas mileage analogy. It is useful to conceptualize these problems as inefficiency with miles per gallon in a car. Because of engine concerns, one day the child gets 35 miles to the gallon and is at peak performance; the next day, he or she is only getting 12 miles to the gallon and runs out of fuel (mental energy and effort) sooner than expected and performance suffers. Barkley (2015) notes that children with ADHD have associated executive functioning deficits and that adults are more successful when they are working with such behaviors when they act as "shepherds" rather than trying to "engineer" these problems out of children's behavioral repertoire. With very young children, adults do act as a their frontal lobes, guiding, instructing, modeling, and directing their behaviors with the expectation that as they mature, they will have internalized the capacities to self-direct and guide their own behaviors with minimal adult intervention. Children with delayed executive functioning skills may always be behind their typically developing peers and need assistance throughout their lives in these areas. Barkley also recommends that tests which evaluate ADL skills be administered routinely in evaluations where there is a suspicion of deficits related to executive functioning skills, such as with ADHD, as these ADL skills can impair functioning across settings.

Clinicians should be aware of the motor, social, emotional, learning, executive skills, and psychiatric problems that are associated with frontal region functioning and how they may be affected by early trauma. Children with executive skills deficits are at a much greater risk for negative outcomes such as social and emotional problems, relationship difficulties, meeting day-to-day task demands, academic and learning disorders, and following rules of social convention. Assessing for executive skills deficits can be problematic as children often perform better on psychological tests than they function in daily life. Interviewing the adults who know the child best along with checklists and questionnaires are useful when combined with relevant standardized measures in an assessment battery. See Baron (2004), McCloskey & Wasserman (2012), Miller (2013), and Flanagan et al. (2013) for excellent discussions on evaluating executive functioning capacities in children. For children with executive skills deficits, interventions such as planning and organizational skill groups, coaching, and individual counseling for skill building can be useful, especially in school and community settings.

Seven

DOMAINS OF IMPAIRMENT: FUNCTIONAL IMPACT OF COMPLEX TRAUMA AND STRESS

Kirby L. Wycoff

INTRODUCTION

There are a number of functional impairments that affect children and young adults who have been impacted by trauma. This chapter will review these functional domains of impact and consider how they can guide the assessment process when working with trauma-impacted youth in school and community settings.

Areas of trauma-affected functioning that are important to assess include the following: intellectual functioning; language; executive functions; learning and memory; social skills; emotional identification; quality of relationships; self-regulation; self-concept and future orientation; and depression, anxiety, and other psychiatric symptoms. This section will outline and help drive the domains of impairment that may be assessed through the trauma-informed lens.

In their seminal article on school-based psychological evaluations that integrate a trauma perspective, Tishelman et al. noted the importance of building a framework for understanding these critical issues. Here, we will focus on the significance of building a framework approach to assessment that ultimately guides the development of interventions. We must have a clear hypothesis and conceptualization of their presenting challenges to match students to a specific service appropriately. This framework also acknowledges (and will be expanding in this section and subsequent chapters) possible challenges of assessing trauma-impacted youth in school settings.

Children will manifest the outcomes of their traumatic exposure across developmental stages and our awareness of typical and atypical child development is salient here (Tishelman et al., 2010). A summary of this was provided in

Section 2. Depending on the child's age at the time of traumatic exposure, different development trajectories can unfold. There is a significant body of literature that provides empirical and reliable data on both short and long-term impacts of children who have been exposed to traumatic events (in Holt et al., 2008; Cleaver et al., 1999; Edleson, 1999; Hester et al., 2000; McGee, 2000; Mullender et al., 2002; Saunders, 2003). At the earliest ages, trauma exposure will likely impact self-regulation, relationships, and self-concept. These children will often demonstrate increased anger, decreased frustration tolerance, and overall non-compliance in pre-school settings (Egeland et al., 1983; Ohmi et al., 2002; Vondra et al., 1989, 1990). They may also demonstrate withdrawal, irritability, and aggression (Ohmi et al., 2002).

Trauma-exposed individuals often experience changes in cognitive abilities as well. Preschoolers impacted by trauma are more rigid in their thinking, approach new problems with less flexibility, and have difficulty trying out multiple different solutions in problem-solving tasks (Egeland et al., 1983). These early challenges worsen as the level of difficulty in higher grades increases. Older children in school struggle with inattention, executive functioning impairment, and an overall reduction in abstract reasoning. They exhibit an impaired ability to think abstractly and envision different solutions to different problems, as well as consider various strategies in solving problems (Beers & DeBellis, 2002).

In addition to challenges within the school settings, some youth might avoid school altogether. Sexually abused teens are routinely noted as having increased behavioral and social challenges and lower overall competence in school-related tasks, as well as being school avoidant (Daignault & Hebert, 2009; Trickett et al., 1994).

When considering the importance of the above-noted tasks as they relate to school functioning, it is no wonder that many of these youth struggles mightily in the school context. These individuals are often disproportionately represented in the disciplinary infraction systems within schools and are referred to special education services (Eckenrode et al., 1993; Shonk & Cicchetti, 2001). It is no surprise that these children often demonstrated reduced grades, higher overall rates of academic failure, and even lower scores on standardized testing (Eckenrode et al., 1993; Leiter & Johnson, 1994). More research needs to be conducted to better understand the impact of trauma on school-related functioning.

Shonk and Cicchetti (2001) found that trauma-exposed preschoolers had lower persistence on challenging tasks and even avoid challenging tasks or exercises (Shonk & Cicchetti, 2001). This could make the entire school day (which is already riddled with frustration and need for persistence in learning new tasks) incredibly overwhelming for trauma-impacted youth. Shonk and Cicchetti

(2001) utilized an organizational perspective on the development to predict the impact of maltreatment on infants, toddlers, and preschoolers. Shonk et al. indicated that the demands for academic engagement and social competencies could cause significant problems in school for a child who had been maltreated (Shonk & Cicchetti, 2001). Shonk and Cicchetti sought to understand the individual child characteristics that might mediate the connection between early maltreatment and later school success. The researchers examined teachers' assessments of their students' academic engagement, social competency, ego resiliency, and ego control. They unpacked the various aspects of academic engagement that might affect maltreated youth disproportionately. Their research found that children who had a history of maltreatment were less engaged academically, demonstrated increased academic risk, had deficits in social relationships, and showed increased externalizing and internalizing behaviors as rated by teachers, school records, and camp counselors (Shonk & Cicchetti, 2001).

Further explorations of youth exposed to abuse or neglect conclude that various aspects of individual histories, academic histories, and disciplinary histories can all negatively impact a young person's success in school. Eckenrode et al. matched a sample of 420 maltreated children in grades K-12 with a group of 420 children who were not maltreated within the same community. This team utilized available social service data and records from the public school system to explore this relationship. The team found that maltreated children had poorer outcomes on all of the metrics that were assessed. Maltreated children did worse on standardized tests, had lower grades, were more likely to repeat a grade, and had higher office referrals for discipline and suspensions (Eckenrode et al., 1993). This trend wherein youth who are impacted by adversity and trauma have poorer outcomes in school has been replicated time and time again (Skiba et al. 2014). Wycoff et al. (2018) further noted the relationship between free and reduced lunch status, disability status, race and disproportionality in suspensions, and expulsions.

Others noted that specific types of traumatic exposure like domestic violence may differentially impact children and the unfolding of their developmental trajectory. Holt et al. (2008) noted that the unique aspects of certain traumas like domestic violence, neglect, or physical abuse may impact children differently than others. The co-occurrence of domestic violence exposure in addition to child abuse, the overall impact on parent capacity, and the impact on child development may increase exposure to other adversities (Holt et al., 2008). Earlier reports suggested that physically abused children may be more aggressive and receive more discipline infractions from teachers when compared with neglected children or control subjects (Hoffman-Plotkin et al., 1984).

The overwhelming evidence suggests that irrespective of the type of abuse, neglect or adversity that a child is exposed to, there is a high likelihood that children exposed to ongoing, chronic adversity may struggle in school. The core domains of functioning that are needed to be successful in school are compromised in those who have experienced adversity. This chapter seeks to explore the various domains of functioning that may be impacted in trauma-exposed children, so that school and community based clinicians can use development assessment batteries that are sensitive to these realities.

ASSESSMENT FRAMEWORK

In building a framework of assessment that includes a trauma-informed lens, it is critical that we consider the ecological context within which the child exists.

Saxe et al. (2007) advocated a model of assessment and treatment of trauma that involves intervening across various levels of the child's ecology. They argued that a child cannot make effective change without involving the surrounding environment, an approach that is consistent with an ecological model of intervention. This concept is integrated into both assessment and treatment, utilizing what they have termed the Trauma Systems Therapy Approach (Saxe et al., 2007). This understanding is multi-faceted, and considers the child as an individual; the child in the context of the familial and caregiving context and the child in the context of the educational, community, cultural, and larger societal context. We concur that the assessment (and intervention approach) must include the "system" of caregiving which means not only immediate caregivers but also the family and school context (Tishelman et al., 2010).

> "In order to assist the school success of traumatized children, we must consider the hypothesis that trauma may be contributing to a child's functioning in the school setting. A second critical presupposition is that individual children's responses to trauma will vary and therefore each child who may be impacted by trauma will need a careful evaluation in order to understand his or her unique profile of skills and deficits. A third premise is that the child's unique learning history, posttraumatic or otherwise, will influence how he or she interacts within the current school context"

> *(Tishelman et al., 2010, p. 282).*

Children may have attributes of bad behavior, acting out, being lazy, having a low cognitive ability, or not caring enough about their education as potential reasons to explain their lack of success in school settings. Furthermore, these youth (as Mateo and Rosyln were at the beginning of this book) are often diagnosed with a wide range of mental health diagnosis including attention deficit hyperactivity disorder (ADHD), conduct disorder, oppositional defiant disorder, anxiety disorders, and depressive disorders, all without ever considering the impact of a trauma history. Understanding the etiology of an individual's distress can drive both the assessment process (not a product, but the *process*) as well as the case conceptualization and intervention process which is intimately connected to assessment.

While single-incident trauma may be readily recognized as causing a change in student functioning, chronic, traumatic stress that covers a wide span of time produces a different clinical presentation in the children we are serving.

As Streeck-Fischer and van der Kolk (2000) noted:

> Isolated traumatic incidents tend to produce discrete conditioned behavioral and biological responses to reminders of the trauma. In contrast, chronic childhood trauma interferes with the capacity to integrate sensory, emotional, and cognitive information into a cohesive whole and sets the stage for unfocused and irrelevant responses to subsequent stress

> *(Streeck-Fischer & van Der Kolk, 2000, p. 903).*

If we consider the impact on a chronically neglected child, they will likely present differently than a child exposed to one single concrete event. However, the functional impairments are just as damaging (Tishelman et al., 2010). Hildyard and Wolfe (2002) pointed out that children exposed to severe neglect in the absence of other concrete traumatic incidents will experience isolation, less opportunity for relationship-building, and less opportunity to build language and develop cognitive skills. These authors noted a number of critical outcomes in three important developmental periods (Infancy/preschool, School-Aged and Younger Adolescents, and Older Adolescents and Adults), and the major developmental processes that are affected. Hildyard et al. (2002) noted that neglected children experience chronic poverty, serious caregiving deficits, parental psychopathology, substance abuse, homelessness, family breakup, and poor pre and postnatal care. These types of things are precisely the type of non-incident specific traumatic stressors which often go unnoticed in school settings.

The importance of recognizing all forms of trauma and adversity is critical if we are to understand and appreciate the needs of this vulnerable population fully and ultimately help them in school and life (Tishelman et al., 2010). We suggest here, as do Tischelman and others (Cole et al., 2005a,b, 2013), that a flexible, trauma-informed approach is appropriate in school settings.

RESILIENCE AND RECOVERY

As we unpack and explore all of the harmful ways in which trauma can impact youth, and the responsibility of school and community-based clinicians to assess not only the history of and exposure to trauma, but also current functional impairment, a note on resilience is appropriate. Not all children exposed to trauma will experience or demonstrate functional impairment as a result of that trauma exposure. Masten and Coatsworth, (1998) in their work on "Lessons from Research on Successful Children" noted that a focus on competence and resilience could foster an improved perspective on how to best help and support children who have experienced adversity. In the public health arena, we refer to these as cases of "positive deviance." The individuals who successfully navigate exposure to trauma and are not negatively impacted in the ways we might expect them to deviate in a positive direction and are the exception from the norm. "Positive Deviants" are those who are successful, when their peers are not. They are essentially "positive outliers." This is a resilience-based approach to social change; individuals that can succeed and function better than their peers, despite facing the same hardships. Marsh and Schroeder (2002) noted:

> "Positive deviance (PD) refers to a phenomenon that exists in many resource-poor communities, that is, the finding that a few individuals and families employ uncommon, beneficial practices that allow them and their children to have better health as compared to their similarly impoverished neighbors"

> *(Marsh and Schroeder. 2002 p. 1).*

Figuring out what worked for some members of a population helps us leverage solutions and interventions for other members of the population. So, in a population of children exposed to community violence, a select number of these children will not experience the negative outcomes that their peers do. Why is that? What additional capacity or resources (internal or external) improved the resiliency of this group? Our ability to learn from positive deviants within the realm of childhood adversity and distress gives us additional tools from which to consider the resiliency puzzle. When considering resiliency in adversity-exposed individuals, highlighting the role of the developmental trajectory can be useful. Masten and Coatsworth (1998) noted that children are protected "not only by the self-righting nature of development but also by the actions of adults, by their actions, by the nurturing of their assets, by opportunities to succeed, and by the experience of success" (p. 216). By considering the role of resilience in the world of adverse childhood experiences, childhood trauma can drive conversations around change and policy.

Ferguson and Horwood noted that studying the pathways of individuals who transcend adversity can provide insight into understanding resilience. They noted two primary mechanisms and theories related to resilience: (i) Protective Processes and (ii) Compensatory Processes. Drawing on the work of Rutter (1979, 1990) and others, Ferguson et al. defined these two mechanisms in the following ways:

1. Protective processes in which the exposure to the resilience factor is beneficial to those exposed to the risk factor but has no benefit (or less benefit) for those not exposed to the risk factor.
2. Compensatory processes in which the resilience factor has an equally beneficial effect on those exposed and those not exposed to adversity (Fergusson & Horwood, 2003, p. 134).

The conceptualization by Ferguson and Horwood was quite relevant to our consideration of utilizing a trauma-informed perspective in assessment in school and community settings. It is critical that we take a strength-based approach to our assessment process before we embark on considering all of the areas that children may be negatively impacted by their history. In the midst of considering how trauma gets in the way of children's functioning, we also actively seek to highlight how children are succeeding in spite of their trauma histories. Utilizing a strength-based approach to assessment, we must consider, look for, and leverage the protective and compensatory factors in children's lives. This approach simply cannot be overstated. If we are to instill hope for a brighter future in the lives of the children and families we work with, we must look not just at what is going wrong, but what is also going right. This way of thinking draws on the interventions highlighted in the literature from Solution-Focused (see Murphy, J. J. (2015) for a more robust discussion on Solution Focused work in schools). As Murphy noted, "Yes, the child has had a rough go of it, and she has experienced trauma and now her brain works differently and she is going to struggle in school" and developed the thought that, "Yes, this child has experienced hardship and adversity, and yes our trauma-informed perspective helps us better understand how that adversity impacts her day to day functioning. But in the midst of that, here is where this child has succeeded, thrived and transcended her life circumstances. Here, we can leverage her strengths. In the places where things are going 'right,' we can instill hope and provide support so that she can meet her fullest potential." One challenge in writing a book about trauma-informed assessments is that it can overemphasize the problems these individuals are experiencing. This book is about assessing for and acknowledging individuals facing difficult, challenging, and traumatic life experiences, but not letting those experiences define them. Our goal is to attract attention to a critical need for assessing and supporting these individuals, but not for labeling them and applying a fixed mindset to their life circumstances. As Hollander-Goldfein et al., (2012) noted:

> Once for example, we assumed that everyone who endured child trauma, combat, a major disaster or terrorist attack would have behavioral health problems, and this did help attract increased attention to trauma's effects. However, what emerged was the impression that everyone touched by trauma was unable to function. Now, in the second half of the twenty-first century, and in part due to the pioneering work in positive psychology, we recognize that not everyone exposed to trauma becomes traumatized, and not all traumatized people remain so forever
>
> *(Hollander-Goldfein et al., 2012, p. xi).*

Hollander-Goldfein noted that individuals impacted by trauma are not defined by it in their "Transcending Trauma" project where they were conducting ethnographic interviews using a grounded theory approach to a qualitative study of Holocaust survivors and in seeking to better understand the impact of intergenerational trauma. The Transcending Trauma Project (TPP) at the Council for Relationships is a nonprofit outpatient therapy center within the Division of Couple and Family Studies, Department of Psychiatry and Jefferson Medical College in Philadelphia, PA. The work of TPP calls forth another critically important aspect of this book on trauma-informed assessments. That is, the goal here is not just to assess, identify, and label those who have been adversely impacted by trauma. Rather, the goal of *any* assessment is that it *drives* intervention. Hollander-Goldfein et al. (2012) and the authors of this book support the notion that we (those that can help) have to both acknowledge the reality of the suffering in the lives of those exposed to trauma and focus on "the capacity to recover, heal, and rebuild after devastating events" (Hollander-Goldfein et al., 2012, p. 5). In our assessment framework, we must not only consider what impairments a child might have but also consider the impact of the larger context in which the child is embedded. The systems way of thinking considers not just the individual parts, but the whole context of the child's life. When we consider the role that the large socio-ecological factors play, we might find other protective factors and compensatory mechanisms. "This suggests that environmental factors can either buffer a child from the full effects of adversity or conversely exacerbate a child's difficulties. Thus, evaluation and intervention with maltreated and traumatized children must integrally include attention to the surrounding settings in his or her life" (Tishelman et al., 2010, p. 280).

As Cook (2005) noted, children might shift areas of competence over time as they are faced with different or increasing stressors, and the developmental process unfolds. "Resilience is a psychological characteristic predicting 'good outcomes in spite of serious threats to adaptation" (Masten, 2001, p. 228). A resilient self-concept likely contains features associated with positive functioning, including optimism, personal control, positive self-regard, and a sense that life is meaningful (Hemenover, 2003; Ryff & Singer, 1998). Cook et al. noted that the following characteristics could function as resiliency factors in children's lives:

1. Positive attachment and connections to emotionally supportive and competent adults within a child's family or community (attachment).
2. Development of cognitive and self-regulation abilities (affect regulation, cognition, altered consciousness, biology).
3. Positive beliefs about oneself (self-concept).
4. Motivation to act effectively in one's environment (behavioral control) (Cook et al., 2010, p. 396).

Zolkoski and Bullock (2012) noted that resiliency contextualizes a child's strengths against her or her adverse experiences. The reader may note that a number of the areas of resilience listed above actually align with the areas of functional impairment that will be covered in this chapter. We will reiterate here again the importance of multi-dimensional assessment, with multiple informants so that areas of impairment and areas of strength are both assessed. If we view the assessment process as the beginning of the intervention process (the first critically informs the latter), we can see the importance of comprehensive assessment frameworks that integrates a holistic understanding of the child's past, present, and future.

EVALUATION DOMAINS AND CORE ISSUES

Tishelman offered one perspective for considering the primary domains of evaluation and related core issues. The National Child Traumatic Stress Network (NCTSN), influenced by Cook et al. (2010) offered a similar yet distinct organization of domains of functioning that have been impacted by trauma. Both Tishelman et al. (2010) and Cook's (2005) full article are a must-read for anyone interested in the trauma-informed perspective of evaluation and assessment. The domains and core issues as reported by Tishelman include the following:

1. Self-Regulation (Domain 1)
   • Deficits in emotion identification
   • Hypervigilance to threat

- Impaired ability to modulate arousal
- Extreme mood states
- Dissociation

2. Physical Functioning (Domain 2)
    - Disconnection from body
    - Physical holding of stress
    - Physical integrity/boundaries
    - Trauma-related injuries

3. Relationships (Domain 3)
    - Sense of self
    - Trust and safety
    - Social skills and competence

4. Academics (Domain 4)
    - Information processing
    - Language development
    - Executive functioning
    - Worldview and personal agency
    - Specific learning disability (Tishelman et al. 2010, p. 288)

Cook et al., (2005) offered a different conceptualization of these domains of functioning and impact that is built from the Complex Trauma White Paper of the NCTSD workgroup on Complex Trauma, supported through Substance Abuse and Mental Health Services Administration (SAMHSA). The original articulation of these domains include the following:

1. Attachment
2. Biology
3. Affect Regulation
4. Dissociation
5. Behavioral Control
6. Cognition
7. Self-Concept (Cook et al., 2005, p. 392)

The remainder of this chapter will be organized by domain and will integrate both the work of Cook et al. and the NCTSN. We will fold Tishelman's excellent conceptualization of the domains of impairment into this organization as well.

Attachment and Relationships

Individuals who have been exposed to chronic, traumatic stress often struggle in their interpersonal relationships. As noted earlier in this book, trauma is essentially an assault at the very core of who we are, how we view ourselves, and how we build relationships. Bloom (1994, 2007, 2008, 2011, 2013) has continually noted that trauma is at its core a violation of boundaries. Healthy and appropriate boundaries are a critical aspect of the development of safe, healthy relationships. Individuals impacted by early exposure to complex trauma often have difficulties with boundaries in their relationships and are often distrustful and suspicious of others. These individuals struggle with understanding and interpreting others' emotions, have difficulty taking the perspective of others into account, and often struggle interpersonally (Cook et al., 2005). The NCTSN further expands on how individuals exposed to chronic, traumatic stress frequently struggle in their relationships with family members, siblings, peers, adults, and even teachers (Cook et al., 2005). These individuals may have difficulties with separating from their caregivers and may be alternatively clingy and rejecting of caregivers.

Early attachment relationships with caregivers provide the template on which all other relationships in an individual's life are built. In the context of these relationships, children build a sense of self, a sense of others, and a sense of self in relation to others (Cook et al., 2005). Among so many other things, children learn how to tolerate distress, how to communicate with others, and how to get their needs met in the context of these caregiver relationships. When the trauma itself happens in the context of that caregiver relationship, the very space where the child is supposed to feel safe and have their needs met is negatively impacted (Fredrich, 2002). Parents who are systematically unavailable to meet their children's needs and/or too preoccupied, distant, punitive, or themselves distressed, simply cannot meet their children's needs. In their inability to respond consistently and reliably, children learn that their world is not a safe place and their own internal resources are inadequate (Cook et al., 2005).

This attachment style can create significant problems for individuals in their lives. For young children, this pattern may result in erratic behavior and for older teenagers may manifest in rigidity and dissociation (Lyons-Ruth & Jacobovitz, 1999). The challenges that these individuals experience in relationships may include themes of helplessness, abandonment, and betrayal (Cook et al., 2005).

When an attachment is severely disrupted (in humans and animals), this often engenders lifelong risk of physical disease and psychosocial dysfunction. This risk occurs along three pathways that react impairments in core biopsychosocial competencies: increased susceptibility to stress (e.g., difficulty focusing attention and modulating arousal); inability to regulate emotions without external assistance (e.g., feeling and acting overwhelmed by intense or numbed emotions); and altered help-seeking (e.g., excessive help-seeking and dependency or social isolation and disengagement).

(Cook et al., 2005, p. 393)

Shonk and Cicchetti (2001) noted that social competencies are a significant aspect of the challenges that trauma-exposed youth experience. They note that forming relationships and working towards individual and social goals are important developmental tasks (Shonk & Cicchetti, 2001). School-aged children do this through their interactions and relationships with others as they learn to negotiate, consider others viewpoints and work together (Shantz & Hartup, 1992). Children's relationships with their peers may tell us about multiple outcomes including school-related difficulties, school withdrawal, aggression, and depression (Parker et al., 1995; Rubin et al., 1998).

The impact of trauma and chronic stress on the quality of attachments and relationships is significant. It is no wonder that at times, these individuals struggle to connect with their teachers and other care-providing adults in their lives. Adults may, in turn, feel rejected and confused by these children, who are often described as difficult to connect with emotionally. The assessment of peer relationships, relationships with teachers, relationships with caregivers, and overall beliefs about self in the world and the context of those relationships is a critical aspect of considering the needs of trauma-exposed youth in school and community settings.

For further expansion on the concept of boundaries and relationships for trauma-impacted individuals, we suggest the reader revisit Dr. Sandra Bloom's conceptualization in Chapter 3.

Thinking and Learning

Thinking and learning are often negatively impacted in individuals who are trauma-exposed, which are core aspects of success in school. Individuals who are raised by abusive and neglectful parents had a notable cognitive impairment as compared to non-abused children. These differences were seen as early as late infancy (Egeland et al., 1983). The impoverished environment is typically associated with poverty and neglectful parents, and infants living in these environments demonstrate expressive and receptive language delays and an overall reduction in IQ (Culp et al., 1991).

Children exposed to trauma often experience significant academic problems and can struggle in both thinking and learning. The impact of a specific, single incident trauma can cause traumatic brain injuries, for example, but there are also related cognitive impairments that result from extreme levels of chronic stress (Tishelman, et al., 2010). The documentation of actual neurobiological changes that result from children being exposed to chronic and traumatic stress is increasing. Evans and Schamberg (2009) noted that when measuring markers of allostatic load (a biological marker of wear and tear on the body related to chronic stress), childhood poverty is inversely related to working memory capacity in young adults. These authors further discuss this income-achievement gap and noted that the longer a child lives in poverty, the worst their later achievement levels become (Evans and Schamberg, 2009). These authors sought to better understand the neurocognitive mechanisms at play in these relationships, especially working memory, which is a requirement for things like language development, reading, and problem-solving. This team hypothesized that childhood poverty would impair working memory in young adults. They further hypothesized that there would be a prospective relationship between childhood poverty and adult working memory, which would be mediated by chronic stress exposure (i.e. poverty → chronic stress → working memory). Both of these hypotheses proved true. They noted that "the proportion of early childhood spent in poverty is also significantly related to working memory in young adulthood [b = –1.01 (SE = 0.44); P < 0.02]. The greater the proportion of life growing up in poverty from birth to age 13 years, the shorter the span of following information 17-year-old adults can accurately hold in their working memory. On average, adults raised in middle-income families could hold in working memory a sequence of 9.44 items, whereas adults who grew up in poverty had a working memory capacity of 8.50 items" (Evans & Schamberg, 2009, para. 10). The overall ability to think and learn is impacted by neurobiological changes in the brain that happen as a result of exposure to chronic adversity and stress. Children who have been involved in the child protective services system, for example, demonstrate cognitive impairments, thought to be in part due to exposure to adversity (Messacappa et al., 2001).

Information processing, language development, and executive functioning (also both connected to working memory capacity) are also impacted in youth who have been exposed to trauma (Tishelman et al., 2010). Likely also impacted by memory impairment, things like sequencing, organization of information, comprehension, and causal relationships are all impaired in children who have trauma exposure (Tishelman et al., 2010).

These youth may have difficulty understanding and being understood in the school setting. Tishelman et al. noted a number of possible manifestations of these impairments:

A. Difficulty following directions
B. Poor production (written, oral, homework, tests)
C. Poor reading skills including comprehension difficulties
D. Poor organization and study skills
E. Auditory processing difficulties (Tishelman et al., 2010)

Cook et al. further note that these children will likely struggle with regulating attentional controls, and may have difficulties focusing and completing tasks as well as planning and anticipating what is coming next (Cook et al., 2010). Executive functioning is commonly impaired in this population as is the capacity for abstract reasoning. Not surprisingly, diagnoses of attention-related disorders are not uncommon in this population. We acknowledge here the neuropsychological underpinnings of ADHD and its clear connection to thinking and learning, but we will expand on the connection between trauma and disruptive behavioral disorders in a subsequent section. DePrince et al., (2009) examined the impact of familial trauma, non-familial trauma, and no trauma in group of children from an ethnically diverse community sample (n = 110, mean age = 10.39). Familial trauma included sexual or physical victimization and witnessing domestic violence (DePrince et al., 2009). This research team used an assessment battery that included memory, behavioral inhibition, processing speed, auditory attention, and interference control to examine these three groups (DePrince et al., 2009). The outcomes indicted that relative to non-familial trauma and no trauma exposure, children exposed to familial trauma performed more poorly on the executive functioning metric that included working memory, inhibition, auditory attention, and processing speed. After taking into account other symptoms like anxiety and disassociation, as well as socioeconomic status (SES) and possible traumatic brain injury (TBI), trauma exposure did contribute to a reduction in basic (i.e. the absence of emotions content) executive functioning (medium effect size). Relative to the implications of this research on practice, they note that Executive Function (EF) problems "may provide one route via which maltreated children become at-risk for peer, academic, psychological, and behavior problems relative to their peers. Recently, intervention strategies have emerged in the anxiety and mood disorder treatment literature that appear to effectively target EFs. As future research continues to specify the relationship between child trauma exposure and EF performance, these innovative treatments may have important practice implications for addressing EF deficits" (Freyd, 2007). In an additional study (N = 29), maltreated children with a posttraumatic stress syndrome (PTSD) diagnosis performed worse than their non-maltreated peers on multiple executive functioning tasks including sustained visual attention (Beers & De Bellis, 2002).

Impairments in cognition, memory, executive functioning, attentional controls, and overall learning directly impact school-aged children's academic achievement. These children are often over-identified in special education populations and more frequently referred for these services. A history of complex trauma often results in reduced grades and performance on standardized academic assessments (Cook et al., 2005). Delaney-Black et al. (2002) assessed 299 urban first-grade students and caregivers in order to explore the association between violence exposure, IQ, and reading deficits. This team examined the connection between violence exposure and trauma-related distress in standardized assessment measures, while controlling for the confounding factors of gender, caregiver IQ, home environment, SES, and parental substance abuse. They found that violence exposure was in fact related to the student's IQ (p = 0.01) and reading ability (p = 0.045). These authors reported that a "child experiencing both violence exposure and trauma-related distress at or above the 90th percentile would be expected to have a 7.5-point (SD, 0.5) decrement in IQ and a 9.8-point (SD, 0.66) decrement in reading achievement" (Delaney-Black, et al. 2002, p. 280). These authors essentially found that trauma-related distress in urban first-grade students was associated with significant reductions in IQ and reading achievement (Delaney-Black et al., 2002). It is clear that children who have been exposed to chronic, traumatic stress struggle with some of the core capacities necessary for school success. Identifying where these areas of impairment are in our assessments will help guide the decision-making and intervention process. In additional to the neuropsychological impacts of adversity and trauma on the developing brain that directly impacts thinking and learning, there is also a clear impact of trauma on overall academic engagement.

Shonk and Cicchetti note the need for intrinsic motivation in school success and further note that an optimal degree of this type of engagement is characterized by self-initiation, task persistence, and self-directed behavioral management (Shonk & Cicchetti, 2001). This issue of internal versus external motivation is a critical one when considering overall success in school, and often predictive of later academic achievement via grades, test scores, referral for specialized services, and potential drop-out risk (Shonk & Cicchetti, 2001). "Children who are intrinsically engaged in school increase their exposure to learning opportunities, whereas those who remain externally regulated are dependent on others' direction, perform in order to obtain rewards (e.g. grades, approval) or to avoid punishments, and may disengage from academic pursuits" (Shonk & Cicchetti, 2001, p. 4). Optimal levels of academic engagement are critical for success in school and life. Shonk & Cicchetti note that in their sample of n = 229 socioeconomically disadvantaged youth (match sample, n = 146 of whom had a maltreatment history) maltreatment was predicted to negatively impact both children's behavior and academic success. Impairments in academic achievement, social competency, and ego resiliency and control were part of the reason why (Shonk & Cicchetti, 2001). These authors go on to note that maltreated toddlers, preschools, and school-aged children reportedly display excessive clinginess and dependency, are less exploratory of their environments, are less autonomous in mastering tasks, and generally exhibit wariness and uncertainty in social situations (Shonk & Cicchetti, 2001; Aber & Allen 1987; Erickson & Hawes, 1989).

It is quite clear that exposure to chronic traumatic stress may create significant challenges in thinking and learning. With all of the tools that the school psychologists already possess in their toolbox on comprehensive assessment, this domain is readily within the scope of their practice. We direct readers to the work of Hale & Fiorello, as well as Hale, Wycoff and Fiorello, for a robust discussion of the assessment of cognition and academic achievement using a concordance-discordance model (C-DM) to assessment.

Physical Health: Brain and Body

Upset and stressed-out brains can't think or behave well. The brain's job is to keep us alive, first and foremost. Its goal is to maintain homeostasis which includes things like maintaining appropriate levels of oxygen, ideal body temperature, and basic functioning. All of these different things come together in any given individual as "homeostatic balance." That is, all of these different functions are kept at optimal, working levels. However, when a stressor occurs (anything that knocks you out of homeostatic balance) the body works hard to re-establish that balance, and that response is called the stress-response (Sapolsky, 1998).

When homeostasis is threatened, the limbic system (the alarm system of the body), which includes the thalamus, hypothalamus, amygdala, and hippocampus, among others, jumps into high alert. Think alarms sounding, flashing lights, and red flags. This is often referred to as the fight-or-flight or freeze response. When this happens, our central nervous system kicks into high gear, which then turns the endocrine system spigot on, flooding the body with heavy-hitting biochemicals like cortisol and adrenaline (Sapolsky, 1998). One of the most robust and easy-to-digest texts on the body and brain's response to stress is provided by neuroendocrinologist and Stanford Professor of Biology, Dr. Robert Sapolsky, who wrote the book *Why Zebra's Don't get Ulcers*. We highly encourage readers to seek out this resource.

Evans and others (Cook et al., 2005; Tishelman et al., 2010; DePrince et al., 2009; Tarullo, & Gunnar, 2006; Ishikawa & Nakamura, 2003) note that the brain and body itself are actually subject to change in individuals who have been exposed to chronic, traumatic stress and adversity. Tishelman et al. (2010) notes four ways in which the physical body may be implicated in trauma response: (i) Disconnection from the body, (ii) Physical Holding of stress, (iii) Physical Integrity and Boundaries, and (iv) Trauma-Related Physical Effects. It is well established in the literature that the architecture of the brain is altered in many of these individuals, particularly when the traumatic stress is chronic and starts at a young age. Understanding the biological mechanisms, or the neurocognitive link between poverty and chronic traumatic stress is an aspect of this work that has been missing until recently (Evans & Schamberg, 2009). Young children exposed to trauma are at risk for underdevelopment in the function of the brain that manages emotions and responds to stress (Cook et al., 2005).

Children who have not been exposed to trauma learn, over time, how to attend to, synthesize, integrate, and give meaning to both their internal and external environments. They do this, instead of a knee-jerk, reflexive response to whatever stimulus is attended to, which is often the case for trauma-exposed individuals. When functioning optimally, this ability to orient to the internal and external environments and respond in kind is believed to occur through a gradual shift from right hemisphere dominance (feeling and sensing) to a primary reliance on the left hemisphere (language, abstract reasoning and long-range planning) and to an integration of neural communication across the two hemispheres (corpus callosum) (Cook et al., 2005, p. 393; De Bellis et al., 2002a,b,c; Kagan, 2003). A full primer on biological and neuropsychological functioning is well beyond the scope of this book, but it is important to be aware that the impact of trauma is felt in both the mind and the body.

As noted in the previous section, working memory is often impaired in individuals exposed to trauma, which could potentially indicate prefrontal cortex, hippocampal, and amygdala involvement (LeDoux, 2003; Lupien et al., 2007; Smith et al., 1998). In their study of veterans using regional cerebral blood flow during the recollection of trauma vs. neutral events, Shin et al., (2006) noted that "results suggest a reciprocal relationship between medial prefrontal cortex and amygdala function in PTSD" (Shin et al., 2006, p. 168). The role of the amygdala in emotional response makes it a reasonable consideration for trauma-exposed individuals (Woon & Hedges, 2008).

The hippocampus, which is an integral component of the limbic system and involved with memory and emotions, is also impacted by trauma. Interestingly, Woon et al. noted that hippocampal volume in children with maltreatment-related PTSD had normal volumes, but adults with PTSD who had a history of maltreatment did not. This perhaps suggests that hippocampal volume maintains itself during early traumatic exposures in childhood, but as those exposures persist into adulthood, there is a cumulative impact which later affects hippocampal volume (Woon & Hedges, 2008).

Both the hippocampus and prefrontal cortex are impacted when an individual is exposed to chronic physiological stress (Lupien et al., 1997a,1997b; 1998, 2000, 2007, 2009). As Evans notes, "chronically elevated physiological stress is a plausible model for how poverty could get into the brain and eventually interfere with achievement" (Evans & Schamberg, 2009, p. 6545).

We know that the brain and the body are inextricably connected. While it is increasingly clear that the brain is impacted by trauma and there are often significant neuropsychological deficits for these individuals, the physical body is also greatly impacted by chronic stress.

Evans and Schamberg (2009) discuss the concept of allostatic load as a measurement for chronic physiological stress. This model that uses allostatic load contributes to the stress-disease literature by noting the cascade of physiological dysregulations that occur when the body is under duress (Juster et al., 2010). Allostatic load, includes neuroendocrine functioning, immune functioning, metabolic functioning, and cardiovascular functioning, and also helps us articulate the cumulative wear and tear on the body as a result of stress (Evans & Schamberg, 2009; Juster et al., 2010). This wear and tear is a result of chronic mobilizations of physiological systems, much like an alarm sounding over and over and over again (Karlamangla et al., 2002; McEwen 2000, 2002, 1998; Seeman et al., 1997 2001a,b, 2004). As Sapolsky (1998) has noted, the body is constantly working to maintain that homeostatic balance. Juster et al. (2010) expand on this, noting the differences between allostasis and homeostasis. *Allostasis* refers to the organism's ability to optimally respond to the fluctuations and demands in the environment (Sterling, 2004; Juster et al., 2010). "Allostasis differs from homeostasis vis-à-vis its emphasis on dynamic rather than static biological set-points, considerations of the brain's role in feedback regulation, and view of health as a whole-body adaptation to contexts" (Juster et al., 2010, para. 3). Allostatic theory drives the idea that the body is working actively in response to external stimuli and environmental factors (Evans & Schamberg, 2009). When those alarm bells are set off time and time and time again, this increases wear and tear, and reduces the effectiveness of the alarm system. Evans notes:

Overexposure to a combination of multiple, activated bodily response systems (e.g., neuronal, endocrine, cardiovascular) alters the ability of the body to respond efficiently to environmental demands. Longer, more frequent exposure to environmental stressors accelerates bodily wear and tear. Chronic and more intensive environmental stressors cause the body to mobilize multiple physiological systems to meet those demands, but at higher levels of activity. Conversely, when environmental demands are low, individuals who have had a higher allostatic load burden will be less efficient in turning off the multiple physiological resources marshaled to deal with chronic demands.

(Evans & Schamberg, 2009, para. 5)

McEwen & Saplosky (1995) note that both catecholamine and glucocorticoids are involved in this stress response, and prolonged exposure to stressors can result in neuronal death (particularly in the hippocampus) and cognitive impairment. McEwen and Sapolsky further note that catecholamine involvement can affect emotionally laden memories (McEwen & Sapolsky, 1995).

The hypothalamic-pituitary-adrenal (HPA) axis is also worth mentioning in the discussion on the impact of stress on the body and brain. McEwen (2004) reports that the HPA axis is one of the major aspects of the neuroendocrine stress responses that support the body in maintaining health and stability in the face of stressors. Dysregulation of the HPA axis is not uncommon in children who have been exposed to early, chronic stressors and adversity (Tarullo & Gunnar, 2006).

"Childhood trauma in humans is associated with sensitization of the neuroendocrine stress response, glucocorticoid resistance, increased central corticotropin-releasing factor (CRF) activity, immune activation, and reduced hippocampal volume, closely paralleling several of the neuroendocrine features of depression. Neuroendocrine changes secondary to early-life stress likely reflect risk to develop depression in response to stress, potentially due to failure of a connected neural circuitry implicated in emotional, neuroendocrine and autonomic control to compensate in response to challenge"

(Heim et al., 2008, p. 693).

There is a wealth of information in the literature that documents the biological and physiological impacts of stress and adversity on the body and brain. While a more robust discussion is beyond the scope of this book, we highly encourage readers to expand on their own understanding of these concepts. What is critically important for school and community based clinicians who are working with traumatized and adversity exposed youth and families is that those stressors absolutely impact both the body and brain. Thorough assessment that drives intervention will help us ultimately alleviate suffering in these populations.

Behavioral Control and Self-Regulation

As we learned in the last section, trauma and adversity have a significant impact on both the body and the brain. They also have a significant negative impact on an individual's ability to manage and regulate their own behaviors. For individuals exposed to chronic adversity and stress, their ability to analyze information and respond to their environments in cognitively and emotionally organized ways is seriously impaired and often results in significant behavioral dysregulation (Cook et al., 2005). This dysregulation is seen in any number of problematic behaviors in the school setting and most of them interfere significantly with the learning process as well as the individual's ability to build and maintain meaningful relationships. It is not uncommon for these individuals to exhibit features of a number of externalizing disorders including attention-related disorders, oppositional defiant disorder, and conduct disorders, all which are notoriously characterized by behaviors that are difficult to manage in the classroom setting. Further difficulties may be noted in deficits in judgment, manipulative behaviors, poor planning and organization, and impairments in goal-directed behaviors (Cook et al., 2005). The results of disorganized attachment that are frequently present in the lives of traumatized youth contribute to all of these challenges. "In older children, adolescents, and adults, disorganized attachment manifests itself in survival-based behaviors that are rigid, extreme, and dissociative. Disorganized attachment behaviors revolve either on themes of helplessness (e.g. abandonment, betrayal, failure, dejection) or coercive control (e.g. blame, rejection, intrusiveness, hostility)" (Cook et al., 2005, p. 390).

These children have difficulty with both over- and under-controlling behavioral patterns as evidenced in rigidity and inflexibility (over controlled), and aggression and other externalizing behaviors (under controlled). Crittenden and DiLalla (1988) notes that these children may struggle with compulsive compliance (over controlled) as one of their coping strategies and this can be evidenced as early as infancy. Cook et al. (2005) further expands that these over- and under-controlled behaviors may relate to the actual traumatic event and may include a component of reenactment, such as aggression, self-injury, and sexualized behaviors (Cook et al., 2005). Children with trauma-exposure may also engage in self-stimulation, avoidance of physical touch or intrusiveness in boundaries, and other risk-taking behaviors including substance use and/or rule-breaking activities (Tishelman et al., 2010). When the brain's coping systems are activated, particularly at a young age, the regulatory systems are impacted. There is often a significant impairment in the individual's ability to modulate overall arousal controls, which in turn can result in problematic behavior in the school setting. A further exploration of the neurological underpinnings of behavioral control and self-regulation can be found in the previous section. It is important for any school or community-based evaluation to consider these types of behaviors as possibly being connected to an early trauma exposure.

Emotional Control and Self-Regulation

As has been noted elsewhere, individuals exposed to chronic adversity and stress struggle with a number of complex changes, of which emotional control is one. Affective identification and regulation is a core aspect of managing and expressing one's emotions. This is often impacted in trauma-exposed individuals and can create significant challenges in school, home, work, and community settings. It has been hypothesized that emotion regulation is a part of the complex symptoms related to early-onset, chronic interpersonal trauma (Ehring & Quack, 2010). It has been reportedly robustly in the literature that emotion regulation development occurs in the context of healthy, transactional caregiving (Calkins & Hill, 2007; Cole et al., 1994). "On the one hand, caregivers' own emotion regulation behavior serves as a model for the developing child as to how to deal with emotional states. In addition, caregivers guide the child in understanding and labeling his/her own emotions and ultimately regulating them in a way to achieve his/her goals" (Ehring & Quack, 2010, p. 588). The literature suggests, as we noted earlier in this chapter in the section on Attachment and Relationships, that poor, disorganized, or pathological attachment is associated with poor emotional regulation skills (Cloitre et al., 2008). This further highlights the importance of the interpersonal context in the transmission of trauma. When the trauma occurs in the context of the relationship that is supposed to represent the predictability of a secure, care providing adult, the negative impacts are substantial. Ehring et al. note that their hypothesis is driven by the theory that chronic, interpersonal trauma that occurs early in life would likely disrupt the development of adaptive emotion regulation, particularly when the perpetrator is in the caregiving role (Ehring & Quack, 2010). These authors suspected that early-onset, interpersonal trauma would lead to more significant impairment in emotion regulation skills. The conceptualization of emotion regulation used by Ehring is based off of the Gratz and Roemer (2004) model. Gratz and Roemer note that the work of Linehan (1993) of emotional dysregulation in borderline personality disorders is part of their conceptualization (Linehan, 1993). Linehan points to deliberate self-harm as one mechanism that might serve an emotion-regulating function for some individuals (Linehan, 1993). Gratz and Roemer further note that the perpetration of violence (not just at self) but even at others (i.e. intimate partner violence) and aggression may function to assist in regulating emotions (Jakupcak et al., 2002; Buchsbaum et al., 2001). Pointing to the reduction of emotional arousal, control of negative emotion, and expression of the emotional experience as key functions in emotional regulation, Gratz and Roemer developed a conceptual model of self-regulation and a related measurement tool. Adaptive emotional regulation includes a key aspect of self-awareness, as the individual needs to monitor and evaluate their own emotional experiences, but also modify its expression. The ability to identify and experience one's emotional experience is a key aspect to healthy functioning. Efforts at avoiding internal experiences and unwanted thoughts and feelings, and difficulty in managing increased physiological arousal, are actually key characteristics in many psychological disorders, and may also be indicated in those exposed to chronic adversity and stress (Hayes et al., 1996). An integrative conceptualization of emotional regulation includes four key dimensions:

1. Awareness and understanding of one's emotions,
2. Acceptance of negative emotions,
3. The ability to successfully engage in goal-directed behavior and control impulsive behavior when experiencing negative emotions, and
4. The ability to use situationally appropriate strategies for emotion regulation (Gratz and Roemer, 2004, p. 2)

Using a sample of 616 trauma survivors, Ehring et al. aimed to better understand the role of trauma type and PTSD symptom severity on emotion regulation difficulties. Ehring et al. built their hypothesis on three general groups of evidence in the literature. The first is based on reports that children exposed to early-onset interpersonal trauma report higher degrees of alexithymia, which refers to a difficulty in identifying and labeling one's own emotional state, than non-traumatized children (Cloitre et al., 1997; McLean et al., 2006; Zlotnick et al., 1996). The second group of evidence is related to an individual's ability to accept negative, unpleasant, or uncomfortable emotions. Reports indicate that when compared to non-traumatized individuals, those who had experienced early-onset interpersonal trauma reported lower tolerance for and difficulty in regulating negative emotions, as well as higher fear of negative emotions (Briere et al., 2007; Ehring & Quack, 2010; Tull et al., 2007). Further, those individuals exposed to early-onset interpersonal trauma reported higher avoidance of those emotions, which related to their resistance to experiencing those negative thoughts and feelings and higher efforts at avoiding them as well (Batten et al., 2001; Marx & Sloan, 2002). These individuals who had early interpersonal trauma also struggled with managing their fear and anger as well as impulses, including self-destructive behavior, and sexual behaviors (Pelcovitz et al., 1997; van der Kolk et al., 1996). All of the literature noted here was based on retrospective study design. Ehring and Quack (2010) designed a prospective study to investigate the temporality of the traumatic events and emotion regulation challenges individuals faced. That is, they sought to clarify if and how the traumatic exposure preceded the emotion regulation challenges (Ehring & Quack, 2010).

In this prospective study of trauma survivors, the research team compared early-onset interpersonal trauma survivors (defined as physical or sexual abuse prior to age 14) with late-onset or non-interpersonal trauma (Ehring & Quack, 2010). They sought to clarify their hypothesis that early-onset, interpersonal trauma would contribute to more pronounced emotional regulation difficulties in the former group. Ehring and Quack (2010)'s hypothesis included the following:

1. Emotion regulation difficulties are significantly related to levels of PTSD symptoms.
2. Survivors of early-onset chronic interpersonal trauma report higher levels of emotion regulation difficulties than survivors of late-onset, early-onset single/repeated, and non-interpersonal traumas.
3. The differences in emotion regulation between the different types of trauma survivors remain significant when controlling for PTSD symptoms (Ehring & Quack, 2010, p. 590).

Using the Difficulties with Emotion Regulation Scale (DERS; Gratz & Roemer, 2004) as well as PTSD exposure and impact measures, the authors reported the following findings:

In line with the hypotheses, PTSD symptom severity was significantly associated with all variables assessing emotion regulation difficulties. In addition, survivors of early-onset chronic interpersonal trauma showed higher scores on these measures than survivors of single-event and/or late-onset traumas. However, when controlling for PTSD symptom severity, the group differences only remained significant for two out of nine variables. The most robust findings were found for the variable "lack of clarity of emotions" (Ehring & Quack, 2010, p. 587).

This team found a significant association between all of the emotional regulation variables and trauma symptom severity (Ehring & Quack, 2010). Early-onset chronic interpersonal trauma, when compared to both non-traumatized controls and also late-onset traumas, reported higher degrees of difficulty with emotion regulation. This suggests that early-onset interpersonal trauma places an individual at a potentially higher risk for later emotional regulation challenges. These authors further reported that levels of PTSD were correlated with the following:

a. reduced levels of clarity and awareness of emotion;
b. low levels of acceptance of negative emotions, higher levels of experiential avoidance, and higher levels of emotion suppression;
c. difficulties engaging in goal-directed behavior when distressed and high levels of impulse control difficulties; and
d. impaired use of functional emotion regulation strategies, including low levels of reappraisal (Ehring & Quack, 2010, para. 31)

The challenge here, as is often the case with individuals who are exposed to chronic, traumatic stress (and particularly at a young age), is that emotion identification and expression are some of the very tools needed to engage in therapeutic interventions. Successful trauma recovery requires adaptive emotional regulation and speaks to the need for evidence-based interventions and treatments that can address these impairments in trauma-exposed individuals. Emotion control and self-regulation is a critical aspect of assessment for the trauma-exposed individuals. Awareness of these challenges can directly inform and drive the intervention process and remains a core consideration for children who have exposure to chronic adversity.

Self-Concept and Future Orientation

Given the number of the functional challenges that have been discussed in this chapter, it is not surprising that trauma-exposed youth often struggle with their self-concept, beliefs about themselves, and overall future orientation. It has been documented here and elsewhere that traumatic experiences can cause damage and impairment to an individual's views about themselves and their role in the world. McAdams (1996) notes the "psychological importance of constructing a coherent life narrative that reflects and links together who we were, who we are now, and who we hope to become" (McAdams, 1996; Hemenover, 2003). Horowitz (1986) expands that traumatic events often interfere with and provide inconsistent information about the individual's view of themselves and their life narrative. These individuals struggle to integrate their ideas about themselves with the things that have happened to them or what they have experienced.

What exactly is self-concept and how does it develop? Self-concept and self-perception include things such as self-acceptance, positive view of self, personal agency, and mastery. It also includes the perception of the self as able to handle and manage stress, which is often impaired in individuals with trauma exposure. This further includes an individual's perception of their purpose in life, which includes the belief that their live has meaning, value, and goals for the future (Hemenover, 2003). Self-acceptance is related to an individual's ability to maintain a positive view of self, including the understanding that all individuals have both good and bad qualities (Hemenover, 2003).

Future orientation has been examined as a potential protective factor against risky behavior. Future orientation is a multidimensional construct that includes both cognitive and affect aspects (Cabrera, 2009; Nurmi, 1989; Seginer, 2008; Trommsdorff et al., 1978). Generally speaking, this construct has to do with an individual's attitudes and judgments about their future (Cabrera, 2009; Trommsdorff et al., 1978).

Foster care youth are 10 times more likely to receive mental health services than youth in the general population, and those foster care youth who have experienced a form of abuse are 23 times more likely to receive mental health services than those who had not experienced abuse (Shin, 2005). Although only 10% of the general population utilizes special education services, it has been estimated that 25–52% of foster care youth receive special education services due to learning disabilities and severe emotional disturbances (Zetlin & Weinberg, 2004; Cabrera, 2009, p. 272).

In a study of 343 foster care teenagers, interviews were conducted regarding future orientation, mental health, trauma history and exposure, and cognitions related to HIV risk behaviors (Cabrera, 2009). Using the Childhood Trauma Questionnaire (CTQ), lifetime trauma history data was collected. The Life Orientation Test (LOT-R; Scheier et al., 1994) and the Heimberg's Future Time Perspective Inventory (FTPI; Heimberg, 1968) were both used to measure future orientation. The outcomes of this study are noteworthy. While there were no differences found relative to race, gender, and age, overall findings were significant: "Future orientation was significantly associated with mental health, trauma, HIV-related knowledge, attitudes, behavioral intentions, and number of sexual intercourse partners. Furthermore, externalizing behaviors and attitudes toward risky behaviors each partially mediated the relationship between future orientation and number of sexual intercourse partners" (Cabrera, 2009, p. 271).

Future orientation, or the development of future goals, predicts improved psychological outcomes (Hemenover, 2003; Stein et al., 1997). Sense-of-self, which includes views about one's self in the world, is often associated with psychological wellness, and when impaired, psychological distress. As has been noted before, trauma-related impairments in both of these domains frequently stem from disorganized, disrupted, and poor attachment relationships early in life. Cook et al., (2005) notes that there are three main components to a caregiver's responses that will directly impact a child's sense of self and self-concept. These include: "believing and validating their child's experience, tolerating the child's affect, and managing the caregivers' own emotional response. When a caregiver denies the child's experiences, the child is forced to act as if the trauma did not occur. The child also learns he or she cannot trust the primary caregiver and does not learn to use language to deal with adversity" (Cook et al., 2005, p. 395).

In a study that examined the role of trauma disclosure on perceptions of self and psychological distress (n = 50), results indicated that trauma-exposed participants experienced an increase in positive self-perception and a decrease in distress from pre-test to post-test (Hemenover, 2003). In a different study of 18, 24, and 30-month-old infants, Schneider-Rosen and Cicchetti (1991) assessed the extent to which maltreated children developed their awareness of themselves as distinct from others, visual self-recognition using a mirror, and feelings toward oneself. As early as 18 months of age, maltreated children were more likely to respond to mirror self-recognition with neutral or negative affect than non-traumatized control subjects. As discussed earlier in this chapter as it relates to healthy attachment, stable and positive caretaking early in life supports the development of a strong sense of self and views of one's self as being both worthy and competent (Cook et al., 2005). In a study of resilience, abuse and perceived parental support (n = 61), findings indicated that the child's self-concept was associated with all trauma symptoms (except sexual concerns) and accounted for a significant degree of variance relative to trauma symptoms (Reyes et al., 2008). They further found that relative to sexual trauma, the longer the perpetration period, the more negative the child's self-concept.

It is abundantly clear that individuals who have been exposed to trauma struggle in multiple areas of functioning, least of not which is the often overwhelming sense of shame and poor self-concept they have. The fundamental belief that they are not good enough, or worthy enough is perhaps more damaging than any other of the trauma-related outcomes. As can be imagined, this could wreak havoc on a child's ability to be successful in school and community settings and needs to be central in any assessment and subsequent intervention plan.

Dissociation

Dissociation and alterations in consciousness are one area where trauma-exposed individuals often experience dysfunction and impairment. Putnam reports that children who have been exposed to chronic maltreatment tend to make three specific dissociative alterations that interfere with their awareness of self (Putnam, 1997).

1. Automatization of behavior (i.e. deficits in judgment, planning and organized, goal-directed behavior)
2. Compartmentalizing of painful memory and feelings
3. Detachment from awareness of emotions and self

As Felitti and Anda noted when they were first working with obese sexual abuse survivors, the originations of the behaviors (and we would suggest the dissociations), were adaptive at one time. At one point, they served a protective function for the individual experiencing the trauma. Putnam (1997) noted that these dissociations "are understood as failures in basic developmental processes, such as the consolidation of identity and maturation of metacognitive integrative functions" (Putnam, 1997, p. 2). The intersection of memory and survival is relevant here. Memory gaps and notable missing information in recollections often associated with dissociation are not uncommon in trauma-exposed youth. These dissociative periods can occur intermittently throughout the day and create notable gaps in the youth's acquisition of the content that is delivered throughout the school day. For obvious reasons, this can wreak havoc on the learning process for trauma-impacted individuals.

SUMMARY

This chapter highlights a number of the major domains of functioning that may be resilience-based in trauma and adversity exposed youth. Using a trauma-informed lens in school-based psychological evaluations carries a number of important considerations. We encourage readers to read the work of Tishelman et al. (2010) and Cook et al. (2005) for a robust discussion on utilizing the trauma-informed lens in school settings. We suggest here a number of considerations in both school and community-based trauma-informed assessments for youth exposed to chronic, toxic stress and adversity.

Tishelman et al., (2010) and others (How Traumatized Children Learn (HTCL); Cole et al., 2005a,b) suggested the need for school-wide systems level approaches that address trauma competency across the organization and improve outcomes for all children. The Flexible Framework utilized by the Safe and Supportive Schools Commission of MA (which resulted from the work of Susan Cole and others at the Trauma Policy and the resulting publication "Helping Traumatic Children Learn") is one important avenue for pursuing a whole school, trauma-informed perspective. Tishelman's work seeks to build on the work presented in "How Traumatized Children Learn" and offers important considerations for trauma-informed assessments in school settings.

It should be well within the repertoire of the school-based clinical to consider the role of chronic, traumatic stress and adversity in a child's presenting clinical picture and related functioning. This includes the exceedingly important role of differential diagnosis and the consideration that traumatic exposure and chronic adversity may play a role in a child's presentation, but certainly does not always (Tishelman et al., 2010). Trauma may be related to the youth who is struggling, but is also may not be. As Tishelman et al. note: "Adopting a 'trauma lens' can ensure that trauma is considered as a hypothesis when appropriate, but should not be used to overshadow other important etiologies for a child's presentation or lead to an overemphasis on trauma as an explanatory variable when other factors are more salient" (Tishelman et al., 2010, p. 282). As we move forward in Chapter 9, we will begin to consider different levels of assessment including screening, formal individual assessments, and assessments of familial context. This will include a robust conversation on ethical considerations and challenges to conducting trauma-informed assessments in school settings.

Section Three

TRAUMA-INFORMED ASSESSMENT FRAMEWORK

Eight

CONSIDERATIONS FOR TRAUMA SCREENING IN SCHOOL AND COMMUNITY SETTINGS

Kirby L. Wycoff

Trauma-related screenings are one mechanism by which clinicians can be made aware of children in need. Trauma-related screenings in the school setting however, require careful consideration. In community health and public health settings, universal screenings allow stakeholders to assess and identify members of the population who are most in need. The Centers for Disease Control and Prevention partner with states to survey entire populations, in order to assess health-related, risk-related and overall wellness characteristics of states, cities and towns across the country. The YBFRSS (Youth Behavioral Surveillance Rating System) is one such tool is used to assess overall population health and wellness. Interestingly, only 39 states in the United States integrate the ACEs module in their annual state-level surveillance. Wycoff et al. (2018) are currently building partnerships with the Department of Elementary and Secondary Education, the Department of Public Health, and the Department of Children and Youth Services among others to better integrate and interpret state and county-level datasets. The goal of this interdisciplinary research is to more accurately identify vulnerable populations within the community and drive subsequent resource allocation and interventional programming.

When considered carefully, and when placed within a responsive system, trauma-related screenings have a role in both community health and public health sectors as well as within the school context (Rossen and Cowan, 2013). It is critical, however, that we consider the system's ability to respond appropriately to the data acquired by the screening. Further, the risks and benefits of collecting this data must be weighed against the possible risk of activating some traumatized youth. For some systems, this type of screening may do more harm than good. It is important to note the idea of screening for trauma exposure in schools is relatively recent. For some systems, who are well equipped to respond to student need, there MAY be utility in universal screening. Any screening endeavor internal or external to the school setting must be done with the intent of linking those who are in need of services to suitable resources and interventions. Eklund and Rossen (2016) authored a brief "Guidance for Trauma Screening in Schools: A Product of the Defending Childhood State Policy Initiative" which was supported through a grant from the Office of Juvenile Justice and Delinquency Prevention and the National Center for Mental Health and Juvenile Justice. Eklund and Rossen note that despite an increasing number of available tools for screening and assessment of trauma in schools, there is relatively little support in the literature to address using these practices in the school setting (Eklund & Rossen, 2016). This chapter will explore the use and practical considerations of screening for trauma exposure and impact in the school setting.

INTRODUCTION

There is clear evidence in the literature that early identification of challenges and needs can create more positive outcomes for individuals who are struggling. This literature has driven much of the educational policy and legislation related to universal screening measures in the school context (IDA 2004; New Freedom Commission on Mental Health 2003; Eklund & Rossen, 2016). With the rise of the Response to Intervention (RTI) movement in education, Tier 1 interventions and universal screenings are becoming increasingly prevalent. Largely borrowed from the field of prevention science and public health, the idea of giving everyone in a population (i.e. all children within a school or a district) an intervention or assessment (screening) grows out of the belief that assessing everyone in the population will yield meaningful benefits. That is, probing all members of the population will help target which members of that population are in need of more specialized and intensive support and services. A Tier 1 intervention, which is ultimately a universal assessment program, seeks to survey all members in an articulated target population.

Universal screening is a preventative, proactive approach to helping identify members of a community who may be at risk for future challenges (Eklund & Rossen, 2016; Eklund & Dowdy, 2014; Jenkins et al., 2007). The information collected from these brief and efficient measures is then analyzed and interpreted. This data then drives decision-making to ascertain which members of the target population need a higher level of service or support (Eklund & Rossen, 2016).

In March 2014, the U.S. Department of Health and Human Services authored a publication entitled "Birth to 5: Watch Me Thrive! A Compendium of Screening Measures for Young Children." This publication highlights a number of specific measures that can be used for general screening of this population, but also calls attention to technical aspects of utilizing screening approaches to identification of at-risk members of the population.

It is critically important that screenings are conducted using reliable, valid screening tools that are clinically suitable and relevant for the age, culture, and language of the child who is being screened (Shepard et al., 1998). The technical skill of the clinician who is leading the screening and more importantly, interpreting the outcomes, is also of great importance. Moodi et al., (2014) note the purpose of screenings is to assess a brief period in time indicating the need for additional support. Screening provides a snapshot of a child's current functioning and behavioral, social, physical, educational, or mental health status. The outcomes of the screenings are used to determine if and when additional, more comprehensive evaluations or referral to interventions are needed (Florida Partnership for School Readiness, 2004). Moodi et al. note a number of important considerations for screenings that clinicians and practitioners should be mindful of:

- Screenings are designed to be brief (30 minutes or less)
- Screenings cannot capture the full range of current functioning
- Screenings are designed to identify risk or potential areas of risk
- Screenings only indicate the possibility of a potential concern or risk
- Screenings must be followed by additional follow-up and comprehensive evaluation to confirm or disconfirm red flags that may have been raised (Moodi et al., 2014, p. 2)

Moodi et al. further note there are notable differences between the screening process and the full, comprehensive assessment process. "Assessment refers to an ongoing, continual process of observing, gathering, recording, and interpreting information to answer questions" about a child's functioning (Moodi et al., 2014, p. 3). They noted a number of differences between screeners and full, comprehensive assessments:

- Assessments can be used for multiple purposes including hypothesis testing about a child's current challenges, identification purposes, and driving the intervention process; screenings are only used to monitor current functioning or indicate those at risk
- Assessments seek to establish a child's performance over time; screenings are focused on one specific point in time
- Assessments are typically more robust processes which involve collecting information from multiple sources, across multiple domains of

> functioning; screenings typically reflect a brief probe directly to the
> child, parent, teacher, or care provider (Moodi et al., 2014, p. 2)

As is the case in school settings, screeners are often the precursor to the full, comprehensive evaluation process. That is, when a student or family is noted as needing additional support (based on the screening probes), this indicates to the intervention team some additional actions need to take place. This is a critically important aspect of screenings in schools (and other settings), as one of the most critical aspects of asking individuals if they are struggling is having something to support them with if the answer is yes. Providing universal screenings without having mechanisms in place to support those in need is problematic, and potentially, unethical.

Eklund et al. (2014) and others (Jenkins et al., 2007; Eklund & Rossen, 2016) noted that when data helps connect children and families with needed support, these brief and efficient measures can be part of a comprehensive, practice approach to meeting individual needs. Schools, which represent a captive audience of children and families, might make screening tools particularly useful as we have access to a large number of youths in this setting. This is especially so in light of the many barriers that often exist for accessing community-based care (Eklund 2016; Levitt et al., 2007; Glover & Albers, 2007). While there is clear evidence of the utility of universal and early screeners as a mechanism to support children, only one in eight schools actually have adapted these measures (Bruhn et al., 2014). Eklund and Dowdy note that there is evidence for using screenings to help identify at-risk students who may be otherwise unknown to school staff (Eklund & Dowdy, 2014). However there are also a number of barriers on the implementation of universal screenings. Chafouleas et al., (2010) as well as Eklund and Rossen (2016) note these barriers may include limited time and resources in school building, concerns about ethical considerations and consent, and overall lack of awareness of using universal screening procedures. These barriers as well as the overall use of trauma-related screening measures will be discussed in this chapter. This discussion will include addressing ethical considerations, developmental considerations, and technical considerations in tool selection, among other topics.

CONSIDERATIONS FOR TRAUMA SCREENING IN SCHOOLS

Eklund and Rossen (2016) note a number of logistical considerations that are relevant to the implementation of universal trauma-informed screening in school settings. When a school is developing a trauma screening protocol, these areas must be considered before implementation. As noted by Eklund and Rossen, these include:

- Identifying which concern(s) to examine (e.g. internalizing behaviors, trauma symptoms, sources of adversity, or stress)
- Identifying which screening tool to use
- Examining costs associated with purchasing screening measures
- Calculating personnel time, training, and effort needed to administer measures, score data, and analyze and interpret findings, as well as connect data to interventions
- Identifying who will complete the measures (e.g. teacher, parent, student)
- Ensuring that adolescents, parents and school personnel are aware of the purposes and use of screening tools (e.g. informed consent)
- Determining the number and timing of screening administrations (e.g. Fall, Spring) (Eklund & Rossen, 2016, p. 4)

It has been well-established that increased exposure to trauma is predictive of short and long-term academic and health-related issues. It would be quite realistic to assume early screening and identification of these possible exposures would be helpful for children and families who are at-risk for later problems (Alisic et al., 2011; Eklund, 2016). Having mechanisms in place to help identify these individuals is a reasonable solution for helping schools and communities respond to those most in need. Issues like tool selection, informant selection, informed consent, and the time and resources needed to conduct assessment are all important areas of consideration in developing a trauma screening protocol.

CONFIDENTIALITY

While this book seeks to help guide understanding for both school and clinical-based mental health professionals, there are important distinctions between these two settings which are relevant to trauma-informed assessments. One critically important consideration that is specific to the school setting is the management of sensitive information and disclosures. Typically in a community-based mental health setting parents have chosen to take their children for an evaluation or have been mandated to do so. In a school setting, parents or guardians may have no interest in having a professional evaluate, assess, or provide services to their child. This may be related to concerns about a child disclosing information that would potentially result in Child Protective Services or Judicial involvement. School-based staff may have concerns about a child who they suspect is witnessing domestic violence in the home, or is the victim of sexual or physical abuse, and have no way to confirm this information. Children delay and avoid disclosing maltreatment for a whole host of reasons, and their parents may be resistant to openly sharing this information with school-based personnel for a number of reasons as well (Tishelman et al., 2010). The ability of school-based personnel to get fully informed consent for an evaluation and partner with parents and guardians in helping their children is particularly complex when a trauma history is suspected. This includes fully notifying the parents about the possibility of what will happen if abuse is disclosed; this will require a mandated report to child protective services. In the event that a disclosure is made, how school psychologists, guidance counselors, adjustment counselors, and other school-based mental health professionals handle that information and its sharing (on a strict need-to-know basis, which may be articulated and interpreted differently) is absolutely essential. As Tishelman et al. (2010) note, schools do not always have consistent policies for ensuring that sensitive information is treated with discretion. When a child makes a disclosure of personal information, there may be times when the information is disseminated in ways that can be embarrassing or shaming to a child or family, or can lead to negative perceptions or responses to the child and their family by school personnel. Without a clear sense of where disclosed information will be shared, parents might be understandably cautious about conveying information, even if it could be otherwise beneficial to a child for his or her private information to be communicated to a teacher or other responsible adults at school. In the absence of assurance that information related to trauma would be handled with care and reasonable confidentiality, a child and family cannot be certain that the child will not be stigmatized or that the information will not create further family difficulties (e.g. concerns about involvement with child protection, or potential criminal or immigration proceedings) (Tishelman et al., 2010, p. 284).

In the absence of knowing where and how their information will be used, parents may have serious concerns about sharing information with schools (Tishelman et al., 2010). As clinicians who are considering screening procedures in school or community settings, working with parents to understand how information will be handled and used is critical.

INFORMED CONSENT AND FAMILY RIGHTS

Related to the topic of confidentiality, the issue of informed consent and parental rights is an important one. When asking about exposure to trauma, parents must fully understand their rights and understand what they are providing consent for if they chose to do so. As noted in the previous section, informing parents of their rights to decline consent and understanding how the information will be used if they do give consent is necessary.

In a sample of Elementary School children (n = 402), 34 % (n = 138) of the children who were screened experienced one or more traumatic events, and 75.4% of those who experienced at least one traumatic event indicated moderate-to-high levels of post-traumatic stress symptoms (Gonzalez et al., 2016). Of great concern, however, is that less than half of these students whose parents were asked to take part gave their child consent to do so. Selection bias is a concern, if we consider that parents who know their children might have had exposure to trauma chose not to let their child participate in the screening. The authors indicate that "a total of 1,050 parental consent forms were distributed with 789 (73%) returned and 417 (53%) providing consent for child screening. Of these, 402 children completed the screening for exposure to traumatic events. Parents provided written consent for screening but did not take part in any of the described screening procedures" (Gonzalez et al., 2016, para. 10). This may lead us to wonder if the outcomes found by Gonzalez et al. are possibly an underestimation of the scope of trauma exposure across that population.

There are two different consent methods used in research and clinical practice. One is "active" consent and the other is "passive consent." *Active consent* refers to parents signing a document that specifically indicates whether their child can or cannot take part. *Passive consent* refers to the practice of implying consent is given, unless the parent specifically requests that their child not take part. A parent not sending a consent form back assumes that the parent is agreeing to their child's involvement. Passive consent requires the parent to send the form back saying "no" to their child's participation; active consent requires them to send a form back if they are saying "yes" to their child's participation. The use of passive consent is controversial in many settings, particularly in schools where there are high rates of illiteracy and non-English speaking families (Eklund & Rossen, 2016). Despite these concerns, Ellickson and Hawes (1989) note that passive consent may be a viable alternative to active consent, when additional privacy safeguards are put in place. The differences in using active versus passive consent are particularly salient when considering the issue of universal screenings on sensitive, trauma-related topics. While passive consent may result in higher response rates and more subjects (see Blodgett, 2012; Eklund & Rossen, 2016), we suggest active consent should be used when engaging in screeners related to trauma exposure and impact.

Blodgett (2012) further expands that active consent procedures alone are not enough to ensure full parental understanding. He suggests a comprehensive, informed consent process includes fully ensuring parents and caregivers are able to understand the potential benefits and risks of participation, and generally believe that their sensitive and personal family information will be handled professionally and respectfully (Blodgett, 2012). In his discussion on the trauma-informed work that is being conducted in the state of Washington, Blodgett notes that analogous to the RTI model, the team is using the common three-tier public health model. In this model, interventions are embedded in a systems framework and include trauma-informed classrooms; evidence-based social-emotional learning practices; trauma-informed decision-making for children who are struggling behaviorally and academically related to their trauma history; and providing brief small group and individual clinical services using trauma-focused interventions for those members of the population who are in most need (Blodgett, 2012). This mode integrates and bridges the school-based service delivery with public health service providers. He notes that in this large-scale, state-wide implementation, there is equal emphasis on reduction of the impact of trauma on individuals who had been exposed, while also promoting social-emotional development for all children. This is consistent with the notion that trauma-informed schools are good for all children, not only those who have been exposed to trauma (Cole et al., 2013) Blodgett notes that the efforts in Washington state are funded through the U.S. Department of Justice and the Bill and Melinda Gates Foundation, in partnership with the US Administration of Children and Families and the Washington State Department of Health, which directly funded components of the adversity screening and assessment processes in the schools. This is an important consideration because it speaks to the collaborative opportunities that are possible to pursue across sectors and disciplines. This is consistent with the approach advocated for elsewhere, that suggests when local Departments of Education are willing and able to partner with other human-service organizations, like Departments of Health, State Education Boards, Departments of Social Services, and Departments of Children and Youth, more focused and collaborative attention can be given to supporting a community's most vulnerable members (Wycoff et al., 2018).

Blodgett notes that the single most important lesson learned through the state-wide initiative was that screening and assessment of trauma exposure and adversity in school settings must be meaningful to both the mission and context of the system that is adopting those practices (Blodgett, 2012). He noted:

> If the resulting knowledge does not drive practice improvement in meaningful ways, then the fact of adversity is not helpful information. As a

result, screening and assessment are tools within a broader discussion of organizational change and practice change. The 'soft skills' of leadership and staff engagement, organizational development and decision-making, working with resistance, and partnership are integral to the success of these efforts. This lesson aligns fully with the recommendations from Implementation Science and the practical lessons of innovation diffusion.

(Blodgett, 2012, p. 2–3)

The lessons from Washington state also indicate that ascertaining an overall "adverse childhood experience (ACE) Dose Exposure" is more critical that the specific questions that are asked in the screening process. While clarity of questions is obviously important, initial data suggests that the cumulative exposures on core domains are so robust, that focusing on specific trauma details may not be necessary when trying to identify those in the population who are at the most risk (Blodgett, 2012).

Blodgett (2012) noted that there are a number of core domains of ACE dose exposure that are useful to consider in a trauma screening. These include disruptions in caregiver relationships (due to divorce, death, and illness), reduced caregiver capacity (due to behavioral health problems, child maltreatment, mental illness, and substance abuse), and family and community violence and safety (homelessness, and whether basic material needs are met). We suggest here, as have Blodgett (2012) and others (Eklund & Rossen, 2016), that consent is not just the end product that we need to receive back from parents. Rather, it is a process, wherein caregivers must be our partners. That is, "informed consent has to be treated as a central development task and parents need to fully understand the implications if they answer affirmatively to some questions. The increased risk with more detailed questions needs to be justified by our need to know. Our initial experience suggests that outside of formal treatment and research settings, justification of the risk is difficult to defend" (Blodgett, 2012, p. 3). The clarity we provide parents when requesting their consent to ask their children these questions is critical and will be further discussed in subsequent sections as we consider how we handle the information we collect through screenings.

As Blodgett suggests (see the initial Head Start study findings), practitioners can avoid triggering questions, while still accessing productive ACE dose exposure that can help us better understand an individual's risk for future challenges (Blodgett, 2012). We will continue to explore the concept of a "Need to Know" framework in the next section on safety and follow-up.

SAFETY AND FOLLOW-UP

Whenever we systematically ask about any individual's exposure to adversity and trauma, the likelihood we get an answer that concerns us is high. There are real safety and ethical issues that need to be taken into consideration when querying anyone, especially minors, about their adversity exposure (Blodgett, 2012). Unlike adults, who may no longer be in the threatening or dangerous environment that is connected to the adversity exposure, the same is not always true for youths. When asking these questions of minors, the risks are simply higher. One of the most important risks is the need for mandated child maltreatment and abuse reporting, and there may be increased reporting demands when we ask minors more direct questions about their possible trauma exposure (Blodgett, 2012). Additional risks that need to be considered are the potential damage to professional relationships between parents and clinicians (Blodgett, 2012). This is particularly salient when we consider the introduction of ACE-related and trauma questions into a non-treatment professional relationship (e.g. teacher–parent relationship) wherein the social contract for services has not yet addressed issues like confidentiality mandated reporting (Blodgett, 2012).

Blodgett proposes a "need to know/consent to share" decision-making tree that can help school-based clinicians guide their screening process. Blodgett references the study in Washington's Head Start programs, noting that for families and clients who were already engaged in services, a detailed child maltreatment and risk profile was collected. However, for the more general screening of the entire population, the questions were focused on information that would lead to eligibility for services, (more general questions) and did not include specific information that would require follow-up action (Blodgett, 2012). He notes that "a decision tree in terms of what information, when, and for what purpose is the most constructive way to build effective ACEs and trauma screening and assessment practices" (Blodgett, 2012, p. 4). This also highlights the imperative of linking screening and assessment data to action plans and interventions. Schools can invest in the process of developing screening processes and decision trees relative to what information is collected, and when and how that information is used, in order to reduce overall risk and still capture the needs of the district.

VOLUNTARY PARTICIPATION

As has been noted in earlier sections of this chapter, ethical decision-making must be considered when building a system-wide trauma and adversity screening process. Blodgett (2012) notes a voluntary universal screening is most appropriate when specifically exploring trauma histories and current impact. It may be that asking about the child's trauma history may also reveal a parental or caregiver trauma history as well. This may be one of the reasons that some caregivers are reluctant to participate in screenings, particularly when they do not have a full understanding of how that information will be used. In the implementation of ACEs screenings in Head Start programs in Washington state, the results indicated that as the parent's ACE history increases, so does that child's ACE's exposure. "In the parents with five or more ACEs, 69% of their children have two or more ACEs and 40% of their children have four or more ACEs" (Blodgett, 2014, p. 10).

Despite this, when parents feel like they fully understand the rationale behind the actual ACE's screening and they feel like they have a choice in participation, they do appear willing to participate. In the voluntary "universal" screening in the Head Start programs, more than 75% of caregivers indicated a willingness to participate (Blodgett, 2012). He notes that while ACE scores in and of themselves may not be distressing, the act of responding to them and disclosing that information (which may, for some, be the first and only disclosure or acknowledgement they have ever made about their trauma history) can be quite distressing. Providing support for both children who have high ACE exposure is important, as is connecting the parents that also indicated high exposure scores to resources. Letting parents know that part of how this information will be used is to connect them and their children with meaningful support may be part of what allows parents to feel comfortable enough to disclose this information. In any service relationship, however, there may still be fear and uncertainty, as well as a great deal of shame and stigma around sharing this information – particularly as it relates to how the information will be used (Blodgett, 2012). The literature on intimate partner violence and advocacy also provides insight around the issue of voluntary disclosure. For someone who has potentially experienced violation of their personal boundaries via trauma of any sort, giving control back to the survivor is essential. As Blodgett notes, "you never take control and choice away from a person exposed to trauma unless the duty to protect children requires you do so. We need to consider the act of discussing adversity as an empowerment process and base our professional decisions on how we conduct ourselves accordingly" (Blodgett, 2012, p. 4). Blodgett notes that given this information and the overall goal to improve and build relationships with children and families, voluntary participation in any level of care, including screenings, is the most trauma-sensitive approach to use (Blodgett, 2012). These authors concur with this assessment.

FEASIBILITY AND PRACTICALITY

There are a number of practical and logistical issues that need to be taken into account when developing school-based screenings. As we have noted earlier, we cannot overstate the significance of connecting screening data to actual interventions, as well as appropriate follow-up for those that endorse exposure to trauma. That said, the staffing and time requirements that are needed for thoughtful, ethical trauma-screenings must also be taken into consideration.

School-based screenings may present practical barriers, including limited funding and staffing to conduct screenings, as well as concerns regarding follow-up after at-risk youth are identified (Levitt et al., 2007). Some may worry that engaging in full-scale, robust screenings may actually detract (or pull resources) from the services that are needed to implement the core mission of the organization (Blodgett, 2012).

> With feasibility and sustainability in mind, assessment measures were selected with consideration of their psychometric properties as well as their low-cost availability and ease of administration and scoring. Several adaptations were made to assessment procedures in order to make them appropriate to the developmental level of children.
>
> *(Gonzalez et al., 2016, para 12)*

Administration may vary from 5 to 10 minutes for students without a trauma or adversity history up to 15–25 minutes for those that do (Eklund & Rossen, 2016; Gonzalez et al. 2016). This does not take into account the time needed to follow-up with personal phone calls and individual meetings with parents and children who have endorsed multiple trauma exposures or high traumatic stress impact.

Blodgett notes that "detailed questions appropriate for adults will result in increased mandated child maltreatment reporting. We are encountering frequent mandated reporting demands when we ask more direct questions. Several lessons seem to be emerging from these challenges: Staff engagement, buy-in, and training are critical needs for adoption of screening. Staff engagement becomes more critical as direct questions involving potentially actionable information are to be included" (Blodgett, 2012, p. 3) Schools will need to consider the time investment necessary to develop and implement a comprehensive screening protocol that includes appropriate and ethical support for those who indicate a high degree of adversity and trauma exposure. Engaging staff and teachers in the process of building the screening protocols and impressing upon the entire school community the why behind the screenings is absolutely critical.

Developmental Appropriateness

Screening for trauma and adversity exposure, like screening for any other social, emotional, behavioral, or academic concern in school or community settings must take into account the developmental level and knowledge base of the target population and informants alike. Eklund and Rossen (2016) reflect that many universal screenings related to trauma (See Gonazlez et al., 2016; Woodbridge et al., 2015) use rating scales or individual interviews. While others (Blodgett, 2012) have used teachers as informants using sentinel and surveillance style screenings, it is important to consider the extent to which teachers feel comfortable screening for trauma and adversity, or even have general knowledge about trauma symptoms and reactions among their students (Eklund & Rossen 2016). When using student self-reported data or even parent-reported data, it is critical that reading levels and language are taking into consideration.

Woodbridge et al. (2015) used an active consent procedure and sent middle school students home with an informational flyer and consent form in English, Spanish, and Chinese. This study population included 4,076 students (of 25,033 in the whole district) in the sixth grade across four academic years (2011–2015) in a diverse school district in Northern California. This form provided information to parents regarding a brief screening process that would assess their child's trauma exposure and related traumatic stress. To address concerns and methodological vulnerabilities around the developmental and language levels of participants, the research team administered the screening within the first two months of school via a group administration of the trauma screener. This generally occurred in the context of a classroom and took approximately 15 minutes for students to complete (Woodbridge et al., 2015). The research administrators read all of the instructions during the screen out loud to participants and examples were provided on how to rate the trauma exposure and distress levels (Woodbridge et al., 2015). Even though only students with parental consent were able to participate, the research team did inform the participating students that at any time, they could decline participation and discontinue the screening. They were further informed that their parents would get general information on the results of the screening, but not specific details of what was disclosed (Woodbridge et al., 2015). As noted in the earlier section on safety and follow-up in trauma screening procedures, in this study, the research team adhered to all legal and ethical requirements for mandated reporting in the state of California. With the administrators of the screening present in the classroom and providing verbal instructions on survey procedures in the small group setting, they were also available for one-on-one support and guidance for any student who needed it during the administration. Once the small-group, classroom-based administration was completed, all screeners were scored per the manualized scoring procedures. In addition to mailing home general results of the screening process, this team specifically addressed the need for follow-up and support to the highest-need students (Woodbridge et al., 2015). These researchers addressed concerns regarding follow-up and support by personally calling all parents of students who had elevated ACE scores from the screener in order to discuss the results and connect families with resources and interventions in the school and community (Woodbridge et al., 2015).

Gonzalez et al. (2016) noted that screening younger children for trauma exposure and impact can present additional challenges. While self-report measures offer one possibility in efficiently collecting data about this topic, screening young children may present developmental and methodological challenges. Things like subjectivity, poor reliability, and poor validity may all be relevant when using self-reports with young children, largely related to their cognitive development and reading abilities (Gonzalez et al, 2016) There are a number of trauma-related tools that can be used in assessment for young children (play therapy, play narrative, etc.), though many of these tools are more appropriate for one-on-one or small group clinical work, not large-scale screenings (Gonazlez et al., 2016; Luby et al., 2007). Despite this, there is increasing evidence for improved reliability and validity in assessment tools for younger children (Luby et al., 2007; Gonzalez et al 2016). Further, in order to address the limited reading skills of some of the youngest children in schools, alternative modes of administration like verbal administration may be useful, just as they were in the older population in the Woodbridge et al. 2015 study.

In addition to adjusting the administration procedures to account for developmental, language and reading abilities, the areas of content within the screening itself may need to be considered. Blodgett (2012) noted additional developmental concerns that are profoundly unique for children with ACE exposure. Two examples of these are homelessness and homeless risk, which were not considered in the original ACE research. He suggests that integrating these aspects of basic resource assessment (clothing, hosing, hygiene, food) in school-aged populations help us better understand and address the cumulative stressors in the lives of children (Blodgett, 2012).

Developmentally appropriate modifications may be necessary in order for school-based clinicians to collect accurate information on both the nature and severity of students' traumatic history and risk (Eklund & Rossen, 2016). Trauma-related screeners have the potential to drive important decisions, and it is critical that the information collected is accurate and collected with the highest ethical and legal standards in mind.

TOOL SELECTION

It is critically important to use measures in the trauma-informed assessment that have strong psychometric properties (e.g. validity and reliability). Standardized measures, or those that are norms for different ages, genders, and cultures, are appropriate for trauma-informed screening. Reliability and validity are important aspects when selecting the appropriate tools for either the screening process or a full, comprehensive evaluation. We will not unpack this topic in great detail, but a quick refresher is necessary. For a more robust discussion on the selection of psychometrically sound, evidence-based measurements tools, please see the full work of Hunsley and Mash (2007).

Understanding the reliability and validity profiles of any specific tool that we may integrate into our screening processes enables us to make appropriate choices. The tool must be psychometrically sound and also be appropriate for the population and specific topic of interest. *Reliability*, or the extent to which a tool is reliable over time, is needed for a tool to be useful, but validity is equally important as well. Without psychometrically sound tools that are appropriately selected for the population and area of interest, the data that is yielded is virtually useless.

Reliability: This refers to the extent that scores or outcomes of a specific measurement tool will remain consistent over time, across administrators and across settings (Moodi et al., 2014). Reliability is the degree to which any instrument or tool produces stable and consistent results over time and across different clinicians. If a person takes a test several different times (i.e. taking the test at time 1, and one year later, taking the test again at time 2) and the results are the same, the test is considered reliable. There are a number of different types of reliability. They include:

- Test-Retest Reliability
- Inter-Rater Reliability
- Internal Consistency (IC) Reliability

Validity: refers to the extent to which the data yielded from the instrument captures what it is meant to capture. That is, does the tool measure what it is supposed to measure?

- Face Validity
- Construct Validity
- Criterion-Related Validity

While reliability is necessary, it alone is not sufficient. For a test to be reliable, it also needs to be valid. For example, if your scale is off by 5 pounds, it reads your weight every day with an excess of 5 pounds. The scale is reliable because it consistently reports the same weight every day, but it is not valid because it adds 5 pounds to your true weight. It is not a valid measure of your weight.

(Phelan & Wren, 2005, para. 12).

In order for a tool to be useful, it must have strong validity and reliability and be meaningful to the setting in which it is being applied. Hunsley et al., (2003) noted that in order for an instrument to be psychometrically sound, it needs to be standardized, normed on a relevant population, and have adequate reliability and validity. But how do we define adequate? It is important to consider psychometric properties in light of how that tool is to be used in any specific context and setting (Hunsley et al., 2007; Streiner & Norman, 2003). So it is not just a question of whether this the "right" tool, but rather, is it the right tool for the job at hand – does it do what we need it to do. Hunsley and Mash, (2007) developed a rating system for clinical tools that focused on nine different categories of consideration in selecting a tool for a certain purpose. These nine categories include "norms, internal consistency, inter-rater reliability, test-retest reliability, content validity, construct validity, validity generalization, sensitivity to treatment change and clinical utility" (Hunsley & Mash, 2007, p. 39). The authors note the absolute importance of making decisions about instrument utility within the context of a specific purpose, goal, or clinical need. The rating categories developed by Hunsley and Mash reflect a range from "not applicable/possible" to "acceptable," "good," and "excellent" (Hunsley & Mash, 2007, p. 39) Their goal was to help practitioners establish what was "good enough" in terms of psychometric strength to use with clinical utility. For example, relative to IC (reliability), they noted that 0.70–0.79 was acceptable, 0.80–0.89 was good, and 0.90+ was excellent (Hunsley & Mash, 2007). Guidelines like these can help guide practitioners in selecting the most suitable tool for the task at hand.

SAMPLE SCREENING PROTOCOL

Gonzalez et al. provided a great deal of detail on their consent and screening procedures which may be useful for us to consider here. While research purposes are different than clinical purposes, the format used here may in part inform the development of screening procedures in your setting. These authors noted that parental consent forms were sent home in September, during the first week of the school year, with all other beginning of the year materials for parents. The materials were sent home with each student in a folder that regularly goes home on the same day each week with important information for parents. That is, the material was positioned in a place and at a time that a parent might be looking for other important information. Each consent form had a place for the parent to check YES or NO for their consent, as well as a location for parental signature. If consent forms were not returned with other school-related materials, reminders and additional copies were sent home in the following two weeks. Teachers were instructed to provide verbal reminders to any parent that they had the opportunity to interact with (such as when dropping off or picking up students from school). In addition to these procedures, an incentive structure was put in place. Teachers were informed that the classroom with the highest return rate (meaning returned consent document, irrespective of whether parents said yes or no) would get a pizza party (Gonzalez et al., 2016).

Blodgett et al. (2012, 2016) of Washington State University utilized an ACE screening process in elementary school children in Spokane, Washington. The participants were elementary school staff who reported on students enrolled in the public school, including grades K-6. The primary population was 2,101 children enrolled in the school, of which 50% were randomly selected for staff review. There were a total of 179 teachers who were trained as first-level reporters. Their ACE's screening process for this district in Spokane utilized a

> sentinel reporting method with data reflecting information in school records or factual professional knowledge, in which teachers and building administrators completed reports of known concerns regarding academic, health, and adverse event exposure. Parent disclosure of information was treated as a factual statement. In participating buildings, fifty percent of the enrolled students were randomly selected for staff review. Using a common reporting form and variable definitions, the research team trained school staff to report what was known and not to report opinion or suspicions. Reports were made as Yes/No responses. No identifying information regarding students was collected. Student descriptive information included grade, gender, race, Free and Reduced Meal eligibility (a poverty indicator), and Special Education enrollment.
>
> *(Blodgett 2012, p. 6)*

The team accounted for a number of academic challenges in their screening calculations including the fact that the student wasn't meeting grade level requirements in one or more core subjects, that attendance was problematic and interfering with learning, and finally, that their school-based behaviors were also interfering with academic progress (Blodgett, 2012). In addition these learning challenges, health concerns were also considered. They included "seizure disorders, speech/language disorders, autism spectrum disorders, asthma, diabetes, obesity, food allergies, serious dental problems or other chronic health conditions identified by the school staff and a pattern of student-reported health" (Blodgett, 2012, p. 6) The team modeled their ACEs scale off of the original scale by Anda and Felitti. An ACE score was calculated based on both lifetime and past year exposures to 10 different adversity-related concerns. The following categories were added: community violence, physical disability and homelessness, and very specific child maltreatment questions were replaced with a general question about Child Protection Services (CPS) involvement with the family. The final list of ACEs included:

> lifetime and past 12 month occurrence of CPS referral or placement, homeless or highly mobile (McKinney- Vento Act eligible), parents' divorce or separation, death of a primary caregiver, family member Adverse events included lifetime and past 12 month occurrence of: CPS referral or placement, homeless or highly mobile, parents' divorce or separation, death of a primary caregiver, family member.

> *(Blodgett et al., 2014, p. 6)*

With this protocol, the research team was able to essentially engage in public-health surveillance data collection, without directly probing the children or families themselves. This method allowed for an overall understanding of the risk factors within the district and identifies children who might need to be referred for a higher level of services. The results indicated that staff identified 45% of their students who had been exposed to one or more adverse events in their lifetime, with 12% of the student populations experiencing three or more adverse events. It is important to note that the methodological approach used here is amenable to implementation in a school setting.

CAUTIONS IN TRAUMA SCREENING

Eklund and Rossen (2016) note a number of cautions for the development of trauma-related screening protocols in schools. While there may be great utility in these screenings in schools, others caution that they may unnecessarily label children and their families. This is often related to the concern that a focus on screening that is not embedded in an entire, whole-school culture of safety and support for all students may create a focus on specific Tier 2 and 3 interventions instead of recognizing the need for a school-wide culture shift. For this reason, it may be useful to consider sentinel surveillance approaches like those used by Blodgett in Washington state which leverage the use of publicly available databases and general understanding of district-wide risk. Wycoff et al. (2018) noted that using publicly available databases (educational, public health, etc.) may provide an over-all assessment of the ACE exposure across communities, and can at times be used in helping leverage stakeholders and improve understanding and rationale for why whole-school, trauma-sensitive approaches are needed. Cole et al. (2013) noted:

> A common reaction to the whole-staff presentation is the notion that trauma sensitivity requires screening and identifying all children who have had traumatic experiences. In fact, this is not recommended and could be quite harmful. In addition to stigmatizing some children, this approach also reinforces the idea that trauma sensitivity is solely about applying interventions to particular children instead of creating a safe, whole-school environment for all children.
>
> *(Cole et al., 2013, p. 54)*

Articulating best practices for school-based screening models for trauma-exposed youth is an area of interest that needs additional research and literature to be more fully understood.

As noted throughout this chapter, issues around identifying reliable, valid, developmentally appropriate measures, that can account for the subjectivity in informant response and provide accurate measures of trauma exposure and impact is of great concern. Further, when considering the role of informant, there is the possibility that parents and children may not have a high degree of agree-ment in reporting on adversity and trauma (Eklund & Rossen, 2016; Shemesh et al., 2005; Stover et al., 2010). Finally, as has been noted elsewhere, the critical link of connecting screening outcomes to interventions is of the utmost impor-tance. With the already established literature on overall incidence of trauma exposure in the US population, there are some schools that have chosen not to ask these specific questions, largely because they are not prepared to respond to the answers they get (Eklund & Rossen, 2016).

> Practical and accurate screening methods, when deployed appropriately and with adequate staff buy-in and commitment, better inform schools about where to focus resources for youth. The same could be said for using trauma screening data to consider how schools can allocate training, professional devel-opment, and/or services to the school community, based on survey results.
>
> *(Eklund & Rossen, 2016, p. 8)*

The same may be true for trauma-related screening protocols. All of the rea-sons noted above indicate the absolute imperative for caution and thoughtfulness when considering the development and implementation of a school-wide trauma screening model. While there may be benefit in the data that results from these screenings, for some the risks may not outweigh the benefits.

TRAUMA SCREENING MEASURES

For schools that have decided to implement screening procedures to better assess their school's overall trauma-related risk, and use that data to drive intervention, the selection of appropriate tools is critical. Some of these tools have been used in clinical settings, and some have been used in research settings, but all may be appropriate for consideration in school-wide approaches. A summary of a few of these tools is noted below. Please note that this list is not exhaustive, and different schools may choose different tools based on their individual needs.

Childhood Trauma Questionnaire (CTR)

This self-report assessment tool examines emotional, physical, and sexual abuse in childhood. It also assesses emotional and physical neglect. This self-report measure includes 28 items and is appropriate for children that age 12 years of age and older. The IC of this tool is 0.81–0.95. The Test-retest (TRT) Reliability of the tool is 0.79–0.86. The validity coefficient of this tool has been reported as 0.50–0.75 (Bernstein & Fink, 1998; Berstein et al., 2003; Berstein et al., 1997; Eklund et al., 2016).

Traumatic Events Screening Inventory For Children – Brief Form (TESI-C-BRIEF)

This assessment tool examines the exposure to direct or witnessing of traumatic events in children between the ages of 6 and 18 years old. There are 21 items of this brief form and it is conducted via a structured interview. The IC of this tool is 0.80. The Interrater Reliability (IR) is 0.73–1.00 (Davis et al., 2000; Eklund et al., 2016; Ford et al., 2002; Ford et al., 2008; Ribbe, 1996).

Traumatic Events Screening Inventory – Child Report Form – Revised (TESI-CRF-R)

The TESI-CRF-R was adapted from the TESI-C interview. This assessment tool is a brief, self-report inventory that examines the occurrence of traumatic events in children aged 6 to 18 years. This includes assessment of hospitalizations, community violence, domestic violence, physical violence, natural disasters, and accidents. This tool assesses both events to which the child was either a witness or a direct victim. Psychometric properties have not yet been reported on this measure, but the properties of the original form above are within acceptable ranges. There is also a TESI-Parent form, which has convergent validity equaling 0.42–0.91 (Ippen et al., 2002; Ribbe, 1996; Eklund et al., 2016).

Trauma Symptom Checklist-Child Version-Post-Traumatic Stress Sub Scale (TSCC-PTS)

This assessment tool is a self-report measure that assesses general traumatic stress symptoms and the impact of trauma on psychological symptomology in children between the ages of 8 and 16 years. The PTS is the 10-item Post-traumatic Stress Sub-scale that allows the opportunity to identify students in distress. The larger assessment tool is 54 items. The TSCC is available in multiple languages and was standardized on a larger normative sample of over 3,000 racially and economically diverse children without known trauma histories. The IC has been reported as between 0.82 and 0.93. (Brier, 1996; Briere et al., 2001; Sadowski & Fridrich, 2000). There is also a Trauma Symptom Checklist for Young Children (TSCYC) for children between the ages of 3 and 12 years.

UCLA PTSD Reaction Index – Adolescent Version (RI-R)

This assessment tool is a revised version of the UCLA Reaction Index (Pynoos et al., 1998). It assesses a child's experiencing of post-traumatic stress symptoms that had occurred in the last month and symptoms related to the Diagnostic and Statistical Manual of Mental Disorders. This tool can be used as a self-report measure or an interview format, which has 48 items in total and can be used with children between the ages of 6 and 18 years of age. Symptoms are rated on a 5-point Likert scale ranging from 0 (none of the time) to 4 (most all the time). This tool is available in multiple languages. Sample items include: "I have upsetting thoughts, pictures or sounds of what happened come into my mind when I do now want them to" and "I watch out for danger or things that I am afraid of" (Rodriguez et al., 1999; Roussos et al., 2005; Steinberg et al., 2004; Steinberg et al., 2013).

Community Violence Exposure Survey (CVES)

This assessment tool is a self-report that measures community violence exposure. This tool assesses for exposure to violent or dangerous events within the community. It may include direct exposure to and witnessing of violent events. These violent events could include homicides, threatening with a weapon, shootings, beatings, and attempted or completed suicide (Richters & Saltzman, 1990; Richters & Martinez, 1993; Lorion & Saltzman, 1993).

Strengths And Difficulties Questionnaire (SDQ)

This assessment tool includes multiple versions; a caregiver report, a teacher report and a youth report. It is a measure that assesses resilience, coping, and strengths in youth between the ages of 3 and 18 years and older. It takes approximately five minutes to complete. The tool has been translated into over 40 languages and assesses positive and negative attributes across five domain scales. These scales include: (i) Emotional Symptoms, (ii) Conduct Problems, (iii) Hyperactivity/Inattention, (iv) Peer Problems, and (v) Prosocial Behavior. This tool was included in the 2001 National Health Interview Survey conducted by the CDC. The psychometric properties for the teacher report are as follows: (IC Min = 0.70, Max = 0.88, Avg = 0.81), (Test Re-Test Min = 0.62, Max = 0.82, Avg = 0.74) and the NCTSN has rated both of these as acceptable. The interrater reliability was rated by NCTSN at questionable: (Inter-Rater Min = 0.25, Max = 0.48, Avg = 0.37) (Goodman, 1997).

CONCLUSION

Screenings of subsections or entire populations within any given organization may provide a useful avenue for prioritizing and triaging the members of those populations that are most in need. There are a number of important considerations that are relevant in trauma and adversity exposure and impact in school settings. Issues like confidentiality, informed consent, parent engagement, and follow-up protocols are essential in building trust and with families and collecting useful and valid information. While there may be valuable information that comes out of the screening process, for some schools, the potential risk does not outweigh the potential benefits. In addition to this, some (Cole et al., 2013) caution against screening procedures so as to not needlessly stigmatize children and their families and unintentionally de-emphasizing the need for school-wide approaches while only focusing on assessment and diagnosis. The gold standard for responding to the needs of trauma and adversity-impacted students includes movement towards school-wide approaches and shifting the overall culture within the school to better understand and respond to our most vulnerable community members. Eklund and Rossen (2016) noted following summary points relative to trauma-screening in schools:

- Screening for exposure to adversity can serve as a useful tool to determine potential risk for stress or trauma among students in schools
- Always obtain active parental informed consent for screening
- Screening tools administered to students may be more accurate than other informants (e.g. teachers or parents), though must be provided at a developmentally appropriate level
- Outcomes of screenings can help identify the severity or degree of need in a school community and help direct resources to support traumatized students
- Schools should consider existing resources and processes to address identified needs prior to implementing trauma screening in schools
- Supports should be provided through a Multi-Tiered System of Support (MTSS) framework, with a trauma-informed approach and implementation of more targeted, intensive interventions as necessary
- Individual services should not be determined solely through the screening process; follow- up assessment and individualized determination of needs are critical (Eklund & Rossen, 2016, p. 10).
- These authors concur with Eklund and Rossen that, for some districts, trauma-related screenings will be appropriate. The ability to which major stakeholders have a better understanding of their population (i.e. by using community-wide and district-wide ACEs surveying) can be used to build a rationale for why districts may need to consider the development of trauma-informed schools. We further note, however, our first choice for how to access this information is via sentinel and surveillance methods and approaches that do not directly assess (and potentially distress) individual students and families. We acknowledge the concern of Cole et al. (2013) regarding the possibility that trauma-focused screenings may stigmatize children and families and may de-emphasize the needs for school-wide culture shifts. We suggest that if trauma and adversity-related screenings are integrated into a district's screening process, the guidelines of Eklund and Rossen should be considered.

Nine

INDIVIDUAL AND FAMILIAL ASSESSMENT TOOLS

Kirby L. Wycoff

INTRODUCTION

The National Child Traumatic Stress Network (NCTSN) is one of the resources highlighted in the first section of this book. The NCTSN is leading the way in helping clinicians, providers, educators, community practitioners, and others in youth-serving organizations better understand the needs of trauma-impacted children. The NCTSN offers robust and comprehensive guidelines on the assessment of both the exposure to trauma and impact of trauma on youth. This framework assessment largely considers not only the possibility of whether or not a PTSD diagnosis exists (see Section 2 for the controversy around the DSM and trauma), but also the extent to which the youth may be impacted by chronic, complex adversity and stress, which is directly related to their functional impairments at the time of the assessment. The assessment framework presented here is built out of the work of the NCTSN and many others (Cole, et al., 2017; Tishelman et al., 2010), as well as the clinical experiences of this book's co-authors. First and foremost, it is critical that the assessment process be viewed as exactly that—a process, not a product. The assessment is not just a written document or deliverable that reports out on all of the information and data that was collected, but rather, reflects the iterative, collaborative process that unfolds between the clinician, client/student, client/student family, related professionals, and any other individual who has vested interest in the individual/student of concern. That is, the multiple informant approach is necessary; as those individuals who exist contextually around the child of interest are also critical. The process of assessment is really just the beginning of the intervention and treatment process. It is the assessment that drives the intervention and provision of services. Essentially, assessment is the first step in the intervention process. This includes a robust case for conceptualization and hypothesis testing about what challenges the child may be experiencing and why. Consistent with the RTI approach that includes a profile of strengths and weaknesses and/or concordance/discordance modeling (Hale et al., 2011), children who reach the highest level of support, and who do not respond to universal or Tier 2 interventions will need an individualized assessment to ascertain their needs.

HYPOTHESIS TESTING AND THE SCIENTIFIC METHOD

Hypothesis testing in assessment simply means that we have ideas or hypothesis about why a particular individual might be struggling. Presumably, this knowledge builds off of the initial referral question and is driven by the individual who brought the youth for services or made the request for an evaluation. These hypotheses are exactly that—a hypothesis, not truths, or known entities, but possibilities. The hypothesis testing model comes from the world of science, and we suggest that it is in fact a scientific inquiry and lens that we are to bring to the assessment process. Hypothesis testing is when you conduct research and try to answer a question. That is, you collect data and try to assess the extent to which your original hypothesis was true or not true. The hypothesis testing models is born out of the scientific method and can be conceptualized like this:

1. Ask a question
2. Do background research
3. Construct a hypothesis
4. Test with an experiment
5. Analyze data and draw conclusions
   - Results align with hypothesis – Continue
   - Results do not align with hypothesis – Return to Step 3 – Use the data to consider alternative hypothesis, collect more data, run the experiment again.
6. Communicate results

Another way of thinking of this as a more cyclical, iterative process can be demonstrated here:

1. Make an observation (What do I notice about a particular child in the setting)
2. Formulate a question (Why do I think that problem is occurring for this child?)

3. Formulate a hypothesis (What do I know to be true for children who typically struggle with this? What do my observations tell me about this child? Based on my expertise, and preliminary observations, what may be a reasonable hypothesis about this child's current difficulties?)
4. Develop a testable prediction (If my hypothesis is correct, the data will indicate these trends)
5. Gather data to test prediction (Build my assessment battery. Where and how will I collect data? Multiple informants, multiple domains of functioning. Be thorough and intentional in building the assessment battery – what do I need to know and what tools do I have at my disposal that will help me test my hypothesis?)
6. Refine, alter, expand or reject my hypothesis (Did the data confirm or disconfirm my original hypothesis? If it did not confirm, then reject, expand or alter it and go back to developing testable predictions and gathering data to test those predictions.)
7. Communicate results (Work with relevant stakeholders, including the client themselves to discuss the results and importantly, what steps can now be taken to ensure the client/student is able to get the support and services that they need to be successful) (Adapted from: https://en.wikipedia.org/wiki/Scientific_method)

As we look towards a framework for trauma-informed assessments, we must predicate that on the understanding of the assessment process in general. The scientific method and hypothesis-testing process provide a strong foundation of inquiry for better understanding any given individual's challenges in any range of contexts.

THE ASSESSMENT FRAMEWORK

The necessity of an assessment framework that considers the potential impact (not definite, but *potential* impact) of trauma as a driving factor in a child's current challenges and impairments cannot be overstated. Even when the referral question has nothing (seemingly) to do with trauma, the trauma-competent professional will build this possibility into their hypothesis testing approach. For example, even though a teacher's referral reports what may seem like straightforward attention deficit symptoms, assessing only for the presence of ADHD with a Conners assessment and other related measures misses the opportunity to explore the possibility to which the observed disregulation is occurring because of the impact of early adversity. As we have noted throughout this book, complex trauma can have far-reaching and significant impacts on multiple areas of functioning and across the developmental trajectory. Our comprehensive approach must include the possibility that exposure to and/or impact of trauma is connected to the child's clinical presentation. It is important to note that not all children with a trauma history or exposure will meet diagnostic criteria for PTSD or even have impairments. This is why it is important to have assessment batteries that are both specific to the referral question and reflective of the hypothesis testing model, and that integrate the possibility of trauma (as well as the possibility of any number of other things) as part of the underlying etiology. It is important to note that like Rosalyn and Mateo at the beginning of this book, children that are refereed to us may have a trauma history, and have often already received any number of other diagnoses when they are referred. These individuals may have already tried a number of different treatments (therapies, medications, etc.) that were focused on addressing a particular presenting problem, without taking into consideration the fact that trauma may actually be playing a greater role.

The National Child Traumatic Stress Network notes a number of key steps to the process of conducting trauma-informed assessments. NCTSN aptly notes that the assessment for complex trauma is by definition, complex. This will require clinicians to assess both a history of traumatic exposure as well as potential current impairment and impact on functioning. Asking very specific questions about the impact of trauma in the building of the assessment battery and process will be essential.

The following are some key steps for conducting a comprehensive assessment of complex trauma:

1. Assess for a wide range of traumatic events. Determine when they occurred so that they can be linked to developmental stages.
2. Assess for a wide range of symptoms (beyond PTSD), risk behaviors, functional impairments, and developmental derailments.
3. Gather information using a variety of techniques (clinical interviews, standardized measures, and behavioral observations).
4. Gather information from a variety of perspectives (child, caregivers, teachers, other providers, etc.).
5. Try to make sense of how each traumatic event might have impacted developmental tasks and derailed future development. Note: this may be challenging given the number of pervasive and chronic traumatic events a child may have experienced throughout his or her young life.
6. Try to link traumatic events to trauma reminders that may trigger symptoms or avoidant behavior. Remember that trauma reminders can

be remembered both in explicit memory and out of awareness in the child's body and emotions" (National Child Traumatic Stress Network, 2017, para. 9, retrieved from: http://www.nctsn.org/trauma-types/complex-trauma/assessment#q2)

It is important to note that even when the referral question does not include trauma or adversity as one of the driving questions or factors in the child's current functioning, the trauma-competent professional will absolutely build this lens (and possibility) into their hypothesis building and testing.

ASSESSMENT GUIDELINES

In the context of assessing children and families who may have been exposed to trauma and adversity, safety is of the utmost importance. Creating a safe place for the assessment to be conducted as well as building a therapeutic alliance with the individual who is being assessed is critical in order to create physical and psychological safety in the context of the assessment process (National Child Traumatic Stress Network, 2017, para. 2, retrieved from: http://www.nctsn.org/trauma-types/complex-trauma/assessment#q2). To this end, parents and their children should have an understanding of what the assessment process will look like, how the data will be collected, and how the information will be used.

As noted in the earlier chapter on trauma-informed screenings, ensuring children and families have a full understanding of the parameters and limitations of confidentiality is critically important. Those participating in the assessment need to understand under what conditions the clinician would need to break confidentiality and report previously unreported neglect and abuse information to the appropriate child protection service organization. A therapeutic relationship should be built with the child and the family, but all actual discussion about traumatic exposure should be conducted in private. This is specifically to protect the child from being queried about this information in the presence of parents, perpetrators (known or unknown), or other individuals who may have an investment in non-disclosure (National Child Traumatic Stress Network, para. 2, retrieved from: http://www.nctsn.org/trauma-types/complex-trauma/assessment#q2).

In addition to creating safety in the context of the assessment it is important to use both multiple informants and multiple tools/techniques and approaches to collect the most robust sample of data as possible. If the child is the client of interest, the child should be an informant. However, additional individuals who interact with that child are also relevant to the assessment process. This includes parents, caregivers, kinship care providers, foster parents, teachers, and any other relevant professionals involved in the child's life, such as case workers and allied health professionals (National Child Traumatic Stress Network, 2017, para. 3, retrieved from: http://www.nctsn.org/trauma-types/complex-trauma/assessment#q2).

Depending on the referral question, context, and goals of the assessment, the specific assessment tools you select will likely vary. A combination of different types of assessment techniques and tools will likely yield the most robust and holistic understanding of the child's difficulties. Behavioral and functional observation of the child in their natural environment as well as a clinical interview with the child and caregivers or other individuals who have knowledge of the child's history will likely be appropriate. Using the domains of functioning that were reviewed in Chapter 7 will help guide the selection of appropriate tools, measures and techniques. Further, it is also critical that assessors take a strength-based, assets-driven approach to understanding the child's areas of strength that serve as resiliency and protective factors. It will be necessary to also select standardized assessment tools with strong psychometric properties that have been normed on populations consistent with the population you are assessing (National Child Traumatic Stress Network, para. 5, retrieved from: http://www.nctsn.org/trauma-types/complex-trauma/assessment#q2). For additional discussion on measurement selection and assessment approaches, see Briere and Spinazzola (2005), Habib and Labruna (2011, 2012), Mash and Barkley (2009), and Nader (2007a,b).

As has been noted elsewhere, collaboration and therapeutic alliance with the child, family, and support team is a critical aspect of engaging in trauma-informed assessment practices. We have noted throughout this book that the "why" behind these types of assessments is to directly link children in need with appropriate and needed supports and services. Assessment that does link directly to follow-up services may fall dangerously short in empowering vulnerable children and their families to get the help they need. This is especially relevant and necessary, as using a trauma-informed perspective in the assessment process often includes gathering information about the family and context within which the child exists. Explaining to parents at the outset (and throughout) the process why certain information is being collected, and how it will be used, is a key ingredient to building therapeutic alliance, safety, and trust within the helping relationship. At the completion of the assessment (and as appropriate, throughout the assessment process), caregivers, family members and legal guardians should be kept informed of the progress of the assessment. Once the assessment is completed, spend clearly-articulated time with the adults to fully understand the outcomes and implications of the data collected. This may mean multiple meetings with various stakeholders (who are in a need-to-know position and for whom the legal guardian has given consent for the information to be shared) in order to help build understanding of who the child is, and why and how they are struggling. This idea of stakeholder investment also builds relationships with the student and family that can be leveraged to inform treatment planning and accessing of follow-up services. Work with the family and the multidisciplinary team to integrate findings and navigate "next steps" in accessing care and supports. Finally, it is important to always remember that an assessment is essentially a snapshot in time. For individuals exposed to trauma, the clinical presentation often shifts. As the child experiences new developmental milestones or stressors, and as other variables in their life shift and change, the outcomes of the assessment and data may also shift. Trauma-exposed children are also more likely than others to gradually disclose trauma experiences over time, as relationship, safety and therapeutic alliance are built (National Child Traumatic Stress Network, 2017, para. 5, retrieved from: http://www.nctsn.org/trauma-types/complex-trauma/assessment#q2).

INDIVIDUAL ASSESSMENT TOOLS

There are a number of assessment tools that one can select to use in the trauma-informed assessment battery. The list below highlights a number of available tools, but is not exhaustive in scope. The tools listed below are done so alphabetically and when available, all psychometric properties are reported. The National Child Traumatic Stress Network has an entire library of assessment tools that can be accessed here: http://www.nctsn.org/trauma-types/complex-trauma/standardized-measures-assess-complex-trauma. In the following list of measures, psychometric properties of each tool will be reported if available. Hodges et al. also provide a comprehensive literature review on the assessment of complex trauma and various tools that can be used. We also encourage readers to view this resource in its entirety.

- As NCTSN notes, and we would agree, every clinician who is working with youth and families should have at least one comprehensive tool that measures multiple domains of functioning. The Child and Adolescent Needs and Strengths – Trauma Questionnaire (CANS) is one such tool. The CANS is a comprehensive assessment tool that collects information relative to traumatic experiences, traumatic stress, overall mental health distress and concerns, various kinds of risk behaviors, daily functioning, and caregiver needs and strengths for both the child and caregiver (The National Child Traumatic Stress Network, 2017, para. 6). We will discuss the CANS, and a number of other tools in more depth below.

Structured Interview for Disorders of Extreme Stress – (SIDES). This assessment tool examines all core domains relative to complex trauma. This includes affect disregulation, somatization, attention, self-perception, relations with others, and systems of meaning. This 45-item assessment tool is a clinician-administered interview and is appropriate for assessment in young adults between 17 years of age and older. There is also a Self-Report Version (SIDES-SR). Both measures typically take between 45 minutes and an hour and a half to complete. This measure helps clarify the presence of complex trauma or DESNOS (Disorders of Extreme Stress – Not Otherwise Specified) (Pelcovitz et al., 1997).

Structured Interview for Disorders of Extreme Stress – (Adolescent Version SIDES-A). This assessment tool assesses the same domains at the tool noted above; however, it can be used in youth between the ages of 12 and 18 years old. It is only used in the clinician-based interview format, not a self-report format (Habib & Labruna, 2011, 2012).

Child and Adolescent Needs and Strengths – Trauma Comprehensive (CANS Trauma). This assessment tool examines core domains of functioning relative to trauma exposure. The domains that are assessed with this tool include attachment, affect disregulation, behavioral control, dissociation, biology, trauma exposure, caregiver functioning, and overall strengths. This clinician-administered rating tool is appropriate for children between the ages of 3 years and 18 years. The NCTSN noted that construct validity of the tool has been evaluated and rated the reliability as acceptable (Inter-rater Reliability Min = 0.77, Max = 0.85, Avg = 0.81). This tool is available for free (Kisiel et al., 2009a,b, 2010).

UCLA PTSD Reaction Index. This assessment tool includes both a caregiver and self-report format and examines trauma exposure, history, and PTSD symptoms. This tool is appropriate for children between the ages of 2 and 9 years and 1 and 17 years. There are 47–48 items and it takes approximately 20 minutes to complete. It is available in English as well as 13 other languages. Sample questions include: "I have upsetting thoughts, pictures or sounds of what happened come into my mind when I do not want them to" (Intrusion Scale) and "I feel like staying by myself and not being with my friends" (Avoidance/Numbing Scale) (Pynoos et al., 1998; Steinberg et al., 2013; Steinberg et al., 2004).

The Devereux Early Childhood Assessment Clinical Form (DECA-C). This assessment tool is a caregiver interview that assesses attachment, behavioral control, affect disregulation, cognition, initiative, depression, and aggression in children between the ages of 2 and 5 years. There are 62 items in the tool and it is estimated to take between 15 and 20 minutes to administer (LeBuffe & Naglieri, 2003).

The Youth Outcome Questionnaire (YOQ-2.01). This assessment tool is a caregiver report that assesses interpersonal distress, somatic concerns, interpersonal relationships, social problems, and behavioral control in youth between the ages of 4 and 17 years. It consists of 64 items and takes approximately 10 minutes to complete (Burlingame et al., 2004; Lambert et al., 1996).

Youth Outcome Questionnaire (YOQ-2.0 SR). This assessment tool is a self-report tool that measures interpersonal distress, somatic concerns, interpersonal relationships, social problems, and behavioral control in youth between the ages of 12 and 18 years (Wells et al., 1996).

Children's Alexithymia Measures (CAM). This assessment tool is an observer report tool that assesses affect disregulation in youth between ages 5 and 17 years. Alexithymia is described as a challenge in affect expression and cognition wherein an individual has difficulty recognizing and expressing feelings. It has 14 items and takes approximately 10–15 minutes to complete. The internal reliability of this tool = 0.92 (Way et al., 2010).

Difficulties in Emotional Regulation Sale (DERS). This assessment tool is a self-report measure that assesses affect dysregulation in individuals between 18 and 60 years of age. There are six scales in this measure and they include: (1) Non-acceptance of emotional responses, (2) Difficulties engaging in goal-directed behavior, (3) Impulse control difficulties, (4) Lack of emotional awareness, (5) Limited access to emotion regulation strategies, and (6) Lack of emotional clarity. It has 36 items and takes approximately 8 minutes to complete. NCTSN noted that construct validity of the tool has been evaluated and rated the reliability as acceptable (Test-Retest Min = 0.57 Max = 0.89, Avg = 0.74) and (Internal Consistency Min = 0.84 Max = 0.93, Avg = 0.86). This tool is available for free (Gratz & Roemer, 2004).

Affect Intensity and Reactivity Measure for Youth (AIR-Y). This assessment tool is a self-report measure that assesses affect dysregulation and mood ratings in youth between the ages of 10 and 17 years. The tool has 27 items and takes approximately 10 minutes to complete (Jones et al., 2009).

Abbreviated Dysregulation Inventory (ADI). This assessment tool is a self-report measure that assesses affect dysregulation, cognition, and behavioral control in youth between the ages of 12 and 18 years. The tool has 30 items and takes approximately 15–30 minutes to complete (Mezzich et al., 1997; da Motta et al., 2016).

Child Dissociative Checklist (CDC). This assessment tool is a caregiver report measure that assesses dissociation in youth between the ages of 5 and 12 years. The tool has 20 items and takes approximately 5 minutes to complete. This tool asks questions about the extent to which the child in question remembers or denies trauma and painful experiences and the extent to which dissociative features may be present. This tool is available for free (Putnam et al., 1990).

Boat Inventory on Animal-Related Experience. This tool specifically asks about the child's relationship with various animals in the home. The tool is built on the theoretical model that acknowledges the link between child abuse, spousal abuse, elder abuse, and animal abuse. This tool can be used as a screener to better understand general risk and violence patterns within the family. Questions ask about relationships with animals as well as the extent to which animals have been hurt in the home. For example when inquiring about coercion and control, "sometimes people make children or adults do mean things to animals, or try to control people with threats of actually hurting an animal (e.g. 'If you tell, I'll kill your dog')" (Boat, 1994).

Adolescent Dissociative Experiences Scale (A-DES). This assessment tool is a self-report measure that assesses dissociation in youth between the ages of 11 and 18 years. The tool has 30 items and takes approximately 15–30 minutes to complete. This tool asks questions about the extent to which the youth completing the assessment remembers trauma and painful experiences, and the extent to which dissociative features may be present. This tool is available for free (Armstrong et al., 1997).

Children's Perceptual Alterations Scale (CPAS). This assessment tool is a self-report measure that assesses dissociation in youth between the ages of 8 and 12 years. The tool has 28 items and takes approximately 15–30 minutes to complete. This assessment tool asks questions about the extent to which the youth is impacted by their trauma and painful experiences, and the extent to which dissociative features may be present. This tool is available for free (Evers-Szostak & Sanders, 1992; Ohan et al., 2002).

Dissociative Features Profile (DFP). This assessment tool is a clinician-report measure that assesses dissociation in youth between the ages of 5 and 17 years. The tool has 28 items and takes approximately 15–30 minutes to complete (Silberg, 2008).

Children's Dissociative Experiences Scale & Post-traumatic Symptom Inventory (CDES & PTSI). This assessment tool is a self-report measure that assesses dissociation in youth between the ages of 6 and 12 years. The tool has 37 items and takes approximately 30 minutes to complete. This tool is specifically designed to be developmentally appropriate and accessible to a younger population. The tool uses a descriptive rating scale that is presented as a Likert scale. The scale is anchored by two scenarios. For example, on the far left the descriptor reads "Sometimes Alice has no memory of important things that happen to her (like the first day of school or a birthday party)" while on the far right would read "Ruth remembers important things that happened to her (like the first day of school or a birthday party)." The Likert scale answer choices (from left to right) would read: "I'm a lot like Alice, I'm a little like Alice, I'm a little like Ruth, I'm a lot like Ruth." This tool is available for free (Cloitre et al., 2009; Stolbach, 1997).

Children's Attributions and Perceptions Scale (CAPS). This assessment tool is a clinician interview measure that assesses trauma-related cognitions in youth between the ages of 7 and 17 years. The tool has 18 items and takes approximately 5–10 minutes to complete. The instrument includes four sub-scales: Feeling different from peers, Personal attributions for negative events, Perceived credibility, and Interpersonal Trust (Mannarino et al., 1994).

Children's Hope Scale. This assessment tool is a self-report measure that assesses trauma-related cognitions in youth between the ages of 8 and 19 years. The tool has 6 items and takes approximately 5 minutes to complete. The assessment tool has a strength-based focus and asks questions that are rated on a 6-point Likert Scale with responses that range from "None of the Time" to "All of the Time." Sample questions include "I am doing just as well as other kids my age," and "When I have a problem, I can come up with lots of ways to solve it." NCTSN noted that construct validity of the tool has been evaluated and rated the reliability as acceptable (Test-Retest Min = 0.73 Max = 0.73, Avg = 0.73) and (Internal Consistency Min = 0.72 Max = 0.86, Avg = 0.77). This tool is available for free (Synder et al., 1997).

Child Sexual Behavior Inventory (CSBI). This assessment tool is a caregiver report measure that assesses sexual trauma-related behavior in youth between the ages of 2 and 12years. The tool has 38 items and takes approximately 10–15 minutes to complete. The inventory includes nine domains: (1) Boundary Problems, (2) Exhibitionism, (3) Gender Role Behavior, (4) Self- Stimulation, (5) Sexual Anxiety, (6) Sexual Interest, (7) Sexual Intrusiveness, (8) Sexual Knowledge, and (9) Voyeuristic Behavior. This tool is available in multiple languages. NCTSN noted that construct validity of the tool has been evaluated and rated the reliability as acceptable (Test-Retest Avg = 0.91), (Internal Consistency Min = 0.92 Max = 0.93, Avg = 0.92), (Inter-Rater, Min = 0.43, Max = 0.79, Avg = 55) (Friedrich, 1997).

Piers-Harris Children's Self-Concept Scale, 2nd ed. (Piers-Harris-2). This assessment tool is a self-report measure that assesses self-concept and self-perception in youth between the ages of 7 and 18 years. The tool has 60 items and takes approximately 10–15 minutes to complete. The primary areas assessed include: Popularity, physical appearance and attributes, freedom from anxiety, intellectual and school status, behavioral adjustment, and happiness and satisfaction (Piers & Harris, 1969; Piers et al., 2002).

Juvenile Victimization Questionnaire (JVQ). This assessment tool can be used either as a caregiver or youth report measure that assesses trauma exposure and history in youth between the ages of 7 and 9 years (caregiver report) and 10 and 17 years (self-report). The tool has 34 items and takes approximately 10–20 minutes to complete. This tool includes five primary domains related to victimization that youth can experience. They are: conventional crime, maltreatment, peer and sibling victimization, sexual victimization, and witnessing and other exposure to violence. Questions include asking the youth about the extent to which (at any time in their life) "did someone else take something away from you that you were carrying or wearing?" or "did someone threaten to hurt you when you thought they might really do it?" or "did you get scared or feel really bad because grown-ups in your life called you names, said mean things to you, or said they didn't want you?" There is both a screener and full assessment version available (Hamby et al., 2004; Finkehor et al., 2005, 2011).

Young Child PTSD Checklist. This assessment tool is a caregiver report measure that assesses trauma exposure and history as well as PTSD-related symptoms and impairment in youth between the ages of 1 and 6 years. The tool has 42 items and takes approximately 20–30 minutes to complete. This tool asks caregivers questions like "Does your child re-enact the trauma in play with dolls or toys? This would be scenes that look just like the trauma. Or does s/he act it out by him/herself or with other kids?" and "Since the trauma(s) has s/he had episodes when s/he seems to freeze? You may have tried to snap him/her out of it but s/he was unresponsive." This tool is available for free (Scheeringa, 2010; Dehon & Scheeringa, 2005).

Dimensions of Stressful Events Rating Scale (DOSE). This assessment tool is a clinician-administered measure that assesses trauma exposure and history in youth between the ages of 6 and 18 years (Fletcher, 1994). The tool has 50 items and takes approximately 30 minutes to complete.

Unlike other instruments designed to assess DSM-IV Criterion A for post-traumatic stress disorder, exposure to a high-magnitude stressor, the Dimensions of Stressful Events (DOSE) scale assesses not different types of stressors but the specific characteristics of high-magnitude stressor events that the literature indicates increase the likelihood of post-traumatic response to the stressful event(s).

(Spilsbury et al., 2008, para. 1)

Clinician Administered PTSD Scale for Children and Adolescents (CAPS-CA). This assessment tool is a clinician-administered youth interview that assesses PTSD symptoms in youth between the ages of 8 and 15 years. The tool has 33 items and takes approximately 50 minutes to complete. It assesses both the frequency and intensity of PTSD symptoms as well as the impact of those symptoms on the children's overall functioning and distress. PTSD symptomology that are assessed include: Re-experiencing, avoidance and numbing, and hyperarousal, as well as the extent to which the youth believes the event was or was not their fault. NCTSN noted that content validity of the tool has been evaluated and rated the reliability as acceptable (Internal Consistency Min = 0.75, Max = 0.81, Avg = 0.78), (Inter-Rater, Min = 0.80 Max = 0.80, Avg = 0.80) (Nader et al., 1996).

Diagnostic Interview for Children and Adolescents (DICA). This assessment tool is a clinician-administered, semi-structured interview that assesses PTSD symptoms in youth between the ages of 6 and 17 years. The PTSD Module has 17 items and takes approximately 10–16 minutes to complete. This tool assesses dissociation, re-experiencing, avoidance, and arousal. Sample questions include "At the time of the traumatic event, did you feel spaced out or dazed?" and "Have you ever been really upset because you saw something that reminded you of the traumatic event." NCTSN noted that content validity of the tool has been evaluated and rated the reliability as acceptable (Internal Consistency Min = 0.76, Max = 0.93, Avg = 0.85) (Reich et al., 2000).

Coping Responses Inventory – Youth (CRI-Y). This assessment tool is a self-report measure that assesses resilience, coping, and strengths in youth between the ages of 12 and 18 years. The tool takes approximately 10–15 minutes to complete (Moos, 1990). Zanini et al. (2010) noted in their assessment of the tool in a culturally diverse population that "youth self-report showed significant positive relation between the avoidance dimension and psychopathological symptoms for boys and girls. Data were discussed with respect to coping theory, assessment, and cultural influences" (Zanini, et al., 2010, para.1).

Children's Coping Strategies Checklist (CCSC). This assessment tool is a self-report measure that assesses resilience, coping, and strengths in youth between the ages of 12 and 18 years. The tool takes approximately 10–15 minutes to complete. This tool is built on the four-factor model of dispositional coping which includes active, distraction, avoidant and support seeking (Ayers & Sandler, 1999, 2000).

The Violence Exposure Scale for Children-Preschool Version (VEX-PV). This assessment tool is a self-report inventory administered in an interview formation that assesses violence exposure in youth between the ages of 4 and 10 years. The tool has 25 items and requires moderate training for the interviewer to administer. It is available in English, Hebrew, and Spanish (Stover & Berkowtiz, 2005). The questions focus on issues related to the violence that the child has been exposed to. There is a story about a character named "Chris" (with pictures included) and there are both male and female versions available. The child is asked if the things that ever happened to the character may have also happened to him or her. Children respond by pointing to a visual thermometer that indicates their response. There are also three validity questions included. Internal Consistency Reliability has been reported at 0.80 for mild violence and 0.86 for severe violence (Fox & Leavitt, 1995; Stover & Berkowtis, 2005).

The Violence Exposure Scale for Children-Revised Parent Report (VEX-RPR). This assessment tool parallels the child report version. Caregivers provide information about their child's exposure to violence. The intended audience is parents or caregivers of pre-school-aged children (Fox & Leavitt, 1995).

History of Victimization Form (HVF). This assessment tool is a self-report measure that assesses maltreatment and abuse as well as family violence events in youth between the ages of 8 and 16 years of age. This form can also be completed via clinical and agency record review as an information-gathering tool (Wolfe et al., 1987).

Diagnostic Infant and Preschool Assessment (DIPA). This assessment tool is a caregiver-report measure that assesses general psychopathology and corresponds with the DSM in youth between the ages of 0 and 6 years of age (Scheeringa & Haslett 2010). Scheeringa et al. (2010) reported.

> The median test–retest intraclass correlation was 0.69, mean 0.61, and values ranged from 0.24 to 0.87. The median test–retest kappa was 0.53, mean 0.52, and values ranged from 0.38 to 0.66. Preliminary data support the DIPA as a reliable and valid measure of symptoms in research and clinical work with very young children. This measure adds a tool that is flexible in covering both DSM-IV syndromes and empirically-validated developmental modifications that can help increase confidence in assessing young children, ensuring coverage of symptoms, and improve access to care.

(Sheeringa et al., 2010, para. 1)

Angie/Andry Cartoon Trauma Scale (ACTS). This assessment tool is a self-report measure that assesses PTSD, violence, and abuse in youth between the ages of 6 and 12 years. The tool demonstrated high internal consistency in an examination of psychometric properties with 208 children with familial trauma (Internal Consistency = 0.70–0.95). Angie/Andy is a child version of the adult measure, SIDES, with a focus on behavioral symptoms of trauma. The items were translated into developmentally appropriate cartoons with accompanying rating scales. The domains assessed include: (1) Dysregulation of Affect and Impulses, (2) Attention and Conscious, (3) Self-Perception, (4) Relations with Others, (5) Somatization, and (6) Systems of meaning (Praver et al., 2000).

FAMILY AND CAREGIVER SYSTEMS TOOLS

As has been noted elsewhere, the importance of assessing not only the child of interest but also the context within which those children exist cannot be overstated. This means that building alliances with family members and caregivers and working collaboratively to understand their strengths and stressors is critical. The measures below reflect some of the tools that are available for us in better assessing the family system. Please note that this is not an exhaustive list. Engaging families is a critical aspect of the work we do and is an essential component in the assessment process. The extent to which families, especially families in distress, feel heard, understood and supported can make the difference between a successful outcome and an unsuccessful outcome. The family and system assessment tools will be listed here for your consideration and we strongly encourage readers to consider including these tools in their comprehensive, trauma-informed assessment battery. When assessing the family system, multiple domains should be considered, including access to resources, self-sufficiency, family functioning, caregiver well-being, parenting behavior, management of challenging behaviors, and child-caregiver relationships. We encourage readers to review the Family Policy Program (1998) through Oregon State University (particularly Chapter 3: Strong, Nurturing Families) that provides a robust review of multiple family-related outcome measures.

Family Assessment Measure-III (FAM)III – Harvey A. Skinner, PhD, Paul D. Steinhauer, MD, Jack Santa-Barbara, PhD

- Examines quality of the dyadic relationships within the family and overall health of the family. Questions include things like use of punishment within the family, sense of belonging within the family, and how problems are resolved within the family.

Nurturing Family Resource Checklist (Oregon State University, Family Policy Program, 1997)

- This tool assessed adequacy of family resources in five areas. They include: basic resources, health and health care, parenting and family relationships, social support, and children's education.

Parent-Child Relationship Inventory (Gerard, 1994)

- This self-report measure of parenting skills and attitudes assesses the domains of attachment and relationships. There are seven domains that are assessed and they include: (1) Parental support, (2) Satisfaction with parenting, (3) Involvement, (4) Communication, (5) Limit-Setting, (6) Autonomy, and (7) Role Orientation

Family Adaptability and Cohesion Scale (Olson et al., 1985)

- Assesses adaptability, flexibility, and cohesion in the family systems. Considers four extremes of family functioning: rigid, chaotic, disengaged and enmeshed (Marsac & Alderfer, 2010; Olson et al., 1985; Wu, 2017)

Child Welfare Trauma Referral Tool (Taylor et al., 2006)

- This tool aids child welfare workers in making trauma-informed decisions when referring families for support and services. It is completed via record review and interview with key informants. The domains assessed include: (1) Trauma exposure/Reminders, (2) Traumatic Stress, (3) Externalizing symptoms, and (4) Relationships and attachment

Attachment Questionnaire for Children (AQC) (Muris et al., 2001)

- This is a single question self-report measure that assesses children's attachment style. Children are given three scenarios and select which scenario most reflects their experience. The styles are: secure, avoidant, and ambivalent.

Inventory of Parent and Peer Attachment (IPPA) (Armsden, 1986)

- This self-report tool is used with adolescents and examines the quality of attachment with both parents and peers as well as the nature of feelings towards attachment figures.

Family Environment Scale (FES) (Moos & Moos, 1994)

- This assessment tool can be completed via caregivers of direct youth report. It assesses the overall caregiver and family functioning as well as a response to trauma. The three sub-scales include family relationship, personal growth, and system maintenance and change.

Parenting Stress Index-Short Form (PSI-SF) (Abidin, 1995)

- This caregiver report tool assesses parental stressors and overall caregiver functioning. It also assesses family functioning and response to trauma. This is the brief version of the Parenting Stress Index (Abidin, 1995). The tool assesses the following domains: (1) Parental distress, (2) Parent-Child Dysfunctional Interaction, and (3) Difficult Child.

Parent Emotional Reaction Questionnaire (PERQ) (Cohen et al., 2004)

- This caregiver report measure assesses caregiver functioning and family functioning. The tool assesses a parent's emotional reactions to the sexual abuse of their children. It asks parents to note the frequency with which they report fear, sadness, guilt, anger, embarrassment, shame, and other emotional preoccupation.

Section Four

TRAUMA-INFORMED INTERVENTION FRAMEWORK

Ten

COMPETENCIES AND COMPONENTS OF TRAUMA-INFORMED INTERVENTIONS

Kirby L. Wycoff

INTRODUCTION

As we have noted elsewhere, the assessment process is an integral aspect of the intervention process. Treatment selection is largely driven out of accurate and appropriate assessments, which drives case conceptualization and in turn, the selection of various intervention techniques and tools. The selection of any given intervention must take into account a number of different considerations. Notably, what does the assessment tell you in terms of the individual's therapeutic needs? How does the assessment process drive the needs of the individual and help clarify and articulate treatment goals? Clarity about a presenting population, and the social, emotional, behavioral, psychological, educational or other needs they may have drives clarity about intervention selection (Maher, 2012). The assessment process essentially reflects a needs assessment of sorts. What does this individual need to meet their therapeutic goals? It is with this in mind that appropriately prepared and trained clinicians can make well-informed decisions about which intervention techniques, tools, and treatment might be most appropriate for any given individual.

Matching the right client to the right therapeutic intervention is an important aspect of treating any individual and it is particularly important for meeting the needs of trauma-exposed youth. Pulling a program off the shelf, without considering the actual needs of a particular client will result in reduced insight and clarity regarding what that client actually needs. As has been noted elsewhere, traumatized youth and their families are as diverse and far-reaching as the clinicians who treat them. The National Child Traumatic Stress Network has outlined a number of considerations for evaluating goodness of fit with a particular treatment model for a specific individual or population. We strongly encourage readers to visit this website for a more robust understanding of effective therapeutic interventions for trauma-exposed individuals: http://www.nctsn.org/resources/topics/treatments-that-work/promising-practices. Relative to interventions and treatment, NCTSN noted the development of treatment fact sheets reflects a partnership between the NCTSN Trauma-Informed Interventions: Clinical and Research Evidence and Culture-Specific Information project and the National Crime Victims Research and Treatment Center at the Medical University of South Carolina. This robust project builds a virtual library of interventions which can be considered for trauma-exposed individuals with a particular focus on the needs of diverse clients (NCTSN, 2017).

In considering which intervention to select, there are a number of factors at stake. These include both the types and levels of support that an individual may need, as well as the appropriateness for a given population in any number of contexts (NCTSN 2017). What might work for one individual in one context might not work for another individual in a different context. NCTSN noted that clinicians need to consider what kind of trauma the individual has been exposed to, and what types of losses may be an issue for that individual (or group of individuals), as well as the functional impairment which the individual is experiencing (NCTSN, 2017). A thorough needs assessment, as indicated by a thorough and robust assessment will guide clinicians in their ability to select the most appropriate intervention and treatment approach for trauma-exposed individuals.

The needs, values, available resources, demographic characteristics, and informed preferences of a provider's service population also influences the type of intervention needed. Factors to consider include:

- Local culture and values of the clientele and the surrounding community
- Developmental factors, including age, cognitive, and social domains
- Socioeconomic factors
- Logistical and other barriers to help-seeking
- Availability of individual/family/community strength-based resources that can be therapeutically leveraged
- Setting in which services are offered (school, residential, clinic, home) (NCTSN, 2017, para. 8)

The "Child Physical and Sexual Abuse: Guidelines for Treatment" project which was supported through a grant (1999-VF-GX-K010) from the Office of Victims of Crime, Office of Justice Programs, in the U.S. Department of Justice,

Saunders et al. developed a number of guidelines for considering the selection of various treatments in working with trauma-exposed youth, with a focus on those who were exposed to physical and sexual abuse.

Saunders et al. noted the critical importance of building standardized guidelines for any service professional who works with trauma-impacted children and families. Mental health professionals, victim advocates, family/juvenile court judges, prosecutors, criminal court judges, child protective services personnel, and any other practitioner (including school-based professionals) who interacts with this population needs to have a clear understanding not only of the impact of trauma, but how to choose the most appropriate interventions for these families. Saunders et al. noted that it is essential that we raise the standard for trauma-impacted youth and families through the adoption and "application of theoretically sound, empirically supported, and clinically accepted mental health treatment procedures" (Saunders et al., 2003, p. 6). As we seek to do here, Saunders et al. sought to raise the awareness of clinicians relative to the available treatment modalities for working with this population and encourage clinicians to consider these guidelines when selecting appropriate interventions. Essential to this is the understanding of both potential benefits and potential risks with any given treatment model. This chapter is not intended to be an exhaustive list of available treatment options or imply that these treatment approaches can replace sound clinical judgment or clinical innovation (Saunders et al., 2003). Saunders et al. noted a multi-step process that is involved in getting the right treatments to the clients that need it. First and foremost, the project team noted the importance of solid research which can help determine which treatments will be most effective for this trauma-exposed population. They then noted that after the development of treatment approaches, the field has to work to disseminate those theoretically sound and empirically supported models. After this, we must focus on training front-line service providers in how to implement and use these treatment modes with trauma-exposed youth and families. "Clinical science can do a wonderful job of developing and testing good treatments. Unfortunately, if the front-line practitioners are not aware of the work and are not trained to use good treatments, child victims will not benefit" (Saunders et al., 2003, p. 7). Finally, as noted by the project team (supported by these authors), in addition to developing sound treatments and disseminating them to clinicians, providers need to make the choices to actually implement those theoretically sound and empirically driven treatment models. We contend that this Essentials book is in large part designed to get the most relevant information about trauma-exposed youth and families into the hands of front-line providers.

CLINICAL COMPETENCIES

Working with trauma-exposed and impacted youth and families is an area of clinical specialty. In order for a provider to be competent (and work within the confines of their scope of practice, as indicated by various ethics codes), the provider must have specialized training and supervision in working with this population. This book is intended as one such resource wherein front-line providers might increase their knowledge, skill, and ability around the impact on and needs of trauma-exposed youth and families. In order for a provider to gain skills and knowledge in working with trauma-exposed youth and families in school and community settings, there are a number of prerequisites that must be considered. First and foremost, the provider should have graduated from an accredited graduate training program in their field of practice, which provides at least basic clinical training in working directly with clients who have mental and behavioral health challenges. Furthermore, the provider should have participated in and successfully completed a supervised training experience including a practicum or internship, consistent with the training standards in their field of practice. We also suggest here that the provider has achieved and demonstrated basic clinical competency and has completed all licensing and certification assessments and processes (nationally and at the state level) that are consistent with their field of practice. Finally, and perhaps most importantly, is that providers who are beginning their work with trauma-exposed individuals should place high value on accessing and engaging in regular, clinical supervision with a more experienced professional who has specifically worked with trauma-exposed and impacted youth and families. As will be noted in the final chapter in this book, working with this population can present unique challenges to the provider and it is essential that a sound supervision model is in place. This is not only considered best practices, but ongoing, regular supervision for new and emerging skills is consistent with multiple ethical codes for service providers.

We suggest here that clinicians who are interested in providing assessment and intervention services to trauma-impacted youth and families have a strong and solid foundation in a case-conceptualization framework. That is, the provider understands and appreciates that assessment and interventions are both part of the case-conceptualization process. Assessment (using a hypothesis testing model) drives our understanding of the individual we are working with, which then informs our case conceptualization, or how we make sense of the individual's current challenges. This then drives the development of a treatment plan, wherein we would select appropriate and relevant interventions to meet specific goals as outlined in the treatment plan. We then move forward with the implementation of the intervention and continue to monitor outcomes and goals in an ongoing and regular way. This process is iterative and reflexive, and the regularly collected data will help further indicate to the clinician the extent to which the intervention is working or not working. If the data does not indicate a positive growth and goal attainment, the clinician will revisit assessment and case conceptualization to better understand the needs of the client, hypothesize why this particular treatment might not be working, and adjust accordingly. Case conceptualization refers to a process (where both assessment and intervention play a critical role) and helps the clinician make sense of the client's current challenges within the context of a certain theoretical framework in order to plan for treatment goals and interventions (Division of Clinical Psychology, 2011; Wycoff, 2013). This process helps us explain and understand the client's symptoms and current struggles or impairments in light of a particular theory or integration of theories (Division of Clinical Psychology, 2011; Wycoff, 2013). This case conceptualization leads directly to the development of goals, intervention strategies, and ultimately, the selection of the most appropriate intervention or treatment. The case conceptualization process helps us identify the best way to move forward with a client in any given setting. There are three big-picture steps which are part of the case conceptualization process and in turn, particularly relevant to both the assessment and selection of interventions with trauma-exposed youth. They include:

1. Client's Presenting Concerns (What brings the client into services at this time, what does the client indicate are their current challenges or concerns?)
2. Hypothesize a framework for which to explain the stated problem (How and why do we believe this individual came to have these difficulties? What do we think the problems might be stemming from? What are their strengths, how have they coped in the past? Here, we note the importance of considering a trauma-informed lens in understanding the client's needs and challenges)
3. Goal setting and Interventions (What are the client's goals for the treatment or intervention? How do we select an intervention which is empirically supported and meets the client's needs?)

Understanding the above noted process of assessing and intervening with all clients is a foundational, prerequisite skill for the provider who is interested in working with trauma-exposed youth and families. We cannot over state the importance of understanding this framework as a process on which trauma informed work can be built.

In their "Prerequisite Clinical Competencies for Implementing Effective, Trauma-Informed Intervention," the National Child Traumatic Stress Network noted a number of specific competencies which they consider prerequisites for implementing any trauma-informed or focused clinical intervention. The NCTSN also noted the critical importance of ensuring core clinical competencies before a provider is trained on a trauma-specific intervention as well as ongoing monitoring and supervision of the implementation of those services and interventions once the provider has begun working with clients.

The NCTSN noted the following core clinical competencies; to review this document in full, please visit http://nctsn.org/sites/default/files/assets/pdfs/nctsn_position_statement_on_clinical_competency.pdf:

1. Basic Assessment: Effectively gather relevant clinical information to assess problems that will be addressed via therapeutic work.
2. Risk Assessment: Effectively assess individuals' likelihood of harming self or others, as well as likelihood the individual may be harmed by others. Include caregiver's ability to ensure the youth's safety.
3. Case Conceptualization: Effectively integrate assessment information to form an understanding and hypothesis about the individual's challenges. Include all sociocultural factors in case conceptualization and formulation.
4. Treatment Planning: Effectively use the case conceptualization information to select the most effective intervention and treatment for the targeted clinical goals.
5. Treatment Engagement: Effectively build a therapeutic alliance with the client and clients' family to address the targeted clinical goals.
6. Treatment Implementation: Effectively implement the intervention of choice to address the targeted clinical goals.
7. Treatment Quality Monitoring: Effectively monitor progress and treatment outcomes on a regular basis and adjust treatment as needed (NCTSN Position Statement, Prerequisite Clinical Competencies for Implementing Effective, Trauma-Informed Interventions, 2015). http://nctsn.org/sites/default/files/assets/pdfs/nctsn_position_statement_on_clinical_competency.pdf

Using the guidelines posited by NCTSN above as well as the authors' focus on case conceptualization skills, interested clinicians can ensure they have the foundational competencies needed to provide high-quality assessment and intervention services to trauma-impacted youth and families.

EVIDENCE-BASED PRACTICES

There are a number of resources and databases which have evaluated the efficacy of treatment programs and interventions that are appropriate for trauma-impacted youth and families. These include, but are not limited to: the "Child Physical and Sexual Abuse: Guidelines for Treatment" project through the Office of Victims of Crime, Office of Justice Programs; the National Child Traumatic Stress Network; the SAMHSA (Substance Abuse and Mental Health Services Administrations) National Registry of Evidence-Based Programs and Practices (NREPP); and the California Evidence-Based Clearinghouse for Child Welfare (CEBC). All links and resources will be available in the appendix of this book.

Saunders et al., 2003 (Child Physical and Sexual Abuse Guidelines for Treatment, OVC) noted the process whereby clinical science drives the development of interventions and treatments. This team noted that innovative treatments are developed and initially used with caution in relevant clinical settings. The outcomes and anecdotal feedback from those clinical settings drives further treatment development. Augmented and revised treatments are then tested again (and often multiple times) back in the clinical (and often clinical research) setting with actual clients. Qualitative data is often collected on how the interventions were received, if there were perceived benefits, and how clients responded to those treatments. After a series of case studies, when it is believed a certain treatment methodology might be useful in a broader context, the treatment is then put through more rigorous scientific inquiry and testing. These are often randomized controlled trials (RCT) where the parameters and variables are closely monitored and the treatment is implemented with the target population (Saunders et al., 2003). These are often conducted in academic and research settings (Saunders et al., 2003). After efficacy has been established in a tightly controlled scientific setting, the treatments are often then put back into the field with real, front-line practitioners for field testing. That is, to evaluate the extent to which under real conditions, with real clients, the treatment creates the desired outcomes or conditions (Saunders et al., 2003). Once the treatment is shown to be effective in the field, it typically moves out into the field for wider dissemination. We will discuss the process by which a treatment becomes "evidence-based" in the next section (Saunders et al., 2003).

The Ideal Clinical Science Process demonstrated this ideal development process by which a new treatment might be determined to be effective for a wider clinical population. Unfortunately, the authors noted that this process is not always followed in the development of new treatments (Saunders et al., 2003).

The Common Clinical Science Process demonstrates that often a therapeutic approach will be developed in clinical settings, but is unfortunately often disseminated before rigorous evaluation has been conducted to ascertain effectiveness. Dissemination often occurs by individual clinicians or group of clinicians (and/or researchers) who have found a particular approach to be useful with a certain clinical population (Saunders et al., 2003). Saunders et al. noted that true effectiveness studies are somewhat rare in practice, but in the field of trauma-exposed youth we are working more to establish efficacy and effectiveness.

While ratings of every single possible trauma treatment are beyond the scope of this work, we encourage readers to read Saunders et al. in full and consider these criterion in their evaluation of a potential treatment model. The following classification system was used to classify levels of empirical support for various interventions:

Treatment Protocol Classification System
1 = Well supported, efficacious treatment
2 = Supported and probably efficacious treatment
3 = Supported and acceptable treatment
4 = Promising and acceptable treatment
5 = Innovative or novel treatment
6 = Concerning treatment (Saunders et al., 2003 p. ii)

This rating system may be useful in guiding the decision-making process for clinicians. We will expand on another rating scale below which may also further help the clinician make decisions about the use of empirically supported treatments and interventions.

Evidence-based practices can first be found in the literature in the early 1990s coming out of the medical field. The term "evidence-based medicine" was defined as "the conscientious, explicit, and judicious use of current best evidence in making decisions about individual patient care" (Sackett et al., 1996, p. 71). Evidence-based practices have been noted as reflecting a movement that seeks to use high-quality, rigorous clinical research to guide clinical decision-making, all while taking into account the client's needs and values (Masic et al., 2008) Essentially, evidence-based medicine, which filtered into other industries and sectors and is now referred to as evidence-based practice, raised the bar for what was acceptable in terms of our understanding of whether or not a given treatment actually worked. "The practice of evidence-based medicine is a process of life-long, self-directed, problem-based learning in which caring for one's own patients creates the need for clinically important information about diagnosis, prognosis, therapy and other clinical and health care issues" (Masic et al., 2008, p. 219). This way of thinking reflected a movement in the health and public health field towards increased accountability and improved evidence of efficacy. In the age of rapid advancements in science and technology, clinicians must continue to evaluate their treatment choices. It integrates clinical expertise of the clinician, the values and needs of the patients, as well as the best available scientific evidence for a chosen intervention or treatment. As has been highlighted elsewhere, hypothesis testing and problem-solving is important in comprehensive assessment: "The revised and improved definition of evidence-based medicine is a systematic approach to clinical problem-solving, which allows the integration of the best available research evidence with clinical expertise and patient values" (Masic et al., 2008, para. 3). The evidence-based practice model has been integrated into the ethical standards and guidelines of multiple professional organizations, and has been adopted across sectors (CEBC, Understanding Evidence Based Practice, 2017). This chapter (and entire book!) is not intended to supplant clinical experience and expertise, but rather complement clinical acumen with external, evidence-driven guidelines which can improve the decision-making and problem-solving of front-line clinicians.

The CEBC and the NREPP have also both done extensive work on establishing a database for empirically supported interventions for a wide range of child and adolescent mental health challenges. The CEBC is funded through the California Department of Social Services' (CDSS) Office of Child Abuse Prevention. As noted on the CEBC's website, which we encourage readers to visit (http://www.cebc4cw.org), the mission of the CEBC is to "advance the effective implementation of evidence-based practices for children and families involved with the child welfare system" (CEBC, 2007, p. 1). The CEBC reports that evidence-based practices (as defined by the Institute of Medicine) include a combination of these three variables: (1) best research evidence, (2) best clinical experience, and (3) consistent with patient values (Institute of Medicine, 2001).

The CEBC seeks to help end users (clinicians and others in child and family serving organizations) to readily understand the quality of research evidence for any specific intervention or treatment (Institute of Medicine, 2001). The metric they use defines evidence of research as a "research study of outcomes that have been published in a peer-reviewed journal" (CEBC, 2017). They further use a continuum-based scale to note the overall quality of the support for any given program. This is a 5-point scale ranging from "Well-Supported" to "Concerning." This scale denotes varying levels of scientific support for any given treatment, intervention or program (CEBC, 2017).

We encourage readers to view and download the CEBC rating scale document here: http://www.cebc4cw.org/files/OverviewOfTheCEBCScientificRatingScale.pdf. In order for an intervention to even be rated, it must include the following pre-requisites: (1) must have a manual or protocol noting how to conduct the intervention, (2) must meet requirements of CEBC topic area of interest (i.e. relative to at-risk youth and families), (3) outcomes of the research must be published in peer reviewed journals, and (4) outcome measures used must have been valid and reliable and administered accurately (CEBC, Overview of the CEBC Scientific Rating Scale 2017, p 1). We will briefly summarize the scaled categories below as this may provide a useful metric for clinicians:

1. Well-Supported by Research Evidence
   - At least two rigorous RCT
   - Effects found to be far better than control
   - Outcomes sustained for at least one (1) year
2. Supported by Research Evidence
   - At least one RCT
   - Effects found to be far better than control
   - Outcomes sustained for at least six (6) months
3. Promising Research Evidence
   - At least 1 study using some type of control group (placebo, wait list, untreated)
   - Effects found to be better than the control
   - Practice comparable to another tool which has been rated as 3 or higher
4. Evidence Fails to Demonstrate Effect
   - Two or more RCT's have has not shown improvements
   - Overall weight of evidence does not support intervention
5. Concerning Practice
   - Overall weight of the evidence suggests negative effect on clients
   - Case study data indicating possible risk of harm causing treatment
   - Empirical basis suggesting risk to clients
6. NR - Not able to be rated on the CEBC Rating Scale
   - Practice has no published outcome data, no peer-reviewed publication, and no control (The California Evidence-Based Clearinghouse for Child Welfare, 2016) http://www.cebc4cw.org/files/OverviewOfTheCEBCScientificRatingScale.pdf

We suggest here that guidelines like these may provide useful frameworks to the front-line provider for considering the selection of interventions and treatments for trauma-exposed individuals. Another useful resource for considering evidence-based practice is SAMHSA's National Registry of Evidence-Based Programs and Practices, which can be found here: http://nrepp.samhsa.gov/landing.aspx.

The NREPP's primary goal is the dissemination of information and translation of research into front-line applicability. The NREPP provides a searchable, online repository developed to help front-line clinicians, providers, and the public learn about evidence-based interventions that are available for use with clinical populations (NREPP, 2017).

The NREPP does not endorse specific interventions or programs, but rather publishes programs that have been reviewed and rated (NREPP, 2017). It has multiple open submission periods throughout the year when researchers or program developers can submit their interventions and protocols for peer review and possible inclusion in the NREPP repository. The minimum requirements for submission to the review panel include the following:

1. The program/intervention must target an outcome related to mental health, substance use or behavioral health.
2. The program/intervention must have been evaluated with at least one study using an experimental or quasi-experimental design.
3. The program/intervention must have collected data on the intervention and control group outcomes.
4. The program/intervention must be published in a peer reviewed journal or publication sometime on or after 1995 (NREPP, 2017, para. 2).

NREPP will review submissions which have been accepted and provide a rating based on the methodological rigor of the research, and the degree of impact the intervention made.

The evaluation is conducted by two professionally trained intervention reviewers using a standardized evaluation methodology. This includes deriving an evidence score related to rigor and fidelity of the program, as well as effect, which is driven by the confidence interval of the effect size (NREPP, 2017). The effect sizes are interpreted as follows:

1. Favorable: Confidence interval lies completely within the favorable range (greater than 0.10)
2. Possibly favorable: Confidence interval spans both the favorable (greater than 0.10) and trivial range (from –0.25 to 0.10)
3. Trivial: Confidence interval lies completely within the trivial range (from –0.25 to 0.10) or spans the harmful and favorable range (from –0.25 to greater than 0.10)

4. Possibly harmful: Confidence interval spans both the harmful (lower than –0.25) and trivial range (from –0.25 to 0.10).
5. Harmful: Confidence interval lies completely within the harmful range (lower than –0.25) (http://nrepp.samhsa.gov/review_process.aspx NREPP, 2017, para. 16).

The evidence score and effect class are collapsed to categorize the intervention into one of seven evidence classes (Class A through Class G). Class A is described as "Highest quality of evidence with confidence interval completely within the favorable range" whereas Class G is described as "Limitations in the study preclude from reporting further on the outcome" (NREPP, 2017, para. 18). For a full description of the evaluation process please visit: http://nrepp.samhsa.gov/review_process.aspx. After this, an outcome score (which comes from evidence classes) and a conceptual framework rating (which comes from the extent to which the program includes goals, activities, and theory of change) are used to derive an overall Outcome Rating (NREPP 2017). Using a color-coded system, each intervention or program is rated with an overall Outcome Evidence Rating. These ratings are listed below:

1. *Effective (Green Check Mark).* The evaluation evidence has strong methodological rigor, and the short-term effect on this outcome is favorable. More specifically, the short-term effect favors the intervention group and the size of the effect is substantial.
2. *Promising (Yellow Check Mark)* The evaluation evidence has sufficient methodological rigor, and the short-term effect on this outcome is likely to be favorable. More specifically, the short-term effect favors the intervention group and the size of the effect is likely to be substantial.
3. *Ineffective (Red X Mark).* The evaluation evidence has sufficient methodological rigor, but there is little to no short-term effect. More specifically, the short-term effect does not favor the intervention group and the size of the effect is negligible. Occasionally, the evidence indicates that there is a negative short-term effect. In these cases, the short-term effect harms the intervention group and the size of the effect is substantial.
4. *Inconclusive (Black Question Mark)* Programs may be classified as inconclusive for two reasons. First, the evaluation evidence has insufficient methodological rigor to determine the impact of the program. Second, the size of the short-term effect could not be calculated. (NREPP, 2017, p. 20, retrieved from: http://nrepp.samhsa.gov/review_process.aspx)

CORE COMPONENTS OF TRAUMA-FOCUSED INTERVENTIONS

The treatment and intervention landscape for trauma-impacted youth and families draws from the literature on a number of other therapeutic models and theories. The U.S. Department of Justice and Department of Health and Human Services (Evidence-Based Practices for Children Exposed to Violence: A Selection from Federal Databases) noted a number of service characteristics which are common across evidence-based practices when working with children exposed to violence. They noted these service characteristics and the key features of a program and include things like length, duration, and intensity of services as well as the target population for the services and the delivery modality of the services. Listed below are both the common features of successful evidence-based programs targeting violence exposed youth, as well as common barriers.

Common Characteristics of Successfully Implemented EBP for Violence-Exposed Youth:

1. Combined home and center-based approach
2. Multi-modal treatment approaches
3. Parent-Child dual approach
4. Parent training and psycho-educational services
5. Developmentally and culturally appropriate services (U.S. Department of Justice and Department of Health and Human Services, Evidence Based Practices for Children Exposed to Violence, 2011, p. 1)

Common Barriers to Implementing EBP for Violence-Exposed Youth:

1. Attrition and retention
2. Mandated reporting
3. Parental motivation and expectations
4. Lack of evidence in practice (U.S. Department of Justice and Department of Health and Human Services, Evidence Based Practices for Children Exposed to Violence, 2011, p. 1)

The National Child Traumatic Stress Network also provides a set of guidelines that are considered core components or aspects of trauma-related interventions and treatments. These are largely drawn from other therapeutic models, but are particularly salient and relevant when working with trauma-exposed youth and families. A number of trauma-related interventions and treatment models include similar underlying techniques. Assessing the client's needs, goals, and values, and the empirical support for any particular treatment will help guide the clinician in selecting the intervention representing the best goodness of fit for the client.

PSYCHOEDUCATION

Psychoeducation is another core component of many trauma-focused interventions. Psychoeducation as a treatment strategy was originally used with families who had a member with a schizophrenia diagnosis (Goldstein & Miklowtiz, 1995). Psychoeducation is used therapeutically in working with youth and families wherein the program is designed to provide information about a specific diagnosis or clinical issue (in this case, trauma) as well as its course, etiology, prognosis, and treatment approaches (Goldstein & Miklowitz, 1995). In working with trauma-exposed youth and families, psychoeducation would focus on the trauma, the impact of trauma, post-traumatic stress reactions, and how to strengthen coping skills (NCTSN, 2017).

EMOTION IDENTIFICATION AND REGULATION

Emotion identification, expression, and regulation skills are another core aspect of many trauma-focused interventions and treatments. Teaching individuals to identify, express, and regulate their emotions is a core component of building coping skills in trauma-exposed youth and families. "An individual's autonomic arousal level, subjective feeling state, and cognitions are potential influences on an individual's expressive displays and behavioral choices in a particular social context" (Mahady-Wilton et al., 2000, p. 227). In more recent years, we have come to understand the expression of emotion as a dynamic and evolving system which is related to other key psychological factors and is amenable to change. They largely involved neural processes which are primarily automatic and somatic and involve awareness of one's own emotional experiences as well as expressive display of that emotional experience (Mahady Wilton et al., 2000). "Expressive display refers to discrete facial expressions, non-verbal behavior, and overt behavioral responses which signal to others an individual's emotional state. Examples of expressive displays would include smiling, weeping, and aggression. Subjective emotional experiences are the personal affective states of the individual, which are typically conceptualized and referred to as 'feelings' (e.g. anger, joy, surprise, distress, etc.)" (Mahady Wilton et al., 2000, p. 227). Managing one's own emotions is central to building healthy relationships as well functioning well in daily activities of living and work, school, and other social experiences. Healthy and adaptive emotional regulation skills serve as the foundation of interpersonal experiences (Mahady Wilton, 2000). The centrality of the emotional regulation process to adaptive psychological functioning must be underscored; in essence, emotional regulation functions to "facilitate task-oriented behavior in the face of distracting events and conditions, and avoid or weaken the stress of negative emotions from failure, loss, or trauma" (Cicchetti et al., 1995, p.8). This is a core component of many trauma-focused interventions and treatment approaches.

TRAUMA NARRATIVE

One additional aspect of treatments for trauma-exposed individuals is in the trauma narrative. Trauma re-telling or narrative has been used in treatments with a wide range of traumatic clinical presentations (Cohen et al. 2016). These include children who have experienced sexual abuse (Deblinger & Heflin, 1996; Cohen & Mannarino, 1993, 1996b, 1997, 1998, 2000; Cohen et al., 2004, 2005, 2006; Deblinger et al., 2005; Pollio & Deblinger, 2017; Runyon et al., https://tfcbt.org/wp-content/uploads/2018/05/FosterCareManual-FINAL.pdf), community based violence (Pynoos & Nadar, 1988; Nader et al., 1999; Nader, 2003, 2007a, 2007b, 2008; Saltzman et al., 2001), domestic violence exposure (Cohen et al., 2011), natural disasters Jaycox et al., 2010), single-episode traumatic events (March et al., 1998), and complex trauma (Murray et al., 2015, O'Callaghan et al., 2013).

Traumas, by definition, are often confusing events wherein our brain and body hold on to various aspects of the story through memories and emotions. Memories, emotions, thoughts, and feelings in the mind and body can all become disjointed and confusing after a traumatic experience. The narrative sequence of what actually happened is often impacted by protective disassociation at the time of the traumatic event. Re-telling the trauma story or trauma narrative (and restructuring the narrative) in the context of a safe and supportive environment (often a therapeutic setting) can help reorganize the trauma experience in a way that makes trauma feel more manageable to process, and provides mastery and understanding for the victim. Additionally, from a behavioral perspective, the re-telling of the trauma narrative (after adequate coping skills have been installed) allows for the unpairing of the associations from the trauma, with the physiological fear that was experienced during the trauma. Cohen et al. (2016) stated "one of the goals of creating the trauma narrative is to unlink thoughts and reminders of discussions of the traumatic event from overwhelming negative emotions such as terror, horror, extreme helplessness, avoidance, anger, anxiety, shame, or rage" (Cohen et al., 2016, p. 172). The trauma narrative gradually builds the child's capacity to manage the discomfort of re-telling the trauma story over time. There is an element of systematic, gradual desensitization which is the mechanism by which the uncoupling of traumatic memory and physiological fear occurs.

However, this alone is not enough. While it was originally conceptualized as an exposure procedure (Deblinger et al., 1990; Cohen et al., 2004, 2005, 2006, 2011, 2016; Deblinger et al., 2005; Pollio & Deblinger, 2017) whereby repeated writing, talking about, and elaboration of the trauma would desensitize the child to the traumatic memories, the technique has since evolved. Work by others (Pennebaker, 1996, 2000) has found the trauma narrative alone is not enough to create symptom reduction and must be partnered with other techniques like adequate coping, stress management, and cognitive processing. Desensitization alone, without other elements of trauma treatment (e.g. Cognitive processing) may be quite distressing (and potential harmful) to the child. "Our current conceptualization of the trauma narrative is in addition to desensitizing the child to traumatic reminders and decreasing avoidance and hyperarousal; this process also helps the child to integrate the traumatic experience into the totality of his or her life. In this way, the trauma is only one part of the child's life experiences and self concept, rather than the defining aspect of both. This distinction involves metacognitive ability; that is, the ability to think about and evaluate one's own thoughts and experiences" (Cohen et al., 2016, p. 173).

The trauma reprocessing and narrative often includes a tangible product from the narrative re-telling. This may include a book, poem, drawing, or painting. It may also include expressive art and movement. It is important to note that while the "product" of the narrative can be useful to clients, it is the actual re-telling and co-constructing of the narrative between the child and the therapist that is thought to be most impactful (Cohen et al., 2016). A sample introductory script for a trauma narrative can be found here:

It is very hard to talk about painful things, and often children and parents try to avoid doing this. In fact, they say things like "let sleeping dogs lie," and wonder if it is a good thing to bring back memories of sad things. We tell kids and parents that if they had been able to put those memories behind them, children would not be having any problems, and they would not be coming here to therapy in the first place. It's like when you fall off a bicycle and skin your knee on the sidewalk, and all that dirt and germs get into the wound. You have two choices about what to do with that wound. You can leave it alone, not wash it off or put any medicine on it, and hope that it gets better all by itself. Sometimes that works fine. But other times, if you do that it will get infected. Infections don't usually get better by leaving them alone; they get worse and worse. Your other choice is to wash the wound out real carefully, getting all the dirt and germs out of there. Than stings, it hurts at first, but then the pain goes away, and it doesn't get infected, and can heal quickly. In the end, once an infection starts, it hurts a lot less to clean it out than to let it get worse and worse. Creating the trauma narrative, or telling the story of what happened, is like cleaning out the wound. It might be a little painful at first, but it hurts less and less as we go on, and then the wound can heal. Just like when you clean out a wound, if you rub it too hard or too fast, it will hurt a lot more than if you go more carefully. We try to go at just the right pace in telling your story so that it never hurts more than a little bit. You can let us know at any point if we are going too fast for you, and we will slow down.

(Cohen et al., 2016, p. 175–176)

While the trauma narrative or re-telling may not be an essential component to all trauma treatments, it is one which has been validated in the literature as having a meaningful impact on client outcomes.

MOTIVATIONAL INTERVIEWING

Motivational interviewing (MI) is a therapeutic strategy which is particularly relevant when working with trauma-exposed youth and families. This model is largely built on the methods of engaging clients and addressing ambivalent feelings about the therapeutic process, and moving clients from a more ambivalent to less ambivalent state (Rollnick et al., 2008). This technique and model is a person-centered approach which essentially works by motivating clients to engage in the therapeutic opportunity. The model is built on four core principles – expressing empathy, avoiding arguing, rolling with resistance, and supporting self-efficacy (Miller & Rollnick, 2012). Motivational interviewing is commonly used in substance abuse work and has been adapted for healthcare settings to help work with clients towards making health-related behavioral changes. The techniques that are central to the MI model may also be quite useful in working with trauma-exposed youth and families, particularly as it relates to engaging clients (NCTSN, 2017). MI further helps clinicians address and explore potential barriers to service, and work with clients to ensure adequate therapeutic progress.

RISK SCREENING AND TRIAGE

Risk screening and triaging are two additional components that are central to providing intervention and treatment to this population. This will allow the provider to identify the clients who are at the highest level of risk and match clients with the level of services that they require (NCTSN, 2017; Yang et al., 2010). Assessing those, for example, who are at risk for future violence is one aspect of ensuring individuals are able to maintain safety (Yang et al., 2010). This risk assessment and triaging includes not only ensuring the individual is not a danger to others, but also ensuring that they are not a danger to themselves and that they are able to be maintained safety in their home environment. The use of risk assessment and triaging allows clinicians to facilitate the immediate response to crisis situations as needed (Grisso et al., 2005).

Irrespective of which choices a clinician makes relative to treatments and interventions, there are a number of useful core essential components. Here we have noted the importance of the psychoeducation, emotion and affect recognition and regulation, trauma narratives, aspects of motivational interviewing, and risk assessment. We will also add parent collaboration, and establishing a sense of safety and security and cultural sensitivity to this list of core essential components of effective trauma treatments. As we consider some of these core components, we will move into a discussion of specific trauma treatments and whom they might be best suited for.

Eleven

TRAUMA-INFORMED INTERVENTIONS AND TREATMENTS

Kirby L. Wycoff

INTRODUCTION

As noted in the previous section, there are a number of core components which are essential in trauma treatment. We will now list and review specific trauma treatments and interventions and the population for whom they might be most appropriate.

These treatment interventions and programs have been gathered from the relevant literature base as well as the databases which are produced and available through the National Child Traumatic Stress Network (NCTSN), SAMHSA's National Registry of Evidence-Based Programs and Practices (NREPP) and The California Evidence Based Clearinghouse for Child Welfare (CEBC). We strongly encourage readers to visit these resources directly for the most robust accounting of available treatments. It is important to note the NCTSN database focuses exclusively on trauma-related treatments, the CEBC focuses on evidence-based treatments and interventions related to child-welfare, and NREPP has a much broader focus on all mental health, behavioral health, and substance abuse issues. The CEBC also describes general treatment and intervention categories, which gives the user a clear sense of how best to match interventions with client needs. We encourage readers to visit the websites below from which the interventions in this section were reviewed and catalogued:

- http://www.cebc4cw.org
- http://www.nctsn.org/resources/topics/treatments-that-work/promising-practices#q3
- http://nrepp.samhsa.gov/AdvancedSearch.aspx

INFANTS, TODDLERS, AND YOUNG CHILDREN

As we consider the public health model of service delivery and the programs that invest in prevention and early intervention, infants, toddlers, and young children are a reasonable population to target for intervention. The literature abounds with risk factors for child maltreatment, which often includes parental stressors, lack of resources, and mental or physical illness. Maternal youth and maternal sociopathy were preceptors for the occurrence of physical abuse, sexual abuse, and neglect (Brown et al., 1998). When risk factors increase from none to greater than four, the likelihood of child abuse or neglect jumps from just 3% to 24% (Brown et al., 1998). Dukewich et al. (1996) examined the connection between risk factors in adolescent mothers including social supports, maternal psychological adjustment, maternal preparation for parenting, child temperament, material psychological predisposition for aggressive coping (perceptions of stress and endorsements of punitive strategies), and future maternal abuse. Preparation for parenting demands including knowledge and attitudes about child development was evidenced to be the strongest single predictor of future child abuse at the hands of an adolescent, primiparous mother (Dukewich et al., 1996). This relationship was impacted by the child's temperament and the mother's predisposition for punitive parenting (Dukewich et al., 1996). Vulnerable parent and child relationships are an obvious area for potential intervention when considering the potential risk for future neglect or maltreatment and later trauma-exposure of children. For this reason, interventions that consider infants, toddlers, and young child often include a parental or family component. The interventions below are targeted toward parent–child relationships, bolstering the supports of under-prepared or under-resourced parents and seeking to reduce the likelihood of future trauma exposure. This list is not exhaustive, but will provider readers with a better understanding of potential avenues to pursue when considering early interventions.

Interventions which focus on attachment disruption in young children, toddlers, and infants is often a common area of focus when considering trauma-exposure in our youngest clients. The CEBC noted that attachment interventions focus on interventions for individuals who have a diagnosis or significant impairment in attachment relationship, such as might be seen in Reactive Attachment Disorder (RAD) or Disinhibited Social Engagement Disorder (DSED) (California Evidence Based Clearinghouse for Child Welfare, 2017, http://www.cebc4cw.org/topic/attachment-interventions-child-adolescent). These diagnoses often include significant disruption to the attachment relationship and may be evidenced as markedly impaired and inappropriate social relatedness, typically evidencing itself before age five (Hornor, 2008). This may be characterized by indiscriminate friendliness (diffuse attachments with any available adult and excessive familiarity with strangers), avoidance of comfort from a caregiver, highly inhibited behaviour with caregivers, ambivalent and contradictory behaviour with caregivers, and significant difficulty forming health relationships (Hornor, 2008). These disruptions and impairments can be evidenced in both inhibited and disinhibited behaviours, and are often the direct result of unavailable caregiving and persistent disregard for the child's needs (WHO, 2004) Typically "gross pathogenic care" must be evidenced for a diagnosis of RAD to be considered (Roberds & Davis, 2011). It should be noted that in the DSM-5, RAD – Indiscriminate Type was relabeled as Disinhibited Social Engagement Disorder (The Diagnostic and Statistical Manual of Mental Disorders, 5th ed.; DSM–5; American Psychiatric Association, 2013; Lyons-Ruth et al., 2015). There is somewhat of a controversy around this relabeling that is beyond the scope of this book. We encourage readers to access the following resources for a more robust discussion on this topic: Lyons-Ruth et al. (2015) and Zeanah et al. (2016).

The CEBC further highlights the controversy around attachment-related diagnoses and interventions, highlighting that some of these interventions have not been consistent with best practices in the past.

Following several child deaths in the early 2000s after using attachment therapy methods such as holding therapy and rebirthing, specific practices have been banned by state legislatures and condemned by Congress. In addition, professional organizations, such as the American Academy of Child & Adolescent Psychiatry (AACAP), the American Professional Society on the Abuse of Children (APSAC), the American Psychiatric Association, and the American Psychology Association, have published warnings regarding these treatments.

(California Evidence-Based Clearinghouse for Child Welfare 2017, para 4, retrieved from: http://www.cebc4cw.org/topic/attachment-interventions-child-adolescent)

Building on the APSAC and AACAP conceptualization, the CEBC does not endorse interventions that include physical domination and coercion. Treatment techniques or attachment parenting techniques involving physical coercion, psychologically or physically enforced holding, physical restraint, physical domination, provoked catharsis, ventilation of rage, age regression, humiliation, withholding or forcing food or water intake, prolonged social isolation, or assuming exaggerated levels of control and domination over a child are contraindicated because of risk of harm and absence of proven benefit and should not be used (Chaffin et al., 2006, p. 86.) Boris and Zeanah (2005) further noted these methods have no empirical support and have been associated with serious death and harm. The position of these authors is consistent with the AACAP, the APSAC and the CEBC.

Despite these significant cautions, there are treatments and interventions that are appropriate and clinically relevant for improving the quality of a child-parent relationship and potentially reducing the likelihood of future maltreatment and abuse. A number of these available treatments are noted below. While this list is not exhaustive and an entire book could be written about (and has been!) focusing on how to best treat infants and young children who have been impacted by trauma, we encourage readers to access the following resource for a more robust discussion on this topic (Osofsky et al., 2017).

Treating Infants and Young Children Impacted by Trauma: Interventions that Promote Healthy Development

Attachment and Biobehavioral Catch-Up (ABC) (NREPP Scientific Rating = Green). This is a parent-training intervention focusing on children between the ages of 6 and 24 months. This intervention focuses on meeting the needs of children who have been exposed to maltreatment or other care disrupts and seeks to target the outcomes of disorganized attachment. The overall therapeutic goal of this intervention for infants and toddlers is to improve the parent–child relationship through increasing positive behaviours and decreasing negative behaviours (Bernard et al., 2012; Dozier et al., 2009; Osofsky et al., 2017). The model includes a number of intervention targets including cultivating nurturance and synchrony as well as psychobiological regulation. This model includes a significant amount of parent coaching and training. This integrates live feedback provided by parent coaches as well as videotaped sessions. This intervention has been rated Green by the NREPP for cognitive functioning, disruptive behaviours, disorders and symptoms, and non-specific mental health disorders and systems. It has been rated Yellow for family cohesion, parenting practices, self-concept and physical health conditions. The principal investigator for this intervention model is Mary Dozier, Ph.D. at the University of Delaware; for more information, visit www.infantcaregiverproject.com) (Bernard et al., 2014; Bernard et al., 2012; Bick & Dozier, 2013; Dozier et al., 2009; Lewis-Morrarty et al., 2012; Lind et al., 2014).

All Babies Cry (ABC) (NREPP Scientific Rating = Yellow) ABC is a primary-prevention and educational program that focuses on the reduction of incidences of child abuse within the first year of life with a particular focus on preventing abusive head trauma (also known as shaken baby syndrome). It is a strength-based program which targets the parents of infants and improves a parent's ability to understand and cope with infant crying. Fussiness and crying in infants is commonly a precursor to maltreatment, and this intervention seeks to normalize that crying in new parents. The authors report the program seeks to promote and develop five factors of resilience that reduce the likelihood of abuse and neglect. They are: (i) parental resilience, (ii) social connections, (iii) knowledge of parenting and child development, (iv) concrete support in times of need, and (v) social and emotional competence of children. The program is considered a very early intervention program with dosing and exposure occurring as early as while the newborn and child are still in the hospital. The primary prevention and mental health promotion intervention is an educational program that provides material and information to the target population during the maternity stay. It includes an educational video, and other multimedia materials. The principal investigator and contact person for the prevention program is Lisa McElaney; for more information visit www.allbabiescry.com (Morrill et al., 2015).

Attachment, Self-Regulation and Competence (ARC): A Comprehensive Framework for Intervention with Complexly Traumatized Youth (2012). The ARC model is built off the attachment system as a primary vehicle through which the child develops their sense of safety and self in the world. The target population for the intervention includes youth between the ages of 2 and 21 years who have experienced complex trauma, and their families. The caregiver relationship becomes the foundation for which the intervention is delivered and focused. The ARC framework is a flexible, component-based intervention for treating children and adolescents who have experienced complex trauma (Blaustein & Kinniburgh, 2010; Kinniburgh et al., 2006, 2017). The intervention addresses the three major domains which are impacted in complex trauma. These include attachment, self-regulation, and developmental competencies. Within these core domains, there are 10 specific targets of the interventions, some of which include the caregivers' management of affect, attunement, affect expression, and modulation. This is a well-researched intervention which has a strong empirical support and is used at a number of NCTSN sites. It is a flexible and adaptive model that has been implemented at a number of different types of youth-serving organizations including inpatient programs, outpatient programs, residential programs, schools, early intervention programs, and within the juvenile justice system. The principal investigator and contact person for this model is Margaret Blaustein, Ph.D. at the Trauma Center at Justice Resource Institute in Brookline, Massachuesttes. www.traumacenter.org. (Blaustein & Kinniburgh, 2010; Kinniburgh et al., 2006, 2017; Arvidson et al., 2011).

Cognitive-Behavioral Therapy for Sexually Abused Preschool Children (CBT-SAP) Cohen and Mannarino (1996a, 1996b, 1996c) compared sexually abused young children (ages 2–7 years) in a Cognitive-Behavioral Therapy (CBT) model versus nondirective supportive therapy over 12 weekly sessions. Each session was 90 minutes and included the therapist and child alone for 45 minutes and the therapist alone with the caregiver for 45 minutes. The intervention included strategies to address some of the problems that can be evidenced in your children who have been sexually abused including ambivalence toward perpetrators, inappropriate sexual behaviours, and the need for establishing safety (Cohen and Mannarino, 1993, 1996b, 1997, 1998, 2000; Cohen et al., 2004, 2005, 2006). The intervention used developmentally appropriate materials like coloring books, dolls, and puppets and also addressed the child's thoughts about sexual abuse and any related fear and anxiety related to the trauma (Silveman et al., 2008). Intervention techniques that were used included thought stopping and progressive muscle relaxation. The sessions for the parents included psychoeducation, cognitive reframing of the traumatic event, and behavioral management of children's inappropriate behaviors, including possible inappropriate sexual behaviors. CBT-SAP demonstrated a greater improvement compared to control groups who were experiencing nondirective supportive therapy. The control group was later eligible for full participation in the CBT-SAP protocol and at that time, improvements were demonstrated in trauma-related symptoms (Cohen & Mannarino, 1997; Cohen & Mannarino, 1998). Of note, this study and intervention program reflects the early work of Cohen and Mannarino and has since been robustly developed into the Trauma-Focused Cognitive Behavior Model which can be used with a wide range of client ages (https://tfcbt.musc.edu).

Child–Parent Relationship Therapy (CPRT) CEBC Scientific Rating = 3 (CEBC, Provisional Rating, 3 = Promising Research Evidence): This is a play-based intervention for parents of children between the ages of 3 and 8 years of age who have challenges with behaviors, emotions, social relationships, and attachment. It is reportedly grounded in Child-Centered Play therapy models and focuses on attachment principles and interpersonal neurobiology. It further focuses on parental skill attainment and enhancing the attachment relationship between the child and the parent through increased attunement. It is conducted in a small group format over the course of 10 weeks and includes video-recorded sessions of play interactions between parents and children in the home. By focusing on creating that secure base and acceptance of the child, the authors noted four "be-with" attitudes that are the focus of this intervention. They include: *I am here, I hear you, I understand* and *I care*. The developer and contact person for this model is: Sue Bratton, Ph.D., LPC, RPT-S at the Center for Play Therapy at the University of North Texas (http://cpt.unt.edu) (Bratton et al., 2006; Bratton et al., 2015; Landreth & Bratton, 2006).

Child-Parent Psychotherapy (CPP). CEBC Scientific Rating = 2 (CEBC 2 = Supported by Research Evidence): CCP is a dyadic attachment-based intervention for children who have been exposed to interpersonal and domestic violence. The intervention is targeted for children between birth and the age of 5 who have experienced trauma, as well as their caregivers. CCP seeks to better understand how the caregiver's relationships affect the child-caregiver relationships. The theoretical underpinnings of the model are based on attachment theory as well as aspects of psychodynamic, developmental trauma and cognitive behavioral theory. Contextual factors like SES, immigration status, and culture are all considered. Over the course of treatment a joint narrative of the trauma experience is co-constructed between child and caregiver with the support of the clinician. Issues of safety, emotional regulation, parental response, and relational reciprocity are all addressed. The treatment duration is a recommended one year in length with weekly sessions lasting between one and a half hours (Lieberman et al., 2005a, 2005b; Cicchetti et al., 2006, 2009; Liberman et al., 2005a, 2005b, 2005c, 2006; Toth et al., 2002; Chandra Ghosh Ippen, PhD (http://www.cebc4cw .org/program/child-parent-psychotherapy/detailed and http://www.nctsn.org/ sites/default/files/assets/pdfs/cpp_general.pdf).

Parent-Child Interaction Therapy (PCIT). (CEBC Scientific Rating = 1 (CEBC 2 = Well supported by research evidence) Parent-Child Interaction Therapy (PCIT) is a well-established intervention for parents and their children between the ages of 2 and 7 years of age. The NCTSN endorses this treatment for children between the ages of 2 and 12 years of age. This intervention specifically targets children who have disruptive behavior problems, aggressive and oppositional disorders, and parent-child relational distress. It is important to note the original PCIT model (Eyberg, 1995) was developed for young children who demonstrate a range of internalizing and externalizing behaviors as well as severe conduct issues like animal cruelly, fire setting, stealing, and lying (Osofsky et al., 2017). Treatment duration largely depends on the goal attainment of the child and parent and is mastery-based instead of being rigidly time-limited. It also was used for child-caregiver relationship distress that was secondary to family disruption (McNeil et al., 1991a, 1991b; Hembree-Kigin & McNeil, 2013; Schuhmann et al., 1998). The original intervention has a strong empirical basis, with strong validity and post-treatment gains (Eyberg et al., 1995, 2001; Schuh-mann et al., 1998) and the model has since been adapted to also include work-ing with trauma-exposed youth and families (Osofsky et al., 2017; Timmer et al., 2005; Schuhmann et al., 1998). Of note, it is one of the few interven-tions that actually works with physically abusive parents (McNeil et al., 1991a, 1991b; Hembree-Kigin & McNeil, 2013; Schuhmann et al., 1998). The goals of the PCIT include improvement of the child-caregiver relationship, a decrease in disruptive and oppositional child behaviors, and an increase in parenting skills including the use of positive discipline practices and an overall decrease in paren-tal stress (McNeil et al., 1991a, 1991b; Hembree-Kigin & McNeil, 2013; Schuh-mann et al., 1998). This intervention is a structured intervention that includes multiple stages to therapy and focuses on coaching sessions with the parent/caregiver and the child. This often includes the use of a transmitter device in the parent's ear while the coach/clinician guides the parent in the interactions through a two-way mirror (Osofsky et al., 2017; Timmer et al., 2005; Schuh-mann et al., 1998). Chaffin et al. (2006) found that in randomly assigned, physi-cally abusive parents, PCIT resulted in only 19% of PCIT condition parents having a reportable physical abuse incident almost two and a half years later com-pared to 49% of parents who participated in the control group. When consider-ing the role PCIT can play in trauma-exposed youth and families it is important to note the systemic, familial issues as well as how family roles can maintain a negative interaction style between parents and children. "Aggression, like child abuse and domestic violence, alters family roles and interaction patterns. After living in a violent home, disruptive behavior by the child can actually serve as a reminder to the parent's own trauma and may elicit trauma symptoms. For example, a child screaming and hitting might trigger behaviors from the mother such as withdrawal, which would inadvertently reinforce the child's behavior. Conversely, that same child's behavior (i.e. screaming and hitting) might elicit an aggressive response from the mother, which could result in repeated physical abuse" (McNeil & Hembree-Kigin, 2010, p. 260; McNeil et al., 1991a, 1991b; Hembree-Kigin & McNeil, 2013; Schuhmann et al., 1998). In addition to teach-ing the direct skills noted above, the model also teaches the caregiver play therapy skills that are child-directed and include the following: (PRIDE): Praise, reflec-tion, imitation, description, and enthusiasm (Osofsky et al., 2017). In seeking to build closer and healthier caregiver-child relationships, this improves the child's prosocial skills, improves the caregiver's parenting strategies, and creates safety, warmth and security for both. This model is an appropriate choice for trauma-exposed youth and families. The founder of the model is Sheile Eyberg and the contact person for this program is Erica Pearl, Psy.D., & Erna Olafson, Ph.D at the Trauma Treatment Training Center, Cincinnati, Children's Hospital (www. ohiocando4kids.org; http://www.cincinnatichildrens.org/TTTC).

In addition to the interventions and treatments noted above, there are a number of other interventions that have a strong empirical base and show a wide range of treatment approaches, and which may be useful in working with this population. We encourage readers to visit the following resources for a more robust review of available treatments for working with trauma-impacted infants, toddlers, and young children.

- The California Evidence-Based Clearinghouse for Child Welfare
- The National Child Traumatic Stress Network
- SAMHSA's National Registry of Evidence-Based Programs and Practices

ELEMENTARY SCHOOL CHILDREN

There are a number of treatments that are appropriate for trauma-exposed children in elementary school. As noted elsewhere, this list is not exhaustive and we encourage readers to review the resources noted above for a more robust discussion on available interventions. It is important to note that a number of the interventions noted in the previous section on infants, toddlers and young children also overlap with elementary aged children (e.g. CPRT; Attachment, Self-Regulation and Competence, and Parent–Child Interaction Therapy)

Bounce Back (NREPP Scientific Rating = Green) Bounce Back is an adaptation of CBITS (Cognitive-Behavioral Intervention for Trauma in Schools) that is a school-based, cognitive-behavioral program for trauma-exposed youth. The Bounce Back version of this model is for children in grades Kindergarten through Grade 5. CBITS (which will be discussed in the next section on treatments for Middle Schoolers) is intended for youth in grades 5 through 12. Bounce Back (Langley et al., 2015). The development team that designed Bounce Back noted that their intention was to integrate two interventions that were already in existence and demonstrated strong empirical support as trauma treatments. These include CBITS (Jaycox et al., 2002, 2009, 2010) and TF-CBT (Trauma-Focused Cognitive-Behavioral Therapy), (Cohen et al. 2005, 2006, 2011, 2016). Langely et al. consulted with these national trauma experts in the development of the Bounce Back treatment approach. Using this feedback, there were a number of specific goals in the development of Bounce Back. These included a group format to maximize the number of children who could be served, doing universal screenings, inviting (but not requiring) parents for participation and psychoeducation, and focusing on psychoeducation in the group format while using individual sessions for the trauma narratives (Langley et al., 2015). As such, Bounce Back follows a similar model as CBITS, with increased parental involvement for the trauma narrative process (similar to TF-CBT) which is typically the case in working with younger, trauma-exposed children (Langley et al., 2015). The goal in creating Bounce Back was to build off of two other successful treatments (e.g. the youth, group-focus of CBITS and the parental involvement aspect of TF-CBT) while including the aspects of both that are known to be effective in trauma treatment: psychoeducation, relaxation training, cognitive coping, and exposure to avoided stimuli (Langley et al., 2015). The program includes a total of 10 group sessions as well as two to three individual sessions and one to three parental or caregiver sessions. Each group session is between 50 and 60 minutes long and each individual session ranges from 30 to 50 minutes long with the intent of making the sessions fit within the parameters of a school day. The 10 group sessions included topics and content around normalizing trauma reactions, feelings identification, physiological arousal, relaxation training, cognitive restructuring, emotional regulation, and coping, among others (Langley et al., 2015).

> Compared with children in the delayed condition, children who received Bounce Back immediately demonstrated significantly greater improvements in parent- and child- reported posttraumatic stress and child-reported anxiety symptoms over the three- month intervention period. Upon receipt of the intervention, the delayed intervention group demonstrated significant improvements in parent- and child-reported posttraumatic stress, depression, and anxiety symptoms. The immediate treatment group maintained or showed continued gains in all symptom domains over the three- month follow-up period (six-month assessment).
>
> *(Langley et al., 2015, p. 853)*

This program has demonstrated efficacy in the reduction of trauma-related distress in the school-aged population, the average effect size was 0.83 (95% CI; 0.49–1.17). The principal investigator is Audra Langley, Ph.D., Executive Director – UCLA Ties for Families and the Program. The program contact is Lisa Jaycox, Ph.D.; for more information, visit www.cbitsprogram.org and www.bouncebackprogram.org.

Trauma-Focused Cognitive Behavioral Therapy (TF-CBT). (NREPP Scientific Rating – Green) Trauma Focused CBT is an individual, psychosocial intervention which is intended to treat trauma-related distress in youth between the ages of 3 and 18 years of age. The focus is on a wide range of trauma-exposures and incorporates sessions with non-abusing parents and/or caregivers (Cohen et al., 2004, 2005, 2006, 2011, 2016). This intervention includes skill development around affect regulation, the relationship between thoughts and behaviors, and trauma processing all while building safety and increasing parenting skills (Cohen et al., 2004, 2005, 2006, 2011, 2016; O'Callaghan et al., 2013; Jensen et al., 2013; Cohen et al., 2011). Depending on the age and needs of the client the model has been implemented in a child-only intervention, as well as various intervention arrangements including caregivers and parents (Silverman et al., 2008). It is typically delivered once a week across 12–18 sessions for 50–90 minutes. TF-CBT has one of the strongest empirical bases for treatment efficacy and validity including multiple randomized controlled trials (RCT's). The model has been studied extensively in the United States and internationally. In low-resource countries, TF-CBT has been implemented by trained lay counselors using an apprentice model for training non-professional community counselors which demonstrated significant improvement in symptoms of traumatized children (mostly rescued from sex trafficking) in Africa (Murray et al., 2013). There is a focus on the therapeutic alliance in this model. The approach is highly collaborative in building relationships with the parents of the trauma-exposed (non-offending) caregivers. The approach is built on a foundation of cognitive therapy, behavioral therapy, and family therapy approaches (Cohen et al., 2004, 2005, 2006, 2011, 2016). The central goals of the treatment include reduction of the negative emotional and behavioral impairments which result from the trauma exposure, correct maladaptive beliefs about the trauma experiences, and provide support for non-offending parents (Cohen et al., 2004, 2005, 2006, 2011, 2016; O'Callaghan et al., 2013; Jensen, et al., 2013; Cohen et al., 2011). The treatment is generally implemented over 12–16 sessions, but as many as 25 sessions for complexly traumatized youth. The specific components of TF-CBT are highlighted using the acronym "PRACTICE." They include: Psychoeducation and Parenting Skills, Relaxation Skills, Affective Expression and Modulation Skills, Cognitive Coping and Processing Skills, Trauma narration and processing, In-vivo mastery of trauma reminders, Conjoint child-parent sessions, and Enhancing safety and future revictimization (Cohen et al., 2004, 2005, 2006, 2011, 2016; O'Callaghan et al., 2013; Jensen et al. 2013; Cohen et al., 2011). It is important to note this intervention provides free online training for clinicians who are interested in implementation. The principal investigator is Judith Cohen, M.D., Professor of Psychiatry (https://tfcbt.org).

The Incredible Years (IY). CEBC Scientific Rating = 1 (CEBC, 1 = Well-Supported by Research Evidence) Incredible Years (IY) is a multi-layered intervention program that provides targeted intervention and psychoeducation for parents, children and teachers. Target populations include parents and teachers of children between ages 3 and 8 years, but also include a range of other curriculums focused on others ages, including the IY Well-Babies program appropriate for parents of children from birth to nine months. The overall goals of the program are to increase social, emotional, and behavioral competence and decrease behavioral and emotional challenges in young children. This program is targeted toward children between ages 4 and 8 years. While not initially intended for trauma-focused treatment, it has been adapted and is appropriate for high-risk populations and those involved in the child welfare system (Webster-Stratton & Reid, 2010). Goals of the program include improving child-adult relationships (teacher-student and parent-child), building positive relationships and attachment, improving parental functioning and proactive classroom management, and increasing the child's overall social competence and emotional regulation. The program can be delivered in a variety of formats depending on the target audience including 1–2 hour individual sessions (for child and parent), as well as classroom-based sessions (2–3 times weekly for 60 sessions). The IY program is rooted in a prevention science framework and developmental and cognitive social learning theory, suggesting that early interventions around the development of prosocial behaviors can be effective in youth outcomes (Webster-Stratton & Reid, 2010). It was first introduced in the 1980s (Webster-Stratton) as a group-based parenting program for reducing behavioral problems and promoting positive social development and has since been modified to meet the needs of parents, teachers, and children. The program has been implemented in multiple countries and translated into a wide range of languages. It can be used flexibly, as a primary prevention program using the public health model, or a specialized intervention for families who need additional support. All three of versions of the program have been endorsed by the Office for Juvenile Justice and Delinquency Prevention (OJJDP) (Webster-Stratton & Reid, 2010). The IY parenting series has been used with maltreating families and those involved in the child welfare systems where there is a specific focus on positive, developmentally appropriate behavior management and parenting practices. There have been a number of revisions that were made to the IY program, some of which are particularly relevant for use in the child welfare population. They include:

1. Parents learn about normal child development so they have appropriate developmental expectations
2. Parents are trained in academic, persistence, social and emotion coaching to help them foster their children's self-regulation and social

skills build their parent-child relationships and decrease attachment difficulties.

3. Parents are helped to set up predictable routines, schedules, and ongoing monitoring

4. Parents learn how to teach their children problem-solving skills

5. Home safety-proofing and monitoring strategies (Webster-Stratton & Reid, 2010, p. 27)

The parenting series is broken down by age group, with different curriculum for parents of infants, toddlers, pre-schoolers, and other children. Again, while not specifically developed for trauma-exposed youth and families, the IY program is an evidence-based program which can work to address and prevent some of the negative impacts and outcomes of distressed families. The developer of this model is Carolyn Webster-Stratton and the contact person is Megan Pahl at www. incredibleyears.com and http://www.cebc4cw.org/program/the-incredible-years.

The next section in this chapter will review trauma-informed interventions and treatments focusing on the middle school population. It is important to note that some of the interventions noted in this section may also apply to middle school-aged students as well.

MIDDLE SCHOOL CHILDREN

In addition to the programs noted above, some of which may overlap with middle school aged children, the following interventions are appropriate to consider for the Middle School population. Some of those that may be appropriate for elementary school children, including Trauma-Focused CBT, may also be appropriate for this population. Again, we encourage readers to visit the following resources for a more robust review of available treatments for working with trauma-impacted infants, toddlers, and young children.

- The California Evidence-Based Clearinghouse for Child Welfare
- The National Child Traumatic Stress Network
- SAMHSA's National Registry of Evidence-Based Programs and Practices

In addition to these publically available databases we encourage readers to review (Silverman et al., 2008).

Cognitive-Behavioral Intervention for Trauma in Schools (CBITS). (NREPP Scientific Rating = Green) CBITS is a school-based, cognitive behavioral intervention program for traumatized youth. CBITS is intended for youth in grades 5–12

(Bounce Back is for grades K-5). The program focuses on cognitive behavioral therapy techniques for the reduction of trauma symptoms in exposed youth. As noted earlier, CBITS was developed with the school context in mind and intended to be implemented in this setting. The program is delivered in a group format and each new skill set is delivered via didactic psychoeducation as well as the use of age-appropriate games and was generalized across sessions using "homework" which was collaboratively developed between student and clinician (Kataoka et al., 2011; Stein et al., 2003). CBITS is typically delivered to groups of 6–8 youths, over the course of 10 sessions and includes between 1 and 3 three individual sessions (for the trauma narrative) as well (Jaycox et al., 2010). In comparing TF-CBT to CBITS the following has been noted "Both CBITS and TF-CBT include cognitive-behavioral skills, such as: psycho-education, relaxation skills, affective modulation skills, cognitive coping skills, trauma narrative, in vivo mastery of trauma reminders, and enhancing safety. However, there are also significant differences between these two models. TF-CBT is provided in conjoint sessions (with parent and child), whereas CBITS is provided in a group format (children only). TF-CBT may be optimal for developing a multiple trauma narrative and for addressing avoidance symptoms, since the therapist can tailor the intervention to each child, while CBITS may offer a more acceptable and feasible approach by overcoming some logistical barriers and stigma" (Jaycox et al., 2010, para. 20). CBITS includes a number of core cognitive-behavioral techniques. A sample session map of eight sessions (plus one individual session, with space for more as needed) that was used in working with traumatized Latino immigrant children can be found here:

1. Session 1 (Group format): Introduction of group members, confidentiality, and group procedures. Explanation of treatment using stories, discussion of reasons for participation (types of trauma)
2. Session 2 (Group format): Education and common reactions to trauma,; relaxation training to combat anxiety
3. Session 3 (Group format): Thoughts of feelings (introduction to cognitive therapy); fear thermometer, linkage between thoughts and feelings; introduction of idea of combating erroneous negative thoughts
4. Session 4 (Group format): Avoidance and coping (introduction to in-vivo exposure); construction of fear hierarchy
5. Session 5 (Individual format): Imaginal exposure to traumatic event (*additional individual sessions as needed)
6. Session 6 (Group format): Social problem-solving (Stop, Think, What's your goal?)

7. Session 7 (Group format): Exposure to trauma memory though drawing/writing
8. Session 8 (Group format): Exposure to trauma memory though Hembree-Kiginwriting
9. Session 9 (Group format): Relapse prevention and graduation ceremony (Kataoka et al., 2011, p. 312).

CBITS has been used with a wide range of racially, culturally, and ethnically diverse student populations. It is currently being used in the general school population in the Los Angeles Unified School District and has parent materials available in both Spanish and English. Note that the intervention below (Support for Students Exposed to Trauma) is a non-clinical version of CBITS that can be delivered by teachers and other school-based staff. For more information on the CBITS model, contact Marleen Wong (marleen.wong@lausd.net) at the LAUSD Community Practice Site, Lisa Jaycox (jaycox@rand.org) or Bradley Stein (stein@rand.org) at the RAND Corporation, or Sheryl Kataoka (skataoka@ucla.edu) at UCLA; also visit www.cbitsprogram.org.

Supports for Students Exposed to Trauma (SSET). (NREPP Scientific Rating = Yellow). Supports for Students Exposed to Trauma (SSET) is the nonclinical version of CBITS, for implementation by nonclinical school staff members like teachers. It is a group, school-based intervention which is intended to provide support for trauma-exposed youth and improve functioning among this population. The goals of SSET are quite similar to CBITS, with a focus on skill-building, and reduction of anxiety, isolation, and school-related behavioral challenges that may be related to the trauma-exposure. These elements include psychoeducation, cognitive coping, gradual in-vivo mastery of trauma triggers and social problem-solving (Jaycox et al., 2009). "The main differences between the two programs are in format (SSET converts the CBITS session format to a lesson plan format), elimination of individual break-out sessions in SSET, elimination of parent sessions in SSET, and changes in the imaginal exposure to trauma that is conducted in CBITS to a more curricular format in SSET" (Jaycox et al., 2009, para. 6). The data outcome of the pilot implementation in the Los Angeles Unified School District demonstrated some reduction among symptoms of students in the SSET intervention and makes this adaptation of CBITS one possible consideration for school-based interventions for trauma-exposed youth (Jaycox et al., 2009). For more information on the CBITS model, contact Marleen Wong (marleen.wong@lausd.net) at the LAUSD Community Practice Site, Lisa Jaycox (jaycox@rand.org) or Bradley Stein (stein@rand.org) at the RAND Corporation, or Sheryl Kataoka (skataoka@ucla.edu) at UCLA; also visit www.cbitsprogram.org.

Coping Power Program (CP). CEBC Scientific Rating = 1 (CEBC, 1 = Well-Supported by Research Evidence). The Coping Power Program, as a few others listed in this chapter (Incredible Years), is primarily focused on prevention and can also be used for those who have been identified as high-risk in the general population. While it does not have a trauma focus per se, it is intended to address social problem-solving and other disruptive behaviors that are often seen in trauma-exposed populations. The Coping Power Program is intended for youth between the ages of 8 and 14 years whose aggression and or other disruptive behaviors impact their healthy functioning and puts them at risk for later delinquency or risk-taking behaviors. The social-cognitive model is the theoretical foundation of the Coping Power. "The contextual social–cognitive model assumes that aggressive children have distortions in their social–cognitive appraisals and deficiencies in their social problem-solving skills and that their parents have deficiencies in their parenting behaviors" (Lochman & Wells, 2002, p. 945). The program is based on the premise that childhood aggression is a risk factor for the development of later delinquency, conduct issues, and overall poor outcomes (Lochman & Wells, 2002; Hishaw et al., Lashey, & Hart, 1993; Loeber, 1990). Aggressive children are at an increased risk for later interpersonal conflict, criminal behaviour, and poor school adjustment. Based on the original work of Novaco (1978) on adult anger models, this program is conceptualized on a similar model of anger arousal in children. This focuses on a sequential cognitive processing wherein the child experiences and then has a certain perception (or misperception) about task demand frustration or interpersonal conflict (Lochman & Wells, 2002). It is not the event that causes the anger, but rather the child's cognitive processing of the frustrating or difficult event/task.

"Aggressive children have cognitive distortions at the appraisal stage of social-cognitive processing because of difficulties in encoding incoming social information and inaccurately interpreting social events and others' intentions. They also have cognitive deficiencies at the problem-solution stage of social-cognitive processes, generating maladaptive solutions for perceived problems and having nonnormative expectations for the usefulness of aggressive and nonaggressive solutions for their social problems" (Lochman & Wells, 2002, p. 947). Hostile attribution bias, which refers to the concept of an individual selectively attending to interpreting social information as hostile when in fact they are neutral, is typically higher in aggressive individuals (Gouze, 1987; Milich & Dodge, 1984). These individuals excessively infer hostility and assume that others are acting toward them in hostile, aggressive, and provocative ways (Katsurada & Sugawara, 1998; Lochman & Dodge, 1994). It has been established in the literature that individuals with a maltreatment history have superior predictions in recognizing fear and sadness (Leist & Dadds, 2009). "Emotion-processing difficulties are a possible consequence of early maltreatment and have been explored as a mechanism through which maltreatment exerts its influence on later behavior" (Leist & Dadds, 2009, p. 240). Typically developing children learn how to recognize and regulate emotion through healthy and responsive child-caregiver relationships. There they also learn how to allocate resources to the most salient emotional cues (Pollack et al., 2001). In the context of maltreatment and abuse in the caregiver dyad, however, when emotional responses of caregivers are less predictable certain emotional cues become indicators of threat (Pollack et al., 2001). Given this literature, a primary prevention program that is built on the social-cognitive processing model, intended to increase children's ability to interpret and manage social interactions, and reduce aggressive behaviors may have great suitability to the trauma-exposed population. This primary prevention program, which was developed as a school-based intervention, is intended to increase pro-social skills and behaviors (Lochman & Wells, 2002; Lochman & Wells, 2004). These include increased self-regulation, social competence, and positive parental involvement and engagement. The model integrates structured, cognitive-behavioral groups along with a parent training component and typically consists of 34 group sessions (with periodic individual sessions) as well a parental component (Wells et al., 2008). The program is typically delivered over a 15–18 month period. The contact person for the Coping Power Program is Nicole Powell, Ph.D., MPH at the University of Alabama; for more information, visit http://www.copingpower.com.

Real Life Heroes (RLH). (NREPP Scientific Rating = No Rating). The Real Life Heroes (RLH) model is based on the cognitive-behavioral theory of treating PTSD in youth. It was originally developed to be used in child and family agencies with children experiencing complex trauma between 6 and 12 years of age, and/or older students who have delays in social, emotional, or cognitive functioning. "An activity-based workbook and manual assists practitioners to promote safety, understanding of the impact of traumas, attachments, affect modulation, coping skills, and trauma reprocessing" (Kagan et al., 2008, p. 5). The model focuses on improvement of attachment relationships and decreasing dysregulation after abuse, neglect, family violence, and other traumatic experiences (Kagan et al., 2008). The program is delivered over 6–18 months with once-weekly sessions of 60–90 minutes, resulting in 36–108 hours of intervention. The duration will largely depend on the individual child's needs and the availability of a non-offending caregiver who can participate in the treatment.

The model provides practitioners with a life storybook, manual, and creative artistic activities as well as psychoeducation information to work with both clients and caregivers. It is built on CBT theory as well as nonverbal creative arts, narrative interventions, and gradual exposure to help restore hope and process trauma memories (Kagan et al., 2008). The life storybook is focused around the metaphor of heroes and provides a step-wide, manualized approach to engaging clients and rebuilding safety, security, skill, attachment, and hope (Kagan et al., 2008). Interactions with caregivers are designed to foster trust and attunement with caregiver. RLH integrates three core aspects of trauma treatment including (i) Emotional regulation, (ii) attachment, and (iii) life story integration (Richardson et al., 2011; Kagan, 2009). The program includes safety planning, psychoeducation on trauma, affect regulation and identification skills, problem solving, and cognitive restructuring (Richardson et al., 2011; Kagan, 2009). The contact person for the RLH program is Richard Kagan, Ph.D., at the Parsons Child and Family Center; for more information, visit www.reallifeheroes.net and http://www.nctsn.org/sites/default/files/assets/ppt/rlh_general%20022213.pdf.

HIGH SCHOOL STUDENTS

In addition to the programs noted above the following interventions are appropriate to consider for the high school population. Some of those that may be appropriate for Middle School children, including Trauma-Focused CBT and CBITS, may be appropriate for this population as well. Again, we encourage readers to visit the following resources for a more robust review of available treatments for working with trauma impacted infants, toddlers and young children.

- The California Evidence-Based Clearinghouse for Child Welfare
- The National Child Traumatic Stress Network
- SAMHSA's National Registry of Evidence-Based Programs and Practices

Seeking Safety for Adolescents (Substance Abuse and Truma Treatment) CEBC Scientific Rating = 3 (CEBC 3 = Promising Research Evidence). The Seeking Safety for Adolescents intervention is targeted at adolescents between the age of 12 and 17 years with a history of trauma and/or substance abuse. This model is built on the premise that for some, PTSD and SUD (Substance Use Disorders) are closely connected, and PTSD and SUD as a dual diagnosis is common in the adult populations. Dual-diagnosis of PTSD and SUD among adolescent populations is less robust, and treatment of these two diagnoses together is even less robust (Najavits et al., 2006). Among men in the US who develop full PTSD, 52% of them develop an alcohol use disorder and 35% develop a drug use disorder. For women, the rates are 28% and 27% (Kesslet et al., 1995; Najavits, 2007). Seeking Safety (SS) is a manualized treatment program that was focused on adult samples with positive outcomes (Najavits, 2007). The SS intervention has since been modified to also treat adolescents and preliminary data is promising. The initial SS model includes a treatment manual with 25 topics addressing three primary domains of functioning: behavioral, cognitive and interpersonal. Embedded within these three central domains of functioning are specific skills which are often impacted in SUD and PTSD. These include things like asking for help and setting boundaries in relationships. The original SS intervention is built on five principles guiding treatment delivery. They are: "(i) Safety as a priority; (ii) integrated treatment of both disorders; (iii) a focus on ideals; (iv) four content areas (cognitive, behavioral, interpersonal and case management); and (v) attention to therapist process" (Najavits, 2007, p. 454). The SS model was then adapted to meet the developmental needs of the adolescent populations, including adjusting the language and delivery to account for the client's age as well as parent contact (if the adolescent was comfortable with doing so). The SS for Adolescents includes a homework component wherein the student commits to one thing they will do between sessions to support their recovery. The intervention is highly flexible with regards to implementation. Sessions can be held for one hour once a week, or one hour twice a week. In the once a week model, treatment would last approximately six months. In the twice a week model, the duration would shrink to three months. The program can be modified to meet the needs of clients and the context within which clients are seen, including schools, outpatient clinics, residential settings, hospitals, and community agencies. In a RCT comparing SS for dual-diagnosis adolescent females compared to treatment as usual (TAU). SS outperformed TAU on multiple parameters including post-treatment substance use, some trauma-related symptoms and cognitions about SUD and PTSD with effect sizes in the moderate-to-high range (Najavits, 2007). Seeking Safety for Adolescents may be one possible intervention which would meet the needs of trauma-impacted, dual diagnosis adolescents. The contact person for this SS model is Lisa M. Najavits, Ph.D., Associate Professor of Psychiatry at Harvard Medical School, Director of Treatment Innovations; for more information, visit www.seekingsafety.org and http://www.cebc4cw.org/program/seeking-safety-for-adolescents/detailed.

Trauma Affect Regulation: Guide for Education and Treatment (TARGET) (NREPP Scientific Rating = Green). Trauma Affect Regulation: Guide for

Education and Treatment (TARGET) is an emotion-regulation, educational, and psychotherapeutic intervention for adults, adolescents, and families. The treatment focuses on traumatic stress symptoms as well as frequent co-occurring diagnosis like addiction, as well as affective and other related trauma-related challenges. The TARGET model was developed (originally for adult populations) on the premise that PSTD symptoms (including physiological arousal and emotional dysregulation) were biological adaptations to real threat (Ford et al., 2011). In this way, TARGET seeks to normalize the trauma response as one that at one point was mobilized to allow the individual to survive. The program is intended to restore more accurate emotional responses. "Restoring affect regulation is described as requiring seven practical steps or skills summarized by an acronym, 'FREEDOM': Focusing the mind on one thought at a time; Recognizing current triggers for emotional reactions; distinguishing dysregulated ('reactive') versus adaptive ('main') Emotions, Evaluations (thoughts), goal Definitions, and behavioral Options; and self-statements affirming that taking responsibility for recovering from intense emotions is crucial not only to one's own personal well-being but also to Making a positive contribution to primary relationships (e.g., as a parent) and the community" (Ford et al., 2011, p. 566). The intervention supports clients in re-establishing adaptive capacity for emotional identification and expression and interpersonal engagement. There is a manualized model that is brief in nature (four sessions) and a longer version of the program that extends 10–14 sessions in length. In a randomized clinical trial, TARGET was compared to relational supportive therapy (enhanced treatment as usual, ETAU) with 59 delinquent girls between the ages of 13 and 17 years. All female participants met full or partial criteria for PTSD. "Both therapies had small-to-medium effect size changes in anxiety, anger, depression, and posttraumatic cognitions. Treatment × Time interactions showed small-to-medium effects favoring TARGET for change in PTSD (intrusive reexperiencing and avoidance) and anxiety symptoms, posttraumatic cognitions, and emotion regulation, and favoring ETAU for change in hope and anger. Results provided preliminary support for TARGET as a potentially efficacious therapy for PTSD with delinquent girls" (Ford et al., 2012a, 2012b, p. 27). Ford et al. (2011) demonstrated significant reductions in anxiety compared to waitlist control as well as an increase in their use of coping skills in mothers with victimization-related PTSD (Ford et al., 2011). Further, a reduction in the severity of PTSD symptoms and post-trauma beliefs about oneself were also improved (Ford et al., 2011). The contact person for this intervention is Julian Ford, Ph.D. Professor of Psychiatry and Law, University of Connecticut; for more information, visit www.advancedtrauma.com and http://nrepp.samhsa.gov/ProgramProfile.aspx?id=1222).

FAMILIES

As has been noted elsewhere, the family system plays a critical role in understanding and treating the needs of trauma-impacted youth. A number of the interventions presented in this section speak to the need for caregiver and/or parent involvement in the treatment of traumatized youth. Whenever possible, we suggest that clinicians partner with caregivers, parents, and families in the treatment of trauma-impacted youth. Given the systemic nature of chronic, complex, traumatic stress and the potentiality of inter-generational trauma, the family system simply cannot be ignored. Irrespective of the choice of intervention, we contend that the family system plays a significant role in reducing the stressors for the entire family and in turn is a critical component to any successful trauma-related intervention. For a more robust discussion of inter-generational family and the role that the family system plays in chronic, traumatic stress, we strongly encourage readers to read the book *It Didn't Start with You* by Mark Wolynn. In addition to those noted above, the interventions below may prove useful in partnering with trauma-impacted families. While some of these interventions are not focused explicitly on trauma, they do focus on a number of the negative outcomes that can occur as a result of trauma, including interpersonal challenges, relationship distress, strained parent-child relationships, substance use, and juvenile justice involvement, among others. A number of the programs listed below can also be delivered as intervention programs and seek to reduce familial stressors that place children at an increased risk of child abuse and maltreatment. The following treatment and prevention programs were documented in public databases and we encourage readers to visit these resources for additional interventions as they may suit the needs of a specific child or family.

1. The California Evidence-Based Clearinghouse for Child Welfare
2. The National Child Traumatic Stress Network
3. SAMHSA's National Registry of Evidence-Based Programs and Practices

Interventions and treatments that include a family system component:

- Child and Family Traumatic Stress Intervention (CFTSI)
- Multidimensional Family Therapy (MDFT)
- Multisystemic Therapy (MST) for Juvenile Offenders
- Multisystemic Therapy for Youth with Problem Sexual Behaviors (MST-PSB)
- Nurturing Parenting Programs (NPP)
- Strengthening Families Program (SFP)

- SafeCare® Home Visiting for Child Well-Being
- Safe Environment for Every Kid (SEEK)
- ACT Raising Safe Kids Program
- Kids Club & Moms Empowerment
- Triple P – Positive Parenting Program® System (System Triple P)
- Circle of Security-Home Visiting-4 (COS-HV4)

Section Five

ETHICAL CONSIDERATIONS IN TRAUMA-INFORMED ASSESSMENT AND INTERVENTION

Twelve

ETHICAL CONSIDERATIONS

Kirby L. Wycoff

VICARIOUS TRAUMA, COMPASSION FATIGUE, AND SECONDARY TRAUMATIC STRESS

No book on trauma-informed services for youth and families would be complete without a conversation on ethical considerations, vicarious trauma (VT), compassion fatigue (CF), and burnout management. When working with the most vulnerable members of our communities, clinicians and other frontline providers are at an increased risk of experiencing significant burnout and vicarious trauma. The need to attend to these issues and engage in robust self-care is not just a matter of aspiration, but a matter of ethical obligation. Caring comes at a cost (Figley, 2002). As mental health providers and frontline responders, it is incumbent upon us to manage ourselves and self-monitor the extent to which that cost of caring is impacting us negatively. In our roles as helpers, we are vulnerable to burnout, and the vicarious trauma of compassion fatigue.

Charles Figley in "Compassion Fatigue: Psychotherapists' Chronic Lack of Self-Care" notes that compassion fatigue is a type of caregiver burnout that focuses on the cost of caring, empathy, and emotional investment in those who are suffering (Figley, 2002). Those in any helping profession are vulnerable to compassion fatigue. However, when our clients come to us with stories of neglect, maltreatment, and other difficult and traumatic life experiences, we are at an even higher risk. Figley notes that "the very act of being compassionate and empathic extracts a cost under most circumstances. In our effort to view the world from the perspective of the suffering we suffer" (Figley, 2002, p. 1434).

In many cases, it is our interest in helping others and our abilities to be empathic and compassionate that brought us to the helping profession in the first place. The very things that brought us to such a field can interfere with our ability to maintain professional objectivity and perspective when we experience compassion fatigue. Post-traumatic stress disorder considers the possibility that the individual may be directly traumatized, or may be indirectly traumatized by virtue of hearing second-hand accounts of the trauma and bearing the distress of those who experiencing the trauma (Figley, 2002). In many ways, secondary traumatic stress (STS) is related to post-traumatic stress disorder. STS is "the natural consequent behaviors and emotions resulting from knowing about a traumatizing event experienced by a significant other – the stress resulting from helping or wanting to help a traumatized or suffering person" (Figley, 1995, p. 3; 2007; Figley et al., 2011) Vicarious Trauma (VT), Compassion fatigue (CF), and STS are terms that are often used interchangeably and all have to do with exposure of traumatizing event through another's experience. These constructs can be considered through the role of working specifically with traumatized clients. Burnout, on the other hand, is typically a more general phenomenon that could occur in any helping profession or service setting (Newell & MacNeil, 2010). In contrast to CF, VT, and STS–which would be relevant for a professional who is specifically exposed to trauma through work with a specific client–burnout refers to "a state of physical, emotional, and mental exhaustion caused by long-term involvement in emotionally demanding situations" (Pines & Aronson, 1988 p. 9). Figley (2002) notes that compassion fatigue often involves a sense of hopelessness for our clients, but is highly treatable once the professional recognizes that they are at risk. However, he notes that burnout may require changing careers and reducing work in the helping profession (Figley, 2002). Burnout is further described as a "syndrome of emotional exhaustion, depersonalization, and reduced personal accomplishment" (Maslach, 1982, p. 3) This chapter is intended to help get clinicians thinking about CF, STS, and VT *before* they become such a high-level issue that the professional may need to consider leaving the field. As such, these issues are among the highest contributors to turnover in the helping professions and are particularly relevant for those working with traumatized clients.

"Compassion fatigue is defined as a state of tension and preoccupation with the traumatized patients by re-experiencing the traumatic events, avoidance/ numbing of reminders, and persistent arousal (e.g. anxiety) associated with the patient. It is a function of bearing witness to the suffering of others" (Figley, 2002, p. 1435). The impact of STS and Vicarious Trauma (VT) often include many of the same symptoms that one would see in PTSD and includes intrusive thoughts, avoidance, and even physiological arousal (Figley, 1995, 2007; Figley et al., 2011; McCann & Pearlman, 1990; Bride, 2007; Bride, 2007; Haley, 1974). For those of us working with youth and families who are experiencing chronic, traumatic stress and who often come to us with a history of adverse childhood experiences, being aware of our vulnerability to compassion fatigue, vicarious trauma, and STS is absolutely essential (Bride, 2007).

Prevalence of Secondary Traumatic Stress and Compassion Fatigue

What is important to know for both new clinicians and seasoned professionals alike is that for those working with high-risk clients, STS and compassion fatigue are quite common. It is increasingly obvious that for those of us on the frontlines of working with society's most vulnerable members, the psychological effects of that trauma extend far beyond those who are directly affected (Bride 2007). Meldrum et al. (2002) found that 27% of professionals who work with traumatized clients experience extreme distress as a result of that work. At the time of the study a total of 54.8% participants reported being distressed and an additional 35.1% reported feeling very or extremely emotionally drained (Meldrum et al., (2002). In a study of 282 masters-level, licensed social workers randomly selected from a southern state in the U.S., 40.5% of respondents indicated that they thought about their work with traumatized clients without intending to (Bride 2007). 19.1% of the sample population experienced physiological distress and 12.4% experienced physiological reactions in response to reminders about their work with traumatized clients (Bride, 2007). Almost all of these professionals (97.8%) indicated that the clients that they worked with did in fact have a trauma history and that their professional work with those clients was largely focused on that trauma. Given the high exposure of these social workers to traumatic content via their work with the clients, it is not surprising that 70.2% of them reported at least one symptom of STS from the last week alone (Bride, 2007).

In a study that assessed the impacts and long-term mental health on the disaster mental health (DMH) workers who provided crisis counseling services to victims in the Oklahoma City bombing, STS was also found to be present (Wee & Myers, 2002). A significant number of the DMH workers (73.5%) were found to be at some level of risk for compassion fatigue. 23.5% of respondents rated at moderate risk, 29.4% rated as high risk, and 20.6% rated as extremely high risk (Wee & Myers, 2002) as measured by the Compassion Fatigue Self-Test for Psychotherapy (Figley, 1995, 2007; Figley et al., 2011). Overall, scores indicated that the entire population of DMH workers was at some level of risk for both compassion fatigue and burnout (Wee & Myers, 2002).

Among 67 Emergency Nurses, who are often exposed to individuals who have been exposed to traumatic events in three general community hospitals in California, 54% of the nurses reported arousal symptoms and irritability. This was closely followed by 52% who reported avoidance and 46% who reported intrusive thoughts about patients (Dominguez-Gomez & Rutledge, 2009). While not mental health professionals, emergency nurses are on the frontlines of being with individuals who have experienced significant trauma. Whereas mental health professionals *hear* about the traumas of their clients, nurses *see* the traumas of their clients. There is much to be learned by considering the interdisciplinary nature of vicarious traumatization, STS, and compassion fatigue. Using an exploratory comparative study in a Southern California healthcare system, RNs in emergency departments who had been in the role for a minimum of six months were assessed for STS (Dominguez-Gomez & Rutledge, 2009). The STS Scale was used to assess intrusion, avoidance, and arousal, as they correspond with the DSM diagnosis of PTSD (Bride, 2007). A total of 46% of the participants (78% of whom were women) reported thinking about their clients when they did not intend to do so and 27% of those reported that reminders of their work with their clients was upsetting to them (Dominguez-Gomez & Rutledge, 2009).. Interestingly, most of the nurses in the sample (92%) denied have ever sought assistance and support for work-related stress, although 52% of them reported engaging in stress management and self-care. A total of 33% of the sample met the criteria for a diagnosis of STS, most often reporting avoidance of clients, challenges with sleep, irritability, intrusive thoughts, reduced activity levels, and emotional numbing. (Dominguez-Gomez & Rutledge, 2009). This issue of normalizing the process of seeking help for our frontline providers must be part of our efforts moving forward.

Training Needs

As we consider how to normalize both the experience of STS and the process of seeking help, considering training and professional development needs is critical. Understanding the emotional risks of entering the helping professions and working with vulnerable populations has not always been addressed in systematic ways in professional training programs (Cunningham, 2004; Courtois, 2002; Shackelford, 2006). The importance of addressing these topics as critical training issues—issues which are as important as theory and therapy techniques for mental health providers—cannot be overstated. All too often, these concerns are folded into existing lectures on other topics around professional development and never truly given the attention that they require in the curriculum. Lerias and Byre

(2003) note that integrating this information into curricula is a best-practices, frontline prevention strategy that is needed but often overlooked for those in the mental health fields. One of the key skills we teach early mental health trainees is on the importance of building a therapeutic alliance with the client. My own graduate students can tell you that we spend a significant amount of time discussing alliance, building rapport, connecting with clients, and building a working, collaborative relationship with those we help. Figley (2002) notes that empathy and emotional energy are often a large part of what brings someone to a role of helping and that the therapeutic alliance and empathic response are core skills in effective service delivery. He cautions, however, that the very things that help us build relationships with clients, like compassion and empathy, come at a cost. Figley notes relevant variables that are foundational to understanding the construct of compassion fatigue. We encourage readers to view this work in full, but will briefly note them here:

- Empathic ability
- Empathic concern
- Exposure to client
- Empathic response
- Compassion stress
- Sense of achievement
- Disengagement
- Prolonged exposure
- Traumatic recollections
- Life disruption

In light of understanding these variables and how they contribute to a mental health clinician's ability to work with traumatized clients, we can better work toward managing and mitigating compassion fatigue. Figley (1995, 2007; Figley et al., 2011) reminds us that there are a number of things that contribute to compassion fatigue. These include overall poor or nonexistent self-care, the clinician's own unresolved trauma, inability or unwillingness to address work related stressors, and an overall lack of satisfaction that is derived from the professional work (Figley, 1995, 2007; Figley et al., 2011).

Psycho-education around compassion fatigue, desensitization to traumatic content, self-assessment of vulnerability, and active and regular self-care planning and engagement are all useful in mitigating the impacts of CF, STS, and VT. The next section of this chapter will further explore issues of self-assessment, self-care planning, and overall mitigation of these issues.

TOOLS FOR SELF-CARE PLANNING AND BURNOUT MANAGEMENT

As noted in the previous section, self-awareness and self management around vicarious trauma, compassion fatigue, and STS are critical. By engaging in regular self-assessment we are better able to plan and adjust accordingly and mitigate the potential negative impacts of these conditions. The following section will review a number of tools that are available to help frontline professionals in their work with traumatized clients. Figley notes "as psychotherapists, we learn to be on the one hand objective and analytical in our professional role as helper. We must put our personal feelings aside and objectively evaluate our clients and administer the best treatments according to best practices guidelines. But on the other hand, we cannot avoid our compassion and empathy. They provide tools required in the art of human service. To see the world as our clients see it enables us to calibrate our services to fit them and to adjust our services to fit how they are responding" (Figley, 2002, pp. 1433–1434). Understanding this fine line can help maximize our impact as mental health providers. These tools can also help us become more aware of both personal and organizational characteristics that are relative to our experiences of STS, CF, and VT and how to adjust them accordingly. Limiting compassion stress, addressing and managing traumatic memories, and managing caseloads are all examples of how we can mitigate these symptoms when we become aware that they are an issue (Figley, 2002). These approaches are intended to be used in concert with appropriate supervision and the clinician's own therapy services as needed. We again contend that adequate and self-sufficient management of compassion fatigue, STS, and vicarious trauma is not just aspirational, but core to the ethical service provision of clients. Aside from being effective, it is well established that impaired clinicians are more likely to harm their clients (Lawson et al., 2007).

Secondary Traumatic Stress Scale (STSS)

Bride et al. (2007) – The Secondary Traumatic Stress Scale (STSS) is a 17-item, self-report measure that assesses intrusion, avoidance, and arousal symptoms that are related to a professional's work with traumatized populations. Symptoms are measured on a Likert Scale that assesses symptom frequency. The tool includes three sub scales: intrusion (five items), avoidance (seven items), and arousal (five items). Some of the intrusion symptoms include things like intrusive thoughts about clients, disturbing dreams about clients, and a sense of reliving clients' trauma. The avoidance symptoms include avoidance of clients, inability to recall client information, and detachment from others. Arousal symptoms include difficulty sleeping, irritability, and difficulty concentrating (Bride et al., 2007).

Professional Quality of Life Scale (ProQOL)

This tool is based on the idea that professional quality of life includes both compassion fatigue as well as the payoffs of the profession, compassion satisfaction. Compassion fatigue integrates the challenging parts of the role while compassion satisfaction refers to the rewarding and validating aspects of the role. Stamm (1995) notes that compassion satisfaction includes "the pleasure you derive from being able to do your work well" (Stamm, 1995, p. 5). This self-report measure includes 30 items that assess compassion satisfaction, burnout, and compassion fatigue/vicarious trauma. Reliabilities for these scales include Compassion Satisfaction (0.87), Burnout (0.72), and Compassion Fatigue (0.80) (Stamm, 2005). This tool is available here for free and we highly encourage readers to explore its use: http://www.proqol.org/ProQol_Test.html.

Mindful Self-Care Scale (MSCS)

The Mindful Self-Care Scale (MSCS) developed by Dr. Catherine Cook-Cottone of the University of Buffalo was developed with the intention of providing practitioners with a clear set of action items that could be integrated into positive self-care. This tool is an outstanding addition to any self-care plan for those in the helping profession, particularly those who work with traumatized youth and families. "Self-care is the daily process of being aware of and attending to one's basic physiological and psychosocial needs including the shaping of one's daily routine, relationships, and environment as needed to promote optimal daily functioning" (Cook-Cottone, 2016, p. 1, 2015; McCusker et al., 2015; Norcross & Guy, 2007) There are six overall domains in the MSCS and these include physical care, supportive relationships, mindful awareness, self-compassion and purpose, mindful relaxation, and supportive structure (Cook-Cottone & Guyker, 2017). This tool is built on the premise that mindful self-care includes an individual's ability to meet their own personal needs while also staying connected and grounded in their outer experience. The scale assesses overall frequency of various mindful-self care items in the last week. Some of the items included topics like exercise, hydration, healthy eating, feeling supported by friends and family, calm awareness of thoughts and feelings, engaging in supportive self-talk, giving permission to feel feelings, engaging in relaxation activities, and maintaining a balance between demands of others and what is important to the individual (Cook-Cottone & Guyker, 2017).

Wheel of Life (WOL)

The Wheel of Life (WOL) tool is a visual representation of a self-care assessment and plan. Originally developed for the coaching industry, it is a visual tool built in a circle formation, similar to that of a clock-face. There are 8–10 categories in the WOL including areas like career, school, family and friends, health, recreation, finances, personal growth, safety, and physical environment, with room for clients to add their own categories as well. Participants self-rate their satisfaction or overall happiness with each section on a scale from 0 to 10. Zero reflects a low score and is indicated as falling close to the center of the circle, whereas a 10 would be scored as high satisfaction and on the outermost edge of the circle. This visual self-assessment allows individuals to get a sense of how balanced their life is and where adjustments may be needed. It is a useful tool for any self-care planning and management in the helping profession and is particularly useful for those working on the frontlines of service provision. This has been adjusted and expanded to also include the five pillars of happiness, which offer a simple but useful tool to be used with graduate-level trainees and seasoned professionals alike (Robson, 2010). We encourage readers to visit this resource to learn more: http://thefivepillarsofhappiness.com/doc/The_Five_Pillars_of_Happiness_-_Exercise_11.pdf.

Professionals working with trauma-exposed youth and families are at a higher risk than others in the helping profession for developing vicarious trauma, STS, and compassion fatigue. Excellent clinical and peer supervision are essential to managing and mitigating these risks when working with high-needs clients. Understanding the role of these conditions as well as how to manage them and have self-awareness around them is what will ultimately allow clinicians to work in this field effectively. We strongly encourage readers to seek out and build robust self-care and supervision plans that allow for the processing and management of our work, when it is so closely connected to the acute and chronic suffering of others. If we recall Dr. Felitti from earlier in the book noting that he wept when he saw the data documenting the enormity of the effects of ACEs, it is no wonder, that those of us on the frontlines are impacted on a daily basis. We owe it to both ourselves and our clients to work toward meaningful management of these common experiences in the helping profession.

Thirteen

EMERGING TREATMENTS AND ADDITIONAL RESOURCES

Kirby L. Wycoff

EMERGING TREATMENTS

There is simply not enough space in this book to write about, review, and discuss all of the possible treatments, interventions and approaches that are available for working with trauma-exposed youth and their families. As authors, we woefully regret that digging deeper into this content is beyond the scope of this book. Aside from the tried and true, well researched and empirically supported approaches to trauma work that were outlined in Section 4, there are a number of other innovative techniques that are being researched and implemented in our field. With our recognition and awareness of the impact that trauma and adversity has on humans, and the seemingly increasing number of individuals who are impacted, innovation in this field is necessary. We point readers' attention to a number of additional treatments below, some of which enjoy a strong empirical support in adult populations, as well as others that are just emerging and still others that are in need of randomized controlled trials to support what has been found in qualitative inquiry. There is great need in the field of traumatology to expand our current understanding of the mechanisms of trauma and in turn, the available treatment options (Schäfer & Fisher, 2011). The mind-body connection is well established in the literature, and particularly relevant and salient in working with trauma-exposed populations (Van Der Kolk, 1994). It perhaps why, increasingly, treatments that involve not just cognitions but also bodily, somatic, and experiential aspects are also emerging. We encourage readers to review the available literature on some of the treatments below that may be useful for this population. It is important to note that this is not at all an exhaustive list, simply an endeavour to call attention to some of the more nontraditional modalities that may be available.

- Equine Assisted Therapy
- Animal Assisted Therapy
- Trauma-Sensitive Yoga
- EMDR For Children (Eye Movement Desensitization and Reprocessing)
- Mindfulness Based Stress Reduction
- Expressive Arts Therapy
- Somatic Trauma Therapy

Animal Assisted Therapy (AAT) and Equine Assisted Therapies (EAT) in particular offer potential promising avenues for healing and wellness among trauma impacted youth and their families. There is a growing body of literature that supports the inclusion of AAT and EAT into therapeutic practices for trauma treatment.

The presence of animals lowers physiological arousal, improves the therapeutic alliance and decreases anxiety, particularly during the processing of traumatic memories (Lefkowitz et al., 2005).

Bachi, et al., (2012) noted that Equine Facilitated Psychotherapy (EFP) can be effective in working with high-risk adolescent females living in residential settings, particularly around issues of relational stability and trust.

Naste et al., (2017) noted that Equine Facilitated Therapy could be a useful treatment for Complex Trauma (EFT-CT) and should be considered for children exposed to multiple, cumulative traumas.

Wycoff and Murphy (2018) found that Equine Assisted Therapy, when combined with Trauma-Focused Cognitive Behavior Group Therapy provided an effective intervention for sexually traumatized adolescent females. When animals are integrated thoughtfully and intentionally into the therapeutic process, they can provide great support and opportunity for post-traumatic growth to impacted individuals (Wycoff and Gupta, 2018).

Readers interested in learning more about how animals can be integrated into therapeutic practices in school and community practice for behavioral and mental health should refer back to Wiley press for future publications by these authors.

There are countless other approaches to working with traumatized individuals but a full review and consideration of those interventions is well beyond the scope of this book. We highly encourage readers to visit the trauma resources and treatments cited throughout this book and in the References section, which may prove useful to the trauma-informed clinician.

References

Aber, J.L. and Allen, J.P. (1987). Effects of maltreatment on young children's socioemotional development: An attachment theory perspective. *Developmental Psychology* 23 (3): 406.

Abidin, R.R. (1995). Parenting stress index. In: *Professional Manual*, 3e. Odessa, FL: Psychological Assessment Resources, Inc.

Abramovitz, R. and Bloom, S.L. (2003). Creating sanctuary in residential treatment for youth: from the "well-ordered asylum" to a "living-learning environment". *Psychiatric Quarterly* 74 (2): 119–135.

Adamaszek, M., Agata, F.D., Ferrucci, R. et al. (2016). Consensus paper: Cerebellum and emotion. *The Cerebellum*:https://doi.org/10.1007/s12311-016-0815-8.

Adams, R.E., Boscarino, J.A., and Figley, C.R. (2006). Compassion fatigue and psychological distress among social workers: a validation study. *American Journal of Orthopsychiatry* 76 (1): 103.

Adams, R.E., Figley, C.R., and Boscarino, J.A. (2008). The compassion fatigue scale: Its use with social workers following urban disaster. *Research on Social Work Practice* 18 (3): 238–250.

Afifi, T.O. et al. (2012). Physical punishment and mental disorders: Results from a nationally representative U.S. sample. *Pediatrics* 130 (2), available at http://pediatrics.aappublications.org/content/early/2012/06/27/peds.2011-2947.

Alisic, E., Zalta, A.K., Van Wesel, F. et al. (2014). Rates of post-traumatic stressdisorder in trauma-exposed children and adolescents: Meta- analysis. *British Journal of Psychiatry* 204: 335–340.

Allen, J.P., Kuperminc, G., Philliber, S., and Herre, K. (1994). Programmatic prevention of adolescent problem behaviors: the role of autonomy, relatedness, and volunteer service in the teen outreach program. *Community Psychology.* 22: 617–638.

American academy of child and adolescent psychiatrists, policy statement, (2012), http://www.aacap.org/aacap/policy_statements/2012/Policy_Statement_on_Corporal_Punishment.aspx

American Academy of Pediatrics (2014). The medical home approach to identifying and responding to exposure to trauma. Available at: https://www.aap.org/en-us/Documents/ttb_medicalhomeapproach.pdf. Accessed August, 2016.

American Educational Research Association, American Psychological Association, & National Council on Measurement in Education (1985). *Standards for Educational and Psychological Testing.* Washington, DC: American Educational Research Association.

American Psychiatric Association (2013). *Diagnostic and Statistical Manual of Mental Disorders*, 5e. Arlington, TX: American Psychiatric Publishing.

American Psychological Association (2006). Evidence-based practices in psychology. *American Psychologist* 61: 271–285. Retrieved from http://www.apa.org/practice/guidelines/evidence-based-statement.aspx.

American Psychological Association (2008). Startling statistics on child maltreatment. *American Psychological Association* 39 (10): 47. http://www.apa.org/monitor/2008/11/maltreatment.aspx.

Anda, R.F., Williamson, D.F., Escobedo, L.G. et al. (1990). Depression and the dynamics of smoking: a national perspective. *JAMA* 264 (12): 1541–1545.

Anda, R.F., Croft, J.B., Felitti, V.J. et al. (1999). Adverse childhood experiences and smoking during adolescence and adulthood. *Journal of the American Medical Association* 282: 1652–1658.

Anda, R.F., Whitfield, C.L., Felitti, V.J. et al. (2002). Adverse childhood experiences, alcoholic parents, and later risk of alcoholism and depression. *Psychiatric services* 53 (8): 1001–1009.

Anda, R.F., Felitti, V.J., Bremner, J.D. et al. (2006a). The enduring effects of abuse and related adverse experiences in childhood. *Archives of Psychiatry and Clinical Neurosciences* 256 (3): 174–186.

Anda, R.F., Felitti, V.J., Walker, J. et al. (2006b). The enduring effects of abuse and related adverse experiences in childhood: A convergence of evidence from neurobiology and epidemiology. *European Archives of Psychiatry and Clinical Neurosciences* 256: 174–186.

Anda, R.F., Felitti, V.J., Bremner, J.D. et al. (2006c). The enduring effects of abuse and related adverse experiences in childhood: A convergence of evidence from neurobiology and epidemiology. *European Archives of Psychiatry and Clinical Neuroscience* 256 (3): 174–186:https://doi.org/10.1007/s00406-005-0624-4.

Anda, R.F., Brown, D.W., Felitti, V.J. et al. (2007). The relationship of adverse childhood experiences to rates of prescribed psychotropic medications in adulthood. *American Journal of Preventive Medicine* 32: 389–394.

Anda, R.F., Brown, D.W., Dube, S.R. et al. (2009). The relationship of adverse childhood experiences to the prevalence, incidence of hospitalization, and rates of prescription drug use of obstructive pulmonary disease in a cohort of adults. *American Journal of Preventive Medicine*.

Anda, R. F., Driscoll, D., Ripley, E, & Hogan, W. (2012) University of Alaska Anchorage College of Health. How can UAA Help Address ACES? What do future leaders need to know? Presentation at the University of Alaska Anchor. College of Health and The Justice Center and the Department of Health Sciences. Anchorage, AK. https://www.youtube.com/watch?v=QLfUi4ssHmY&t=21s

Anthony, E.J. (1974). The syndrome of the psychologically invulnerable child. In: *The Child in his Family: Children at Psychiatric Risk* (ed. E.J. Anthony and C. Koupernik), 529–545. New York: Wiley.

Armsden, G.C. and Greenberg, M.T. (1987). The inventory of parent and peer attachment: Individual differences and their relationship to psychological well-being in adolescence. *Journal of Youth and Adolescence* 16 (5): 427–454.

Armsden, G.C. and Greenberg, M.T. (1989). *Inventory of Parent and Peer Attachment (IPPA)*. Seattle, WA: University of Washington.

Armstrong, J.G., Putnam, F.W., Carlson, E.B. et al. (1997). Development and validation of a measure of adolescent dissociation: The Adolescent Dissociative Experiences Scale. *The Journal of nervous and mental disease* 185 (8): 491–497.

Arnett, J.J. (2007). Emerging adulthood: What is it and what is it good for? *Child Development Perspectives* 1: 68–73.

Arvidson, J., Kinniburgh, K., Howard, K. et al. (2011). Treatment of complex trauma in young children: Developmental and cultural considerations in application of the ARC intervention model. *Journal of Child & Adolescent Trauma* 4 (1): 34–51.

Ashkenazi, S., Black, J.M., Abrams, D.A. et al. (2013). Neurobiological underpinnings of math and reading learning disabilities. *Journal of Learning Disabilities* 46 (6): 549–569.

ASTHO (n.d.). President's challenge: Public health approaches to preventing substance misuse and addiction. *Journal of Public Health Management and Practice* 23 (5): 531.

Ayers, T. S., & Sandler, I. N. (1999). Manual for the children's coping strategies checklist & the How I Coped Under Pressure Scale. Retrieved from Arizona State Prevention Research Center Web site: http://prc.asu.edu.

Ayers, T., & Sandler, I. N. (2000). The children's coping strategies checklist and the how I coped under pressure scale. Unpublished manuscript, Program for Prevention Research, Arizona State University, Tempe, AZ.

Ayers, T.S., Sandier, I.N., West, S.G., and Roosa, M.W. (1996). A dispositional and situational assessment of children's coping: testing alternative models of coping. *Journal of Personality* 64 (4): 923–958.

Bachi, K., Terkel, J., & Teichman, M. (2012). Equine-facilitated psychotherapy for at-risk adolescents: The influence on self-image, self-control and trust. *Clinical Child Psychology and Psychiatry*, 17 (2): 298–312.

Badaruddin, D.H., Andrews, G.L., Boite, S. et al. (2007). Social and behavioral problems of children with agenesis of the corpus callosum. *Child Psychiatry and Human Development* 38 (4): 287–302.

Baker, C.N., Brown, S.M., Wilcox, P.D. et al. (2016). Development and psychometric evaluation of the attitudes related to trauma-informed care (ARTIC) scale. *School Mental Health* 8 (1): 61–76.

Barkley, R.A. (2012). *Executive functions: What they are, how they work and why they evolved.* New York, NY: Guilford Press.

Barkley, R.A. (2015). *Attention Deficit Hyperactivity Disorder: A Handbook for Diagnosis and Treatment*, 4e. New York, NY: The Guilford Press.

Baron, I.S. (2004). *Neuropsychological Evaluation of the Child.* New York, NY: Oxford University Press.

Baron-Cohen, S., Ring, H.A., Bullmore, E.T. et al. (2000). The amygdala theory of autism. *Neuroscience and Biobehavioral Reviews* 24: 355–364.

Barrett, S., Eber, L., and Weist, M. (2013). *Advancing Education Effectiveness: Interconnecting School Mental Health and School-Wide Positive Behavior Support.* Center for School Mental Health.

Barrett, S., Eber, L., and Weist, M.D. (2013). Advancing education effectiveness: An interconnected systems framework for Positive Behavioral Interventions and Supports (PBIS) and school mental health. In: *Center for Positive Behavioral Interventions and Supports (funded by the Office of Special Education Programs, US Department of Education).* Eugene, Oregon: University of Oregon Press.

Batten, S.V., Follette, V.M., and Aban, I.B. (2001). Experiential avoidance and high-risk sexual behavior in survivors of child sexual abuse. *Journal of Child Sexual Abuse* 10: 101–120.

Bauer, P.M., Hanson, J.L., Pierson, R.K. et al. (2009). Cerebellar volume and cognitive functioning in children who experienced early deprivation. *Biological Psychiatry* 66: 1100–1106.

Baweja, S., Santiago, C.D., Vona, P. et al. (2016). Improving implementation of a school-based program for traumatized stduents: Identifying factors that promote teacher support and collaboration. *School Mental Health* 8: 120–131.

Bedeschi, M.F., Bonaglia, M.C., Grasso, R. et al. (2006). Agenesis of the corpus callosum: Clinical and genetic study in 63 young patients. *Pediatric Neurology* 34: 186–193.

Beers, S.R. and De Bellis, M.D. (2002). Neuropsychological function in children with maltreatment-related posttraumatic stress disorder. *American Journal of Psychiatry* 159: 483–486.

Berlin, L.J., Shanahan, M., and Carmody, K.A. (2014). Promoting supportive parenting in new mothers with substance use problems: A pilot randomized trial of residential treatment plus attachment-based parenting program. *Infant Mental Health Journal* 35 (1): 81–85: https://doi.org/10.1002/imhj.21427.

Bernard, K., Dozier, M., Bick, J. et al. (2012). Enhancing attachment organization among maltreated infants: Results of a randomized clinical trial. *Child Development* 83 (2): 623–636: https://doi.org/10.1111/j.1467-8624.2011.01712.x.

Bernard, K., Dozier, M., Bick, J., and Gordon, M.K. (2014). Intervening to enhance cortisol regulation among children at risk for neglect: Results of a randomized clinical trial. *Development and Psychopathology* 1–13. https://doi.org/10.1017/S095457941400073X.

Bernard, K., Dozier, M., Bick, J., and Gordon, M.K. (2015). Intervening to enhance cortisol regulation among at risk children for neglect: Results of a randomized clinical trial. *Development and Psychopathology* 27: 829–841.

Bernard, K., Simons, R., & Dozier, M. (n.d.) Effects of an attachment-based intervention on high-risk mothers' event-related potentials to children's emotions. Manuscript submitted for publication.

Berninger, V.W., Nielsen, K.H., Abbott, R.D., and Raskind, W. (2008). Writing problems in developmental dyslexia: Under reported and under treated. *Journal of School Psychology* 46 (1): 1–21.

Bernstein, D.P. and Fink, L. (1998). *Childhood Trauma Questionnaire: A Retrospective Self-Report Manual.* San Antonio, TX: The Psychological Corporation.

Bernstein, D.P., Ahluvalia, T., Pogge, D., and Handelsman, L. (1997). Validity of the childhood trauma questionnaire in an adolescent psychiatric population. *Journal of the American Academy of Child and Adolescent Psychiatry* 36: 340–348.

Bernstein, D.P., Stein, J.A., Newcomb, M.D. et al. (2003). Development and validation of a brief screening version of the childhood trauma questionnaire. *Child Abuse and Neglect* 27: 169–190.

Bernstein, D., Bertram, R., Kerns, S., Cannata, E., & Barwick, M. (2015). Evidence based practices in North American MSW curricula [video file]. Retrieved from https://ebpconsortium2014.wordpress.com/webinars/ebp-implementation-webinars.

Bertalanffy, L. (1974). General systems theory and psychiatry. In: *American Handbook of Psychiatry*, 2e, vol. 1 (ed. S. Ariete), 1095–1117. New York: Basic Books.

Bertram, R. M., Kerns, S. E., Berstein, D., Mettrick, J., Marsenich, L., & Kanary, P. (2015). Evidence- informed practice in systems of care: Misconceptions and facts. Retrieved from https://ebpconsortium2014.wordpress.com/blog-2.

Bick, J. and Dozier, M. (2013). The effectiveness of an attachment-based intervention in promoting foster mothers' sensitivity toward foster infants. *Infant Mental Health Journal* 34 (2): 95–103: https://doi.org/10.1002/imhj.21373.

Bick, J. and Nelson, C.A. (2016). Early adverse experiences and the developing brain. *Neuropsychopharmacology Reviews* 41: 177–196.

Blalock, J.E. (2005). The immune system as the sixth sense. *Journal of Internal Medicine* 257 (2): 126–138.

Blaustein, M.E. (2013). Childhood trauma and a framework for intervention. In: *Supporting and Educating Traumatized Students: A Guide for School-Based Professionals* (ed. E. Rossen and R. Hull), 1–21. New York, NY: Oxford University Press.

Blaustein, M.E. and Kinniburgh, K.M. (2010). *Treating Traumatic Stress in Children and Adolescents: How to Foster Resilience Through Attachment, Self-regulation, and Competency.* Guilford Press.

Blodgett, C. (2012). *Adopting ACES Screening and Assessment in Child Serving Systems.* Unpublished manuscript,. Spokane, WA: Area Health Education Center, Washington State University.

Blodgett, C. (2013). *A Review of Community Efforts to Mitigate and Prevent Adverse Childhood Experiences and Trauma.* Spokane, WA: Washington State University Area Health Education Center.

Blodgett, C. (2014). *ACEs in Head Start Children and Impact on Development.* Unpublished manuscript. Spokane, WA: Child and Family Research Unit, Washington State University Retrieved from http://ext100.wsu.edu/cafru/wp-content/uploads/sites/65/2015/03/ACEs-in-Head-Start-Children-and-Impact-on-Development-1-14.pdf.

Blodgett, C. (2015). *No School Alone: How Community Risks and Assets Contribute to School and Youth Success.* Washington State Office of Financial Management.

Bloom, S.L. (1994). *The Sanctuary Model. Handbook of Post-traumatic Therapy*, 474–491.

Bloom, S.L. (2007). Loss, trauma, and resilience: Therapeutic work with ambiguous loss. *Psychiatric Services* 58 (3): 419–420.

Bloom, S.L., & Sreedhar, S.Y. (2008). *The Sanctuary Model of Trauma Informed Organizational Change Reclaiming children and youth*, 17 (3): 48–53.

Bloom, S. L. (2011). The Sanctuary Model. Retrieved October 18, 2011, from http://www.sanctuaryweb.com/trauma-informedsystems.php

Bloom, S. (2013). The sanctuary model. In: *Treating Complex Traumatic stress Disorders in Children and Adolescents: Scientific Foundations and Therapeutic Models*, 277–294.

Bloom, S. (2017). *Is there a Connection between Trauma and Violence*. Philadelphia, PA: Training presented at the Strawberry Mansion Sanctuary for Hope.

Bloom, S.L. and Sreedhar, S.Y. (2008). The sanctuary model of trauma-informed organizational change. *Reclaiming children and youth* 17 (3): 48.

Boat, B. (1994). *Boat Inventory on Animal-related Experiences*. Cincinnati, OH: University of Cincinnati, Department of Psychiatry.

Boney-McCoy, S. and Finkelhor, D. (1995). Psychosocial sequelae of violent victimization in a national youth sample. *Journal of Consulting and Clinical Psychology* 63: 726–736. https://doi.org/10.1037/0022-006X.63.5.726.

Booth, J.R., Wood, L., Lu, D. et al. (2007). The role of the basal ganglia and cerebellum in language processing. *Brain Research* 1133: 136–144.

Boris, N.W. and Zeanah, C.H. Work Group on Quality Issues(2005). Practice parameter for the assessment and treatment of children and adolescents with reactive attachment disorder of infancy and early childhood. *Journal of the American Academy of Child and Adolescent Psychiatry* 44 (11): 1206–1219. http://www.aacap.org/App_Themes/AACAP/docs/practice_parameters/reactive_attachment_practice_parameter.pdf.

Bratton, S., Landreth, G.L., Kellam, T., and Blackard, S.R. (2006). *Child-Parent Relationship Therapy (CPRT) Treatment Manual: A 10 Session Filial Therapy Model for Training Parents.* New York, NY: Routledge.

Bratton, S.C., Opiola, K., and Dafoe, E. (2015). Child–parent relationship therapy: A 10-session filial therapy model. In: *Play Therapy: A Comprehensive Guide to Theory and Practice* (ed. D.A. Crenshaw and A.L. Stewart), 129–140. New York, NY: Guilford.

Braveman, P., Egerter, S., and Williams, D.R. (2011). The social determinants of health: Coming of age. *Annual Review of Public Health* 32 (1): 381–398.

Bremner, J.D. (2006). Traumatic stress: Effects on the brain. *Dialogues in Clinical Neuroscience* 8: 445–461.

Bremner, J.D. and Marmar, C.R. (2002). *Trauma, Memory, and Dissociation*, vol. 54. American Psychiatric Pub.

Bretherton, I. (1992). The origins of attachment theory: John Bowlby and Mary Ainsworth. *Developmental Psychology* 28 (5): 759–775.

Bride, B.E. (2007). Prevalence of secondary traumatic stress among social workers. *Social Work* 52 (1): 63–70.

Bride, B.E., Radey, M., and Figley, C.R. (2007). Measuring compassion fatigue. *Clinical Social Work Journal* 35 (3): 155–163.

Briere, J. (1996). *Trauma Symptom Checklist for Children*. Odessa, FL: Psychological Assessment Resources.

Briere, J. and Rickards, S. (2007). Self-awareness, affect regulation, and relatedness: differential sequels of childhood versus adult victimization experiences. *Journal of Nervous and Mental Disease* 195: 497–503.

Briere, J. and Spinazzola, J. (2005). Phenomenology and psychological assessment of complex posttraumatic states. *Journal of Traumatic Stress: Official Publication of The International Society for Traumatic Stress Studies* 18 (5): 401–412.

Briere, J. and Spinazzola, J. (2009). Assessment of the sequelae of complex trauma. In: *Treating Complex Traumatic Stress Disorders* (ed. C. Courtois and J. Ford), 104–123. New York, NY: Guilford Press.

Briere, J., Johnson, K., Bissada, A. et al. (2001). The trauma symptom checklist for young children (TSCYC): Reliability and association with abuse exposure in a multi-site study. *Child Abuse and Neglect* 25: 1001–1014.

Brock, S.E. and Cowan, K. (2004). Coping after a crisis. *Principal Leadership* 4 (5): 9–13.

Brown, J., Cohen, P., Johnson, J.G., and Salzinger, S. (1998). A longitudinal analysis of risk factors for child maltreatment: Findings of a 17-year prospective study of officially recorded and self-reported child abuse and neglect. *Child Abuse and Neglect* 22 (11): 1065–1078.

Brown, D.W., Anda, R.A., Tiemeier, H. et al. (2009). Adverse childhood experiences and the risk of premature mortality. *American Journal of Preventive Medicine* 37: 389–396.

Brown, S.M., Baker, C.N., and Wilcox, P. (2012). Risking connection trauma training: A pathway toward trauma-informed care in child congregate care settings. *Psychological Trauma: Theory, Research, Practice, and Policy* 4 (5): 507.

Brown, S.M., Baker, C.N., and Wilcox, P. (2013). Risking connection trauma training: A pathway toward trauma-informed care in child congregate care settings. *Psychological Trauma: Theory, Research, Practice, and Policy* 4 (5): 507.

Bruhn, A.L., Woods-Groves, S., and Huddle, S. (2014). A preliminary investigation of emotional and behavioral screening practices in K-12 schools. *Education and Treatment of Children* 37: 611–634.

Bucci, M., Silverio, M., Oh, D., and Harris, N.B. (2016). Toxic stress in children and adolescents. *Advances in Pediatrics* 63: 403–428.

Buchsbaum, B.R., Hickok, G., and Humphries, C. (2001). Role of the left superior temporal gyrus in phonological processing for speech perception and production. *Cognitive Science* 25: 663–678.

Burke, N.J., Hellman, J.L., Scott, B.G. et al. (2011). The impact of adverse childhood experiences on an urban pediatric population. *Child Abuse and Neglect* 35 (6): 408–413.

Burlingame, G.M., Wells, M.G., Lambert, M.J., and Cox, J.C. (2004). Youth outcome questionnaire (Y-OQ). *The Use of Psychological Testing for Treatment Planning and Outcome Assessment, ed* 3: 235–274.

Cabrera, P., Auslander, W., and Polgar, M. (2009). Future orientation of adolescents in foster care: Relationship to trauma, mental health, and HIV risk behaviors. *Journal of Child & Adolescent Trauma* 2 (4): 271–286.

California Department of Social Services' (CDSS) Office of Child Abuse Prevention, California Evidence Based Clearinghouse 2007, (p. 1). http://www.cebc4cw.org

Calkins, S.D. and Hill, A. (2007). Caregiver influences on emerging emotion regulation: Biological and environmental transactions in early development. In: *Handbook* (ed. J.J. Gross).

Cantrell, C., & Longest, K. (2009). Evidence Based Assessment of Children and Adolescents Related to Trauma. 17th Oklahoma Conference on Child Abuse and Neglect and Healthy Families.

Carrion, V.G. and Steiner, H. (2000). Trauma and dissociation in delinquent adolescents. *Journal of the American Academy of Child and Adolescent Psychiatry* 39 (3): 353–359.

Carrion, V.G. and Wong, S.S. (2012). Can traumatic stress alter the brain? Understanding the implications of early trauma on brain development and learning. *Journal of Adolescent Health* 51 (2): S23–S28.

Carrion, V.G., Weems, C.F., Eliez, S. et al. (2001). Attenuation of frontal asymmetry in pediatric posstraumatic stress disorder. *Biological Psychiatry* 50: 943–951.

Carrión, V.G., Haas, B.W., Garrett, A. et al. (2009). Reduced hippocampal activity in youth with posttraumatic stress symptoms: an FMRI study. *Journal of pediatric psychology* 35 (5): 559–569.

Carrion, V.G., Haas, B.W., Garrett, A. et al. (2010a). Reduced hippocampal activity in youth with posttraumatic stress symptoms: An fMRI study. *Journal of Pediatric Psychology* 35: 559–569.

Carrion, V.G., Weems, C.F., Reichert, K. et al. (2010b). Decreased prefrontal cortical volume associated with increased bedtime cortisol in traumatized youth. *Biological Psychiatry* 68 (5): 491–493.

Cates, W. (1982). Epidemiology: Applying principles to clinical practice. *Contemp Ob/Gyn* 20: 147–161.

Center on the Developing Child at Harvard University (2011) Building the Brain's Air Traffic Control System: How Early Experiences Shape the Development of Executive Function: Working Paper No. 11. http://www.developingchild.Harvard.edu.

Centers for Disease Control and Prevention (2010). *Establishing a Holistic Framework to Reduce Inequities in HIV, Viral Hepatitis, STDs, and Tuberculosis in the United States.* Atlanta, GA: CDC.

Chadwick, E. (1842). Report on the sanitary condition of the laboring population of Great: Britain: supplementary report on the results of special inquiry into the practice of interment in towns (Vol. 1). HM Stationery Office.

Chaffin, M., Hanson, R., Saunders, B.E. et al. (2006). Report of the APSAC task force on attachment therapy, reactive attachment disorder, and attachment problems. *Child Maltreatment* 11 (1): 76–89. http://depts.washington.edu/hcsats/PDF/AttachmentTaskForceAPSAC.pdf.

Chafouleas, S.M., Kilgus, S.P., and Wallach, N. (2010). Ethical dilemmas in school-based behavioral screening. *Assessment for Effective Intervention* 35: 245–252.

Chafouleas, S.M., Johnson, A.H., Overstreet, S., and Santos, N.M. (2016). Toward a blueprint for trauma-informed service delivery in schools. *School Mental Health* 8 (1): 144–162.

Chapman, D.P., Whitfield, C.L., Felitti, V.J. et al. (2004). Adverse childhood experiences and the risk of depressive disorders in adulthood. *Journal of Affective Disorders* 82: 217–225. https://doi.org/10.1016/j.jad.2003.12.013.

Chen, E., Matthews, K.A., and Boyce, W.T. (2002). Socioeconomic differences in children's health: How and why do these relationships change with age? *Psychological Bulletin* 128: 295–329.

Child Welfare Trauma Training Toolkit: The Invisible Suitcase, (2008). The National Child Traumatic Stress Network. Retrieved from http://www.kscourts.org/court-administration/Legal_Institute_on_Adverse_Childhood_Exp/The%20Invisible%20Suitcase.pdf.

Cicchetti, D. and Toth, S. (1995). A developmental psychopathology perspective on child abuse and neglect. *Journal of the American Academy of Child and Adolescent Psychiatry* 34: 541–564.

Cicchetti, D. and Toth, S.L. (2009). The past achievements and future promises of developmental psychopathology: The coming of age of a discipline. *Journal of Child Psychology and Psychiatry* 50 (1–2): 16–25.

Cicchetti, D., Ackerman, B.P., and Izard, C.E. (1995). Emotions and emotion regulation in developmental psychopathology. *Development and Psychopathology* 7: 1–10.

Cicchetti, D., Toth, S.L., and Rogosch, F.A. (1999). The efficacy of Toddler-Parent psychotherapy to increase attachment security in off-spring of depressed mothers. *Attachment & Human Development* 1 (1): 34–66.

Cicchetti, D., Rogosch, F.A., and Toth, S.L. (2006). Fostering secure attachment in infants in maltreating families through preventive interventions. *Development and psychopathology* 18 (3): 623–649.

Clark, D. (2005). *The Brain and Behavior*. Cambridge University Press.

Clarke, A. (2013). Sanctuary in action. *Children Australia* 38 (3): 95–99.

Clarke, D.D. (2017). Childhood disrupted: How your biography becomes your biology, and how you can heal: by Donna Jackson Nakazawa. *The Permanente Journal* 21.

Classen, C., Koopman, C., and Spiegel, D. (1993). Trauma and dissociation. *Bulletin of the Menninger Clinic* 57 (2): 178.

Cleaver, H., Unell, I., and Aldgate, J. (1999). *Children's Needs – Parenting Capacity, the Impact of Parental Mental Illness, Problem Alcohol and Drug Use, and Domestic Violence on children's Development*. London: The Stationary Office.

Clements, K. and Turpin, G. (1996). The life events scale for students: validation for use with British samples. *Personality and Individual Differences* 20 (6): 747–751.

Cloitre, M., Scarvalone, P., and Difede, J. (1997). Posttraumatic stress disorder, self- and interpersonal dysfunction among sexually retraumatized women. *Journal of Traumatic Stress* 10: 437–452.

Cloitre, M., Koenen, K.C., Cohen, L.R., and Han, H. (2002). Skills training in affective and interpersonal regulation followed by exposure: A phase-based treatment for PTSD related to childhood abuse. *Journal of Consulting and Clinical Psychology* 70: 1067–1074.

Cloitre, M., Stovall-McClough, K.C., and Levitt, J.T. (2004). Treating life-impairing problems beyond PTSD: Reply to Cahill, Zoellner, Feeny, and Riggs (2004). *Journal of Consulting and Clinical Psychology* 72: 549–551.

Cloitre, M., Miranda, R., Stovall-McClough, K.C., and Han, H. (2005). Beyond PTSD: Emotion regulation and interpersonal problems as predictors of functional impairment in survivors of childhood abuse. *Behavior Therapy* 36: 119–124.

Cloitre, M., Stovall-McClough, C., Zorbas, P., and Charuvastra, A. (2008). Attachment organization, emotion regulation, and expectations of support in a clinical sample of women with childhood abuse histories. *Journal of Traumatic Stress* 21: 282–289.

Cloitre, M., Stolbach, B.C., Herman, J.L. et al. (2009). A developmental approach to complex PTSD: Childhood and adult cumulative trauma as predictors of symptom complexity. *Journal of traumatic stress* 22 (5): 399–408.

Cohen, J.A. and Mannarino, A.P. (1996a). Factors that mediate treatment outcome of sexually abused preschool children. *Journal of the American Academy of Child and Adolescent Psychiatry* 34 (10): 1402–1410.

Cohen, J.A. and Mannarino, A.P. (1996b). Family-related variables and psychological symptom formation in sexually abused girls. *Journal of Child Sexual Abuse* 5 (1): 105–120.

Cohen, J.A. and Mannarino, A.P. (1996c). A treatment outcome study for sexually abused preschool children: Initial findings. *Journal of the American Academy of Child and Adolescent Psychiatry* 34: 42–50.

Cohen, J.A. and Mannarino, A.P. (1997). A treatment study for sexually abused preschool children: Outcome during a one-year follow-up. *Journal of the American Academy of Child and Adolescent Psychiatry* 36: 1228–1235.

Cohen, J.A. and Mannarino, A.P. (1998). Interventions for sexually abused children: Initial treatment outcome findings. *Child Maltreatment* 3: 17–26.

Cohen, J.A. and Mannarino, A.P. (2000). Predictors of treatment outcome in sexually abused children. *Child Abuse and Neglect* 24: 983–994.

Cohen, J.A. and Mannarino, A.P. (2008). Trauma-focused cognitive behavioural therapy for children and parents. *Child and Adolescent Mental Health* 13 (4): 158–162.

Cohen, J.A., Deblinger, E., Mannarino, A.P., and Steer, R.A. (2004). A multisite, randomized controlled trial for children with sexual abuse–related PTSD symptoms. *Journal of the American Academy of Child & Adolescent Psychiatry* 43 (4): 393–402.

Cohen, J.A., Mannarino, A.P., and Knudsen, K. (2005). Treating sexually abused children: 1 year follow-up of a randomized controlled trial. *Child Abuse and Neglect* 29: 135–145.

Cohen, J.A., Mannarino, A.P., and Deblinger, E. (2006). *Treating Trauma and Traumatic Grief in Children and Adolescents.* New York, NY: Guilford Press.

Cohen, J.A., Mannarino, A.P., and Iyengar, S. (2011). Community treatment of posttraumatic stress disorder for children exposed to intimate partner violence. *Archives of Pediatric and Adolescent Medicine* 165 (1): 16–21.

Cohen, J.A., Mannarino, A.P., and Deblinger, E. (2016). *Treating Trauma and Traumatic Grief in Children and Adolescents.* Guilford Publications.

Cole, P.M., Michel, M.K., and Teti, L.O. (1994). The development of emotion regulation and dysregulation: A clinical perspective. *Monographs of the Society for Research in Child Development* 59: 73–100.

Cole, S., Greenwald O'Brien, J., Gadd, M.G. et al. (2005a). *Helping Traumatized Children Learn.* Boston, MA: Massachusetts Advocates for Children.

Cole, S.F., O'Brien, J.G., Gadd, M.G. et al. (2005b). *Helping Traumatized Children Learn: Supportive School Environments for Children Traumatized by Family Violence.* Boston, MA: Massachusetts Advocates for Children, Trauma and Learning Policy Initiative.

Cole, S.F., Eisner, A., Gregory, M., and Ristuccia, J. (2013). *Helping Traumatized Children Learn II: Creating and Advocating for Trauma-Sensitive Schools.* Boston, MA: Massachusetts Advocates for Children, Trauma and Learning Policy Initiative.

Compton school district lawsuit equating trauma with disabilities proceeds, (2015), www.scpr.org/news/2015/09/30/54748/compton-school-district-lawsuit-equating-trauma-wi/

Conners-Burrow, N.A., Kramer, T.L., Sigel, B.A. et al. (2013). Trauma-informed care training in a child welfare system: Moving it to the front line. *Children and Youth Services Review* 35 (11): 1830–1835.

Conrad, C.D., Galea, L.A., Kuroda, Y., and McEwen, B.S. (1996). Chronic stress impairs rat spatial memory on the Y maze, and this effect is blocked by tianeptine treatment. *Behavioral Neuroscience* 110 (6): 1321.

Conradi, L. and Wilson, C. (2010). Managing traumatized children: A trauma systems perspective. *Current Opinion in Pediatrics* 22 (5): 621–625.

Conradi, L., Wherry, J., and Kisiel, C. (2011). Linking child welfare and mental health using trauma-informed screening and assessment practices. *Child Welfare* 90 (6): 129–147. Available at: Consumer Health Complete - EBSCOhost, Ipswich (MA). Accessed September 24, 2013.

Cook, A., Spinazzola, J., Ford, J. et al. (2005). Complex trauma in children and adolescents. *Psychiatric Annals* 35 (5): 390.

Cook, A., Spinazzola, J., Ford, J. et al. (2007). Complex trauma in children and adolescents. *Focal Point* 21 (1): 4–8.

Cook, A., Spinazzola, J., Ford, J. et al. (2017). Complex trauma in children and adolescents. *Psychiatric annals* 35 (5): 390–398.

Cook-Cottone, C. P. (2014). The Mindful Self-Care Scale: Self-care as a tool to promote physical, emotional, and cognitive well-being.

Cook-Cottone, C.P. (2015a). *Mindfulness and Yoga for Self-regulation: A Primer for Mental Health Professionals.* New York, NY: Springer.

Cook-Cottone, C. (2016). Embodied self-regulation and mindful self-care in the prevention of eating disorders. *Eating disorders* 24 (1): 98–105.

Cook-Cottone, C.P. and Guyker, W. (2017). The development and validation of the mindful self-care scale (MSCS): An assent of practices that support positive embodiment. *Mindfulness* 1–15. https://doi.org/10.1007/s12671-017-0759-1.

Courtois, C.A. (2002). Education in trauma practice: Traumatic stress studies, the need for curricula inclusion. *Journal of Trauma Practice* 1 (1): 33–57.

Cowan, K.C., Vaillancourt, K., Rossen, E., and Pollitt, K. (2013). *A Framework for Safe and Successful Schools [Brief]*. Bethesda, MD: National Association of School Psychologists.

Cozby, P.C. (2001). *Measurement Concepts. Methods in Behavioral Research*, 7e. CA: Mayfield Publishing Company.

Crick, N.R. and Dodge, K.A. (1996). Social information processing mechanisms in reactive and proactive aggression. *Child Development* 67 (3): 993–1002.

Crittenden, P.M. and DiLalla, D.L. (1988). Compulsive compliance: the development of an inhibitory coping strategy in infancy. *Journal of Abnormal Child Psychology* 16 (5): 585–599.

Cronbach, L.J. (1971). Test validation. In: *Educational Measurement*, 2e (ed. R.L. Thorndike). Washington, DC: American Council on Education.

Crouch, J.L., Hanson, R.F., Saunders, B.E. et al. (2000). Income, race/ethnicity, and exposure to violence in youth: Results from the national survey of adolescents. *Journal of Community Psychology* 28 (6): 625–641.

Crozier, J.C. and Barth, R.P. (2005). Cognitive and academic functioning in maltreated children. *Children and Schools* 27: 197–206.

Crozier, J.C., Van Voorhees, E.E., Hooper, S.R. & De Bellis, M.D. (2013). ND Chapter 53. Effects of Abuse and Neglect on Brain Development.

Culp, R., Watkins, R., Lawrence, H. et al. (1991). Mal- treated children's language and speech development: abused, neglected, and abused and neglected. *First Language* 11 (33 Pt 3): 377–389.

Cummings, J.L. and Miller, B.L. (2007). Conceptual and clinical aspects of the frontal lobes. In: *The Human Frontal Lobes: Functions and Disorders*, vol. 2007, 12–21.

Cunningham, M. (2004). Teaching social workers about trauma: Reducing the risks of vicarious traumatization.

Daignault, I.V. and Hebert, M. (2009). Profiles of school adaptation: Social, behavioral and academic functioning in sexually abused girls. *Child Abuse & Neglect* 33: 102–115.

Davies, D. (2011). *Child Development: A Practitioner's Guide*, 3e. New York, NY: The Guilford Press.

Davis, W.B., Mooney, D., Racusin, R. et al. (2000). Predicting post- traumatic stress after hospitalization for pediatric injury. *Journal of the American Academy of Child and Adolescent Psychiatry* 39: 576–583.

Davis, A.S., Moss, L.E., Nogin, M.M., and Webb, N.E. (2015). Neuropsychology of child maltreatment and implications for school psychologists. *Psychology in the Schools* 52 (1): 77–91.

Dawson, D. and Guare, R. (2010). *Executive Skills in Children and Adolescents: A Practical Guide to Assessment and Intervention*, 2e. New York, NY: The Guilford Press.

De Bellis, M.D. and Abigali Zisk, A.B. (2014). The biological effects of childhood trauma. *Child and Adolescent Psychiatric Clinics of North America* 23 (2): 185–222.

De Bellis, M.D. and Thomas, L.A. (2003). Biologic findings of post-traumatic stress disorder and child maltreatment. *Current psychiatry reports* 5 (2): 108–117.

De Bellis, M.D. and Zisk, A. (2014). The biological effects of childhood trauma. *Child and Adolescent Psychiatric Clinics* 23 (2): 185–222.

De Bellis, M.D., Keshavan, M.S., Clark, D.B. et al. (1999). Developmental traumatology part II: Brain development. *Biological Psychiatry* 45: 1271–1284.

De Bellis, M.D., Keshavan, M.S., Spencer, S., and Hall, J. (2000). N-acetylaspartate concentration in the anterior cingulate in maltreated children and adolescents with PTSD. *American Journal of Psychiatry* 157: 1175–1177.

De Bellis, M.D., Hall, J., Boring, A.M., and Frustaci, & Moritz, G. (2001). A pilot longitudinal study of hippocampal volumes in pediatric maltreatment-related posttraumatic stress disorder. *Biological Psychiatry* 50 (4): 305–309.

De Bellis, M.D., Keshavan, M.S., and Shifett, H. (2002a). Brain structures in pediatric maltreatment-re- lated posttraumatic stress disorder: a sociode- mographically matched study. *Biological Psychiatry* 52 (11): 1066–1078.

De Bellis, M.D., Keshavan, M., Schifflett, H. et al. (2002b). Brain structures in pediatric maltreatment-related posttraumatic stress disorder: A sociodemographically matched study. *Biological Psychiatry* 52: 1066–1078.

De Bellis, M.D., Keshavan, M.S., Frustaci, K. et al. (2002c). Superior temporal gyrus volumes in maltreated children and adolescents with PTSD. *Biological Psychiatry* 51: 544–552.

De Bellis, M.D., Hooper, S.R., Spratt, E.G., and Wooley, D.P. (2009). Neuropsychological findings in childhood neglect and their relationships to pediatric ptsd. *Journal of the International Neuropsychological Society* 15: 868–878.

De Bellis, M.D., Hooper, S.R., Chen, M.S. et al. (2015). Posterior structural brain volumes differ in maltreated youth with and without chronic posttraumatic stress disorder. *Developmental Psychopathology* 27 (4 Pt 2): 1555–1576.

De Brito, S.A., Viding, E., Sebastian, C.L. et al. (2013). Reduced orbitofrontal and temporal grey matter in a community sample of maltreated children. *Journal of Child Psychology and Psychiatry* 54 (1): 105–112.

De Prince, A.P. (2005). Social cognition and revictimization risk. *Journal of Trauma and Dissociation* 6: 125–141.

De Prince, A.P. and Freyd, J.J. (1999). Dissociation, attention and memory. *Psychological Science* 10: 449–452.

Deblinger, E., Mannarino, A.P., Cohen, J.A., and Steer, R.A. (2006). A follow-up study of a multisite, randomized, controlled trial for children with sexual abuse-related PTSD symptoms. *Journal of the American Academy of Child & Adolescent Psychiatry* 45 (12): 1474–1484.

Deblinger, E., Mannarino, A.P., Cohen, J.A. et al. (2011). Trauma-focused cognitive behavioral therapy for children: impact of the trauma narrative and treatment length. *Depression and Anxiety* 28 (1): 67–75.

Deering, D. (1996). Compassion fatigue: Coping with secondary traumatic stress disorder in those who treat the traumatized. *Journal of Psychosocial Nursing and Mental Health Services* 34 (11): 52–52.

Dehon, C. and Scheeringa, M.S. (2005). Screening for preschool posttraumatic stress disorder with the Child Behavior Checklist. *Journal of Pediatric Psychology* 31 (4): 431–435.

Delaney-Black, V., Covington, C., Ondersma, S.J. et al. (2002). Violence exposure, trauma, and IQ and/or reading deficits among urban children. *Archives of Pediatrics and Adolescent Medicine* 156 (3): 280–285.

DePrince, A.P., Weinzierl, K.M., and Combs, M.D. (2009). Executive function performance in a trauma exposure in a community sample of children. *Child Abuse and Neglect* 33 (6): 353–361.

Dictionary of Epidemiology (2001). *Dictionary of Epidemiology*, 4e. New York, NY: Oxford University Press.

Division of Clinical Psychology (2011). *Good Practice Guidelines on the Use of Psychological Formulation*. Leicester: The British Psychological Association.

Dominguez-Gomez, E. and Rutledge, D.N. (2009). Prevalence of secondary traumatic stress among emergency nurses. *Journal of Emergency Nursing* 35 (3): 199–204.

Dong, M., Dube, S.R., Felitti, V.J. et al. (2003). Adverse childhood experiences and self-reported liver disease: New insights into a causal pathway. *Archives of Internal Medicine* 163: 1949–1956.

Dong, M., Anda, R.F., Felitti, V.J. et al. (2004a). The interrelatedness of multiple forms of childhood abuse, neglect, and household dysfunction. *Child Abuse and Neglect* 28: 771–784.

Dong, M., Giles, W.H., Felitti, V.J. et al. (2004b). Insights into causal pathways for ischemic heart disease: Adverse childhood experiences study. *Circulation* 110: 1761–1766.

Dozier, M., Lindhiem, O., Lewis, E. et al. (2009). Effects of a foster parent training program on young children's attachment behaviors: preliminary evidence from a randomized clinical trial. *Child Adolescent Social Work Journal* 26: 321–332: https://doi.org/10.1007/s10560-009-0165-1.

Dube, S.R., Anda, R.F., Felitti, V.J. et al. (2001). Childhood abuse, household dysfunction, and the risk of attempted suicide throughout the life span: Findings from the adverse childhood experiences study. *Journal of the American Medical Association JAMA* 286: 3089–3096.

Dube, S.R., Anda, R.F., Felitti, V.J. et al. (2002). Adverse childhood experiences and personal alcohol abuse as an adult. *Addictive Behaviors* 27: 713–725.

Dube, S.R., Anda, R.F., Felitti, V.J. et al. (2003a). Childhood abuse, neglect, and household dysfunction and the risk of illicit drug use: The adverse childhood experiences study. *Pediatrics* 111: 564–572.

Dube, S.R., Felitti, V.J., Dong, M. et al. (2003b). The impact of adverse childhood experiences on health problems: Evidence from four birth cohorts dating back to 1900. *Preventive Medicine* 37: 268–277.

Dube, S.R., Miller, J.W., Brown, D.W. et al. (2006). Adverse childhood experiences and the association with ever using alcohol and initiating alcohol use during adolescence. *Journal of Adolescent Health* 38 (4): 444: e1–e10.

Dube, S.R., Fairweather, D., Pearson, W. et al. (2009). Cumulative childhood stress and autoimmune diseases in adults. *Psychosomatic Medicine* 71: 243–250.

Dukewich, T.L., Borkowski, J.G., and Whitman, T.L. (1996). Adolescent mothers and child abuse potential: An evaluation of risk factors. *Child Abuse and Neglect* 20 (11): 1031–1047.

Dupper, D.R. and Amy, E. (2008). Montgomery Dingus, corporal punishment in US public schools: A continuing challenge for school social workers. *Children and Schools* 30 (4): 243–250. available at http://ewasteschools.pbworks.com/f/Corporal_punishment_2009.pdf.

Eckenrode, J., Laird, M., and Doris, J. (1993). School performance and disciplinary problems among abused and neglected children. *Developmental Psychology* 29: 53–62.

Edleson, J.L. (1999). The overlap between child maltreatment and woman battering. *Violence Against Women* 5 (2): 134–154.

Edwards, V., Holden, G.W., Felitti, V.J., and Anda, R.F. (2003). Relationship between multiple forms of childhood maltreatment and adult mental health in community respondents: Results from the Adverse Childhood Experiences Study. *American Journal of Psychiatry* 160 (8): 1453–1461.

Edwards, V.J., Anda, R.F., Gu, D. et al. (2007). Adverse childhood experiences and smoking persistence in adults with smoking-related symptoms and illness. *The Permanente Journal* 11: 5–13.

Egeland, B., Sroufe, A., and Erickson, M. (1983). The developmental consequences of different patterns of maltreatment. *Child Abuse and Neglect* 7: 459–469.

Eger, C. (2014). Mass. Gov. Patrick signs controversial gun control bill into law. Retrieved on August 2, 2017 from http://www.masslive.com/politics/index.ssf/2014/08/gov_deval_patrick_signs_gun_bi.htmlhttp://www.masslive.com/politics/index.ssf/2014/08/gov_deval_patrick_signs_gun_bi.html.

Ehring, T. and Quack, D. (2010). Emotion regulation difficulties in trauma survivors: The role of trauma type and PTSD symptom severity. *Behavior Therapy* 41 (4): 587–598.

Eklund, K. and Dowdy, E. (2014). Screening for behavioral and emotional risk versus traditional school identification methods. *School Mental Health* 6 (1): 40–49.

Eklund, K. and Rossen, E. (2016). *Guidance for Trauma Screenings in Schools: A Product of Defending Childhood, State Policy Initiative*. The National Center for Mental Health and Juvenile Justice.

Eklund, K. and Tanner, N. (2014). Providing multi-tiered systems of support for behavior: Conducting behavior screening at school. *Principal Leadership* 10: 50–52.

Ellickson, P.L. and Hawes, J.A. (1989). An assessment of active versus passive methods for obtaining parental consent. *Evaluation Review* 13 (1): 45–55.

End Corporal Punishment, (2017) http://www/endcorporalpunsihment.org/pages/pdfs/GlobalProgress.pdf

Esaki, N., Benamati, J., Yanosy, S. et al. (2014). The sanctuary model: theoretical framework. *Families in Society: The Journal of Contemporary Human Services*.

Etkin, A., Egner, T., and Kalisch (2011). Emotional processing in anterior cingulate and medial prefrontal cortex. *Trends in Cognitive Sciences* 15 (2): 85–93.

Evans, G.W. and English, K. (2002). The environment of poverty: Multiple stressor exposure, psychophysiological stress and socioemotional adjustment. *Child Development* 73: 1238–1248.

Evans, G.W. and Kim, P. (2013). Childhood poverty, chronic stress, self? Regulation, and coping. *Child Development Perspectives* 7 (1): 43–48.

Evans, G.W. and Schamberg, M.A. (2009). Childhood poverty, chronic stress, and adult working memory. *Proceedings of the National Academy of Sciences* 106 (16): 6545–6549.

Evarts, E.V. and Thach, W.T. (1969). Motor mechanisms of the CNS: Cererocellular interrealtions. *Annual Review of Physiology* 31: 451–498.

Evers-Szostak, M. and Sanders, S. (1992). The Children's Perceptual Alteration Scale (CPAS): A measure of children's dissociation. In: *Dissociation: Progress in the Dissociative Disorders*.

Eyberg, S.M., Boggs, S.R., and Algina, J. (1995). Parent-child interaction therapy: a psychosocial model for the treatment of young children with conduct problem behavior and their families. *Psychopharmacology bulletin*.

Eyberg, S.M., Funderburk, B.W., Hembree-Kigin, T.L. et al. (2001). Parent-child interaction therapy with behavior problem children: One and two year maintenance of treatment effects in the family. *Child & Family Behavior Therapy* 23 (4): 1–20.

Farmer, E.M., Burns, B.J., Phillips, S.D. et al. (2003). Pathways into and through mental health services for children and adolescents. *Psychiatric Services* 54 (1): 60–66.

Farmer-Dougan, V.A., Heidenreich, B.A., and Wise, L.A. (2011). Functional neuroanatomy of structures of the hindbrain, midbrain and diencephalon, and basal ganglia. In: *Handbook of Pediatric Neuropsychology* (ed. A.S. Davis), 121–146. New York, NY: Springer Publishing Company.

Feifer, S.G. (2010). Assessing and intervening with children with reading disorders. In: *Best Practices in school neuropsychology: Guidelines for effective practice, assessment and evidenced-based intervention* (ed. D. Miller), 483–504.

Feifer, S.G. (2013). *The neuropsychology of written language disorders: A framework for effective interventions*. MD: School Neuropsych Press.

Feifer, S.G. and De Fina (2005). *The neurospchology of mathematics: Diagnosis and intervention.* MD: The Neuropsych Press.

Feifer, S.G. and Della Toffalo, D.A. (2007). *Integrating RTI with Cognitive Neuropsychology: A Scientific Approach to Reading.* School Neuropsych Press.

Felitti, V.J. (2002). The relation between adverse childhood experiences and adult health: Turning gold into lead. *The Permanente Journal* 6 (1): 44–47.

Felitti, V.J. and Anda, R.F. (2009). *The Hidden Epidemic: The Impact of Early Life Trauma on Health and Disease* (ed. R. Lanius and E. Vermetten). Cambridge University Press.

Felitti, V.J. and Anda, R.F. (2010). The relationship of adverse childhood experiences to adult medical disease, psychiatric disorders and sexual behavior: Implications for healthcare. In: *The impact of early life trauma on health and disease: The hidden epidemic*, 77–87. Retrieved from: https://www.theannainstitute.org/LV%20FINAL%202-7-09.pdf

Felitti, V.J., Anda, R.F., Nordenberg, D. et al. (1998a). The relationship of adult health status to childhood abuse and household dysfunction. *American Journal of Preventive Medicine* 14: 245–258.

Felitti, V.J., Anda, R.F., Nordenberg, D. et al. (1998b). Relationship of childhood abuse and household dysfunction to many of the leading causes of death in adults: The adverse childhood experiences (ACE) study. *American Journal of Preventive Medicine* 14 (4): 245–258.

Felitti, V.J., Anda, R.F., Nordenberg, D. et al. (1998c). Relationship of childhood abuse and household dysfunction to many of the leading causes of death in adults. *American Journal of Preventive Medicine* 14: 245–258.

Fergusson, D.M. and Horwood, L.J. (2003). Resilience to childhood adversity: Results of a 21-year study. In: *Resilience and vulnerability: Adaptation in the context of childhood adversities*, 130–155. Cambridge University Press.

Figley, C.R. (1995). Compassion fatigue: Toward a new understanding of the costs of caring. In B. H. Stamm (Ed.), Secondary traumatic stress: Self-care issues for clinicians, researchers, and educators (pp. 3–28). Baltimore, MD, US: The Sidran Press.

Figley, C.R. (2002). Compassion fatigue: Psychotherapists' chronic lack of self care. *Journal of Clinical Psychology* 58 (11): 1433–1441.

Figley, C.R. (2007). The art and science of caring for others without forgetting self-care. In:.

Figley, C.R. and Stamm, B.H. (1996). Psychometric review of compassion fatigue self test. In: *Measurement of stress, trauma, and adaptation*, 127–130.

Figley, C.R., Lovre, C., and Figley, K.R. (2011). Compassion fatigue, vulnerability, and resilience in practitioners working with traumatized children. In: *Post-traumatic Syndromes in Childhood and Adolescence: A Handbook of Research and Practice*, 417–432.

Finkelhor, D., Hamby, S.L., Ormrod, R., and Turner, H. (2005). The Juvenile Victimization Questionnaire: reliability, validity, and national norms. *Child abuse & neglect* 29 (4): 383–412.

Finkelhor, D., Hamby, S.L., Ormrod, R.K. et al. (2011). The Juvenile Victimization Questionnaire (JVQ). *Adolescent Psychiatry* 39 (7): 829–840.

Finkelhor, D., Turner, H.A., Shattuck, A., and Hamby, S.L. (2013). Violence, crime, and abuse exposure in a national sample of children and youth: an update. *JAMA pediatrics* 167 (7): 614–621.

Finkelhor, D., Shattuck, A., Turner, H., and Hamby, S. (2015). A revised inventory of adverse childhood experiences. *Child Abuse and Neglect* 48: 13–21.

Fixsen, D.L., Blase, K.A., Naoom, S.F. et al. (2009). *Implementation: The Missing Link Between Research and Practice*, vol. 1. NIRN implementation brief.

Flanagan, D.P., Ortiz, S.O., and Alfonso (2013). *Essentials of cross battery assessment*, 3e. NJ: John Wiley and Sons.

Fletcher, K. E. (1994). Dimensions of stressful events rating scale. Unpublished manuscript, Department of Psychiatry, University of Massachusetts Medical Center, Worcester.

Fletcher-Janzen, E. (2017). The neurodevelopmental model of assessment and intervention. Workshop presented at the meeting of the National Association of School Psychologists Annual Conference, San Antonio, TX.

Florida Partnership for School Readiness (2004). *Birth to three screening and assessment resource guide*. Jacksonville, FL: University of North Florida.

Flynn, C.P. (1999). Animal abuse in childhood and later support for interpersonal violence in families. *Society and Animals* 7 (2): 161–172.

Foderaro JF: Personal communication, 1991

Foderaro, J. (2001). Creating a non-violent environment: keeping sanctuary safe. In: *Violence: A Public Health Menace and a Public Health Approach* (ed. S.L. Bloom), 57–82. London: Karnac.

Ford, J.D. (2008). Diagnosis of traumatic stress disorders (DSM and ICD). In: *Encyclopedia of Psychological Trauma* (ed. G. Reyes, J.D. Elhai and J.D. Ford), 200–208. Hoboken, NJ: Wiley.

Ford, J.D. and Hawke, J. (2012). Trauma affect regulation psychoeducation group and milieu intervention outcomes in juvenile detention facilities. *Journal of Aggression, Maltreatment and Trauma* 21 (4): 365–384:https://doi.org/10.1080/10926771.2012.673538.

Ford, J.D., Racusin, R., Ellis, C.G. et al. (2000). Child maltreatment, other trauma exposure, and posttraumatic symptomatology among children with oppositional defiant and attention deficit hyperactivity disorders. *Child Maltreatment* 5 (3): 205–217.

Ford, J.D., Racusin, R., Rogers, K. et al. (2002). *Traumatic Events Screening Inventory for Children (TESI-C) Version 8.4*. Dartmouth, VT: National Center for PTSD and Dartmouth Child Psychiatry Research Group.

Ford, J.D., Steinberg, K.L., and Zhang, W. (2011). A randomized clinical trial comparing affect regulation and social problem-solving psychotherapies for mothers with victimization-related PTSD. *Behavior Therapy* 42 (4): 560–578.

Ford, J., Blaustein, M., Cloitre, M. et al. (2012a). Developmental trauma disorder-focused interventions for traumatized children and adolescents. In: *Treating complex traumatic stress disorders in children: An evidence-based guide* (ed. J.D. Ford and C.A. Courtois). New York, NY: Guilford Press.

Ford, J.D., Steinberg, K.L., Hawke, J. et al. (2012b). Randomized trial comparison of emotion regulation and relational psychotherapies for PTSD with girls involved in delinquency. *Journal of Clinical Child and Adolescent Psychology* 41 (1): 27–37.

Ford, J.D., Chang, R., Levine, J., and Zhang, W. (2013). Randomized clinical trial comparing affect regulation and supportive group therapies for victimization-related PTSD with incarcerated women. *Behavior Therapy* 44 (2): 262–276: https://doi.org/10.1016/j.beth.2012.10.003.

Fox, N.A. and Leavitt, L.A. (1995). *The Violence Exposure Scale for Children-Revised (VEX-R)*. College Park, MD: University of Maryland.

Freyd, J.J., DePrince, A.P., and Gleaves, D. (2007). The state of betrayal trauma theory: Reply to McNally—conceptual issues and future directions. *Memory* 15: 295–311.

Friedrich, W.N. (1997). *Child Sexual Behavior Inventory: Professional Manual*. Odessa, FL: Psychological Assessment Resources.

Friedrich, W.N. (2002). *Psychological Assessment of Sexually Abused Children and their Families*. Thousand Oaks, CA: Sage Publications.

Fristad, M.A., Gavazzi, S.M., and Mackinaw-Koons, B. (2003). Family psychoeducation: an adjunctive intervention for children with bipolar disorder. *Biological Psychiatry* 53 (11): 1000–1008.

Gabel, L.A., Gibson, C.J., Gruen, J.R., and LoTurco, J. (2010). Progress towards a cellulat neurobiology of reading disability. *Neurobiological Disabilites* 38 (2): 173–180.

Garmezy, N. (1974). The study of competence in children at risk for severe psychopathology. In: *Children at Psychiatric Risk*, vol. 3 (ed. E.J. Anthony and C. Koupernik) The child in his family, 77–97. New York: Wiley.

Gazzaniga, M.S., Ivry, R.B., and Mangun, G.R. (2014). *Cognitive Neuroscience: The Biology of the Mind*, 4e. New York, NY: W.W. Norton & Company.

Gerard, A.B. (1994). *Parent-child relationship inventory*. Los Angeles, CA: Western psychological services.

Gershoff, E.T. (2013). Spanking and child development: We know enough now to stop hitting our children. *Child Development Perspective* 7: 133–137. https://www.ncbi.nlm.nih.gov/pmc/articles/PMC3768154.

Gershoff, E. T. (2002). Corporal punishment by parents and associated child behaviors and experiences: a meta-analytic and theoretical review. *Psychological Bulletin* 128 (4): 539–579.

Gershoff, E.T. and Grogan-Taylor, A. (2016). Spanking and child outcomes: Old controversies and new meta-analysis. *Journal of Family Psychology* 30 (4): 453–469.

Glover, T.A. and Albers, C.A. (2007). Considerations for evaluating universal assessments. *Journal of School Psychology* 45: 117–135. https://doi.org/10.1016/j.jsp.2006.05.005.

Goldman, P.S. (1971). Functional development of the prefrontal cortex in early life and the problem of neuronal plasticity. *Experimental Neurology* 66: 366–387.

Goldstein, M.J. and Miklowitz, D.J. (1995). The effectiveness of psychoeducational family therapy in the treatment of schizophrenic disorders. *Journal of Marital and Family Therapy* 21: 361–376.

Gonzalez, A., Monzon, N., Solis, D. et al. (2016). Trauma exposure in elementary school children: description of screening procedures, level of exposure, and stress symptoms. *School Mental Health* 8: 77–88.

Goodman, R. (1997). The strengths and difficulties questionnaire: A research note. *Journal of Child Psychology and Psychiatry* 38 (5): 581–586.

Gouze, K.R. (1987). Attention and social problem solving as correlats of aggression in preschool males. *Journal of Abnormal Child Psychology* 15: 181–197.

Graczyk, P.A., Domitrovich, C.E., and Zins, J.E. (2003). Facilitating the implementation of evidence-based prevention and mental health promotion efforts in schools. In: *Handbook of School Mental Health Advancing Practice and Research*, 301–318. Boston, MA: Springer.

Grasso, D.J., Ford, J.D., and Lindheim, O. (2016). A patient-centered decision-support tool informed by history of interpersonal violence: "Will this treatment work for me?". *Journal of Interpersonal Violence* 31 (3): 465–480: https://doi.org/10.1177/0886260514555870.

Gratz, K.L. and Roemer, L. (2004). Multidimensional assessment of emotion regulation and dysregulation: Development, factor structure, and initial validation of the difficulties in emotion regulation scale. *Journal of Psychopathology and Behavioral Assessment* 26 (1): 41–54.

Greenwald, R. (2002). The role of trauma in conduct disorder. *Journal of Aggression, Maltreatment and Trauma* 6 (1): 5–23.

Greenwood, M. (1935). *Epidemics and crowd-diseases*. London: Williams Norgate.

Grisso, T., Vincent, G., and Seagrave, D. (Eds.). (2005). *Mental health screening and assessment in juvenile justice*. Guilford Press.

Gunnar, M.R. and Donzella, B. (2001). Social regulation of the of the LHPA axis in early human development. *Psychoneuroendocrinology* 27: 199–220.

Gunnar, M.R. and Quevedo, K. (2007). The neurobiology of stress and development. *Annual Review of Psychology* 58: 145–173.

Gunnar, M.R. and Vazquez, D.M. (2001). Low cortisol and a flattening of expected rhythm: Potential indices of risk in human development. *Development and Psychopathology* 13: 515–737.

Gwinn, C. (2015). *Cheering for the children: Creating pathways to hope for children exposed to trauma*. Wheatmark, Inc.

Habib, M. and Labruna, V. (2011). Clinical considerations in assessing trauma and PTSD in adolescents. *Journal of Child & Adolescent Trauma* 4 (3): 198–216.

Habib, M., Labruna, V., and Newman, J. (2012). Implementation of a manually guided group treatment: A phenomenological approach to treating traumatized adolescents in residential settings. *Journal of Child and Adolescent Trauma*.

Hale, J.B. and Fiorello, K.A. (2004). *School Neuropsychology: A practitioner's handbook*. New York, NY: Guilford Press.

Hale, J.B., Wycoff, K.L., and Fiorello, C.A. (2011). RTI and cognitive hypothesis testing for identification and intervention of specific learning disabilities: The best of both worlds. In: *Essentials of Specific Learning Disability Identification*, 173–201.

Haley, S.A. (1974). When the patient reports atrocities: Specific treatment considerations of the Vietnam veteran. *Archives of General Psychiatry* 30 (2): 191–196.

Hamby, S.L., Finkelhor, D., Ormrod, R.K., and Turner, H.A. (2004). *The Juvenile Victimization Questionnaire (JVQ): Administration and Scoring Manual*. Durham, NH: Crimes Against Children Research Center.

Hamby, S., Finkelhor, D., Turner, H., & Kracke, K. (2011). The Juvenile Victimization Questionnaire toolkit. Retrieved from http://www.unh.edu/ccrc/jvq/index_new.html.

Hanson, J.L., Chung, M.K., Avants, B.A. et al. (2010). Early stress is associated with alterations in the orbitofrontal cortex: A tensor-based morphometry investigation of brain structure and behavioral risk. *Journal of Neuroscience* 30 (22): 7466–7472.

Hart, H. and Rubia, K. (2012). Neuroimaging and child abuse: a critical review. *Frontiers in Human Neuroscience* 6: 52124: https://doi.org/10.3389/fnhum.2012.00052.

Hatfield, D. and Ogles, B. (2004). The use of outcome measures by psychologists in clinical practice. *Professional Psychology Research Practice* 35 (5): 485–491. Available at: PsycINFO, Ipswich (MA). accessed 27 September 2013.

Hawkins, S. and Radcliffe, J. (2006). Current measures of PTSD for children and adolescents. *Journal of Pediatric Psychology* 31 (4): 420–430. Available at: PsycINFO, Ipswich (MA). accessed 27 September 2013.

Hayes, S.C., Wilson, K.G., Gifford, E.V. et al. (1996). Experiential avoidance and behavioral disorders: A functional dimensional approach to diagnosis and treatment. *Journal of Consulting and Clinical Psychology* 64: 1152–1168.

Heim, C., Newport, D.J., Mletzko, T. et al. (2008). The link between childhood trauma and depression: insights from HPA axis studies in humans. *Psychoneuroendocrinology* 33 (6): 693–710.

Heimberg, L.K. (1968). The measurement of future time perspective (Doctoral dissertation, Vanderbilt University, 1968). *Dissertation Abstracts International* 24 (4): 1686–1687.

Hembree-Kigin, T.L. and McNeil, C.B. (2013). *Parent—child Interaction Therapy*. Springer Science & Business Media.

Hemenover, S.H. (2003). The good, the bad, and the healthy: impacts of emotional disclosure of trauma on resilient self-concept and psychological distress. *Personality and Social Psychology Bulletin* 29 (10): 1236–1244.

Herman, J.P., Ostrander, M.M., Mueller, N.K., and Figueiredo, H. (2005). Limbic system mechanisms of stress regulation: hypothalamo-pituitary-adrenocortical axis. *Progress in Neuro-Psychopharmacology and Biological Psychiatry* 29 (8): 1201–1213.

Hermans, H.J.M. and Hermans-Jansen, E. (1995). *Self-narratives: The Construction of Meaning in Psychotherapy*. New York: Guilford.

Hester, M., Pearson, C., and Harwin, N. (2000). *Making an impact: Children and domestic violence: A reader*. London: Jessica Kingsley Publications.

Hildyard, K.L. and Wolfe, D.A. (2002). Child neglect: Developmental issues and outcomes. *Child Abuse and Neglect* 26 (6-7): 679–695.

Hillis, S.D., Anda, R.F., Dube, S.R. et al. (2004). The association between adolescent pregnancy, long-term psychosocial outcomes, and fetal death. *Pediatrics* 113: 320–327.

Hillis, S.D., Anda, R.F., Dube, S.R. et al. (2010). The protective effect of family strengths in childhood against adolescent pregnancy and its long-term psychosocial consequences. *The Permanente Journal* 14 (3): 18.

Hinkley, L.B., Marco, E.J., Findlay, A.M. et al. (2012). The role of corpus callosum development in functional connectivity and cognitive processing. *PLoS One* 7 (8): e39804.

Hishaw, S.P., Lahey, D.B., and Hart, E.L. (1993). Issues of taxonomy and comorbidity in the development of conduct disorder. *Developmental and Psychopathology* 5: 31–34.

Hobfoll, S.E. and London, P. (1986). The relationship of self-concept and social support to emotional distress among women during war. *Journal of Social and Clinical Psychology* 4 (2): 189–203.

Hoffman-Plotkin, D. and Twentyman, C.T. (1984). A multimodal assessment of behavioral and cognitive deficits in abused and neglected preschoolers. *Child Development* 55: 794–802.

Holden, G.W., Coleman, S.W., and Schmidt, K.L. (1995). Why 3-year-old children get spanked: Parent and child determinants as reported by college-educated mothers. *Merrill-Palmer Quarterly* 41: 431–452.

Hollander-Goldfein, B., Isserman, N., and Goldenberg, J.E. (2012). *Transcending Trauma: Survival, Resilience and Clinical Implications in Survivor Families*, vol. 40. Routledge.

Holt, S., Buckley, H., and Whelan, S. (2008). The impact of exposure to domestic violence on children and young people: A review of the literature. *Child Abuse and Neglect* 32 (8): 797–810.

Hornor, G. (2008). Reactive attachment disorder. *Journal of Pediatric Health Care* 22 (4): 234–239.

Horwitz, A.V., Widom, C.S., McLaughlin, J., and White, H.R. (2001). The impact of childhood abuse and neglect on adult mental health: a prospective study. *Journal of Health and Social Behavior* 42: 184–201. https://doi.org/10.2307/3090177.

Hoye, J., Asok, A., Bernard, K., Roth, T.L., Rosen, J. B., & Dozier, M. (2013). Intervening early to protect telomeres: Results of a randomized clinical trial. Unpublished manuscript.

Hoyme, H.E., Kalberg, W.O., Elliot, A.J. et al. (2016). Updated clinical guidelines for diagnosing fetal alcohol spectrum disorders. *Pediatrics* 138 (2): pii:e20154256.

Huber, M., Knottnerus, J.A., Green, L. et al. (2003). Interacting mediators of allostasis and allostatic load: towards an understanding of resilience in aging. *Metabolism* 52 (suppl 2): 10–16.

Huber, M., Knottnerus, J.A., Green, L. et al. (2011a). How should we define health? *BMJ: British Medical Journal* 343.

Huber, M., Knottnerus, J.A., Green, L. et al. (2011b). How should we define health? *BMJ: British Medical Journal* 343.

Hughes, K., Bellis, M.A., Hardcastle, K.A. et al. (2017). The effect of multiple adverse childhood experiences on health: a systematic review and meta-analysis. *The Lancet Public Health* 2 (8): e356–e366.

Hunsley, J. and Mash, E.J. (2007). Evidence-based assessment. *Annual Review of Clinical Psychology* 3: 29–51.

Hunsley, J., Lee, C.M., and Wood, J. (2003). Controversial and questionable assessment techniques. In: *Science and Pseudoscience in Clinical Psychology* (ed. S.O. Lilienfeld, S.J. Lynn and J. Lohr), 39–76. New York: Guilford.

Hussey, J.M., Chang, J.J., and Kotch, J.B. (2006). Child maltreatment in the United States: prevalence, risk factors, and adolescent health consequences. *Pediatrics* 118 (3): 933–942.

Hyman, I.A. (1995). Corporal punishment, psychological maltreatment, violence, and punitiveness in America: Research, advocacy, and public policy. *Applied and Preventive Psychology* 4: 113–130.

Institute of Medicine (2001). *Crossing the quality chasm: A new health system for the 21st century*. Washington, DC: National Academy Press.

Ippen, C. G., Ford, J., Racusin, R., Acker, M., Bosquet, M., Rogers, K., et al. (2002). Traumatic Events Screening Inventory—Children. Retrieved at http://www.ptsd.va.gov/ professional/ pages/assessments/assessment-pdf/TESI-C.pdf/.

Ishikawa, A. and Nakamura, S. (2003). Convergence and interaction of hippocampal and amygdala projections within the prefrontal cortex in the rat. *Journal of Neuroscience* 23: 9987–9995.

Jacoby, N., Overfield, J., Binder, E.B., and Heim, C.M. (2016). Stress neurobiology and developmental psychopathology. In: *Developmental Psychopathology, Developmental Neuroscience* (ed. D. Cicchetti), 787–831.

Jakupcak, M., Lisak, D., and Roemer, L. (2002). The role of masculine ideology and masculine gender role stress in men's perpetration of relationship violence. *Psychology of Men & Masculinity* 3 (2): 97.

Jaycox, L.H. (2004). *Cognitive behavioral intervention for trauma in schools*. Longmont, CO: Sopris West Educational Services.

Jaycox, L.H., Stein, B.D., Kataoka, S.H. et al. (2002). Violence exposure, post-traumatic stress disorder, and depressive symptoms among recent immigrant schoolchildren. *Journal of the American Academy of Child and Adolescent Psychiatry* 41 (9): 1104–1110.

Jaycox, L.H., Tanielian, T.L., Sharma, P. et al. (2007). Schools' mental health responses after Hurricanes Katrina and Rita. *Psychiatric Services* 58 (10): 1339–1343.

Jaycox, L.H., Langley, A.K., Stein, B.D. et al. (2009). Support for students exposed to trauma: A pilot study. *School Mental Health* 1 (2): 49–60.

Jaycox, L.H., Cohen, J.A., Mannarino, A.P. et al. (2010). Children's mental health care following Hurricane Katrina: A field trial of trauma-focused psychotherapies. *Journal of Traumatic Stress* 23 (2): 223–231.

Jenkins, J.R., Hudson, R.F., and Johnson, E.S. (2007). Screening for At-Risk Readers in a Response to. *School Psychology Review* 36 (4): 582–600.

Jensen, T.K., Holt, T., Ormhauga, S.M. et al. (2013). A randomized effectiveness study comparing trauma-focused cognitive behavioral therapy with therapy as usual for youth. *Journal of Clinical Child and Adolescent Psychology* 0 (0): 1–14: https://doi.org/10.1080/ 15374416.2013.822307.

Jeret, J.S., Serur, D., Wisniewski, E., and Fisch, C. (1986). Frequency of agenesis of the corpus callosum in developmentally disabled population determined by computerized tomography. *Pediatric Neuroscience* 12: 101–103.

Johnson, S.B., Riley, A.W., Granger, D.A., and Riis, J. (2013). The science of early life toxic stress for pediatric practice and advocacy. *Pediatrics* 131: 319–327:https://doi.org/10.1542/peds.2012-0469.

Jones, R.E., Leen-Feldner, E.W., Olatunji, B.O. et al. (2009). Psychometric properties of the Affect Intensity and Reactivity Measure adapted for Youth (AIR–Y). *Psychological Assessment* 21 (2): 162.

Jones, D.J., Lewis, T., Litrownik, A. et al. (2013). Linking childhood sexual abuse and early adolescent risk behavior: The intervening role of internalizing and externalizing problems. *Journal of abnormal child psychology* 41 (1): 139–150.

Juster, R.P., McEwen, B.S., and Lupien, S.J. (2010). Allostatic load biomarkers of chronic stress and impact on health and cognition. *Neuroscience and Biobehavioral Reviews* 35 (1): 2–16.

Kagan, J. (2003). *Surprise, Uncertainty and Mental Structures*. Cambridge, MA: Harvard University Press.

Kagan, R. (2004). *Rebuilding attachments with traumatized children; healing from losses, violence, abuse and neglect*. New York, NY: Routledge.

Kagan, R. (2007a). *Real life heroes; a life storybook for children*, 2e. New York, NY: Routledge.

Kagan, R. (2007b). *Real life heroes practitioner's manual*. New York, NY: Routledge.

Kagan, R. (2009). Transforming Troubled Children into Tomorrow's Heroes. In: *Treating traumatized children: Risk, resilience and recovery* (ed. D. Brom, R. Pat-Horenczyk and J. Ford). New York, NY: Routledge.

Kagan, R. and Spinazzola, J. (2013). Real life heroes in residential treatment: Implementation of an integrated model of trauma and resiliency-focused treatment for children and adolescents with complex PTSD. *Journal of Family Violence* 28 (7): 705–715.

Kagan, R., Douglas, A., Hornik, J., and Kratz, S. (2008). Real life heroes pilot study: Evaluation of a treatment model for children with traumatic stress. *Journal of Child and Adolescent Trauma* 1: 5–22.

Karatekin, C. (2017). Adverse Childhood Experiences (ACEs), stress and mental health in college students. *Stress and Health* 34 (1): 36–45.

Karlamangla, A.S., Singer, B.H., McEwen, B.S. et al. (2002). Allostatic load as a predictor of functional decline: MacArthur studies of successful aging. *Journal of Clinical Epidemiology* 29: 696–710.

Karlén, J.L., Ludvigsson, J., Hedmark, M. et al. (2015). Early psychosocial exposures, hair cortisol levels, and disease risk. *Pediatrics* 135 (6).

Kataoka, S.H., Stein, B.D., Jaycox, L.H. et al. (2003). A school-based mental health program for traumatized Latino immigrant children. *Journal of the American Academy of Child and Adolescent Psychiatry* 42 (3): 311–318.

Kataoka, S., Stein, B.D., Nadeem, E., and Wong, M. (2007). Who gets care? Mental health service use following a school-based suicide prevention program. *Journal of the American Academy of Child and Adolescent Psychiatry* 46 (10): 1341–1348.

Kataoka, S., Jaycox, L.H., Wong, M. et al. (2011). Effects on school outcomes in low-income minority youth: Preliminary findings from a community-partnered study of a school trauma intervention. *Ethnicity and Disease* 21 (3 0 1): S1-71–S1-77.

Katsurada, E. and Sugawara, A.I. (1998). The relationship betwen hostile attribution bias and aggressive behavior in preschoolers. *Early Childhood Research Quarterly* 13: 623–636.

Kaufer, D.I. (2007). The dorsolateral and cingulate cortex. In: *The human frontal lobes*, 2e (ed. B.L. Miller and J.L. Cummings), 44–58.

Kaufmann, R.B., Spitz, A.M., Strauss, L.T. et al. (1998). The decline in US teen pregnancy rates, 1990–1995. *Pediatrics* 102 (5): 1141–1147.

Kelly, P.A., Viding, E., Wallace, G.L. et al. (2013). Cortical thickness, surface area, and gyrification abnormalities in children exposed to maltreatment: Neural markers for vulnerability? *Biological Psychiatry* 74 (11): 845–852.

Kelly, P.A., Viding, E., Puetz, V.B. et al. (2015). Sex differences in socioemotional functioning, attentional bias, and gray matter volume in maltreated children: A multilevel investigation. *Development and Psychopathology* 27: 1591–1609.

Kendall-Tackett, K.A., Williams, L.M., and Finkelhor, D. (1993). Impact of sexual abuse on children: A review and synthesis of recent empirical studies. *Psychological Bulletin* 113: 164–180. https://doi.org/10.1037/0033-2909.113.1.164.

Kennedy, D.P., Glascher, J., Tyszka, J.M., and Adolphs, R. (2009). Personal space regulation by the human amygdala. *Nature Neuroscience* 12 (10): 1226–1227.

Keough, K.K. and Markus, H.R. (1998). On being well: The role of the self in building the bridge from philosophy to biology. *Psychological Inquiry* 9: 49–53.

Kessler, R.C. and Magee, W.J. (1993). Childhood adversities and adult depression: basic patterns of association in a US national survey. *Psychological Medicine*. 23: 679–690.

Kessler, R.C. and Magee, W.J. (1994). Childhood family violence and adult recurrent depression. *Journal of Health and Social Behavior* 35: 13–27.

Kessler, R.C., Sonnega, A., Bromet, E. et al. (1995). Posttraumatic stress disorder in the National Comorbidity Survey. *Archives of general psychiatry* 52 (12): 1048–1060.

Kessler, R.C., Davis, C.G., and Kendler, K.S. (1997). Childhood adversity and adult psychiatric disorder in the US National Comorbidity Survey. *Psychological Medicine*. 27: 1101–1119. https://doi.org/10.1017/S0033291797005588.

Kessler, R.C., Rose, S., Koenen, K.C. et al. (2014). How well can post-traumatic stress disorder be predicted from pre-trauma risk factors? An exploratory study in the WHO World Mental Health Surveys. *World Psychiatry* 13 (3): 265–274.

Khantzian, E.J. (1987). The self-medication hypothesis of addictive disorders: focus on heroin and cocaine dependence. In: *The cocaine crisis*, 65–74. Boston, MA: Springer.

Kilpatrick, D.G., Ruggiero, K.J., Acierno, R. et al. (2003). Violence and risk of PTSD, major depression, substance abuse/dependence, and cormorbidity: Results from the National Survey of Adolescents. *Journal of Consulting and Clinical Psychology* 71: 692–700. https://doi.org/10.1037/0022-006X.71.4.692.

Kindig, D. and Stoddart, G. (2003). What is population health? *American Journal of Public Health* 93 (3): 380–383.

King, L.A. (2001). The health benefits of writing about life goals. *Personality and Social Psychology Bulletin* 27: 798–807.

Kinniburgh, K. J., Blaustein, M., Spinazzola, J., & Van der Kolk, B. A. (2006). ARC: Attachment, self-regulation and competency. A comprehensive framework for intervention with complexly traumatized youth. Unpublished manuscript.

Kinniburgh, K.J., Blaustein, M., Spinazzola, J., and Van der Kolk, B.A. (2017). Attachment, Self-Regulation, and Competency: A comprehensive intervention framework for children with complex trauma. *Psychiatric annals* 35 (5): 424–430.

Kirby, D. (2001). *Emerging Answers: Research Findings on Programs to Reduce Teen Pregnancy*. Washington, DC: National Campaign to Prevent Teen Pregnancy.

Kisiel, C., Blaustein, M.E., Fogler, J. et al. (2009a). Treating children with traumatic experiences: understanding and assessing needs & strengths. In: *Behavioral health care: Assessment, service planning, & total clinical outcomes management* (ed. J.S. Lyons and D.A. Weiner), 17.1–17.18. Kingston, NJ: Civic Research Institute.

Kisiel, C., Fehrenbach, T., Small, L. et al. (2009b). Assessment of complex trauma exposure, responses, and service needs among children and adolescents in child welfare. *Journal of Child Adolescent Trauma* 2 (3): 143–160.

Kisiel, C., Lyons, J.S., Blaustein, M. et al. (2010). *Child and adolescent needs and strengths (CANS) manual: The NCTSN CANS Comprehensive–Trauma Version: A Comprehensive Information Integration Tool for Children and Adolescents Exposed to Traumatic Events*. National Center for Child Traumatic Stress.

Kisiel, C., Conradi, L., Fehrenbach, T. et al. (2014). Assessing the effects of trauma in children and adolescents in practice settings. *Journal of Child and Adolescent Psychiatric Clinics of North America* 23: 223–242.

Ko, S.J., Ford, J.D., Kassam-Adams, N. et al. (2008). Creating trauma-informed systems: child welfare, education, first responders, health care, juvenile justice. *Professional Psychology: Research and Practice* 39 (4): 396.

Kolb, B. and Whishaw, I.Q. (2015). *Fundamentals of Human Neuropsychology*, 7e. New York, NY: Worth Publishers.

Kramer, T.L., Sigel, B.A., Conners-Burrow, N.A. et al. (2013). A statewide introduction of trauma-informed care in a child welfare system. *Children and Youth Services Review* 35 (1): 19–24.

Kravitz, D.J., Saleem, K.S., Baker, C.I. et al. (2013). The ventral visual pathway: An expanded neural framework for the processing of object quality. *Trends in Cognitive Neuroscience* 17 (1): 26–49.

Kurtz, P.D., Gaudin, J.M. Jr., Wodarski, J.S., and Howing, P.T. (1993). Maltreatment and the school-aged child: school performance consequences. *Child Abuse Neglect* 17: 581–589.

Laghezza, L., Delvecchio, E., Pazzagli, C., and Mazzeschi, C. (2014). The family assessment measure III (FAM III) in an Italian sample. *BPA-Applied Psychology Bulletin (Bollettino di Psicologia Applicata)* 62: 269.

Lambert, M.J., Burlingame, G.M., Umphress, V. et al. (1996). The reliability and validity of the Outcome Questionnaire. *Clinical Psychology & Psychotherapy: An International Journal of Theory and Practice* 3 (4): 249–258.

Landreth, G. and Bratton, S. (2006). *Child-Parent Relationship Therapy (CPRT): A 10-session filial therapy model*. New York, NY: Bruner-Routledge Publishing.

Langley, A.K., Gonzalez, A., Sugar, C.A. et al. (2015). Bounce back: Effectiveness of an elementary school-based intervention for multicultural children exposed to traumatic events. *Journal of Consulting and Clinical Psychology* 83 (5): 853.

Lanius, R.A., Vermetten, E., and Pain, C. (2010). *The impact of early life trauma on health and disease: The hidden epidemic*. Cambridge University Press.

Lansford, J.E., Dodge, K.A., Pettit, G.S. et al. (2002). A 12-year study of the long term effects of early child maltreatment on psychological, behavioral, and academic problems in adolescence. *Archives of Pediatric Adolescent Medicine* 156 (8): 824–830.

Lapping, K., Marsh, D.R., Rosenbaum, J. et al. (2002). The positive deviance approach: Challenges and opportunities for the future. *Food and Nutrition Bulletin* 23 (4_supp l2): 128–135.

Lasser, K., Boyd, J.W., Woolhandler, S. et al. (2000). Smoking and mental illness: a population-based prevalence study. *JAMA* 284 (20): 2606–2610.

Last, J.M. (ed.) (2001). *Dictionary of Epidemiology*, 4e. New York: Oxford University Press.

Lawson, G. and Myers, J.E. (2011). Wellness, professional quality of life, and career-sustaining Behaviors: What keeps us well? *Journal of Counseling and Development* 89 (2): 163–171.

Lawson, G., Venart, E., Hazier, R.J., and Kottler, J.A. (2007). Toward a culture of counselor wellness. *The Journal of Humanistic Counseling, Education and Development* 46: 5–19.

Layne, C.M., Ippen, C.G., Strand, V. et al. (2011). The Core Curriculum on Childhood Trauma: A tool for training a trauma-informed workforce. Psychological Trauma: Theory, Research. *Practice, and Policy* 3 (3): 243.

Lebel, C., Roussotte, F., and Sowell, E.R. (2011). Imaging the impact of prenatal alcohol exposure on the structure of the developing brain. *Neuropsychology Review* 21: 102–118.

LeBuffe, P.A. and Naglieri, J.A. (2003). *The Devereux Early Childhood Assessment Clinical Form (DECA-C): A Measure of Behaviors Related to Risk and Resilience in Preschool Children*. Lewisville, NC: Kaplan Press.

LeDoux, J. (2003). The emotional brain, fear, and the amygdala. *Cellular and Molecular Neurobiology* 23: 727–738.

Leeb, R.T. (2008). Child maltreatment surveillance: Uniform definitions for public health and recommended data elements. In: *Centers for Disease Control and Prevention*. National: Center for Injury Prevention and Control.

Lees, D.G. and Ronan, K.R. (2008). Engagement and effectiveness of parent management training (Incredible Years) for solo high-risk mothers: A multiple baseline evaluation. *Behaviour Change* 25 (2): 109–128.

Lefkowitz, C., Prout, M., Bleiberg, J., Paharia, I., & Debiak, D. (2005). Animal-assisted prolonged exposure: A treatment for survivors of sexual assault suffering posttraumat stress disorder. *Society & Animals*, 13 (4): 275–296.

Leist, T. and Dadds, M.R. (2009). Adolescents' ability to read different emotional faces relates to their history of maltreatment and type of psychopathology. *Clinical Child Psychology and Psychiatry* 14 (2): 237–250.

Leiter, J. and Johnson, M. (1994). Child maltreatment and school performance. *American Journal of Education* 102: 154–189.

Lenore, C. (1991). Terr, Childhood Traumas: An outline and overview, 148 AM. *Journal of Psychiatry* 10: 11.

Lenta, P. (2012). Corporal punishment of children. *Social Theory and Practice* 38 (4): 689–716.

Lerias, D. and Byre, M.K. (2003). Vicarious traumatization: Symptoms and predictors. *Stress and Health* 19: 129–138.

Levitt, J.M., Saka, N., Romanelli, L.H., and Hoagwood, K. (2007). Early identification of mental health problems in schools: The status of instrumentation. *Journal of School Psychology.* 45 (2): 163–191.

Lewis-Morrarty, E., Dozier, M., Bernard, K. et al. (2012). Cognitive flexibility and theory of mind outcomes among foster children: Preschool follow-up results of a randomized clinical trial. *Journal of Adolescent Health* 51 (2): S17–S22.

Lieberman, A.F., Van Horn, P., and Ippen, C.G. (2005a). Toward evidence-based treatment: Child-parent psychotherapy with preschoolers exposed to marital violence. *Journal of the American Academy of Child & Adolescent Psychiatry* 44 (12): 1241–1248.

Lieberman, V.H., Van Horn, P., and Ippen, G.C. (2005c). Toward evidence-based treatment: child–parent psychotherapy with preschoolers exposed to marital violence. *Journal of American Academy of Child Adolescence Psychiatry* 44 (81): 12.

Lieberman, A.F., Ghosh Ippen, C., and Van Horn, P. (2006). Child-Parent Psychotherapy: 6-month follow-up of a randomized controlled trial. *Journal of the American Academy of Child and Adolescent Psychiatry* 45 (8): 913–918.

Lightfoot, C., Cole, M., and Cole, S.R. (2013). *The Development of Children*, 7e. New York, NY: Worth Publishers.

Lind, T., Bernard, K., Ross, E., and Dozier, M. (2014). Intervention effects on negative affect of CPS-referred children: Results of a randomized clinical trial. *Child Abuse and Neglect* 38: 1459–1467.

Linehan, M. (1993). *Cognitive–behavioral Treatment of Borderline per - sonality Disorder*. New York: The Guilford Press.

Lochman, J.E. and Dodge, K.A. (1994). Social cognitive processes of severely violent, moderately aggressive and non aggressive boys. *Journal of Consulting and Clinical Psychology* 62: 366–374.

Lochman, J.E. and Wells, K.C. (2002). Contextual social-cognitive mediators and child outcome: A test of the theoretical model in the coping power program. *Development and Psychopathology* 14: 945–967.

Lochman, J.E. and Wells, K.C. (2004). The coping power program for preadolescent aggressive boys and their parents: outcome effects at the 1-year follow-up. *Journal of Consulting and Clinical Psychology* 72 (4): 571.

Lochman, J.E., Wells, K.C., and Murray, M. (2007). The coping power program: Preventive intervention at the middle school transition. In: *Preventing youth substance abuse: Science-based programs for children and adolescents* (ed. P. Tolan, J. Szapocznik and S. Sambrano), 185–210. Washington, DC: American Psychological Association.

Lochman, J.E., Wells, K.C., and Lenhart, L.A. (2008). *Coping power child group program: Facilitator guide*. New York, NY: Oxford.

Loeber, R. (1990). Development and risk factors of juvenile antisocial behavior and delinquency. *Clinical Psychology Review* 10: 1–42.

Logan-Greene, P., Green, S., Nurius, P.S., and Longhi, D. (2014). Distinct contributions of adverse childhood experiences and resilience resources: a cohort analysis of adult physical and mental health. *Social Work in Health Care* 53 (8): 776–797.

Lorion, R.P. and Saltzman, W. (1993). Children's exposure to community violence: Following a path from concern to research to action. *Psychiatry* 56 (1): 55–65.

Loundeback, J. (2016). Compton trauma lawsuit near resolution? Chronicle of Social Change. http://laschoolreport.com/compton-trauma-lawsuit-near-resolution.

Lupien, S.J. and BS, M.E. (1997). The acute effects of corticosteroids on cognition: Integration of animal and human model studies. *Brain Res Rev* 24: 1–27.

Lupien, S.J., Gaudreau, S., Tchiteya, B.M. et al. (1997). Stress-induced declarative memory impairments in healthy elderly subjects: Relationship with cortisol reactivity. *The Journal of Clinical Endocrinology and Metabolism* 82: 2070–2075.

Lupien, S.J., DeLeon, M., DeSanti, S. et al. (1998). Longitudinal increase in cortisol during human aging predicts hippocampal atrophy and memory deficits. *Nat Neurosci* 1: 69–73.

Lupien, S.J., Gillin, C., and Hauger, R.L. (1999). Working memory is more sensitive than declarative memory to the acute effects of corticosteroids: A dose-response study. *Behavioral Neuroscience* 113: 420–430.

Lupien, S.J., Maheu, F., Tu, M. et al. (2007). The effect of stress and stress hormones on human cognition: Implications for the field of brain and cognition. *Brain and Cognition* 65: 209–237.

Lupien, S.J., McEwen, B.S., Gunnar, M.R., and Heim, C. (2009). Effects of stress throughout the lifespan on the brain, behavior, and cognition. *Nature Reviews: Neuroscience* 10 (6): 434–445.

Lyons, J.S., Griffin, E., Fazio, M., and Lyons, M.B. (1999). *Child and Adolescent Needs and Strengths: An Information Integration Tool for Children and Adolescents with Mental Health Challenges (CANS-MH), Manual*. Chicago, IL: Buddin Praed Foundation, 558 Willow Rd., Winnetka, IL 60093.

Lyons-Ruth, K. and Jacobovitz, D. (1999). Attachment dis- organization: unresolved loss, relational violence, and lapses in behavioral and attentional strategies. In: *Handbook of Attachment: Theory, Research, and Clinical Application* (ed. J. Cassidy and P.R. Shaver), 520–554. New York, NY: The Guilford Press.

Lyons-Ruth, K., Zeanah, C.H., and Gleason, M.M. (2015). Commentary: Should we move away from an attachment framework for understanding disinhibited social engagement disorder (DSED)? A commentary on Zeanah and Gleason (2015). *Journal of Child Psychology and Psychiatry* 56 (3): 223–227.

MacKenzie, M.J., Nicklas, E., Waldfogel, J., and Brooks-Gunn, J. (2012). Corporal punishment and child behavioral and cognitive outcomes through 5 years-of-age: Evidence from a contemporary urban birth cohort study. *Infant Child Development* 21 (1): 3–33.

Maggio, V., Granana, N.E., Richaudeau, A. et al. (2014). Behavior problems in children with specific language impairment. *Journal of Neurology* 29 (2): 194–202.

Mahady Wilton, M.M., Craig, W.M., and Pepler, D.J. (2000). Emotional regulation and display in classroom victims of bullying: Characteristic expressions of affect, coping styles and relevant contextual factors. *Social Development* 9 (2): 226–245.

Maher, C.A. (2012). *Planning and Evaluating Human Services Programs: A Resource Guide for Practitioners*. AuthorHouse.

Mannarino, A.P., Cohen, J.A., and Berman, S.R. (1994). The Children's Attributions and Perceptions Scale: A new measure of sexual abuse-related factors. *Journal of Clinical Child Psychology* 23 (2): 204–211.

Marien, P., Ackermann, H., Adamaszek, M. et al. (2014). Consensus paper: Language and the cerebellum: An ongoing dilemma. *Cerebellum* 13: 386–410.

Markou, A., Kosten, T.R., and Koob, G.F. (1998). Neurobiological similarities in depression and drug dependence: a self-medication hypothesis. *Neuropsychopharmacology* 18 (3): 135–174.

Marrow, M., Knudsen, K., Olafson, E., and Bucher, S. (2012). The value of implementing TARGET within a trauma-informed juvenile justice setting. *Journal of Child and Adolescent Trauma* 5: 257–270.

Marsac, M.L. and Alderfer, M.A. (2010). Psychometric properties of the FACES-IV in a pediatric oncology population. *Journal of Pediatric Psychology* 36 (5): 528–538.

Marsh, D.R. and Schroeder, D.G. (2002). The positive deviance approach to improve health outcomes: experience and evidence from the field – Preface. *Food and Nutrition Bulletin* 23 (4_supp l2): 3–6.

Marsh, D.R., Schroeder, D.G., Dearden, K.A. et al. (2004). The power of positive deviance. *BMJ: British Medical Journal* 329 (7475): 1177.

Marsh, A.A., Finger, E.C., Mitchell, D. et al. (2008). Reduced amygdala response to fearful expressions in children and adults with callous-unemotional traits and disruptive behavior disorders. *American Journal of Psychiatry* 165 (6): 712–720.

Marx, B.P. and Sloan, D.M. (2002). The role of emotion in the psychological functioning of adult survivors of childhood sexual abuse. *Behavior Therapy* 33: 563–577.

Mash, E.J. and Barkley, R.A. (eds.) (2009). *Assessment of Childhood Disorders*. Guilford Press.

Masic, I., Miokovic, M., and Muhamedagic, B. (2008). Evidence based medicine–new approaches and challenges. *Acta Informatica Medica* 16 (4): 219.

Maslach, C. (1982). *The burnout syndrome. Burnout – the cost of caring*. New York, NY: Prentice-Hall.

Maslach, C. (1982). *Burnout: The Cost Of Caring*. Englewood Cliffs, NJ: Prentice Hall.

Maslach, C. and Jackson, S.E. (1981). The measurement of experienced burnout. *Journal of Occupational Behavior* 2 (2): 99–113.

Maslach, C., Schaufeli, W.B., and Leiter, M.P. (2001). Job burnout. *Annual Review of Psychology* 52: 397–422.

Mass Legal Services. (2007). The Legislative Process in Massachusetts. Retrieved on September 4, 2017 from https://www.masslegalservices.org/content/legislative-process-massachusetts-0.

Massachusetts Department of Criminal Justice Information System. (2014) Changes to Laws Concerning Firearms Licensing and Gun Sales in Massachusetts. Retrieved on September 2, 2017 from http://www.mass.gov/eopss/agencies/dcjis/key-changes-to-the-massachusetts-gun-laws-august-2014.html.

Masten, A.S. (2001). Ordinary magic: Resilience processes in development. *American psychologist* 56 (3): 227.

Masten, A. and Coatsworth, J.D. (1998). The development of competence in favorable and unfavorable environments: Lessons from research in successful children. *American Psychologist* 53: 205–220.

Mayes, S.D., Calhoun, S.L., and Crowell, E.W. (2000). Learning disabilities and adhd: overlapping spectrum disorders. *Journal of Learning Disabilities* 33 (5): 417–424.

McAdams, D.P. (1996). Personality, modernity, and the storied self: A contemporary framework for studying persons. *Psychological Inquiry* 7: 295–321.

McCann, I.L. and Pearlman, L.A. (1990). Vicarious traumatization: A contextual model for understanding the effects of trauma on helpers. *Journal of Traumatic Stress* 3 (1): 131–149.

McCann, I.L. and Pearlman, L.A. (1990). Vicarious traumatization: A framework for understanding the psychological effects of working with victims. *Journal of Traumatic Stress* 3 (1): 131–149.

McCloskey, G. and Wasserman, J. (2012). *Essentials of executive function assessment.* NJ: Wiley.

McCrory, E., De Brito, S.A., and Viding (2010). Research review: The neurobiology and genetics of maltreatment and adversity. *Journal of Child Psychology and Psychiatry* 51 (10): 1079–1095.

McCusker, J., Cole, M.G., Yaffe, M. et al. (2015). A randomized trial of a depression self-care toolkit with or without lay telephone coaching for primary care patients with chronic physical conditions. *General Hospital Psychiatry* 37 (3): 257–265:https://doi.org/10.1016/j.genhosppsych.2015.03.007.

McEwen, B.S. (1998). Protective and damaging effects of stress mediators. *The New England Journal of Medicine* 238: 171–179.

McEwen, B.S. (2000). The neurobiology of stress: From serendipity to clinical relevance. *Brain Research* 886: 172–189.

McEwen, B.S. (2002). *The end of stress as we know it.* Washington, DC: John Henry Press.

McEwen, B.S. (2004). Protection and damage from acute and chronic stress: allostasis and allostatic overload and relevance to the pathophysiology of psychiatric disorders. *Annals of the New York Academy of Sciences* 1032 (1): 1–7.

McEwen, B.S. and Sapolsky, R.M. (1995). Stress and cognitive function. *Current Opinion in Neurobiology* 5 (2): 205–216.

McGee, C. (2000). *Childhood experiences of domestic violence.* London: Jessica Kingsley Publishers.

McGovern, L., Miller, G., and Hughes-Cromwick, P. (2014). *Health Policy Brief: The Relative Contribution of Multiple Determinants to Health Outcomes.* Health Affairs.

McLean, L.M., Toner, B., Jackson, J. et al. (2006). The relationship between childhood sexual abuse, complex post-traumatic stress disorder and alexithymia in two outpatient samples: Examination of women treated in community and institutional clinics. *Journal of Child Sexual Abuse* 15: 1–17.

McMullen, J., O'Callaghan, P., Shannon, C. et al. (2013). Group trauma-focused cognitive-behavioural therapy with former child soldiers and other war-affected boys in the DR Congo: A randomised controlled trial. *Journal of Child Psychology and Psychiatry* 54 (11): 1231–1241:https://doi.org/10.1111/jcpp.12094.

McNeil, C.B., Eyberg, S., Hembree Eisenstadt, T. et al. (1991). Parent-child interaction therapy with behavior problem children: Generalization of treatment effects to the school setting. *Journal of Clinical Child and Adolescent Psychology* 20 (2): 140–151.

Meany, M. (2010). Epigenetics and the biological definition of gene x environment interactions. *Child Development* 81 (1): 41–97.

Meldrum, L., King, R., and Spooner, D. (2002). Compassion fatigue in community mental health case managers. In: *Treating Compassion Fatigue* (ed. C.R. Figley). New York, NY: Brunner/Rutledge.

Merrick, M. (2017). *Preventing Early Adversity through Policies, Norms and Programs.* National Center for Injury Prevention and Control. Mobilizing Action for Resilient Communities, Brown Bag Lunch Series.

Mersky, J.P., Topitzes, J., and Reynolds, A.J. (2013). Impacts of adverse childhood experiences on health, mental health, and substance use in early adulthood: A cohort study of an urban, minority sample in the US. *Child Abuse and Neglect* 37 (11): 917–925.

Mezzacappa, E., Kindlon, D., and Earls, F. (2001). Child abuse and performance task assess- ments of executive functions in boys. *Journal of Child Psychology and Psychiatry* 42: 1041–1048.

Mezzich, A.C., Tarter, R.E., Giancola, P.R. et al. (1997). Substance use and risky sexual behaviors in female adolescents. *Drug Alcohol Depend* 44: 157–166.

Milich, R. and Dodge, K.A. (1984). Social information processing in child psychiatric populations. *Journal of Abnormal Child Psychology* 12: 471–490.

Miller, B.L. (2007). The human frontal lobes: An introduction. In: *The human frontal lobes*, 2e (ed. B.L. Miller and J.L. Cummings), 3–11. New York, NY: The Guilford Press.

Miller, D.C. (2013). *Essentials of school neuropsychological assessment*, 2e. NJ: Wiley.

Miller, W.R. and Rollnick, S. (2012). *Motivational interviewing: Helping people change*. Guilford Press.

Mizoguchi, K., Yuzurihara, M., Ishige, A. et al. (2000). Chronic stress induces impairment of spatial working memory because of prefrontal dopaminergic dysfunction. *Journal of Neuroscience* 20 (4): 1568–1574.

Moodi, S., Daneri, P., Goldhagen, S., Halle, T., Green, K., & LaMonte, L. (2014). Early Childhood Developmental Screening: Compendium of Measures for Children Ages Birth to Five. (OPRE Report 201411) Washington, DC: Office of Planning, Research and Evaluation, Administration for Children and Families, U.S. Department of Health and Human Services.

Moos, R.H. (1990). *Coping Responses Inventory-Youth Form. Center for Health Care Evaluation*. Stanford University.

Moos, R.H. and Moos, B.S. (1994). *Family Environment Scale Manual*. Consulting Psychologists Press.

Morrill, A.C., McElaney, L., Peixotto, B. et al. (2015). Evaluation of all babies cry, a second generation universal abusive head trauma prevention program. *Journal of community psychology* 43 (3): 296–314.

Morrow, G. (1987). *The compassionate school: A practical guide to educating abused and traumatized children*. Prentice Hall.

Moskal, B.M. and Leydens, J.A. (2000). Scoring rubric development: Validity and reliability. *Practical Assessment, Research and Evaluation* 7 (10). [Available online: http://pareonline.net/getvn.asp?v=7&n=10.

da Motta, C.D.A., Rijo, D., Vagos, P., and Sousa, B. (2016). The Abbreviated Dysregulation Inventory: Dimensionality and Psychometric Properties in Portuguese Adolescents. *Journal of Child and Family Studies* 1–10.

Moylan, C.A., Herrenkohl, T.I., Sousa, C. et al. (2010). The effects of child abuse and exposure to domestic violence on adolescent internalizing and externalizing behavior problems. *Journal of Family Violence* 25 (1): 53–63.

Mullender, A., Hague, G., Iman, U. et al. (2002). *Children's perspectives on domestic violence*. London: Sage.

Murgatroyd, C. and Spengler, D. (2011). Epigenetics of early child development. *Frontiers in Psychiatry* 2: https://doi.org/10.3389/fpsyt.2011.00016.

Muris, P., Meesters, C., van Melick, M., and Zwambag, L. (2001). Selfreported attachment style, attachment quality, and symptoms of anxiety and depression in young adolescents. *Personality and Individual Differences* 30: 809–818.

Murphy, J.J. (2015). *Solution-focused counseling in schools*. John Wiley & Sons.

Murphy, L.B. and Moriarty, A.E. (1976). *Vulnerability, Coping, and Growth: From Infancy to Adolescence*. New Haven, CT: Yale University Press.

Murray, L.K., Familiar, I., Skavenski, S. et al. (2013). An evaluation of trauma focused cognitive behavioral therapy for children in Zambia. *Child Abuse and Neglect* 37 (12): 1175–1185.

Murray, L.K., Skavenski, S., Kane, J.C. et al. (2015). Effectiveness of trauma-focused cognitive behavioral therapy among trauma-affected children in Lusaka, Zambia: A randomized clinical trial. *Journal of American Medical Association Pediatrics* 169 (8): 761–769:https://doi.org/10.1001/jamapediatrics.2015.0580.

Myers, D., & Wee, D. F. (2002). Strategies for managing disaster mental health worker stress.

Nader, K. (2003). *Walking among us: Culture and trauma. The Child Survivor of Traumatic Stress*, vol. 4, 1–8. [Available on line at www.ummed.edu/k/kfletche/kidsurv.html].

Nader, K. (2007a). Culture and the assessment of trauma in youths. In: *Cross-cultural assessment of psychological trauma and PTSD* (ed. J.P. Wilson and C. Tang), 169–196. New York, NY: Springer Science Business Media.

Nader, K. (2007b). Assessment of the child following crisis: The Challenge of Differential Diagnosis. In: *Play Therapy with Children in Crisis: Individual, group, and family treatment*, 3e (ed. N.B. Webb), 21–44. New York: Guilford.

Nader, K. (2008). *Understanding and Assessing trauma in children and adolescents: Measures, Methods, and Youth in Context*. New York: Routledge.

Nader, K., Kriegler, J.A., Blake, D.D. et al. (1996). *Clinician Administered PTSD Scale, Child and Adolescent Version*. White River Junction, VT: National Center for PTSD.

Nader, K., Dubrow, N., and Stamm, B. (eds.) (1999). *Honoring differences: Cultural Issues in the Treatment of Trauma and Loss*. Philadelphia: Taylor & Francis.

Najavits, L.M. (2002). *Seeking Safety: A treatment manual for PTSD and substance abuse*. New York, NY: Guilford.

Najavits, L.M. (2007). Seeking Safety: an evidence-based model for substance abuse and trauma/PTSD. In: *Therapist's guide to evidence-based relapse prevention: Practical resources for the mental health professional* (ed. K.A. Witkiewitz and G.A. Marlatt), 141–167. San Diego, CA: Elsevier Press.

Najavits, L.M. (2009). Seeking safety: An implementation guide. In: *Substance Abuse Treatment for Youth and Adults: Clinician's Guide to Evidence-Based Practice* (ed. A. Rubin and D.W. Springer), 311–348. Hoboken, NJ: Wiley.

Najavits, L.M., Gallop, R.J., and Weiss, R.D. (2006). Seeking safety therapy for adolescent girls with PTSD and substance use disorder: A randomized controlled trial. *The Journal of Behavioral Health Services and Research* 33: 453–463.

Nakazawa, D.J. (2015). *Childhood disrupted: How your biography becomes your biology, and how you can heal*. Simon and Schuster.

Naste, T.M., Price, M., Karol, J., Martin, L., Murphy, K., Miguel, J., & Spinazzola, J. (2017). Equine Facilitated Therapy for Complex Trauma (EFT-CT). *Journal of Child & Adolescent Trauma*, 1–15.

National Association of School Psychologists (NASP) (n.d.) https://www.nasponline.org/research-and-policy/public-policy-institute-(ppi)

National Association of Social Workers (2013). NASW standards for social work practice in child welfare. Retrieved from http://www.socialworkers.org/practice/standards/index.asp.

National Child Traumatic Stress Network (2016) Defining trauma and child traumatic stress. Retrieved from http://www.nctsn.org/content/defining-trauma-and-child-traumatic-stress

National Child Traumatic Stress Network Empirically Supported Treatments and Promising Practices, (n.d.) https://www.nctsn.org/treatments-and-practices/treatments-that-work

National Human Genome Research Institute Fact Sheet: Epigenomics, 2016.

National Institute of Health/U.S. National Library of Medicine (2017). *The Immune Response*. Bethesda, MD: MedlinePlus Retrieved from http://medlineplus.gov/ency/article/00821.

National Scientific Council on the Developing Child. (2004). Young children develop in an environment of relationships. Working Paper No. 1. Retrieved from www.developingchild.net. © 2004, National Scientific Council on the Developing Child, Center on the Developing Child at Harvard University.

National Scientific Council on the Developing Child (2005/2014). Excessive Stress Disrupts the Architecture of the Developing Brain: Working Paper No. 3. Updated Edition, http://developingchild.harvard.edu

National Scientific Council on the Developing Child (2006). Early Exposure to Toxic Substances Damages Brain Architecture: Working Paper # 4.

National Scientific Council on the Developing Child (2007). The Timing and Quality of Early Experiences Combine to Shape Brain Architecture: Working Paper # 5.

National Scientific Council on the Developing Child (2010). Early Experiences Can Alter Gene Expression and Affect Long-Term Development: Working Paper No. 10. Retrieved from http://www.developingchild.harvard.edu

National Scientific Council on the Developing Child. (2012). The Science of Neglect: The Persistent Absence of Responsive Care Disrupts the Developing Brain: Working Paper 12.

NCTSN Position Statement: Prerequisite Clinical Competencies for Implementing Effective, Trauma-informed Intervention. 2015.

Newell, J.M. and MacNeil, G.A. (2010). Professional burnout, vicarious trauma, secondary traumatic stress, and compassion fatigue. *Best Practices in Mental Health* 6 (2): 57–68.

Newman, E., Weathers, F.W., Nader, K. et al. (2004). *Clinician-Administered PTSD Scale for Children and Adolescents (CAPS-CA)*. Los Angeles: Western Psychological Services.

Ngo, V., Langley, A., Kataoka, S.H. et al. (2008). Providingevidence-based practice to ethnically diverse youths: Examples from the cognitive behavioral intervention for trauma in schools (CBITS) program. *Journal of the American Academy of Child and Adolescent Psychiatry* 47 (8): 858–862.

Noggle, C.A., Horowitz, J.L., and Davis, A.S. (2011). Neuroimaging and pediatric neuropsychology: Implications for clinical practice. In: *Handbook of Pediatric Neuropsychology* (ed. A. Davis), 1065–1076.

Norcross, J.C. and Guy, J.D. (2007). *Leaving it at the office: A Guide to Psychotherapist Self-care*. New York, NY: The Guildford Press.

Norman, R.E., Byambaa, M., De, R. et al. (2012). The long-term health consequences of child physical abuse, emotional abuse, and neglect: a systematic review and meta-analysis. *PLoS medicine* 9 (11): e1001349.

Novaco, R.W. (1978). Anger and coping with stress: Cognitive behavioral interventions. In: *Cognitive behavioral therapy: Research and application* (ed. J.P. Foreyet and D.P. Rathjen). New York, NY: Plenum Press.

Nurmi, J.E. (1989). Development of orientation to the future during early adolescence: a four-year longitudinal study and two cross-sectional comparisons. *International Journal of Psychology* 24 (1-5): 195–214.

O'Connor, T.G., Moynihan, J.A., and Caserta, M.T. (2014). Annual research review: The neuroinflammation hypothesis for stress and psychopathology in children-developmental psychoneuroimmunology. *Journal of Child Psychology and Psychiatry* 55 (6): 615–631.

O'Callaghan, P., McMullen, J., Shannon, C. et al. (2013). A randomized controlled trial of trauma focused cognitive therapy for sexually exploited, war-affected Congolese girls. *Journal of American Academy of Child and Adolescent Psychiatry* 52 (4): 539–569.

Office of the Surgeon General (2016). *Facing Addiction in America: The Surgeon General's Report on Alcohol, Drugs, and Health*. Washington, DC: US Department of Health & Human Services.

Ogar, J. and Gorno-Tempini, M.L. (2007). The orbitofrontal cortex and the insula. In: *The human frontal lobes*, 2e (ed. B.L. Miller and J.L. Cummings), 59–67.

Ohan, J.L., Myers, K., and Collett, B.R. (2002). Ten-year review of rating scales. IV: Scales assessing trauma and its effects. *Journal of the American Academy of Child & Adolescent Psychiatry* 41 (12): 1401–1422.

Ohmi, H., Kojima, S., Awai, Y. et al. (2002). Post-traumatic stress disorder in pre-school aged children after a gas explosion. *European Journal of Pediatrics* 161 (12): 643–648.

Olij, J. (2005). Trauma awareness, healing, and group counseling in secondary schools. *Intervention* 3 (1): 51–57.

Olson, D., Portner, J., and Lavee, Y. (1985). *Family Adaptability and Cohesion Evaluation Scale (FACES III)*. St Paul, MN: University of Minnesota.

Olson, D.H., Gorall, D.M., and Tiesel, J.W. (2006). *FACES-IV Package: Administration*. Minneapolis, MN: Life Innovations, Inc.

Oregon State University, Family Policy Program, 1997, https://health.oregonstate.edu/sites/health.oregonstate.edu/files/sbhs/pdf/BR2Ch5.pdf

Osofsky, J.D. (1999). The impact of violence on children. *The Future of Children* 9 (3): 33–34.

Osofsky, J.D. (2003). Prevalence of children's exposure to domestic violence and child maltreatment: Implications for prevention and intervention. *Clinical Child and Family Psychology Review* 6 (3): 161–170.

Osofsky, J.D., Stepka, P.T., and King, L.S. (2017). *Treating infants and young children impacted by trauma: Interventions that promote healthy development*. American Psychological Association.

Overstreet, S. and Chafouleas, S.M. (2016). Trauma-informed schools: Introduction to the special issue. *School Mental Health* 8 (1): 1–6.

Palta, R. (2015) KPCC: The Voice of Southern California. Compton school district lawsuit equating trauma with disabilities proceeds, http://www.scpr.orgnews/2015/09/30/54748/compton-school-district-lawsuit-equating-trauma-wi/

Park, S., Kim, B.-N., Choi, N.-H. et al. (2014). The effect of persistent posttraumatic stress disorder symptoms on executive functions in preadolescent children witnessing a single accident of death. *Anxiety, Stress & Coping: An International Journal* 27: 241–252.

Parker, J.G., Rubin, K.H., Price, J.M., and DeRosier, M.E. (1995). Peer relationships, child development, and adjustment: A developmental psy- chopathology perspective. In: *Developmental Psychopathology*, vol. 2. Risk, disorder, and adaptation (ed. D. Cicchetti and D.J. Cohen), 96–161. New York: Wiley.

Pearlin, I.L. (1999). The stress process revisited: Reflections on concepts and their interrelationships. In: *Sociology of Mental Health* (ed. C.S. Aneshensel and J.C. Phelan), 395–415. New York, NY: Kluwer Academic/Plenum.

Pearlman, L.A. and Saakvitne, K.W. (1995a). Treating therapists with vicarious traumatization and secondary traumatic stress disorders. In: *Compassion fatigue: Coping with secondary traumatic stress disorder in those who treat the traumatized*, vol. 23 (ed. C.R. Figley), 150–177. Philadelphia, PA: Brunner/Mazel.

Pearlman, L.A. and Saakvitne, K.W. (1995b). *Trauma and the therapist: Countertransference and vicarious Traumatization in Psychotherapy with incest Survivors*. New York: W.W. Norton.

Pears, K. and Fisher, P.A. (2005). Develpmental, cognitive, and neuropsychological functioning in preschool aged foster children: Associations with prior maltreatment and placement history. *Journal of Developmental and Behavioral Pediatrics* 26: 112–122.

Pechtel, P. and Pizzagalli, D.A. (2011). Effects of early life stress on cognitive and affective function: An integrated review of human literature. *Psychopharmacology* 214 (1): 55–70.

Pelcovitz, D., van der Kolk, B.D., Roth, S. et al. (1997). Development of a criteria set and a structured interview for disorders of extreme stress (SIDES). *Journal of Traumatic Stress* 10: 3–16.

Penke, I., Munoz-Maniega, S., Murray, C. et al. (2010). A general factor of brain white matter integrity predicts information processing speed in healthy older people. *Journal of Neuroscience* 30: 7569–7574.

Pennebaker, J.W. (2000). The effects of traumatic disclosure on physical and mental health: The values of writing and talking about upsetting events. In J.M. Violanti, D. Paton and C. Dunning (Eds.), *Posttraumatic stress intervention: Challenges, issues, and perspectives* (97–114). IL: Springfield, Charles C Thomas Publisher.

Pennebaker, J.W. and Francis, M.E. (1996). Cognitive, emotional, and language processes in disclosure: Physical health and adjustment. *Cognition and Emotion* 10: 601–626.

Perfect, M.M., Turley, M.R., Carlson, J.S. et al. (2016). School related outcomes of traumatic exposure and traumatic stress symptoms in students: A systematic review of the literature. *School Mental Health* 8: 7–43. http://dx.doi.org/10.1007/s12310-016-9175-2.

Perry, B.D. and Pollard, R. (1998). Homeostasis, stress, trauma, and adaptation: A neurodevelopmental view of childhood trauma. *Child and adolescent psychiatric clinics of North America* 7 (1): 33–51.

Perry, B.D., Pollard, R.A., Blaicley, T.L. et al. (1995). Childhood trauma, the neurobiology of adaptation, and "use-dependent" development of the brain: How "states" become "traits". *Infant Mental Health Journal* 16 (4): 271–291.

Peter P., et al.. Compton Unified School District 2015.

Phillips, J.R., Hewedi, D.H., Eissa, A.M., and Moustafa, A.A. (2015). The cerebellum and psychiatric disorders. *Frontiers in Public Health* 3: 66:https://doi.org/10.3389/fpubh.2015.00066.

Piers, E. V., & Harris, D. B. (1969). Children's self-concept scale. Nashville, Tenn.: Counselor Recordings and Tests.

Piers, E. V., Herzberg, D. S., & Harris, D. B. (2002). Piers-Harris Children's Self-concept Scale:(PHCSCS). Western Psychological Services.

Pines, A. and Aronson, E. (1988). *Career burnout: Causes and Cures*. New York, NY: The Free Press.

Pires, S.A. (2002). *Building systems of care: A primer*. National Technical Assistance Center for Children's Mental Health, Georgetown University Child Development Center.

Pokorny, S.B., Jason, L.A., Schoeny, M.E. et al. (2001). Do participation rates change when active consent procedures replace passive consent. *Evaluation Review* 25 (5): 567–580.

Pollack, S.D., Cicchetti, D., Klorman, R., and Brumaghim, J.T. (1997). Cognitive brain eventrelated potentials and emotion processing in maltreated children. *Child Development* 68: 773–787.

Pollack, S.D., Cicchetti, D., Hornung, K., and Reed, A. (2000). Recognizing emotion in faces: Developmental effects of child abuse and neglect. *Developmental Psychology* 36: 679–688.

Pollack, S.D., Klorman, R., Thatcher, J.E., and Cicchetti, D. (2001). P3b reflects maltreated children's reactions to facial displays of emotion. *Psychophysiology* 38: 267–274.

Pollio, E. and Deblinger, E. (2017). Trauma-focused cognitive behavioural therapy for young children: clinical considerations. *European journal of psychotraumatology* 8 (sup7): 1433929.

Porche, M.V., Costello, D.M., and Rosen-Reynoso (2016). Adverse family experiences, child mental health and educational outcomes for a national sample of students. *School Mental Health* 8: 44–60: https://doi.org/10.1007/s12310-016-9174-3.

Praver, F., DiGiuseppe, R., Pelcovitz, D. et al. (2000). A preliminary study of a cartoon measure for children's reactions to chronic trauma. *Child Maltreatment* 5 (3): 273–285.

Prewitt, E. (2016). New elementary and secondary education law includes specific "trauma-informed practices" provisions. Retrieved from: http://www.acesconnection.com/g/aces-in-education/blog/new-elementary-and-secondary-education-law-includes-specific-trauma-informed-practices-provisions.

Public Counsel Opportunity Under Law, University of California-Irvine Law School https://www.newark.rutgers.edu/news/rutgers-center-law-inequality-and-metropolitan-equity-clime-sponsors-may-5-conference-trauma

Purves, D., Augustine, G.J., Fitzpatrick, D. et al. (eds.) (2008). *Neuroscience*, 4e. MA: Sinauer Associates.

Putnam, F. (1990). *Child Dissociative Checklist (v3. 0)*. Washington DC: NIMH.

Putnam, F.W. (1997). *Dissociation in Children and Adolescents: A Developmental Perspective.* New York, NY: The Guilford Press.

Pynoos, R.S., Rodriguez, N., Steinberg, A.S. et al. (1998). *The UCLA PTSD reaction index for DSM IV (Revision 1)*. Los Angeles: UCLA Trauma Psychiatry Program.

Ramirez, M., Paik, A., Sanchagrin, K., and Heimer, K. (2012). Violent peers, network centrality, and intimate partner violence perpetration by young men. *Journal of Adolescent Health* 51 (5): 503–509.

Range, L.M., Embry, T., and MacLeod, T. (2001). Active and passive consent: a comparison of actual research with children. *Ethical Human Sciences and Services* 3 (1): 23–31.

Reich, W. (2000). Diagnostic interview for children and adolescents (DICA). *Journal of the American Academy of Child & Adolescent Psychiatry* 39 (1): 59–66.

Reid, M.J. and Webster-Stratton, C. (2001). The Incredible Years parent, teacher, and child intervention: Targeting multiple areas of risk for a young child with pervasive conduct problems using a flexible, manualized, treatment program. *Journal of Cognitive and Behavior Practice* 8: 377–386.

Reyes, C.J. (2008). Exploring the relations among the nature of the abuse, perceived parental support, and child's self-concept and trauma symptoms among sexually abused children. *Journal of Child Sexual Abuse* 17 (1): 51–70.

Reyes, J.A. and Elias, M.J. (2011). Fostering social–emotional resilience among Latino youth. *Psychology in the Schools* 48 (7): 723–737.

Ribbe, D. (1996). Psychometric review of traumatic events screening inventory for children (TESI-C). In: *Measurement of stress, trauma, and adaptation* (ed. B.H. Stamm), 386–387.

Richardson, M., Kagan, R., Henry, J. et al. (2011). *HEROES Project Three Month Evaluation Report*. Albany, NY: Parsons Child and Family Center.

Richardson, M., Kagan, R., Henry, J. et al. (2012). *HEROES Project Six Month Data Analysis*. Albany, NY: Parsons Child and Family Center.

Richters, J.E. and Martinez, P. (1993). The NIMH community violence project: I. Children as victims of and witnesses to violence. *Psychiatry* 56 (1): 7–21.

Richters, J. E., & Saltzman, W. (1990). Survey of exposure to community violence: Self-report version. JE Richters.

Ridgard, T., Laracy, S., DuPaul, G. et al. (2015). *Trauma-Informed Care in Schools: A Social Justice Imperative*. NASP.

Ridgard, T.J., Laracu, S.D., Dupaul, G.J. et al. (2015). Trauma-Informed Care in Schools: A Social Justice Imperative.(cover story). *Communique* (0164775X) 44 (2): 1–15.

Rivard, J.C., Bloom, S.L., McCorkle, D., and Abramovitz, R. (2005). Preliminary results of a study examining the implementation and effects of a trauma recovery framework for youths in residential treatment. *Therapeutic Community: The International Journal for Therapeutic and Supportive Organizations* 26 (1): 83–96.

Roberds, E.L. and Davis, A.S. (2011). Reactive attachment disorder. In: *Encyclopedia of Child Behavior and Development*, 1217–1219. Springer US.

Roberts, M.W. and Powers, S.W. (1990). Adjusting chair timeout enforcement procedures for oppositional children. *Behavioral Therapy* 21: 257–271.

Robson, D. (2010). *The five pillars of happiness: Your new life step by step*. Wizard Publishing.

Rodriguez, N., Steinberg, A., and Pynoos, R.S. (1999). *UCLA PTSD index for DSM IV Instrument Information: Child version, Parent Version, Adolescent Version*. Los Angeles, CA: UCLA Trauma Psychiatry Services.

Rodríguez-Sierra, O.E., Goswami, S., Turesson, H.K., and Pare, D. (2016). Altered responsiveness of BNST and amygdala neurons in trauma-induced anxiety. *Translational psychiatry* 6 (7): e857.

Rollnick, S. and Miller, W.R. (1995). What is motivational interviewing? *Behavioural and Cognitive Psychotherapy* 23 (4): 325–334.

Rollnick, S., Miller, W.R., Butler, C.C., and Aloia, M.S. (2008). Motivational interviewing in health care: helping patients change behavior. *Journal of Chromic Obstructive Pulmonary Disease* 5 (3): 203.

Rosenblat, J.D. and McIntyre, R.S. (2016). Bipolar disorder and inflammation. *Psychiatric Clinics of North America* 39: 125–137. https://doi.org/10.1016/j.psc.2015.09.006.

Rosenblat, J.D., Cha, D.S., Mansur, R.B. et al. (2014). Inflamed moods: A review of the interactions between inflammation and mood disorders. *Progress in Neuro-Psychopharmacology & Biological Psychiatry* 53: 23–34.

Rossen, E. and Cowan, K. (2013). The role of schools in supporting traumatized students. *Principal's Research Review* 8 (6): 1–8.

Rossen, E. and Hull, R. (eds.) (2013). *Supporting and educating traumatized students: A guide for school-based professionals*. New York, NY: Oxford University Press.

Roussos, A., Goenjian, A.K., Steinberg, A.M. et al. (2005). Post-traumatic stress and depressive reactions among children and adolescents after the 1999 earthquake in Ano Liosia, Greece. *American Journal of Psychiatry* 162: 530–537.

Rubin, K.H., Bukowski, W., and Parker, J.G. (1998). Peer interactions, relationships, and groups. In: *Hand–Book of Child Psychology*, 5e, vol. 3 (ed. W. Damon and N. Eisenberg). Social, emo.

Runyon, M.K., Deblinger, E., and Steer, R.A. (2014). PTSD symptom cluster profits of youth who have experienced sexual or physical abuse. *Child Abuse and Neglect* 38 (1): 114–122.

Runyon, M. K., Pollio, E., & Cohen, J. Trauma-Focused Cognitive Behavioral Therapy for Children in Foster Care: An Implementation Manual Esther Deblinger, Ph. D. Anthony P. Mannarino, Ph.D.

Rutgers University Law School's "Center on Law, Inequality, and Metropolitan Equity" (May 5, 2017) Mark Rosenbaum

Rutter, M. (1979). Protective factors in children's responses to stress and disadvantage. In: *Primary Prevention of Psychopathology*, vol. 3. Social competence in children (ed. M.W. Kent and J.E. Rolf), 49–74. Hanover, NH: University Press of New England.

Rutter, M. (1990). Psychosocial resilience and protective mechanisms. In: *Risk and Protective Factors in the Development of Psychopathology* (ed. J.R.A.S. Masten, D. Cicchetti, K.H. Nuechterlein and S. Weintraub), 181–1214. New York: Cambridge University Press.

Ryff, C.D. (1989). Happiness is everything, or is it? Explorations on the meaning of psychological well-being. *Journal of Personality and Social Psychology* 57: 1069–1081. Charles C Thomas.

Ryff, C.D. and Singer, B. (1998). The contours of positive human health. *Psychological inquiry* 9 (1): 1–28.

Sackett, D.L., Rosenberg, W.M., Gray, J.A. et al. (1996). Evidence based medicine: What it is and what it isn't. *British Medical Journal* 312: 71–72. Retrieved from http://www.ncbi.nlm.nih.gov/pmc/articles/PMC2349778/pdf/bmj00524-0009.pdf.

Safe and Supportive Schools Commission (2017). Massachusetts General Laws, chapter 69, section 1P. In: *An Act Relative to the Reduction of Gun Violence*. Safe and Supportive Schools Commission Retrieved on August 31, 2017 from https://malegislature.gov/Laws/SessionLaws/Acts/2014/Chapter284.

Saigh, P.A., Mroueh, M., and Bremner, J.D. (1997). Scholastic impairments among traumatized adolescents. *Behaviour Research and Therapy* 35: 429–436.

Saltzman, W.R., Pynoos, R.S., Layne, C.M. et al. (2001). Trauma-and grief-focused intervention for adolescents exposed to community violence: Results of a school-based screening and group treatment protocol. *Group Dynamics: Theory, Research, and Practice* 5 (4): 291.

Saltzman, K.M., Weems, C.F., and Carrion, V.G. (2005). IQ and posttraumatic stress symptoms in children exposed to interpersonal violence. *Child Psychiatry and Human Development*:https://doi.org/10.1007/s10578-005-002-5.

SAMHSA's National Registry of Evidence-Based Programs and Practices, which can be found here: Retrieved 2017 http://nrepp.samhsa.gov/landing.aspx.

Santiago, C.D., Lennon, J.M., Fuller, A.K. et al. (2014). Examining the impact of a family treatment component for CBITS: When and for whom is it helpful? *Journal of Family Psychology* 28 (4): 560.

Sapolsky, R. (2004). *The cognitive neurosciences, stress and cognition*, vol. 3 (ed. M. Gazzaniga). Cambridge, MA: MIT Press.

Sapolsky, R.M., Romero, L.M., and Munck, A.U. (2000a). How do glucocorticoids influence stress responses? Integrating permissive, suppressive, stimulatory, and preparative actions. *Endocrine Reviews* 21 (1): 55–89.

Sapolsky, R., Romero, L., and Munck, A. (2000b). How do glucocorticoids influence stress responses: Integrating permissive, stimulatory, and preparative actions. *Endocrine Review* 21: 55–89.

Sar, V., Taycan, O., Bolat, N. et al. (2010). Childhood trauma and dissociation in schizophrenia. *Psychopathology* 43 (1): 33–40.

Sarazin, M., Pillon, B., Giannakopoulos, P. et al. (1998). Clinico-metabolic dissociation of cognitive functions and social behavior in frontal lobe lesions. *Neurology* 51: 142–148.

Sattler, J.M. (2008). *Assessment of Children:Cognitive Foundations*, 5e. San Diego, CA: Sattler.

Saunders, B.E. (2003). Understanding children exposed to violence: Towards an integration of overlapping fields. *Journal of Interpersonal Violence* 18 (4): 356–376.

Saunders, B.E., Berliner, L., & Hanson, R.F. (Eds.). (2003). Child Physical and Sexual Abuse: Gudelines for Treamtnet (Final Report: January 15, 2003). Charleston, SC: National Crime Victims Research and Treatment Center.

Saxe, G.N. and Ellis, B.H. (2012). *Collaborative treatment of traumatized children and teens: The trauma systems therapy approach*. Guilford Press.

Saxe, G.N., Ellis, B.H., and Kaplow, J.B. (2007). *Collaborative Treatment of Traumatized Children and Teens: The Trauma Systems Therapy Approach*. New York, NY: Guilford Press.

Schäfer, I. and Fisher, H.L. (2011). Childhood trauma and post-traumatic stress disorder in patients with psychosis: clinical challenges and emerging treatments. *Current Opinion in Psychiatry* 24 (6): 514–518.

Scheeringa, M.S. (2010). *Young child PTSD Checklist*. New Orleans, LA: Tulane University.

Scheeringa, M.S. and Haslett, N. (2010). The reliability and criterion validity of the diagnostic infant and preschool assessment: A new diagnostic instrument for young children. *Child Psychiatry and Human Development* 41 (3): 299–312.

Scheier, M., Carver, C., and Bridges, M. (1994). Distinguishing optimism from neuroticism (and trait anxiety, self-mastery, and self-esteem): A reevaluation of the Life Orientation Test. *Journal of Personality and Social Psychology* 67 (6): 1063–1078.

Schilling, E.A., Aseltine, R.H., and Gore, S. (2007). Adverse childhood experiences and mental health in young adults: a longitudinal survey. *BMC Public Health* 7 (1): 30.

Schneider-Rosen, K. and Cicchetti, D. (1991). Early self- knowledge and emotional development: Visual self-recognition and affective reactions to mirror self-images in maltreated and non- maltreated toddlers. *Development and Psychopathology*.

Schoenberg, S. (2014). Gov. Deval Patrick signs gun bill into law saying, "It's a good bill, an important bill." Retrieved on September 2, 2017 from http://www.masslive.com/politics/index.ssf/2014/08/gov_deval_patrick_signs_gun_bi.html

School, H.M. (2016). *Understanding the stress response: Chronic activation of this survival mechanism impairs health.* Harvard Publishing Retrieved at http://www.health.harvard.edu/staying-healthy/understanding-the-stress-response.

Schore, A.N. (2001). The effects of early relational trauma on right brain development, affect regulation, and infant mental health. *Infant Mental Health Journal* 22 (1–2): 201–269.

Schuhmann, E.M., Foote, R.C., Eyberg, S.M. et al. (1998). Efficacy of parent-child interaction therapy: Interim report of a randomized trial with short-term maintenance. *Journal of clinical child psychology* 27 (1): 34–45.

Schulkin, J. (2004). *Allostasis, Homeostasis, and the Costs of Adaptation*, 17. Cambridge: Cambridge University Press.

Scott, G.R. (1996). *The History of Corporal Punishment.* London: Senate.

Seckl, J.R. and Meany, M.J. (2006). Glucocorticoid "programming" and PTSD risk. *Annals of the New York Academy of Science* 1071: 351–378.

Seedat, S., Nyamai, C., Njenga, F. et al. (2004). Trauma exposure and post-traumatic stress symptoms in urban African schools survey in CapeTown and Nairobi. *The British Journal of Psychiatry* 184 (2): 169–175.

Seeman, T.E., McEwen, B.S., Rowe, J.W., and Singer, B.H. (2001a). Allostatic load as a marker of cumulative biological risk: MacArthur studies of successful aging. *Proceedings of the National Academy of Sciences* 98 (8): 4770–4775.

Seeman, T., McEwen, B., Rowe, J., and Singer, B. (2001b). Allostatic load as a marker of cumulative biological risk. *Proceedings of the National Academy of Sciences* 98: 4770–4775.

Seeman, T.E. et al. (2004). Cumulative biological risk and socioeconomic differences in mortality: MacArthur studies of successful aging. *Social Science and Medicine* 58: 1985–1997.

Seginer, R. (2008). Future orientation in times of threat and challenge: How resilient adolescents construct their future. *International Journal of Behavioral Development* 32 (4): 272–282.

Shackelford, K. (2006). Preparation of undergraduate social work students to cope with the effects of indirect trauma. Unpublished Doctoral Dissertation. Department of Social Work: University of Mississippi.

Shantz, C.U. and Hartup, W.W. (eds.) (1992). *Conflict in Child and Adolescent Development.* New York: Cambridge University Press.

Shapiro, S.L., Brown, K.W., and Biegel, G.M. (2007). Teaching self-care to caregivers: effects of mindfulness-based stress reduction on the mental health of therapists in training. *Training and Education in Professional Psychology* 1 (2): 105.

Shaywitz, S.E. (2003). *Overcoming dyslexia: A New and Complete Science-based Program for Reading Problems at any Level.* Knopf.

Shaywitz, S. (2004). *Overcoming Dyslexia.* New York, NY: Random House.

Shaywitz, S.E. and Shaywitz, B.A. (2004). Reading disability and the brain. *Educational leadership* 61 (6): 6–11.

Shaywitz, S.E. and Shaywitz, B.A. (2008). Paying attention to reading: the neurobiology of reading and dyslexia. *Development and psychopathology* 20 (4): 1329–1349.

Shaywitz, B.A., Shaywitz, S.E., Pugh, K.R. et al. (2002). Disruption of posterior brain systems for reading in children with developmental dyslexia. *Biological Psychiatry* 52 (2): 101–110.

Sheehan, M.J. and Watson, M.W. (2008). Reciprocal influences between maternal discipline techniques and aggression in children and adolescents. *Aggressive Behavior* 34: 245–255.

Shemesh, E., Newcorn, J.H., Rockmore, L. et al. (2005). Comparison of parent and child reports of emotional trauma symptoms in pediatric outpatient settings. *Pediatrics* 115: e582–e589:https://doi.org/10.1542/peds.2004-2201.

Shepard, L., Kagan, S.L., and Wurtz, E. (eds.) (1998). *Principles and recommendations for early childhood assessments: The National Education Goals Panel*. Goal 1 Early Childhood Assessments Resource Group.

Sher, K.J., Gershuny, B.S., Peterson, L., and Raskin, G. (1997). The role of childhood stressors in the intergenerational transmission of alcohol use disorders. *Journal of Studies on Alcohol and Drugs* 58: 414–427.

Shevelkin, A.V., Ihenatu, C., and Pletnikov, M.V. (2014). Preclinical models of neurodevelopmental disorders: Focus on the cerebellum. *Review Neuroscience* 25 (2): 177–194.

Shin, S. (2005). Need for and actual use of mental health service by adolescents in the foster care system. *Children and Youth Services Review* 27: 1071–1083.

Shin, L.M., Rauch, S.L., and Pitman, R.K. (2006). Amygdala, medial prefrontal cortex, and hippocampal function in PTSD. *Annals of the New York Academy of Sciences* 1071 (1): 67–79.

Shonk, S.M. and Cicchetti, D. (2001). Maltreatment, competency deficits, and risk for academic and behavioral maladjustment. *Developmental Psychology* 37: 3–17.

Shonkoff, J.P. and Phillips, D. (eds.) (2000). *From neurons to neighborhoods: The science of early childhood development. Committee on Integrating the Science of Early Childhood Development*. Washington, DC: National Academy Press.

Shonkoff, J.P., Garner, A.S., CSiegel, B.S. et al. (2012). The lifelong effects of early childhood adversity and toxic stress. *Pediatrics* 129: e232–e246: https://doi.org/10.2542/peds.2011-2663.

Silverman, W.K., Ortiz, C.D., Viswesvaran, C. et al. (2008). Evidence-based psychosocial treatments for children and adolescents exposed to traumatic events. *Journal of Clinical Child and Adolescent Psychology* 37 (1): 156–183.

Singer, M.I., Anglin, T.M., Song, L.Y., and Lunghofer, L. (1995). Adolescents' exposure to violence and associated symptoms of psychological trauma. *JAMA* 273: 477–482. https://doi.org/10.1001/jama.286.24.3089.

Skiba, R.J., Chung, C.G., Trachok, M. et al. (2014). Parsing disciplinary disproportionality: Contributions of infraction, student, and school characteristics to out-of-school suspension and expulsion. *American Educational Research Journal* 51 (4): 640–670.

Smith, E.E., Jonides, J., Marshuetz, C., and Koeppe, R.A. (1998). Components of verbal memory: Evidence from neuroimaging. *Proceedings of the National Academy of Sciences of the United States of America* 95: 876–882.

Snyder, C.R. (1994). *The psychology of hope: You can get there from here*. Simon and Schuster.

Snyder, C.R., Hoza, B., Pelham, W.E. et al. (1997). The development and validation of the children's hope scale. *Journal of Pediatric Psychology* 22: 399–421.

Spauwen, J., Krabbendam, L., Lieb, R. et al. (2006). Impact of psychological trauma on the development of psychotic symptoms: relationship with psychosis proneness. *The British Journal of Psychiatry* 188 (6): 527–533.

Spilsbury, J.C., Fletcher, K.E., Creeden, R., and Friedman, S. (2008). Psychometric properties of the dimensions of stressful events rating scale. *Traumatology* 14 (4): 116–130.

Squire, L.R., Stark, C.E.L., and Clark, R.E. (2004). The medial temporal lobe. *Annual Review of Neuroscience* 27: 279–306.

Sroufe, L.A., Carlson, E.A., Levy, A.K., and Egeland (1999). Implications of attachment theory for developmental psychopathology. *Development and Psychopathology* 11: 1–13.

Stamm, B. (1995). *Secondary traumatic stress: Self-care issues for clinicians, researchers, and educators*. The Sidran Press.

Stamm, B. H. (2005). The ProQOL manual. Retrieved July, 16, 2007.

Stearns, P. (2006). *Childhood in world history*. New York, NY: Routledge.

Stein, N., Folkman, S., Trabasso, T., and Richards, T.A. (1997). Appraisal and goal processes as predictors of psychological well- being in bereaved caregivers. *Journal of Personality and Social Psychology* 72: 872–884.

Stein, B.D., Jaycox, L.H., Kataoka, S.H. et al. (2003). A mental health intervention for schoolchildren exposed to violence: a randomized controlled trial. *JAMA* 290 (5): 603–611. (Main outcome study associated with Study 1: Kataoka et al., 2011 – assessed impacts on trauma symptoms, depression, classroom conduct, internalizing problems, learning problems, and psychosocial dysfunction).

Stein, B.D., Jaycox, L.H., Langley, A. et al. (2007). Active parental consent for a school-based community violence screening: comparing distribution methods. *Journal of school health* 77 (3): 116–120.

Steinberg, M.S. and Dodge, K.A. (1983). Attributional bias in aggressive adolescent boys and girls. *Journal of Social and Clinical Psychology* 1 (4): 312–321.

Steinberg, A.M., Brymer, M.J., Decker, K.B., and Pynoos, R.S. (2004). The University of California at Los Angeles post-traumatic stress disorder reaction index. *Current Psychiatry Reports* 6: 96–100.

Steinberg, A.M., Brymer, M.J., Kim, S. et al. (2013). Psychometric properties of the UCLA PTSD reaction index: Part 1. *Journal of Traumatic Stress* 26: 1–9.

Stephan, S., Green, M., Rosen-Gill, E., Sullivan, K., & Pitchford, J. (2017). Implementation and Evaluation of Trauma-informed Intervention in Baltimore City Schools. School-Based Mental Health Programs for Children Exposed to Trauma; 23rd International Society for Traumatic Stress Studies Annual Meeting; Nov 14–17, Baltimore, Maryland.

Sterling, P. (2004). Principles of allostasis: optimal design, predictive regulation, pathophysiology and rational therapeutics. In: *Allostasis, homeostasis, and the costs of physiological adaptation* (ed. J. Schulkin), 17–64. New York, NY: Cambridge University Press.

Stevens, J. E. (2013a). The Adverse Childhood Experiences Study - the largest, most important public health study you never heard of - began in an obesity clinic. Retrieved from https://acestoohigh.com/2012/10/03/the-adverse-childhood-experiences-study-the-largest-most-important-public-health-study-you-never-heard-of-began-in-an-obesity-clinic.

Stevens, J. E. (2013b). There's no such thing as a bad kid in these Spokane, WA, trauma-informed elementary schools. ACEs Too High. Retrieved from http://acestoohigh.com/2013/08/20/spokaneschools.

Stiles, J. (2010). The basics of brain development. *Neuropsychological Review (what is full title)* 20: 327–348.

Stiles, J. and Jernigan, T.L. (2010). The basics of brain development. *Neuropsychology review* 20 (4): 327–348.

Stoddard, F.J. (2014). Outcomes of traumatic exposure. *Child and Adolescent Clinics of North America* 23: 243–256.

Stoeckle, C., Gough, P.M., Watkins, K.E., and Devlin, J.T. (2009). Supramarginal gyrus involved in visual word recognition. *Cortex* 45 (9): 1091–1096.

Stolbach, B.C. (1997). *The children's Dissociative Experiences Scale and Posttraumatic Symptom Inventory: RATIONALE, Development, and Validation of a self-report Measure*. University of Colorado: Doctoral dissertation.

Stover, C.S. and Berkowitz, S. (2005). Assessing violence exposure and trauma symptoms in young children: A critical review of measures. *Journal of Traumatic Stress* 18 (6): 707–717.

Stover, C.S., Hahn, H., Im, J.J.Y., and Berkowitz, S. (2010). Agreement of parent and child reports of trauma exposure and symptoms in the early aftermath of a traumatic event. *Psychological Trauma: Theory, Research, Practice, and Policy* 2: 159–168. https://doi.org/10.1037/a0019156.

Strand, V., Sarmiento, T., and Pasquale, L. (2005). Assessment and screening tools for trauma in children and adolescents: A review. *Trauma Violence and Abuse* 6 (1): 55–78.

Straus, M.A. (2001). *Beating the devil out of them: Corporal punishment in American families and its effects on children*. Transaction Publishers.

Straus, M.A. and Paschall, M.J. (2009). Corporal punishment by mothers and development of children's cognitive ability: a longitudinal study of two nationally representative age cohorts. *Journal of Aggression Maltreatment and Trauma* 18: 459–483.

Streeck-Fischer, A. and van der Kolk, B. (2000). Down will come baby, cradle and all: Diagnostic and therapeutic implications of chronic trauma on child development. *Australian and New Zealand Journal of Psychiatry* 34: 903–918.

Stuss, D.T. and Alexander, M.P. (2007). Is there a dysexecutive syndrome? *Philosophical Transactions of the Royal Society of London B: Biological Sciences* 362 (1481): 901–915.

Stuss, D.T., Gallup, G.G., and Alexander, M.P. (2001). The frontal lobes are necessary for "theory of mind". *Brain* 124: 279–286.

Substance Abuse and Mental Health Services Administration (2014). *Trauma-Informed Care in Behavioral Health Services. Treatment Improvement Protocol (TIP) Series 57*. HHS Publication No. (SMA) 13-4801. Rockville, MD: Substance Abuse and Mental Health Services Administration Retrieved From https://store.samhsa.gov/shin/content/SMA14-4816/SMA14-4816.pdf.

Swain-Bradway, J., Johnson, J., Eber, L. et al. (2015). *Interconnecting school mental health and school-wide positive behavior support*, 282. School Mental Health: Global Challenges and Opportunities.

Talwar, V., Carlson, S.M., and Lee, K. (2011). Effects of a punitive environment on children's executive functioning: A natural experiment. *Social Development*.

Tarullo, A.R. and Gunnar, M.R. (2006). Child maltreatment and the developing HPA axis. *Hormones and Behavior* 50: 632–639.

Taylor, N., Steinburg, A., and Wilson, C. (2006). *The Child Welfare Trauma Referral Tool*. San Diego, CA: Chadwick Center for Children and Families, Rady Children's Hospital San Diego, CA.

Teicher, M.H. (2000). Wounds that time won't heal: The neurobiology of child abuse. *Cerebrum* 2 (4).

Teicher, M.H. and Samson, J.A. (2016). Annual research review: Enduring neurobiological effects of childhood abuse and neglect. *Journal of Child Psychology and Psychiatry* https://doi.org/10.1111/jcpp.12507.

Teicher, M.H., Dumont, N.L., Ito, Y. et al. (2004). Childhood neglect is associated with reduced corpus callosum area. *Biological Psychiatry* 56: 80–85.

Teicher, M.H., Anderson, C.M., and Polcari, A. (2012). Childhood maltreatment is associated with reduced volume in the hippocampal subfields CA3, dentate gyrus and subiculum. *Proceedings from the National Academy of the United States PNAS*. Published online February 13, 2012. http://www.pnas.org/cgi/doi/10.1073/pnas.1115396109.

Terr, L.C. (1991). Childhood traumas: An outline and overview. *American Journal of Psychiatry* 148: 10–20.

Texas Classroom Teachers Association (2017) https://tcta.org/node/13128-corporal_punishment_and_use_of_force

The Center for the Enhancement of Teaching. (n.d.) How to improve test reliability and validity: Implications for grading. [Available online: http://oct.sfsu.edu/assessment/evaluating/htmls/improve_rel_val.html].

The Center on the Developing Child at Harvard University: (2011) https://developingchild.harvard.edu

The President's New Freedom Commission on Mental Health 2003 Retrieved from http://govinfo.library.unt.edu/mentalhealthcommission/reports/reports.htm.

The Sanctuary Model (2012). Community Meetings. Re- trieved from http://www.sanctuaryweb.com/community- meetings.php.

The Sanctuary Model (2012). Red Flag Meetings. Retrieved from http://www.sanctuaryweb.com/red-flag-reviews.php

Thoits, P.A. (2010). Stress and health: Major findings and policy implications. *Journal of Health And Social Behavior* 51 (1_suppl): S41–S53.

Timmer, S.G., Urquiza, A.J., Zebell, N.M., and McGrath, J.M. (2005). Parent-child interaction therapy: Application to maltreating parent-child dyads. *Child Abuse & Neglect* 29 (7): 825–842.

Tishelman, A.C., Haney, P., O'Brien, J.G., and Blaustein, M.E. (2010). A framework for school-based psychological evaluations: Utilizing a 'trauma lens'. *Journal of Child and Adolescent Trauma* 3 (4): 279–302.

Tomoda, A., Suzuki, H., Rabi, K. et al. (2009). Reduced prefrontal cortical Gray matter volume in young adults exposed to harsh corporal punishment. *Neuroimage* 47 (Suppl 2): T66–T67.

Tomoda, A., Yi-Shin Sheu, B.S., Rabi, K. et al. (2011). Exposure to parental verbal abuse is associated with increased grey matter volume in superior temporal gyrus. *Neuroimage* 54: 280–286.

Toth, S.L., Maughan, A., Manly, J.T. et al. (2002). The relative efficacy of two interventions in altering maltreated preschool children's representational models: Implications for attachment theory. *Development and Psychopathology* 14: 877–908.

Tottenham, N. and Sheridan, M.A. (2009). A review of adversity, the amygdala and the hippocampus: A consideration of developmental timing. *Frontiers in Human Neuroscience* 3: 68.

Trickett, P., McBride-Chang, C., and Putnam, F. (1994). The classroom performance and behavior of sexually abused females. *Development & Psychopathology* 6: 183–194.

Trommsdorff, G., Lamm, H., and Schmidt, R. (1978). A longitudinal study of adolescents' future orientation (time perspective). *Journal of Youth and Adolescence* 8 (2): 131–147.

Tull, M.T., Jakupcak, M., McFadden, M.E., and Roemer, L. (2007). The role of negative affect intensity and the fear of emotions in posttraumatic stress symptom severity among victims of childhood interpersonal violence. *Journal of Nervous and Mental Disease* 195: 580–587.

Tupler, L.A. and De Bellis, M.D. (2006). Segmented hippocampal volume in children and adolescents with posttraumatic stress disorder. *Biological Psychiatry* 59 (6): 523–529.

Turner, H.A., Finkelhor, D., and Ormrod, R. (2006). The effect of lifetime victimization on the mental health of children and adolescents. *Social Science Medicine.* 62: 13–27. https://doi.org/10.1016/j.socscimed.2005.05.030.

Turnock, B.J. (2012). *Public health*. Jones & Bartlett Publishers.

Tuval-Mashiach, R., Freedman, S., Bargai, N. et al. (2004). Coping with trauma: Narrative and cognitive perspectives. *Psychiatry: Interpersonal and Biological Processes* 67 (3): 280–293.

U.S Department of Justice, U.S. Department of Health and Human Services (2011). *Evidence-Based Practices for Children Exposed to Violence: A Selection from Federal Databases.* U.S Department of Justice, U.S. Department of Health and Human Services.

U.S. Department of Justice, U.S. Department of Health and Human Services (2011). *Evidence-Based Practices for Children Exposed to Violence: A Selection from Federal Databases.* Safe Start Center http://www.safestartcenter.org_pdf_Evidence-Based-Practices-Matrix_2011.

Understanding Evidence-Based Practices (2017) downloaded from www.cebc4cw.org - Rev. 1 September 2017.

UNICEF (n.d.) Hidden in Plain Site.

United Nation's Children's Fund (2014). *Hidden in plain sight: A statistical analysis of violence against children*. New York, NY: UNICEF.

Van de Weijer-Bergsma, E., Kroesbergen, E.H., and Van Luit, J.E.H. (2015). Verbal and visual spatial working memory and mathematical ability in different domains throughout primary school. *Memory and Cognition* 43: 367–378.

Van der Kolk, B.A. (1994). The body keeps the score: Memory and the evolving psychobiology of post-traumatic stress. *Harvard Review of Psychiatry* 1 (5): 253–265.

Van der Kolk, B.A. (2005). Developmental trauma disorder: Toward a rational diagnosis for children with complex trauma histories. *Psychiatric Annals* 35 (5): 401–408.

Van der Kolk, B.A., Pelcovitz, D., Roth, S. et al. (1996). Dissociation, somatization, and affect dysregulation: The complexity of adaptation to trauma. *American Journal of Psychiatry* 153: 83–93.

Van der Kolk, B.A., Roth, S., Pelcovitz, D. et al. (2005). Disorders of extreme stress: The empirical foundation of a complex adaptation to trauma. *Journal of Traumatic Stress* 18 (5): 389–399.

Vargha-Khadem, F., Gadian, D.G., Watkins, K.E. et al. (1997). Differential effects of early hippocampal pathology on episodic and semantic memory. *Science* 277: 376–380.

Viezel, K.D., Freer, B.D., Lowell, A., and Castillo, J.A. (2015). Cognitive abilities of maltreated children. *Psychology in the Schools* 52: 92–106.

Villodas, M.T., Cromer, K.D., Moses, J.O. et al. (2016). Unstable child welfare permanent placements and early adolescent physical and mental health: the roles of adverse childhood experiences and post-traumatic stress. *Child Abuse and Neglect* 62: 76–88.

Vincent, G.M. (2011). *Screening and assessment in juvenile justice systems: Identifying mental health needs and risk of reoffending*. Washington, DC: Technical Assistance Partnership for Child and Family Mental Health Retrieved from http://www.tapartnership.org/docs/jjResource_screeningAssessment.pdf.

Von Bertalanffy, L. (1950). An outline of general system theory. *The British Journal for the Philosophy of science* 1 (2): 134.

Von Bertalanffy, L. (1968). General System Theory. New York, 41973 40.

Von Bertalanffy, L. and Rapoport, A. (1956). General systems. *Yearbook of the society for the Advancement of General System Theory* 1: 1–10.

Vondra, J.I., Barnett, D., and Cicchetti, D. (1989). Perceived and actual competence among maltreated and comparison school children. *Development and Psychopathology* I: Til-255.

Vondra, J.I., Barnett, D., and Cicchetti, D. (1990). Self-concept, motivation, and competence among preschoolers from maltreating and comparison families. *Child Abuse & Neglect* 14 (4): 525–540.

Wagner, M., Kutash, K., Duchnowski, A.J. et al. (2005). The children and youth we serve: A national picture of the characteristics of students with emotional disturbances receiving special education. *Journal of emotional and behavioral disorders* 13 (2): 79–96.

Walkley, M. and Cox, T.L. (2013). Building trauma-informed schools and communities. *Children and Schools* 35 (2): 123–126.

Wandall, B.A. and Yeatman, J.D. (2012). Biological development of reading circuits. *Current Opinion in Neurobiology* 23 (2): 261–268.

Warrier, C., Wong, P., Penhune, V. et al. (2009). Relating structure to function: Heschl's gyrus and acoustic processing. *Journal of Neuroscience* 7 (29): 61–69.

Watson, S., Chilton, R., Fairchild, H., and Whewell, P. (2006). Association between childhood trauma and dissociation among patients with borderline personality disorder. *Australian and New Zealand Journal of Psychiatry* 40 (5): 478–481.

Way, I.F., Applegate, B., Cai, X. et al. (2010). Children's Alexithymia Measure (CAM): a new instrument for screening difficulties with emotional expression. *Journal of Child & Adolescent Trauma* 3 (4): 303–318.

Weatherbee, T.G., Dye, K.E., Bissonnette, A., and Mills, A.J. (2009). Valuation theory and organizational change: Towards a sociopsychological method of intervention. *Journal of Change Management* 9 (2): 195–213.

Webster-Stratton, C. and Reid, M. (2010). Adapting the Incredible Years, an evidence-based parenting programme, for families involved in the child welfare system. *Journal of Children's Services* 5 (1): 25–42.

Wee, D.F. and Myers, D. (2002). Stress responses of mental health workers following disaster: The Oklahoma City bombing. In: *Psychosocial stress series, no. 24. Treating compassion fatigue* (ed. C.R. Figley), 57–83. New York, NY: Brunner-Rutledge.

Weist, M.D. and Evans, S.W. (2005). Expanded school mental health: Challenges and opportunities in an emerging field. *Journal of Youth and Adolescence* 34 (1): 3–6.

Weist, M.D. and Murray, M. (2008). Advancing school mental health promotion globally. *Advances in School Mental Health Promotion* 1 (sup1): 2–12.

Wells, M.G., Burlingame, G.M., Lambert, M.J. et al. (1996). Conceptualization and measurement of patient change during psychotherapy: Development of the Outcome Questionnaire and Youth Outcome Questionnaire. *Psychotherapy: Theory, Research, Practice, Training* 33 (2): 275.

Wells, K.C., Lochman, J.E., and Lenhart, L.A. (2008). *Coping Power parent group program: Facilitator guide*. Oxford: New York, NY.

Werker, J. and Tees, R. (2005). Speech perception as a window for understanding plasticity and commitment in language systems of the brain. *Developmental Psycholbiology* 46: 233–251.

Werner, E.E. and Smith, R.S. (1982). *Vulnerable but invincible: A Study of Resilient Children*. New York: McGraw-Hill.

Whitfield, C.L., Dube, S.R., Felitti, V.J., and Anda, R.F. (2005a). Adverse childhood experiences and hallucinations. *Child Abuse and Neglect* 29 (7): 797–810.

Whitfield, C.L., Dube, S.R., Felitti, V.J., and Anda, R.F. (2005b). Adverse childhood experiences and subsequent hallucinations. *Child Abuse and Neglect* 29: 797–810.

Williamson, D.F., Thompson, T.J., Anda, R.F. et al. (2002). Body weight and obesity in adults and self-reported abuse in childhood. *International Journal of Obesity* 26 (8): 1075.

Williams-Taylor, L. (2007). Evidence-based programs and practices: What does it all mean? Retrieved from http://www.evidencebasedassociates.com/reports/research_review.pdf.

Wolfe, V. V., Gentile, C., & Bourdeau, P. (1987). History of victimization form. Unpublished assessment instrument, London Health Science Centre, London, Ontario, Canada.

Wolfe, V.V., Gentile, C., and Wolfe, D.A. (1989). The impact of sexual abuse on children: A PTSD formulation. *Behavior Therapy* 20 (2): 215–228.

Woodbridge, M.W., Sumi, W.C., Thornton, S.P. et al. (2015). *Screening for trauma in early adolescence: Findings from a diverse school district*. School Mental Health.

Woon, F.L. and Hedges, D.W. (2008). Hippocampal and amygdala volumes in children and adults with childhood maltreatment-related posttraumatic stress disorder: A meta-analysis. *Hippocampus* 18 (8): 729–736.

World Health Organization (2000). *The World Health Report 2000: Health systems: Improving performance*. World Health Organization.

World Health Organization (2002). *The World Health Report 2002: Reducing Risks, Promoting Healthy Life*. Geneva: World Health Organization.

World Health Organization. (2004). The importance of caregiver-child interactions for the survival and healthy development of young children: A review.

World Health Organization Commission on Social Determinants of Health and World Health Organization (2008). *Closing the gap in a generation: Health equity through action on the social determinants of health: Commission on Social Determinants of Health final report*. World Health Organization.

Wu, J. (2017). Family Adaptability and Cohesion Scale. https://www.nctsn.org/measures/family-adaptability-and-cohesion-scale

Wycoff, K.L. (2013). *Case Conceptualization in School-Based Mental Health: School Psychologists Role in Case Formulation and Measuring Impact on Students*. Worcester State University.

Wycoff, K.L., Conroy, T., Briesacher, A. (2018, February) Race, Class, Discipline and ACE's: Complexities and Solutions in Urban Settings. National Association of School Psychology National Conference, Chicago, Illinois.

Wycoff, K.L., & Murphy, V. (2018). Equine-Assisted Group Therapy for Adolescent Sexual Trauma Survivors: Development, Implementation, and Outcomes. In Equine-Assisted Mental Health for Healing Trauma (pp. 84–106). Routledge.

Wycoff, K.L., & Gupta, M. (2018). Ethical Considerations in Equine-Assisted Interventions: Meeting the Needs of Both Human and Horse. In Equine-Assisted Mental Health Interventions (pp. 23–38). Routledge.

Wycoff, K.L., Gauthier, R., Conroy, T., Briesacher, A., Boykins, N. (June 14, 2017) Principal Cocker College Prep, New Orleans (Personal communication).

Yang, M., Wong, S.C., and Coid, J. (2010). The efficacy of violence prediction: a meta-analytic comparison of nine risk assessment tools. *Psychological Bulletin* 136 (5): 740.

Zahr, N.M., Rohlfing, T., Pfefferbaum, A., and Sullivan, E.V. (2009). Problem solving, working memory and motor correlates of association and commissural fiber bundles in normal aging: A quantitative fiber tracking study. *Neuroimage* 44: 1050–1062.

Zanini, D.S., Helenides, M., Forns, M., and Kirchner, T. (2010). Psychometric properties of the coping response inventory with brazilian adolescents. *Psychological reports* 107 (2): 617–628.

Zeanah, C.H., Chesher, T., Boris, N.W. et al. (2016). Practice parameter for the assessment and treatment of children and adolescents with reactive attachment disorder and disinhibited social engagement disorder. *Journal of the American Academy of Child and Adolescent Psychiatry* 55 (11): 990–1003.

Zero to Three (2012). FAQ's on the brain. Retrieved from http://www.zerotothree.org/childdevelopment/brain-development/faqs-on-the-brain.html.

Zero to Three (n.d.) https://www.zerotothree.org/policy-and-advocacy

Zetlin, A. and Weinberg, L. (2004). Understanding the plight of foster youth and improving their educational opportunities. *Child Abuse & Neglect* 28: 917–923.

Zhang, J., Zhao, G., Li, X. et al. (2009). Positive future orientation as a mediator between traumatic events and mental health among children affected by HIV/AIDS in rural China. *AIDS Care* 21 (12): 1508–1516.

Zlotnick, C., Zakriski, A.L., Shea, M.T. et al. (1996). The long-term sequelae of sexual abuse: Support for a complex posttraumatic stress disorder. *Journal of Traumatic Stress* 9: 195–205.

Zolkoski, S.M. and Bullock, L.M. (2012). Resilience in children and youth: A review. *Children and youth services review* 34 (12): 2295–2303.

Index

A

Abuse, category, 18
Academic difficulties, 122–123
Academics (domain), 136
Acetylcholine, 101
Active consent, 163
  procedure, usage, 169
Activities of daily living (ADLs),
    110, 123–125
ACT Raising Safe Kids Program, 240
Adaptive functioning, 89
Addiction risk, ACE impact, 27–29
Addictions, ranking, 28
Adolescence, 89
Adolescent Dissociative Experiences
    Scale (A-DES), 190
Adrenocorticotropin (ACTH),
    release, 104
Adult illness, childhood adversity
    (relationship), 27
Adverse Childhood Experiences
    (ACEs), 3, 7
  Dose Exposure, 165
  effects, 4, 250
  exposure
    categories, 27
    elimination, 33
    impact, 20
  history, suicidality (relationship), 25
  inventory questions, 11–12
  medical impact, 27

number, drug use problems
    (relationship), 29
  reactions, frequency, 21
  risk factor, 21
  scores (increase), teenage pregnancy
    risk increase (relationship), 30
  screening process, 173
Adverse Childhood Experiences
    Study, 7
Affect Intensity and Reactivity
    Measure for Youth (AIR-Y),
    189
Affective dysregulation, 95
Affective identification, 147
Affect regulation, 135,
    136
Agenesis, 115
Age regression, 222
Aggressive disorders, 225
Alarm system, effectiveness
    (reduction), 145
Alcoholism addiction, 28
All Babies Cry (ABC), 223
Allostasis, 19–20
Allostatic load, 20, 139, 144
Altered consciousness, 135
Alzheimer's disease, 101
  ACE impact, 20
American Academy of Child &
    Adolescent Psychiatry
    (AACAP), 83, 221

American Professional Society on the
Abuse of Children
(APSAC), 221
Americans with Disabilities
Act (ADA), 62
Amygdala, 111–113
functions, 112
risk factors, 112–113
Andrus Children's Center,
partnership, 47
Angie/Andry Cartoon Trauma Scale
(ACTS), 195
Animal Assisted Therapy, 252
Anterior cingulate cortex (ACC),
121
dysfunction, biological markers,
120
Antisocial behavior, 22
Anxiety, 22
disorders, 115
experience, 21
presence, population
percentage, 24–25
Assessments
basic assessment, 206
framework, 183–185
guidelines, 185–187
individual assessment
tools, 187–195
risk assessment, 206
Assessments, screeners (differences), 159–160
At-risk students, identification,
160
Attachment, 92, 98–99, 135–136

attachment-related diagnoses/
interventions, 221
disruption, 138–139
relationships, 137–138
Attachment and Biobehavioral
Catch-Up (ABC), 222
Attachment Questionnaire for
Children (AQC), 196
Attachment, Self-Regulation and
Competence (ARC), 223–224
Attentional controls, impairment,
141
Attention deficit hyperactivity
disorder (ADHD), 62, 131
neuropsychological under-
pinnings, 140
presence, 183–184
Attention dysregulation, 95
Atypical brain development,
childhood trauma toxic
(association), 102–103
Auditory processing difficulties, 140
Autistic Spectrum Disorders
(ASDs), 115
Automaticity, 122
Axon terminals, 101

B
Behavioral control, 135–136
self-regulation, relationship,
146–147
Behavioral dysregulation, 95, 106
Behavioral Health and Public Schools
Task Force, 68
Behavioral reenactments, 50

Behavioral regulation, 99
Behavioral Risk Factor Surveillance System (BRFSS), 44
Behavior, automatization, 153
Bill H. 4376, 67–68
Biology, 135–136
Biopsychosocial competencies, impairments, 138
Bipolar disorder, 115
Boat Inventory on Animal-Related Experience, 190
Body
  coping response, impact, 19–20
  physical health, 142–146
  response systems, overexposure, 145
Body mass index (BMI), 10
Bounce Back, 227–228
Boundary problems, 191
Bowlby, John, 92
Boykins, Nicole, 70
Brain
  brain-behavior-pathology relationships, clinical associations, 106
  circuit functions, system classifications, 102
  complex trauma, impact, 93
  developing brain, stress glucocorticoid role (relationship), 105–106
  development, 89, 100–102
    atypical brain development, childhood trauma toxic (association), 102–103
    effects, 99
  intra-lobe connections, 116
  physical health, 142–146
  plasticity, 84
  regions of interest (ROI), visualization (improvement), 107
Broca's area, location, 120
Brown v. Board of Education (ruling), 63
Burnout management, 243
  tools, 248–250

C
California Department of Social Services (CDSS), Office of Child Abuse Prevention, 209
California Evidence-Based Clearinghouse for Child Welfare (CEBC), 207, 209, 219, 231
  categories, 210
  rating scale, 210
  Scientific Rating, 225–227, 234
Cancer, ACE impact, 20
Caregivers
  child perspective, 5
  system tools, 195–197
Case conceptualization, 206
"Center on Law, Inequality, and Metropolitan Equity" (Rutgers University Law School), 64
Centers for Disease Control and Prevention (CDC), childhood essentials, 43–44
Central corticotropin-releasing factor (CRF) activity, 145
Cerebellum, functions/risk factors, 115–116

Cerebrum/cerebral cortex, 109–110
  functions, 109–110
  risk factors, 110
Chicago Longitudinal Study (CLS)
    data, usage, 23
Child and Adolescent Needs and
    Strengths - Trauma Question-
    naire (CANS), 187–188
Child and Family Traumatic Stress
    Intervention (CFTSI), 239
Child-Centered Play therapy mod-
    els, 224–225
Child development, 79
  basics, 84
  learning, 230
  study, 79–84
  tenets, 89–92
Child Development (Feldman), 85
Child Dissociative Checklist
    (CDC), 190
Childhood trauma
  sensitization, association, 145
  toxic, atypical brain development
    (association), 102–103
  types, 96–98
Childhood Trauma Questionnaire
    (CTR), 151, 176
Child-Parent Center (CPC)
    program, 23
Child-Parent Psychotherapy
    (CPP), 225
Child-Parent Relationship Therapy
    (CPRT), 224–225, 227
"Child Physical and Sexual Abuse,"
    202–203, 207

Child Protection Services (CPS)
    involvement, questions, 174
Child Protective Services
  family involvement, 4
  involvement, 161–162
Children
  adversity, adult illness
    (relationship), 27
  aggression problems, 113
  attainments, 84–89
  developmental periods,
    84–89
  development, knowledge, 223
  early years, importance, 90–91
  elementary school children, trauma
    treatment, 227–231
  environments, support, 91–92
  functioning domains, 84–89
  impact (ACE information), 17
  middle school children, trauma
    (treatment), 231–236
  neglect, 97
  relationships, 92
  resiliency factors, 135
  scientific study, 79–84
  self-beliefs, 5
  social-emotional development,
    164
  trauma
    assumptions, 134
    exposure, 109–110
  traumatic stress, scope/impact, 43
  treatment, NCTSN endorse-
    ment, 225–226
  welfare, 79–84

young children, trauma-informed interventions/ treatments, 220–227

Children's Alexithymia Measures (CAM), 189

Children's Attribution and Perceptions Scale (CAPS), 191

Children's Coping Strategies Checklist (CCSC), 193–194

Children's Dissociative Experiences Scale (CDES), 190–191

Children's Hope Scale, 191

Children's Perceptual Alterations Scale (CPAS), 190

Child Sexual Behavior Inventory (CSBI), 191

Child Welfare Trauma Referral Tool, 196

Chronic diseases, likelihood, 21

Chronic interpersonal trauma, 147

Chronic lower respiratory diseases, ACE impact, 20

Chronic Obstructive Pulmonary Disease (COPD), 26

Chronic stress
impact, 138
mediation, 27

Chronic stressors, 6

Circle of Security-Home Visiting-4 (COS-HV4), 240

Clients, presenting concerns, 205

Clinical competencies, 204–206

Clinically significant depression/ anxiety, prevalence, 24–25

Clinical science process, 208f

Clinician Administered PTSD Scale for Children and Adolescents (CAPS-CA), 193

Cognition, 99, 135–136
impairments, 141

Cognitive abilities, development, 135

Cognitive-Behavioral Intervention for Trauma in Schools (CBITS), 227–228, 231–232

Cognitive-Behavioral Therapy for Sexually Abused Preschool Children (CBT-SAP), 224

Cognitive flexibility, 122

Collaboration
principle, 42
trauma-informed approach principle, 74

Communities
impact, ACE information, 17
settings, trauma screening (considerations), 157

Community Violence Exposure Survey (CVES), 177–178

Compassion fatigue (CF), 243–244
prevalence, 245–247

"Compassion Fatigue" (Figley), 243

Compassion stress, 247

Compensatory processes, 133

Complex trauma
assessment, steps, 184–185
functional impact, 127
impact, 93–94
impairment areas, 98–99

National Traumatic Stress Network
definition, 93
result, childhood adverse experiences (impact), 98
Complex Trauma White Paper
(NCTSD), 136
Compton (California), trauma-informed schooling movement, 61–66
Compton Unified School District
(CUSD), 61–66
Computed tomography (CT), 107
Concentration problems, 51
Concept formation, 123
Concordance-discordance model
(C-DM), 142
Conduct problems, 178
Confidentiality, 161–162
Conjoint child-parent sessions, 229
Conners assessment, 183–184
Constructivist self-development
theory, 48–49
Construct Validity, 171
Coping Power Program
(CP), 234–235
Coping Responses Inventory—Youth
(CRI-Y), 193
Coping skills, 215
Coronary Artery Disease (CAD), 26
Corporal punishment, usage, 81–83
Corpus callosum, 113–115
development, 114
functions/risk factors, 114–115
Corticotropin-releasing hormone
(CRH), release, 104

Cortisol, role, 104–105
Criterion-Related Validity, 171
Cross-system leadership/training,
impact, 72
Cross-teaming structures, impact,
72
Cultural/historical/gender issues
principle, 42
trauma-informed approach
principle, 74

D
Data
analysis, 182
data-based decision making,
usage, 71
Declarative memory, 117
Democracy, commitment, 55
Dendrites, 101
Depression
experience, 21
presence, population
percentage, 24–25
rates, 22
Developing brain, stress glucocorticoid role (relationship), 105–106
Developmental trauma
disorder, 94–96
criteria, 95–96
Development of Children, The
(Lightfoot/Cole/Cole), 85
Development, promotion, 222
Devereux Early Childhood Assessment Clinical Form
(DECA-C), 188–189

Diabetes
  ACE impact, 20
  likelihood, 21
Diagnostic Infant and Preschool
    Assessment (DIPA), 194
Diagnostic Interview for Children and
    Adolescents (DICA), 193
Diagnostic Statistical Manual of
    Mental Disorders (DSM)
  clinical diagnosis basis, 94
  criteria, 95–96
  DSM-5, 96, 98, 108, 221
Difficulties with Emotion Regulation
    Scale (DERS), 149, 189
Diffusion tensor imaging (DTI),
    107
Digestive issues, likelihood, 21
Dimensions of Stressful Events Rating
    Scale (DOSE), 192–193
Disaster mental health (DMH), 245
Disengagement, 247
Disinhibited Social Engagement
    Disorder (DSED), 220
Dissociation, 51, 99, 106,
    136, 138, 153
Dissociative Features Profile
    (DFP), 190
Domains, articulation, 136
Domains of impairment, 127
  assessment of framework, 130–131
Domestic violence, ACE exposure
    category, 27
Dopamine, 101
Dorsolateral prefrontal cortex
    (DLPFC), 120–121

Drug use problems, ACE number
    (relationship), 29
Dysregulation
  HPA axis dysregulation, 145
  types, 95–96

E
Early adolescence, 88–89
  cognitive development, 88
  language development, 88
  social/emotional/moral
      development, 89
Early childhood
  cognitive development, 86
  language development, 86
  moral development, 87
  social/emotional develop-
      ment, 86–87
  time frame, 86–87
  trauma, neurobiological alterations
      (association), 108–110
Early-onset chronic interpersonal
    trauma, survivors, 149
Early-onset interpersonal trauma, 150
Effect sizes, 211
Effort allocation/regulation, 124
Electroencephalogram (EEG),
    19, 107–108
Electroencephalographic brain waves,
    differences, 117
Elementary school children, trauma
    treatment, 227–231
Emerging treatments, 251–252
Emotional abuse, ACE exposure
    category, 27

Emotional child abuse, 97

Emotional control, self-regulation (relationship), 147–150

Emotional dysregulation, 106, 147

Emotional intelligence, commitment, 54

Emotional neglect, ACE exposure category, 27

Emotional regulation, 123–125
  integrative conceptualization, 148

Emotion regulation
  conceptualization, 147
  differences, 149
  difficulties, 148
  levels, increase, 149
  strategies, 148

Emotions
  awareness, 150
  awareness/understanding, 148
  clarity, absence, 149
  identification/regulation, 214–215
  suppression levels, increase, 150

Empathic ability/concern, 247

Empowerment
  principle, 42
  trauma-informed approach principle, 74

Enhanced treatment as usual (ETAU), 238

Environmental stressors, exposure, 145

Epigenetics, role, 89–90

Equine Assisted Therapy, 252

"Essentials for Childhood" framework, 44

Ethics, considerations, 243

Evaluation domains, core issues, 135–152

Evidence-based practices (EBPs), 207–212
  implementation, characteristics/ barriers, 213
  range, 72

Excessive Stress Disrupts the Architecture of the Developing Brain, 102

Executive functioning, 94, 139
  impairments, 141

Executive Function (EF) problems, 140

Executive skills, 121–123

Exhibitionism, 191

Expressive Arts Therapy, 252

Eye Movement Desensitization and Reprocessing (EMDR for Children), 252

F

Face Validity, 171

Facial expressions, reference, 214

Familial assessment tools, 181

Families
  Child Protection Services (CPS) involvement, questions, 174
  impact, ACE information, 17
  rights, informed consent (relationship), 162–165
  systems tools, 195–197
  trauma, treatment, 239–240

Family Adaptability and Cohesion Scale, 196

Family Assessment Measure-III
(FAM III), 195
Family Environment Scale (FES), 196
Family Policy Program, review, 195
Feelings, compartmentalization, 153
Flashbacks, 50, 51
Flexible framework (Flexible Frame-
work), 66–67, 154
FREEDOM, 238
Frontal lobes, organization, 120
Frontal regions, 119–122
executive functions, 121–122
functions, 120–121
risk factors, 122
Functional emotion regulation
strategies, usage
(impairment), 150
Functional magnetic resonance
imaging (fMRI), 107
Future orientation, self-concept
(relationship), 150–152
Future Time Perspective Inventory
(FTPI), 151

G

Glial cells, 100–101
Glucocorticoids, 105
resistance, 145
Goal-directed behavior, 153
enagement, ability, 148
Goal setting, interventions, 205
Goodness of fit, evaluation, 202
Grooming, 97
Gross pathogenic care, evidence, 221
Growth/change, commitment, 55
Gun violence, reduction, 67–68

H

Head Start programs, ACE screenings
(usage), 167
Healing, vision, 53
Health
initiatives, 39–44
policy, 39–44
economic policy, relationship,
36
social determinants, 35–36
social gradient, 38–39
WHO definition, 37
Heart disease, ACE impact, 20
High school students, trauma
(treatment), 236–238
Hippocampal volume, reduction,
145
Hippocampus, 110–111
functions, 110–111
risk factors, 111
History of Victimization Form
(HVF), 194
Homeostatic balance, 142
House Bill 4376, 67–68
Household criminal, ACE exposure
category, 27
Household dysfunction, 19
How Traumatized Children Learn
(HTCL), 153
Hyperactivity/inattention, 178
Hyperarousal, 50, 52, 106
Hypogenesis, 115
Hypothalamic-Pituitary-
Adrenocortical (HPA) axis,
104–105, 145
dysregulation, 145

Hypothalamic-Pituitary-Adrenocortical (HPA) stress system, negative feedback loop, 110
Hypothesis testing, 182–183

I

Ideal Clinical Science Process, development process, 207–208
Immune activation, 145
Impairment, domains. *See* Domains of impairment
Impulse control difficulties, 150
Impulsive behavior, control, 148
Incredible Years (IY), 229–230
  Well-Babies program, 230
Individual assessment tools, 181, 187–195
Infants
  trauma-informed interventions/ treatments, 220–227
  treatment, trauma (impact), 224–229
Infants, Children, and Adolescents (Berk/Meyers), 85
Influenza, ACE impact, 20
Information processing, 139
Informed consent, family rights (relationship), 162–165
Inhibition, 123
Injection drug use, addiction, 28
Inpatient hospital programs, Sanctuary Model creation, 46
Inquiry, commitment, 55
"Inquiry into the Sanitary Conditions of the Laboring Population of Great Britain, An" (Chadwick), 38

Institutionalized children, Sanctuary Model definition change, 56
Intentional self-harm, ACE impact, 20
Interconnected Systems Framework (ISF), 70, 71
  economic/social benefits, 72
  model, features, 71
Internal consistency (IC) reliability, 171
Interpersonal trauma, history, 111
Inter-Rater Reliability, 171
Interventions, empirical support, 208
Intrusion Scale, 188
Inventory of Parent and Peer Attachment (IPPA), 196
Invisible backpack, 5
Irritability, 50
Isolationism, 52

J

Juvenile Victimization Questionnaire (JVQ), 192

K

Kaiser Health Appraisal Questionnaire, 32
Kaiser Health Plan patients, identification, 12–13
Kids Club & Moms Empowerment, 240
Kingmade, John B., 82–83

L

Language development, 94, 139
Late-onset trauma, 149

Latino immigrant children, trauma, 232–233
LAUSD Community Practice Site, 233
Learning, 94
  impact, 138–142
"Lessons from Research on Successful Children" (Masten/Coatsworth), 132
Letter-sound integration, 118–119
Life disruption, 247
Life expectancy risk, ACE impact, 33–34
Life experiences, victims, 50
Life Orientation Test (LOT-R), 151
Likert scale, 177
Limbic system, 110–122
Liver issues, likelihood, 21
Lung disease, likelihood, 21

M

Magnetic resonance imaging (MRI), 107
  scans, usage, 111
Major depressive disorder, 115
Maltreatment, histories (reporting), 106–107
Mantel-Haenszel statistical analysis, usage, 32
Massachusetts Advocates for Children (MAC), 66
Maternal and Child Health Bureau (MCHB), 70
McKinney-Vento Act, 174
Medial temporal lobe, dysfunction, 117–118

Memory, 94
  compartmentalization, 153
  declarative memory, 117
  impairments, 141
Mental health, 89
  risk, ACE impact, 22–26
Mental illness, ACE exposure category, 27
Metacognitive integrative functions, identity/maturation (consolidation), 153
Middle childhood
  cognitive development, 87
  time frame, 87
Middle school children, trauma (treatment), 231–236
Mindfulness Based Stress Reduction, 252
Mindful Self-Care Scale (MSCS), 249–250
Motivational interviewing (MI), 217
Multi-dimensional assessment, 135
Multidimensional Family Therapy (MDFT), 239
Multisystemic Therapy (MST), 239
Multisystemic Therapy for Youth with Problem Sexual Behaviors (MST-PSB), 241
Multi-Tiered System of Support (MTSS) framework, 179
Mutuality
  principle, 42
  trauma-informed approach principle, 74
Mutual self-help (principle), 42

N

National American Association for the Study of Obesity, 10

National Child Traumatic Stress Network (NCTSN), 42, 135, 181, 219, 231
core clinical competencies, 206
guidelines, 213
trauma-informed assessments, conducting, 184
Trauma-Informed Interventions, 202

National Institute of Mental Health (NIMH)
grant data, 56
research study, 46

National Registry of Evidence-Based Programs and Practices (NREPP), 207, 209, 219, 231
goal, 211
Outcome Evidence Rating, 212
Scientific Rating, 222, 227, 235, 237
submission, requirements, 211

National Survey of Children's Exposure to Violence, 59

National Traumatic Stress Network, complex trauma definition, 93

National Vital Statistics Report (NVSR), 20

Nature, influence, 89–90

Negative emotions, acceptance, 148

Neglect, 19, 97

Nephritis/nephrotic syndrome/ nephrosis, ACE impact, 20

Neurobiological alterations, early childhood trauma (association), 108–110

Neuroendocrine stress response, 145

Neuroimaging, 106–122
methods, 107–108

Neurons, myelination, 105–106

Neurotransmitters, 101–102

Nightmares, 51

Non-interpersonal trauma, 149

Non-touching behaviors, 97

Non-treatment professional relationship, 166

Non-verbal behavior, reference, 214

Nonviolence, commitment, 55

Norepinephrine, 101

Nurture, influence, 89–90

Nurturing Family Resource Checklist, 196

Nurturing Parenting Programs (NPP), 239

O

Occipital lobe, projections, 118

Odds ratio, 21

Office for Juvenile Justice and Delinquency Prevention (OJJDP), 230

Office of Special Education Programs (OSEPs), 70

Office of Victims of Crime (OVC), 207

Open communication, commitment, 55

Oppositional disorders, 225

Orbitofrontal cortex (OFC), 117
Organization
  core mission, implementation, 168
  skills, problems, 140
Organizational skills, 122, 123
Outcome Evidence Rating
      (NREPP), 212

P

PA Child Welfare Training
      Program, 85
Parental resilience, 223
Parent-Child Interaction Therapy
      (PCIT), 225–227
Parent-child relational distress, 225
Parent-Child Relationship
      Inventory, 196
Parent Emotional Reaction Question-
      naire (PERQ), 197
Parenting, knowledge, 223
Parenting Stress Index-Short Form
      (PSI-SF), 197
Parent training, 213
Passive consent, 163
Patient Health Question-
      naire (PHQ), 24
Peer problems, 178
Peer support
  principle, 42
  trauma-informed approach
      principle, 74
Peer victimization, 192
Performance deficits, 123–124
Personnel time/training, calcu-
      lation, 161

Peter P., et al. v. Compton Unified
      School District (CUSD), 61–63
Physical abuse
  ACE exposure category, 27
  harm, 81–82
Physical disease, risk, 137
Physical functioning (domain),
      136
Physical health, 89
  brain/body, 142–146
  risk, ACE impact, 26–27
Physical neglect, ACE exposure
      category, 27
Physical touch, avoidance, 146
Physiological dysregulation, 95
Physiological homeostasis,
      maintenance, 19
Physiological systems, chronic
      mobilizations, 145
Piers-Harris Children's Self-Concept
      Scale, 2nd ed. (Piers-
      Harris-2), 191–192
Planning, 123
  skills, 122
Pneumonia, ACE impact, 20
Policy learning initiative, trauma
      (relationship), 66–68
Positive attachment/connections,
      135
Positive Behavioral Interventions and
      Supports (PBIS), 70–71
Positive deviance (PD), 132
Positive Parenting Program System
      (Triple P), 240
Positive stress, 102–103

Posttraumatic stress disorder (PTSD), 236–237
DSM diagnosis, 63, 248
dual-diagnosis, 238–239
levels, correlation, 150
rates, increase, 60
symptoms, 22, 50
emergence/reemergence, 51–52
Post-traumatic Symptom Inventory (PTSI), 190–191
Praise, reflection, imitation, description, and enthusiasm (PRIDE), 226–227
Prediction, development, 183
Prefrontal cortex, division, 120
Pre-teenagers
language development, 87
moral development, 88
social/emotional development, 88
time frame, 87–88
Prevalence, term (usage), 18–19
Problem explanation, framework (hypothesis), 205
Problem-solving, 114
abilities, 94
Professional Quality of Life Scale (ProQOL), 249
Progress-monitoring, usage, 71
Prosocial behavior, 178
Protective processes, 133
Provoked catharsis, 222
Pseudo-hallucinations, 50
Psychoeducation, 214
Psycho-educational services, 213
Psychoeducation and Parenting Skills, Relaxation Skills, Affective Expression and Modulation Skills, Cognitive Coping and Processing Skills (PRACTICE), 229
Psychometric properties, 177
Psychosis, 22
Psychosocial dysfunction, risk, 137
Psychosomatic symptoms, 51
Public health
historical context, 37–39
trauma-informed movement, relationship, 35

R

Rage
control, inability, 50
ventilation, 222
RAND Corporation, 233
Randomized controlled trials (RCTs), 207, 237
Reactive Attachment Disorder (RAD), 220–221
Reading skills, problems, 140
Realizes Recognizes Responds Re-traumatization (4 Rs), 41, 72
Real Life Heroes (RLH), 235–236
Reconnection (trauma treatment stage), 52
Reconstruction (trauma treatment stage), 51–52
Referral questions, impact, 186
Regions of interest (ROI), 119
visualization, improvement, 107
Rehabilitation Act, 62
Relational dysregulation, 95–96
Relationships (domain), 136
Reliability, term (usage), 171
Resilience/recovery, 132–135
Response inhibition, 123

Response to Intervention (RTI)
  approach, 182
  education movement, 158
Response to intervention (RTI)
    model, 65–66
Results, communication, 183
Re-traumatization, 41
Retrieval fluency, 123
Risk
  assessment, 206
  screening, 217–218
Risky behaviors, 27
  likelihood, 21

S

Safe and Supportive Schools
    Commission for the State of
    Massachusetts, 68
SafeCare, 240
Safe Environment for Every Kid
    (SEEK), 240
Safety
  principle, 41
  trauma-informed approach
      principle, 74
  trauma treatment stage, 51
Safety, emotional management, loss,
    and future (S.E.L.F.), 54
Sanctuary Model, 44–55
  commitments, 54–55
  components, 53
  cultural sensitivity, 53
  grant, implementation/
      assessment, 56
  history, 45–48
  inpatient hospital programs,
      46

institutionalized children, definition
    change, 56
  pillars, 54
  programs, 47–48
  theoretical framework, 48–49
  toolkit, 54
  trauma survivors, relation-
      ship, 50–53
School mental health (SMH),
    70–71
Schools
  confidentiality, 161–162
  corporal punishment, 81
  role, 68
  school-based mental health profes-
      sionals, impact, 162
  school-based mental health services,
      impact, 61
  school-based screenings,
      barriers, 168
  screening methods, benefits, 175
  settings
    adversity, 164–165
    trauma screening, considerations,
        147
    trauma screening, considerations,
        157, 160–161
Scientific method, 182–183
Screeners, assessments (differ-
    ences), 159–160
Screening. See Trauma
  administrations, number/timing
      (determination), 161
  feasibility/practicality, 168–170
  methods, benefits, 175
  protocol, 172–174
  safety/follow-up, 166

tools
  identification, 161
  selection, 171–172
usage, 159
voluntary participation, 166–167
Secondary traumatic stress
    (STS), 243–244
  impact, 244–245
  prevalence, 245–247
  training, needs, 246–247
Secondary Traumatic Stress Scale
    (STSS), 248–249
Self-acceptance, 151
Self-awareness, 248
Self-care planning, tools, 248–250
Self-concept, 135–136
    future orientation, relation-
      ship, 150–152
Self-development theory, 48–49
Self dysregulation, 95–96
Self-help attempts, 27
Self-management, 248
Self monitoring, 123
Self-rated health/life satisfaction,
    problems (likelihood), 21
Self-regulation
  abilities, development, 135
  behavioral control, relation-
      ship, 146–147
  domain, 135–136
  emotional control, relationship,
      147–150
Self-stimulation, 146, 191
Sensory information, process-
    ing, 109–110
Sentinel reporting method, 173
Serotonin, 101

Seven Sanctuary Commitments, 54
Sexual abuse, ACE exposure
    category, 27
Sexual anxiety, 191
Sexual behavior risk, ACE
    impact, 29–33
Sexual Interest/Intrusiveness,
    191
Sexually Transmitted Infection (STI),
    likelihood, 21
Sexual victimization, 192
Shared decision-making, 53
Sibling victimization, 192
Sleep disturbance, 51
Smoking addiction, 28
Social competency, 123–125
Social connections, 223
Social justice policy, 38–39
Social learning, commitment, 55
Social responsibility, commitment,
    55
Socio-economic status
    (SES), 140, 225
  cohort, tracking, 23
Somatic Trauma Therapy, 252
"Stages of Treatment," 51
Strengthening Families Program
    (SFP), 239
Strengths and Difficulties Question-
    naire (SDQ), 178
Stress
  glucocorticoids (role), developing
      brain (relationship), 105–106
  impact, 127
  positive stress, 102–103
  response, 104–105
  secondary traumatic stress, 243

stress-related disorders, vulnerability, 89
stress-related outcomes, 102
systems, 103–106
Stroke, ACE impact, 20
Structural connectivity, 113–115
Structured Interview for Disorders of Extreme Stress (SIDES), 188
Structured Interview for Disorders of Extreme Stress - Adolescent Version (SIDES-A), 188
Structured Interview for Disorders of Extreme Stress Self-Report Version (SIDES-SR), 188
Study skills, problems, 140
Substance abuse, ACE exposure category, 27
Substance Abuse and Mental Health Services Administration (SAMHSA), 39, 72, 207, 219, 231
    Complex Trauma White Paper, 136
    trauma-informed approaches, 40–41
Substance Use Disorders (SUD), 236–237
Suicidal ideation, 25
Suicidality, 22
    ACE history, relationship, 25
Suicide
    ACE impact, 20
    attempt, likelihood, 21
Superior temporal gyrus (STG), 116
Supplementary motor cortex (SMC), 121

Supports for Students Exposed to Trauma (SSET), 233
Supramarginal gyri, gray matter (presence), 117
Sustained attention, 123
Sympathetic-adrenomedullary (SAM) system, 104
Systems theory, 49

T
Target population/informants, developmental appropriateness, 169–170
Teenagers
    impact, ACE information, 17
    pregnancy risk (increase), ACE score increase (relationship), 30
Temporal lobe, 116
Temporal-parietal regions, 116–119
    functions, 117–118
    risk factors, 118–119
Test-Retest
    data, 189
    reliability, 171
Test-retest (TRT)
    kappa, 194
    reliability, 176
Texas Classroom Teachers Association (TCTA), corporal punishment definition, 82
Thinking, impact, 138–142
Threat, immediate response, 104
Toddlers, trauma-informed interventions/treatments, 220–227
Toxic stress, 99

Toxic, term (usage), 103

Training, needs, 246–247

Transactional caregiving, 147

Transcending Trauma Project (TPP), 134

Trauma

behavioral health effects, recognition, 40

childhood trauma, types, 96–98

complex trauma, impact, 93

definition, 40

developmental trauma disorder, 94–96

early childhood trauma, neurobiological alterations (association), 108–110

elementary school children, trauma treatment, 229–233

experience, 52

exposure, 51

screening/assessment, 164–165

high school students, trauma (treatment), 236–238

history, 93, 184

impact, 138

initiatives, 40

middle school children, trauma (treatment), 231–236

narrative, 215–217

neurotoxic effects, 119

policy learning initiative, relationship, 66–68

reprocessing, 216

resilience/recovery, 132–135

safety/follow-up, 166

survivors, Sanctuary Model (relationship), 50–53

trauma-exposed preschoolers, persistence, 128–129

trauma-exposed youth, 203–205

experience, 138

trauma-focused interventions, core components, 213

trauma-informed

approaches, 69, 74–75

trauma-informed assessment

conducting, 184

tool selection, 171–172

trauma-informed care

models, 44–57

evidence base, 55–57

trauma-informed care services/ training, expansion, 40

trauma-informed culture, ethos, 55–56

trauma-informed interventions, 219

competencies/components, 201

trauma-informed movement, public health (relationship), 35

trauma-informed programs, creation, 43

trauma-informed rubric, usage, 118–119

trauma-informed schools, 59–61

culture, 82

movement, 61–66

trauma-informed screenings, 185

trauma-informed treatments, 219

trauma-related screening protocols, 175

trauma-sensitive approaches, 175

trauma-specific interventions, development/promotion, 40

treatment, understanding, 52

type, role, 149

vicarious trauma (VT), 243

Trauma Affect Regulation: Guide for Education and Treatment (TARGET), 237–238

Trauma and Learning Policy Initiative (TLPI), 66

Trauma-Focused Cognitive-Behavioral Therapy (TF-CBT), 227–229, 231, 232, 236

Trauma screening

cautions, 174–176

considerations, 157, 160–161

measures, 176–178

Trauma-Sensitive Yoga, 252

Trauma Symptom Checklist-Child Version-Post-Traumatic Stress Sub Scale (TSCC-PTS), 177

Trauma Symptom Checklist for Young Children (TSCYC), 177

Trauma Systems Therapy Approach, 130

Trauma Theory, 54

Traumatic brain injury (TBI), 140

Traumatic Events Screening Inventory - Child Report Form - Revised (TESI-CRF-R), 176–177

Traumatic Events Screening Inventory for Children—Brief Form (TESI-C-BRIEF), 176

Traumatic incidents, isolation, 131

Traumatized children, school success (assistance), 130

Trauma Treatment Training Center (TTTC), 227

Treatment

planning/engagement/ implementation, 206

protocol classification system, 208

quality monitoring, 206

Triage, 217–218

Trustworthiness/transparency

principle, 41

trauma-informed approach principle, 74

U

UCLA PTSD Reaction Index - Adolescent Version (RI-R), 177–178, 188

Unintentional injuries, ACE impact, 20

Utah Code, abuse guilt, 81

V

Validity, term (usage), 171–172

Ventral pathway representations, 118

Vicarious trauma (VT), 243, 244

impact, 244–245

Violence

expectations/unacceptability, 51

witness, prevalence, 60

Violence-exposed youth, EBP implementation (characteristics/ barriers), 213

Violence Exposure Scale for Children-
    Preschool Version
    (VEX-PV), 194
Violence Exposure Scale for Children-
    Revised Parent Report
    (VEX-RPR), 194
Visual-spatial capacities, 94
Voice/choice (principle), 42
Voluntary participation, 166–167
Voyeuristic Behavior, 191

W
Wernicke's area, 117
Wheel of Life (WOL), 250
Whole-staff presentation,
    175
Word attack, 118
Working memory, 121–122
    problems, 122

World Health Organization (WHO),
    health definition, 37
Written language, 123

Y
Young Child PTSD Checklist, 192
Young children
    attachment disruption, 220–221
    trauma exposure, screening, 170
    trauma-informed interventions/
        treatments, 220–227
    treatment, trauma
        (impact), 222–227
Youth Behavioral Surveillance Rating
    System (YBFRSS), 157
Youth, impairments (manifesta-
    tions), 140
Youth Outcome Questionnaire
    (YOQ-2.01), 189